Arts and Cultural Sponsorship

Manfred Bruhn · Lorenz Pöllmann

Arts and Cultural Sponsorship

Systematic Planning of Partnerships Between Actors in the Cultural Sector and Businesses

Springer

Manfred Bruhn
Universität Basel
Basel, Switzerland

Lorenz Pöllmann
Media University of Applied Sciences
Berlin, Germany

ISBN 978-3-658-50078-8 ISBN 978-3-658-50079-5 (eBook)
https://doi.org/10.1007/978-3-658-50079-5

Translation from the German language edition: "Kultursponsoring" by Manfred Bruhn and Lorenz Pöllmann, © Der/die Herausgeber bzw. der/die Autor(en), exklusiv lizenziert an Springer Fachmedien Wiesbaden GmbH, ein Teil von Springer Nature 2025. Published by Springer Fachmedien Wiesbaden. All Rights Reserved.

This book is a translation of the original German edition "Kultursponsoring" by Manfred Bruhn and Lorenz Pöllmann, published by Springer Fachmedien Wiesbaden GmbH in 2025. The translation was done with the help of an artificial intelligence machine translation tool. A subsequent human revision was done primarily in terms of content, so that the book will read stylistically differently from a conventional translation. Springer Nature works continuously to further the development of tools for the production of books and on the related technologies to support the authors.

This Springer imprint is published by the registered company Springer Fachmedien Wiesbaden GmbH, part of Springer Nature.
The registered company address is: Abraham-Lincoln-Str. 46, 65189 Wiesbaden, Germany

Preface

Arts and cultural sponsorship combines the cultural engagement of corporate sponsorship with strategic marketing communication. It is based on external cooperation with cultural institutions and internal collaboration with the various communication departments within the company. The resulting complexity of arts and cultural sponsorship makes this communication instrument particularly appealing for both academic analysis and practical implementation.

In marketing, (arts and culture) sponsoring has long been considered a highly successful tool for effectively and efficiently achieving specific marketing and communication objectives. This success story has also been significantly shaped by the repeated new editions of the foundational work "Sponsoring" by Manfred Bruhn, first published in 1987. Even in the most recent edition of this continually revised and expanded work on the systematic planning and integrative use of sponsoring, greater attention has been given to its areas of application in sports, culture, the environment, social causes, and the media.

The latest edition of the book by

Manfred Bruhn: Sponsoring. Systematische Planung und integrativer Einsatz (Sponsoring. Systematic Planning and Integrative Application), 6th ed., Wiesbaden 2018

will not be continued in its previous form. The areas of application in sponsorship have become so differentiated that it now seems necessary to write separate treatises on the manifestations. A book on "sports sponsorship" (Bruhn Rohlmann, Springer Gabler 2024[1]) has already been published, and with the present book "arts and cultural sponsorship," another specific in-depth exploration of the various forms of sponsorship is being offered. This allows the specific features of each area of application to be better addressed. This is also achieved through a two-person author team, each contributing their expertise to the individual specialized titles.

---

[1]Bruhn, M. and Rohlmann, P. (2024): Sports Sponsorship: Prerequisites and practical examples for successful partnerships, Wiesbaden, Springer Gabler.

The focus of this book is to demonstrate the full range of diverse applications of arts and cultural sponsorship as a component of integrated communication. The systematic presentation of the individual development stages involved in creating a sponsorship concept enables readers to identify the opportunities and risks associated with the use of arts and cultural sponsorship, and, building on this, to develop an independent, company-specific arts and cultural sponsorship strategy.

The structure of the book aims to provide a selective examination of the individual components of an arts and cultural sponsorship concept. To this end, arts and cultural sponsorship is based on a systematic planning process, with each phase of the planning process addressed specifically. First, Chaps. 1 to 3 lay the foundations for a holistic understanding of arts and cultural sponsorship and the actors involved in arts and cultural sponsorship. Starting with Chap. 4, the planning process is examined. This is subdivided into an analysis phase (Chap. 5), the definition of objectives (Chap. 6), the development of a sponsorship strategy (Chap. 7), the selection of sponsorships (Chap. 8), the operational design of arts and cultural sponsorship (Chap. 9), the integration of arts and cultural sponsorship into marketing and corporate communications (Chap. 10), as well as performance evaluation (Chap. 11). Finally, Chap. 12 derives and discusses trends in the development of arts and cultural sponsorship. The discussion is illustrated with several practical examples and case studies. In addition, each chapter concludes with a list of key points summarizing the central statements.

For this book, the manuscript of the 6th edition of the book sponsoring (Bruhn 2018)[2] was revised, shortened in many places, and supplemented and further developed with numerous new sections. For example, a comprehensive chapter on financing arts and culture (Chap. 3) has been added to adequately address the situation of cooperating cultural institutions. A newly developed arts and cultural sponsorship canvas (Chap. 4) provides a foundation for the practical development of sponsorship concepts, and a sample questionnaire (Chap. 11) supports evaluation. In addition, numerous new models and theoretical approaches have been developed and integrated, such as the polarity profile for integrating a cultural brand into a sponsorship cooperation, the risk analysis of arts and cultural sponsorship projects, the sponsorship portfolio analysis, a sponsorship-specific consumer typology, and several others.

The book is aimed equally at students and practitioners. For students, its primary purpose is to provide an understanding of how the communication instrument of arts and cultural sponsorship fits into the communication mix of corporate sponsorship, and to familiarize them with the perspective of those responsible for sponsorship within corporate sponsorship. Among practitioners, we wish to address both sponsoring corporate entities and sponsored organizations, as well as agencies and media, offering them

[2]Bruhn, M. (2018): Sponsoring. Systematic Planning and Integrative Application, 6th edition, Wiesbaden, Springer Gabler.

support in the development of successful sponsorship strategies. For these readers, numerous practical aids are integrated, especially in Chaps. 2 to 12, such as the arts and cultural sponsorship canvas (Chap. 4) for conducting workshops, as well as the inclusion of numerous guiding questions intended to support the development of individual concepts. In addition, the case studies from the perspectives of both sponsored organizations and sponsors provide practical insights and serve as sources of inspiration and reflection for one's own arts and cultural sponsorship strategy. The following case studies of sponsors and cultural institutions are included in the book:

- Alfred Kärcher SE Co. KG (Chap. 1)
- BMW Group (Chap. 2)
- Gewandhaus Orchestra (Chap. 3)
- Pandion AG (Chap. 6)
- DHL Group (Chap. 7)
- Bayer AG (Chap. 8)
- Beatbox Germany (Chap. 9)

This publication would not have been possible in its present form without the dedicated support of our interview partners, colleagues, and contributors. Therefore, our heartfelt thanks go to the following individuals:

Judith Dissler, Christian Fanghänel, Michael Fritz, Prof. Dr. Thomas Girst, Dr. Thomas Helfrich, Tanita Helm, Martina Jenny, Dr. Gregor Lichtner, Pedro Muñoz, Prof. Dr. Andine Müller, Sebastian Nagel, Eva Nieuweboer, Linda Österle, Marvin Pöttgen, Prof. Andreas Schulz, Antoinette Stocker, Hans-Conrad Walter and Nadine Zuberbühler.

We would also like to express our sincere gratitude to our publishing partner, Springer Gabler Verlag, and in particular to Ms. Barbara Roscher and Ms. Birgit Borstelmann for their patience, numerous suggestions, their dedicated and commendable commitment, as well as for their thorough editing of the manuscript.

Finally, a brief formal note. In the text, for the sake of simplicity and in line with the standard practice in scientific publications, we generally use the generic masculine form. This is not intended to discriminate against or devalue any gender or attitude toward equality. All gender identities are explicitly included wherever it is relevant to the statement.

We would be pleased if this publication captures the interest of its readers and provides inspiration for conceptual and methodological work in the field of arts and cultural sponsorship. It can be expected that the intensive professional discussion on the topic of arts and cultural sponsorship will continue to be pursued with commitment in the future, and we are therefore grateful for suggestions of any kind.

Basel and Berlin
in July 2024

Manfred Bruhn
Lorenz Pöllmann

Contents

1 Term and Fundamentals of Arts and Cultural Sponsorship 1
1.1 From Patronage to Arts and Cultural Sponsorship 2
1.2 Characteristics of Arts and Cultural Sponsorship 6
1.3 Typology of Arts and Cultural Sponsorship 8
1.4 Success Chain of Arts and Cultural Sponsorship 10
1.4.1 Case Study: Arts and Cultural Sponsorship by Alfred Kärcher SE & Co. KG 13

2 Forms of Cultural Sponsorship 21
2.1 Term of Arts and Cultural Funding and Arts and Cultural Sponsoring 22
2.2 Classifications of Arts and Cultural Sponsorship 24
2.3 Actors in the Process of Arts and Cultural Sponsorship 32
2.4 Arts and Cultural Sponsorship From a Marketing Perspective 34
2.5 Arts and Cultural Sponsorship From the Sponsors' Perspective 36
2.6 Arts and Cultural Sponsorship From the Perspective of the Sponsored 41
2.6.1 Case Study: The BMW Group's Cultural Engagement 45

3 Classification of Arts and Cultural Sponsorship in the Financing of Arts and Culture 53
3.1 Fundamentals and Instruments of Financing Arts and Culture 54
3.2 Public Private Arts and Cultural Funding 57
3.3 Donation System and Fundraising 65
3.4 Arts and Cultural Sponsorship as a Form of Private Third-Party Funding 74
3.5 Own Revenues in Distinction to Arts and Cultural Sponsorship 76
3.6 Crowdfunding as a Form of Arts and Cultural Sponsorship 80
3.6.1 Case Study Gewandhausorchester: Arts and Cultural Sponsorship from the Perspective of an Orchestra 84

4 Management Process of Arts and Cultural Sponsorship and Arts and Cultural Sponsorship Canvas ... 93
4.1 Phases of a Management Process for Arts and Cultural Sponsorship ... 94
4.2 Areas of Action of an Arts and Cultural Sponsorship Canvas ... 97

5 Situation Analysis in Arts and Cultural Sponsorship ... 113
5.1 Relevance of a Situation Analysis in Arts and Cultural Sponsorship ... 113
5.2 Internal Analysis ... 115
5.3 External Analysis ... 120
5.3.1 Cultural Organization-Related Analysis ... 120
5.3.2 Market, Competition, and Environment Analysis ... 124

6 Goals and Target Groups of Arts and Cultural Sponsorship ... 129
6.1 Defining the Goals and Motives of Arts and Cultural Sponsorship ... 130
6.2 Target Group Planning in Arts and Cultural Sponsorship ... 135
6.2.1 Case Study: Concept of Arts and Cultural Sponsorship at Pandion AG ... 147

7 Strategy Development of Arts and Cultural Sponsorship ... 155
7.1 Strategy Dimensions of Arts and Cultural Sponsorship ... 155
7.2 Strategic Guidelines in Arts and Cultural Sponsorship and Arts and Cultural Sponsorship Philosophy ... 158
7.3 Types of Strategy in Arts and Cultural Sponsorship ... 162
7.3.1 Case Study: Cultural Engagement of the DHL Group ... 170

8 Selection of Arts and Cultural Sponsorships ... 181
8.1 Levels of the Selection Decision ... 181
8.2 Initial Selection of Arts and Cultural Sectors According to the Affinity Concept ... 182
8.3 Detailed Selection by Cultural Offerings and Sectors ... 186
8.4 Termination of Sponsorship Agreements ... 188
8.4.1 Case Study: Strategy of arts and cultural sponsorship at Bayer AG ... 193

9 Operational Design of Arts and Cultural Sponsorship ... 201
9.1 Development of Individual Measures for Arts and Cultural Sponsorship ... 202
9.1.1 Contribution and Consideration in Arts and Cultural Sponsorship ... 202
9.1.2 Services Provided by External Specialists ... 208
9.2 Valuation of Sponsorship Benefits ... 210
9.3 Calculation of the Sponsorship Budget ... 214

9.4 Legal Framework of Arts and Cultural Sponsorship (in Germany) 217
9.4.1 General Legal and Tax Assessment of Arts and Cultural Sponsorship 217
9.4.2 Sponsorship and Compliance Regulations 219
9.5 Elements of a Cultural Sponsorship Contract (With Case Study Beatbox Germany) 222
9.5.1 Case Study Beatbox Germany: Arts and Cultural Sponsorship from the Perspective of a Cultural Event 224

10 Classification of Arts and Cultural Sponsorship in Marketing and Corporate Communications 233
10.1 Integration of Arts and Cultural Sponsorship into Marketing and Corporate Communication 234
10.2 Integration of Arts and Cultural Sponsorship into the Communication Mix of Corporate Sponsorship 237
10.3 Integration of Arts and Cultural Sponsorship into the Sponsoring Mix of Corporate Sponsorship 249
10.4 Decision Levels in the Corporate Hierarchy 251

11 Performance Evaluation in Arts and Cultural Sponsorship 255
11.1 Methods of Performance Evaluation in Arts and Cultural Sponsorship 256
11.2 Questionnaire for Performance Evaluation in Arts and Cultural Sponsorship 265
11.3 Problems of Performance Evaluation in Arts and Cultural Sponsorship 273
11.4 Criteria and Award Winners of Successful Sponsorship Activities 275

12 Trends in the Use of Arts and Cultural Sponsorship 279
12.1 Sponsorship from the Perspective of the Involved Stakeholders 279
12.2 Tendencies from the Perspective of Sponsors 281
12.2.1 Planning Basis of Sponsoring 281
12.2.2 Sponsoring as a Creative Instrument of Marketing and Corporate Communication 283
12.2.3 Development of a Sponsoring Mix for Corporate Sponsorship 285
12.2.4 Collaboration with Sponsoring Agencies 287
12.3 Tendencies from the Perspective of Cultural Organizations 290
12.4 Tendencies from the Perspective of Cultural Policy 295

References 299

List of Figures

Fig. 1.1	Forms of corporate sponsorship	5
Fig. 1.2	Typology of sponsorship	9
Fig. 1.3	Success Chain of arts and cultural sponsorship	11
Fig. 1.4	The Charles and Hubertus Chapel of Aachen Cathedral	14
Fig. 1.5	Test cleaning using the low-pressure particle blasting method	15
Fig. 1.6	Start of the test phase at the Charles and Hubertus Chapel of Aachen Cathedral	15
Fig. 1.7	Advertisements for cleaning projects in before-and-after comparison	17
Fig. 2.1	Typology of corporate sponsors as cultural supporters	23
Fig. 2.2	classification of various art and arts and cultural sectors	25
Fig. 2.3	Forms of cultural sponsorship	29
Fig. 2.4	Support of cultural sectors by corporate sponsorship in Germany	32
Fig. 2.5	The "Magic Triangle" of arts and cultural sponsorship	33
Fig. 2.6	Sponsorship from the perspective of sponsors and sponsored parties	35
Fig. 2.7	Forms of sponsorship from the sponsors' perspective	37
Fig. 2.8	Performance categories in sponsorship	43
Fig. 2.9	Forms of sponsorship from the perspective of the sponsees	46
Fig. 2.10	BMW-sponsored cultural event "Staatsoper für alle" 2014	48
Fig. 2.11	BMW H2R Project: Olafur Eliasson's installation "Your mobile expectations" 2007 at the Pinakothek der Moderne, Munich	48
Fig. 2.12	BMW Factory Leipzig by Zaha Hadid	50
Fig. 3.1	Structure of the cultural sector according to the three-sector model	55
Fig. 3.2	Sources of financing arts and cultural	56
Fig. 3.3	Five-year comparison of public cultural expenditure in Germany	58
Fig. 3.4	Public private expenditure for culture per inhabitant in 2020 by federal state (including municipal expenditure)	58

Fig. 3.5 Development and distribution of public cultural expenditure by sector in a five-year comparison 59
Fig. 3.6 Share of cultural expenditure in total public spending 60
Fig. 3.7 Comparison of cultural expenditure in Germany, Austria, and Switzerland 61
Fig. 3.8 Systematics of public arts and cultural funding. 65
Fig. 3.9 Stages of a donor pyramid 69
Fig. 3.10 Selection of examples of prices and durations for chair sponsorships (as of January 2023). 73
Fig. 3.11 Rock am Ring and Rock im Park—2022 Festival Edition Warsteiner 78
Fig. 3.12 Breakdown of own revenues at Theater Basel in the 2021/2022 season. 79
Fig. 3.13 Breakdown of the financing of Theater Basel in the 2021/2022 season. 79
Fig. 3.14 Sponsorship benefits of the crowdfunding campaign “NICHTS” (2023) 83
Fig. 3.15 Full financing of the open-air concert “Klassik airleben” in Leipzig’s Rosental through sponsorship income. 85
Fig. 3.16 Presentation of the Sponsors Club on the Gewandhaus Orchestra website. 87
Fig. 3.17 Presentation of sponsors in the Gewandhausorchester’s season program 89
Fig. 3.18 Example of the integration of a program sponsor in the Gewandhausorchester’s season program 89
Fig. 4.1 Planning process for arts and cultural sponsorship from a corporate perspective 95
Fig. 4.2 Use of the Canvas model in a sponsorship workshop 98
Fig. 4.3 Action areas of the arts and cultural sponsorship Canvas 100
Fig. 4.4 Chronology of typical milestones in a sponsorship collaboration. 108
Fig. 5.1 Branding process in arts and cultural sponsorship. 116
Fig. 5.2 Polarity profile for positioning (top) and comparison with the cooperating cultural brand (bottom) 117
Fig. 5.3 Staging the sponsor with its own resources using the example of DB Cargo. 119
Fig. 5.4 Risk analysis of cultural sponsorship projects. 121
Fig. 5.5 Media coverage (screenshots) of sponsor demands in response to criticism of Documenta 2022. 123
Fig. 5.6 sponsorship portfolio analysis 125
Fig. 6.1 Target group potentials in arts and cultural sponsorship 136
Fig. 6.2 Gender distribution of the Berlin cultural audience. 137

Fig. 6.3 Age distribution of the Berlin cultural audience 138
Fig. 6.4 Educational level of the Berlin cultural audience 138
Fig. 6.5 Information behavior of the Berlin cultural audience 140
Fig. 6.6 Characteristics of the Sinus Milieus 142
Fig. 6.7 Sinus Milieus 2022 in Germany. 143
Fig. 6.8 Sinus Milieus 2022 in Austria 143
Fig. 6.9 Sinus Milieus 2019 in Switzerland 144
Fig. 6.10 Personae of the State Museums of Berlin 145
Fig. 6.11 Example of a cultural sponsorship-specific audience segmentation 146
Fig. 6.12 Light installation by the artist Djeff in the exhibition Once only Once in the premises of Pandion AG 150
Fig. 6.13 Sculpture by the artist Djeff in the exhibition Once only Once sponsored by Pandion AG 150
Fig. 6.14 Poster announcement for the art exhibition Berlin Bishkek Art Weeks sponsored by Pandion. 151
Fig. 7.1 Dimensions of a sponsorship strategy 157
Fig. 7.2 Decision matrix for the selection of sponsorships 161
Fig. 7.3 Types of strategy in arts and cultural sponsorship based on the affinity concept. 162
Fig. 7.4 PayPal as a festival sponsor and the provision of charging stations for NFC chips in festival wristbands 163
Fig. 7.5 Summary presentation of different types of strategy in arts and cultural sponsorship 166
Fig. 7.6 Manifestations in arts and cultural sponsorship (exemplary presentation) 168
Fig. 7.7 Media utilization of the cultural engagement of Kreissparkasse Böblingen using the example of support for “Jugend musiziert” 171
Fig. 7.8 Exhibition of Beethoven’s ear trumpet as part of the DHL project “BTHVN on Tour”. 173
Fig. 7.9 DHL presentation with a post office branch at Wacken Openair 2023 175
Fig. 7.10 Interior view of the post office branch at Wacken Openair 2023. 175
Fig. 7.11 Limited special edition stamp for Wacken Openair 2023 176
Fig. 8.1 Lines of connection and patterns of justification for corporate sponsorship in arts and cultural sponsorship 183
Fig. 8.2 Image of classical and modern cultural events 185
Fig. 8.3 Press release by Commerzbank AG on the termination of the arts and cultural sponsorship of the English Theatre 192
Fig. 8.4 Singer-songwriter Wallis Bird with the band Spark at the stARTfestival 2023 in the Erholungshaus Leverkusen (Photo: Hanne Engwald) 194

Fig. 8.5 Communication of Bayer AG's cultural engagement on LinkedIn 196
Fig. 8.6 Communication of Bayer AG's cultural engagement on Instagram 197
Fig. 8.7 Communication of Bayer AG's cultural engagement on the Bayer culture homepage 198
Fig. 9.1 Possibilities for sponsorship in various arts and cultural sectors. 203
Fig. 9.2 Advertising rates Arte Magazin 213
Fig. 9.3 Cultural event German Beatbox Championship in Berlin 225
Fig. 9.4 Logo integration of sponsors at the German Beatbox Championship in Berlin 228
Fig. 9.5 Social media channels of Beatbox Germany (as of July 2023) 229
Fig. 10.1 Sponsorship in combination with other instruments of the communication mix 237
Fig. 10.2 Integration of sponsorship with other communication instruments. 238
Fig. 10.3 Example of integration of sponsorship into media advertising: Advertisement by Hirslanden Klinik St. Anna in the program booklet of the Lucerne Symphony Orchestra for the 2022/2023 season. 241
Fig. 10.4 Example of integration of sponsorship into media advertising: Advertisement by Luzerner Kantonalbank in the program booklet of the Lucerne Symphony Orchestra for the 2022/2023 season 242
Fig. 10.5 Integration of sponsorship into sales promotion: Landing page of the Coca-Cola sweepstake 243
Fig. 10.6 Reciprocal references between sponsor and sponsored party using the example of Deutsche Bank and Berlin Philharmoniker (2023). 246
Fig. 10.7 Dedicated website for communication of arts and cultural sponsorship using the example of the Deutsche Bank art program 247
Fig. 10.8 Connection of arts and cultural sponsorship and event marketing using the example of Hermes. 248
Fig. 10.9 Organizational position of the person with primary responsibility for sponsorship. 252
Fig. 11.1 Example of an audience survey on sponsor impact: excerpts from the Lollaplooza 2023 Berlin questionnaire 261
Fig. 11.2 Attention values of sponsorship for selected cultural events. 262
Fig. 11.3 Example of a polarity profile in the context of a sponsorship image study 263
Fig. 12.1 Example of wild posting in an environment unfavorable to the sponsor's image 284
Fig. 12.2 horizontal and vertical sponsoring mix 286
Fig. 12.3 Example of a hierarchy of guiding idea and campaign messages in various cultural sponsorship areas 287

Term and Fundamentals of Arts and Cultural Sponsorship

1

Contents

1.1 From Patronage to Arts and Cultural Sponsorship 2
1.2 Characteristics of Arts and Cultural Sponsorship 6
1.3 Typology of Arts and Cultural Sponsorship 8
1.4 Success Chain of Arts and Cultural Sponsorship 10

Abstract

Sponsoring has developed into a significant segment within the communications sector. While arguments based on product benefits and additional services often no longer provide sufficient differentiation from competitors, corporate sponsorships are increasingly seeking communication tools that offer experiential value and enable targeted audience engagement. Both of these are found in sponsoring, which has now often become an established component of the communication mix. This chapter outlines the development of sponsoring, identifies key characteristics, and defines a typology that distinguishes between various forms of arts and cultural sponsorship. Furthermore, a success chain for arts and cultural sponsorship is presented, serving as a conceptual framework for the development of sponsoring activities. Finally, a case study of Alfred Kärcher SE & Co. KG demonstrates the practical implementation of arts and cultural sponsorship.

M. Bruhn and L. Pöllmann, *Arts and Cultural Sponsorship*,
https://doi.org/10.1007/978-3-658-50079-5_1

1.1 From Patronage to Arts and Cultural Sponsorship

Sponsorship has become a familiar and everyday phenomenon. Increasingly, corporate sponsorships from various sectors are making use of the diverse opportunities offered by sponsorship. In cultural events, sports, as well as in the ecological, social, and media sectors, individuals, institutions, and audiovisual programs are specifically supported, and own events are initiated in order to confront participants and spectators with the communication objectives of corporate sponsorship. This confrontation aims to integrate events that are in the public spotlight and thus receive media coverage into the communication activities of corporate sponsorship, in order to achieve communicative effects.

The promotion of culture and sports as well as social welfare by corporate sponsorship or entrepreneurs has a long tradition (see Bruhn, 2018a, below). When considering the historical development of the various **forms of corporate sponsorship**, a general distinction is made between patronage and the donation system as specific forms of philanthropy. The Roman Gaius Cilnius Maecenas (70–8 BC) is regarded as the forefather of the promotion of art and culture. As a friend, helper, and advisor to Emperor Augustus, he gathered and supported the most important poets of his time. Even though Maecenas himself did not always support the arts entirely selflessly: The German term Mäzenatentum (in English: **patronage**) (Hermanns & Marwitz, 2008, p. 45), derived from his name, denotes the support of culture and the community by individuals or organizations out of altruistic motives.

A **patron** thus supports individuals or institutions without expecting specific sponsorship benefits in return. The motivation for such an action may be the self-imposed obligation of a person, a foundation, or a company to use part of the available budget for the benefit of a particular segment of their environment, with artistic, sporting, or socio-political interests taking precedence (Walliser, 1995, p. 10; Hermanns & Marwitz, 2008, p. 45). However, a closer look at the cultural support activities of historical patrons (including Maecenas and the Medici) reveals that even in these cases, there were indeed interests of a political, economic, or communicative nature, and thus not purely selfless (see in detail Rothe, 2001, pp. 212 ff.). Thus, it is possible that historical patrons were genuinely motivated by their love of the arts and sense of social responsibility. Nevertheless, it is also quite conceivable that their actions were driven by an interest in influencing external perceptions and images. Still, the terms patronage and arts and cultural funding (as opposed to arts and cultural sponsorship) remain associated to this day with positively connoted characteristics, from which corporate sponsorships that present themselves as patrons or cultural benefactors benefit (Rothe, 2001, p. 222).

Cultural history repeatedly points to patrons who enabled artistic works and thereby also gained distinction. For example, the Swiss music patron Paul Sacher, who was himself active as a conductor, commissioned numerous compositions, including from Béla Bartok, Igor Stravinsky, Anton Webern, and Henri Dutilleux. Sacher himself is immortalized as the dedicatee of several works. Since 1976, the Paul Sacher Foundation he established has supported musicology by collecting the estates of significant composers—a form of support that also remains associated with the patron's name.

In the case of classical patronage, the patron would provide support even if his or her name or that of the company is not associated with the sponsorship. It is obvious, therefore, that there is hardly any reliable overview of the financial scope of corporate patronage—not only in Germany—since many forms of support are not made public. This is all the more true as the tasks of patrons are now partly assumed by **foundations**, which fulfill their stated purpose from the income generated by their endowment assets (for the involvement of cultural foundations, see Chap. 3).

An evolution of patronage, and thus another specific form of philanthropy, are the activities of corporate sponsorship, referred to in the United States as **corporate giving** and in Germany as donations. These are donation campaigns in which corporate sponsors provide financial or material resources or services free of charge, in awareness of their socio-political responsibility, with the aim of contributing to the solution of societal problems (Porter & Kramer, 2003; Mecking, 2010; Haibach, 2019; Urselmann, 2023). In the United States and other Western countries, this systematic support is found in healthcare institutions, universities, opera houses, and more. In Germany, it primarily finances social and religious associations as well as political parties. From a corporate perspective, tax reasons are the main factor in the allocation of donations; specifically demanded sponsorship benefits from the recipient are rather the exception.

Neither patronage nor donations are equivalent to sponsorship. An examination of the etymological meaning of the word "to sponsor" yields the following interpretations:

Duden to sponsor: (on the basis of a corresponding contract) to provide financial support or support through material goods or services, [co-]finance (in order to receive sponsorship benefits serving advertising or similar purposes).

The American Heritage 1. One who assumes responsibility for another person or a group during a period of instruction, apprenticeship, or probation. 2. One who vouches for the suitability of a candidate for admission. 3. A legislator who proposes and urges adoption of a bill. 4. One who presents a candidate for baptism or confirmation; a godparent. 5. One that finances a project or an event carried out by another person or group, especially a business enterprise that pays for radio or television programming in return for advertising time.

Grimm's Dictionary Spons: fiancé, fiancée, referring to the heavenly bridegroom and heavenly bride. Spunse: beloved. Alte Spunse: pejorative for an unchaste girl. Sponsieren: 1. to accept as a spons: to become engaged, to marry, 2. more commonly: to behave like bride and groom, in a secular sense: of sensual courtship: to sponsor, to act as a matchmaker. Sponsiererin, f. she who courts, woos, a euphemistic term for a procuress. Sponsierung: wooing.

If one sets aside the medieval definition according to the Brothers Grimm, "sponsoring" is primarily associated with terms such as "guarantee" and "partnership." In contrast to patronage and donations, corporate sponsorship, in which companies act as sponsors, links their involvement to their own communication objectives. These objectives are achieved by agreeing on specific sponsorship benefits with the sponsored party and by publicizing the sponsorship through the use of other communication tools, such as media advertising, sales promotion, or their own social media activities.

An analysis of the development of the understanding of sponsorship in the academic field reveals a comprehensive discussion of the term, distinguishing between phase- and event-oriented definitions as well as enumerative-explanatory and contract-oriented approaches (Ahlert et al., 2007, pp. 14 ff.; Bagusat & Marwitz, 2008, pp. 5 ff.; Bruhn, 2018a, pp. 3 ff.). For a comprehensive overview of the discourse on sponsorship in the English-language literature, see Walliser 2003 and Cornwell et al. 2005. When examining developments in practice, it becomes clear that in recent years, a sometimes very diffuse understanding of the **conceptual content of sponsorship** has emerged among corporate sponsors, sponsored parties, media representatives, politicians, and the general public (for the debate on the definition of the term, see also Weiland, 2017, p. 23). This has led to the situation where, in everyday language, almost any form of support, promotion, business transaction, etc. between individuals, groups, or organizations is mistakenly referred to as "sponsoring" (examples include a mother's regular allowance to her son or a manufacturer's advertising subsidies to its retail partners). In the actual sense, however, this has nothing to do with sponsorship.

A clear definition of sponsorship is not only relevant from an academic perspective. In practice, it is repeatedly evident that divergent understandings of sponsorship lead to misunderstandings and occasionally to unsuccessful cooperation efforts. This is the case, for example, when sponsorship is equated with donation. In such cases, the sponsor is not offered appropriate sponsorship benefits, even though they expect them.

The previous discussion shows that the differences between the **forms of corporate sponsorship** presented are primarily based on different emphases regarding the motives for support. These are supplemented by varying conditions attached to the allocation of funding by patrons, donors, and sponsors. Figure 1.1 illustrates the differences between the three forms of corporate sponsorship mentioned above using various characteristics.

Based on these fundamental distinguishing features, the **term sponsorship** is defined as follows (Bruhn, 2018a, p. 5):

Sponsorship

- means the analysis, planning, implementation, and control of all activities,
- that involve the provision of money, goods, services, or know-how by corporate sponsors and institutions
- to support individuals and/or organizations in the fields of sports, culture, social affairs, environment, and/or the media

Forms of business support			
Characteristics	**Type of support**		
	Patronage	**Donations**	**Sponsorship**
Type of sponsor	Private individuals, foundations	Private individuals, companies	Companies
Motive(s) for sponsorship	Exclusively funding motives (altruistic)	Funding motive dominant, possible tax benefits (public benefit)	Motive for promotion and Achievement of communication goals (self-interest)
Cooperation with sponsored parties	Partially (via funding areas)	No	Yes (implementation of sponsorships)
Media impact	No (rather private)	Hardly	Yes (public)
Use in the field of sport	Very rare	Rarely	Dominant
Use in the fields of arts and culture	Dominant	Frequently	Frequently
Use in the social/ ecological field	Frequent	Dominant	Frequent
Use in the media sector	Non-existent	Non-existent	Dominant
Decision-makers in the company	Entrepreneur	Finance departement	Company management, marketing, communication

Fig. 1.1 Forms of corporate sponsorship. (Source: Bruhn, 2018a, p. 4)

- under contractual regulation of the sponsor's contribution and the sponsored party's return,
- in order to simultaneously achieve marketing and corporate communication objectives.

Accordingly, one speaks of a **sponsorship** when the sponsor and the sponsored party have agreed to jointly carry out a specific project within a defined period under certain conditions (Bruhn, 2018a, p. 5).

Arts and cultural sponsorship in particular initially means that corporate sponsors present themselves in a cultural context by supporting artists, cultural actors or cultural institutions. The specific features of arts and cultural sponsorship are discussed below and then form the basis for a definition.

On the State of Research

Arts and cultural sponsorship is examined in the literature from various perspectives. On the one hand, arts and cultural sponsorship is studied from the **perspective of sponsors** (see Lamprecht, 2014; Vance et al., 2016; Bruhn, 2018b) and is understood as an instrument of corporate communication (see, among others, Fuchs & Unger, 2014, p. 309 f.; Bruhn, 2018c).

As a financing instrument and a means of procurement marketing, arts and cultural sponsorship is, on the other hand, addressed from the **perspective of the sponsored cultural institutions** and as a task of arts and cultural management (Heinze, 1999, 2008; Litzel et al., 2003; Pöllmann, 2011; Bortoluzzi Dubach, 2011; Haltern, 2014; Frohne et al., 2015; Hoppe & Heinze, 2016; Gottschalk, 2016; Gerlach-March & Pöllmann, 2019; Hausmann, 2021).

In addition to these two fundamental perspectives, **research on arts and cultural sponsorship** also includes studies on specific manifestations:

- With regard to geographic regions, such as Brazil (de Alcântara et al., 2019), Germany (Weiland, 2017), Greece (Moysidou, 2020), Sweden (Gianneschi & Broberg, 2019), Switzerland (Fischer & Schmidli, 2022), or Turkey (Bulut & Yumrukaya, 2009).
- Analysis of individual case studies (Ryan, 2018; Lund & Greyser, 2019).
- With regard to areas of application, such as arts and cultural sponsorship in monument preservation (Dolores et al., 2017, 2019, 2021; Settembre Blundo et al., 2017).
- On impact assessment (Schwaiger, 2003; Hohenauer & Reinecke, 2016; Wozniak, 2016; Hewelt, 2008; Lee & Yoon, 2021; Batt et al., 2021), also in comparison to other forms of sponsorship such as sports sponsorship (Toscani & Prendergast, 2019).
- On legal issues (Maniatis, 2017).
- On the area of tension between cultural organizations and protest critical of sponsorship (Chong, 2012; Serafini & Garrard, 2019).

1.2 Characteristics of Arts and Cultural Sponsorship

An analysis of the specific characteristics of arts and cultural sponsorship shows that the use of various forms of arts and cultural sponsorship as an instrument of marketing and corporate communication is sometimes based on heterogeneous intentions, with different rules and principles to be considered. Regardless of the different objectives and approaches, the following six **characteristics of arts and cultural sponsorship** can be highlighted, which are common to all sponsoring activities:

1. Arts and cultural sponsorship is based on the principle of **performance and consideration**. The sponsor provides support, such as money, goods, and services, with the expectation of receiving a specific return from the sponsored party. For example, the sponsored party may offer the promotional use of the sponsor's brand or company name as a return. In addition, the sponsor may be granted communicative use of the sponsorship, for example as part of their public private relations (Meenaghan, 1983;

Meenaghan & Flood, 1983; Cornwell & Maignan, 1998; Meenaghan & Shipley, 1999, Koth, 2000, pp. 5 f.).

2. Arts and cultural sponsorship is not simply the purchase of advertising space for a fee. Rather, in sponsorship, the **sponsorship motivation** towards the sponsored party is expressed, as the sponsor also identifies with the objectives of the sponsored party. Through its supportive character and the backing of activities considered important by society, a sponsor can generate goodwill to an extent not possible through media advertising. The extent to which reputation is positively influenced depends not only on the respective sponsoring activities, but also on how much a corporate sponsorship exploits a sponsorship for self-serving purposes and displaces the idea of support (Meenaghan & Shipley, 1999, p. 340).
3. For corporate sponsorship, arts and cultural sponsorship is a communication instrument. Sponsorship fulfills **communicative functions** for sponsors, which can be provided directly by the sponsored party, conveyed through the media, or even created by the sponsor themselves (Bruhn, 2018a, p. 6).
4. Arts and cultural sponsorship must undergo a **systematic planning and decision-making process**. It is not sufficient to simply provide resources to a sponsored party and wait for the hoped-for effect. Instead, measures must be planned, organized, implemented, and controlled on the basis of a situation analysis and goal formulation. This necessity for a systematic planning and decision-making process applies equally to sponsors and sponsored parties.
5. One of the main objectives of arts and cultural sponsorship is **image transfer**. The special feature of image transfer in sponsorship lies in the determinants that contribute to a particular brand or corporate image (Meenaghan & Shipley, 1999). While in classic communication instruments, such as media advertising, the message of an advertising measure and the medium through which it is communicated independently influence image transfer, in sponsorship, message and medium cannot be separated. The object of a sponsorship engagement embodies both the message and the medium itself. Empirical studies have shown that the derived image from a sponsorship largely depends on the form in which the sponsorship appears (Christensen, 2006; Huber & Matthes, 2007). Precise image dimensions are further derived from the specific activities within a sponsorship category.
6. From a corporate perspective, arts and cultural sponsorship is a component of **integrated communication.** Thus, sponsorship by corporate sponsors is not used in isolation, but in conjunction with other marketing and communication instruments. A clear distinction between sponsorship and other communication instruments and forms of corporate sponsorship is not always possible in sponsorship practice based on the characteristics mentioned. Rather, a number of hybrid forms have emerged, each requiring the presence of the listed characteristics, but assigning them different levels of importance.

1.3 Typology of Arts and Cultural Sponsorship

Arts and cultural sponsorship can be differentiated not only by the forms of support mentioned above, but also by the intentions of the sponsors. Given the divergent motives of sponsors, the diverse application possibilities, and the heterogeneous degree of utilization of sponsorship for marketing and corporate communications, it is advisable from the perspective of corporate sponsorship to establish a typology within sponsorship. Figure 1.2 illustrates that three **types of sponsorship** have been distinguished: altruistic, promotion-oriented, and traditional sponsorship. Recently, there has also been some debate about an instrumentalized form of arts and cultural sponsorship.

Type 1: Altruistic Sponsorship
In altruistic sponsorship within corporate sponsorship, altruistic motives are paramount, often rooted in the company's philosophy. A defining feature is that the corporate sponsorship's involvement is communicated to the public only very discreetly. This form of sponsorship is primarily observed in the support of cultural, social, and other non-commercial institutions. Therefore, altruistic engagement is significantly more common in arts and cultural sponsorship than, for example, in sports sponsorship. Support is usually provided directly by the corporate sponsor itself or through company-specific foundations (e.g., Allianz Kulturstiftung). However, it should be noted that discreet arts and cultural sponsorship is not necessarily altruistic. A popular benefit in arts and cultural sponsorship, for instance, is the allocation of exclusive tickets to cultural events, which a sponsor can pass on to deserving employees, partners, or clients. In this case, while the sponsorship commitment is not communicated to the general public, it is still not altruistic.

Type 2: Promotion-Oriented Sponsorship
In promotion-oriented sponsorship, the motivation to support takes precedence over the intended communicative effect. This form of sponsorship is characterized by the fact that the sponsoring company's mention, for example in a specific sponsorship, is not mandatory but is desired. The company's involvement is usually presented to the public as part of public private relations activities, without professional and systematic planning. Promotion-oriented sponsorship is primarily used in the social, environmental, and cultural sectors. Numerous art prizes and scholarships awarded by corporate sponsors as part of their cultural engagement can be cited as examples of promotion-oriented arts and cultural sponsorship. Typically, no specific benefit or obligation regarding the mention of the sponsor is agreed upon with the prizewinners or scholarship recipients.

Type 3: Traditional Sponsorship
Traditional sponsorship is characterized by sponsors making it a condition to be mentioned in the sponsorships. The basis of the engagement is the intended communicative

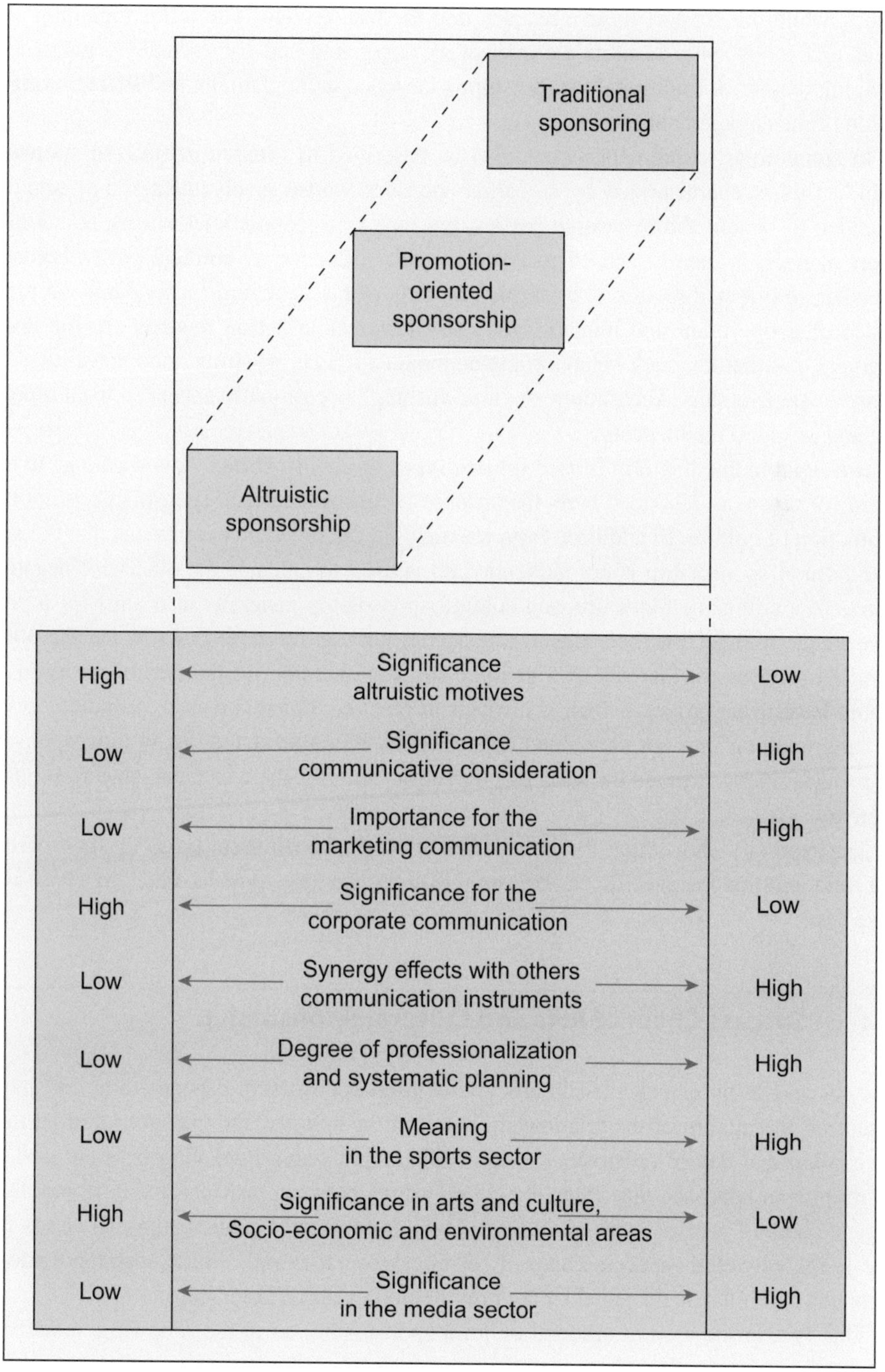

Fig. 1.2 Typology of sponsorship. (Source: Bruhn, 2018a, p. 8)

effect, while the support motive recedes into the background. The terms regarding services and sponsorship benefits are intensively negotiated and contractually regulated. A defining feature of traditional sponsorship is the systematic planning and strategic orientation of the engagement.

In some areas, certain forms can also be described as **"instrumentalized sponsorship"**. This is characterized by so-called sponsors whose involvement is not actually intended to benefit the sponsored parties, but rather, in a sometimes covert, sometimes overt manner, is merely abused to leverage their influence as political power holders, speculation-oriented investors, or similar. In view of the disregard for fundamental principles of cooperation and human rights, and responsible action towards art, the environment, and nature, such behavior is tantamount to **"arts washing"** and constitutes an abuse of sponsorship. Accusations of "arts washing" occasionally appear in local reporting and as social media posts.

It is notable that the term is used for two **types of arts washing**: "arts washing" in the narrower sense, as described here: the purpose of arts and cultural sponsorship is not the promotion of culture. In addition, "arts washing" in the broader sense means that the arts and cultural sponsorship is not authentic and is used to enhance the otherwise negative image of a company. Since arts and cultural sponsorship generally also aims for a positive image transfer for the sponsor, this accusation can be made quickly. On the other hand, in such cases, the lack of a genuine support intention on the part of the sponsor would have to be proven, which is difficult in practice. For this reason, purported cases of "arts washing" are not mentioned here. Overall, it can be stated that in most sponsorship engagements, despite the strategic marketing benefits, there is a real, sincere support motive.

The typology shows that the boundaries between the different types of sponsorship are fluid and that the specific classification of a sponsorship must be made on a case-by-case basis.

1.4 Success Chain of Arts and Cultural Sponsorship

The success of an engagement in arts and cultural sponsorship depends to a very large extent on the quality of the relationship between the sponsor and the sponsored parties. To explain and design (customer) relationships, relationship marketing is often used. It represents an approach that views the relationships between provider and customer as a logical chain of process steps, in order to build and intensify relationships. The basis for this is the so-called "success chain of relationship marketing," which specifies various elements that must be managed by the provider to develop relationships.

This is also the case in arts and cultural sponsorship, so in the following, a success **chain of arts and cultural sponsorship** will be used as the basis for further considerations in the individual chapters. The success chain is a helpful explanatory approach for identifying the individual relevant influencing factors for arts and cultural sponsorship. The success chain is shown in Fig. 1.3.

The success chain is essentially a **causal chain** and takes into account pre-economic constructs, i.e., consumer-related objectives that precede economic success and determine economic success on the provider side, such as sales. These components of the chain of effectiveness must be established and maintained by the company. The theoretical model is based on the causal relationships between psychological constructs, customers' behavioral intentions and actual behavior, and economic success.

Thus, the following **links in a success chain** can be distinguished:

1. Company input,
2. Psychological effects,
3. Behavioral effects,
4. Company output.

Crucial in the **interpretation of the success chain** is the connection between provider-related and customer-related (impact) variables. The key question is which entrepreneurial measures (input) can be used to achieve which psychological effects among customers. Furthermore, it is necessary to determine which psychological effects among

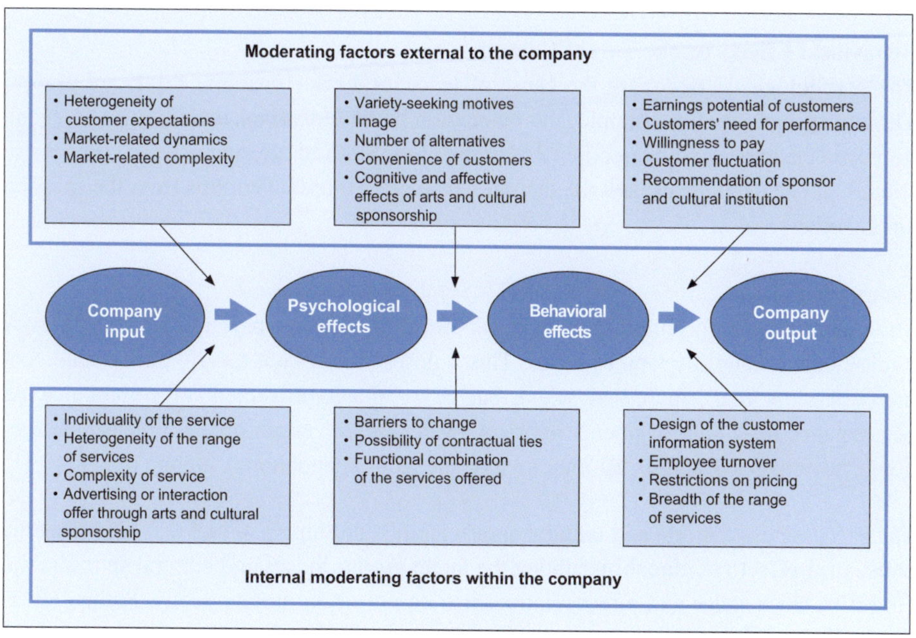

Fig. 1.3 Success Chain of arts and cultural sponsorship. (Source: Bruhn, 2018a, p. 509)

customers lead to which behavioral outcomes. Finally, the influence of customer behavior on economic success must be examined. In this respect, it is a matter of analyzing various cause-and-effect relationships (Bruhn, 2016, p. 73). Since there are not always clear relationships between the different links in the chain, both internal and external moderating factors must also be taken into account (Bruhn, 2016, p. 72).

The success **chain of arts and cultural sponsorship** can be interpreted for the individual links in the chain as follows:

Company Input
A corporate sponsor has reached an agreement with a cultural institution on a cultural sponsorship and implements it as part of its marketing and corporate communications. This constitutes an advertising or interaction offer for the company's target groups. The corporate sponsor hopes for positive effects on its communication objectives.

Psychological Effects on the Target Groups
The target groups perceive the arts and cultural sponsorships, either through individual invitations or through other forms of advertising perception. Psychological effects arise among the target groups, i.e., they become aware of the arts and cultural sponsorship (cognitive effects) and they evaluate the sponsorship and the associated advertising measures as positive or negative (affective effects). This influences the acceptance of the company's cultural sponsorship by the various target groups.

Behavioral Effects on the Target Groups
The psychological effects are the cause of behavioral effects among the target groups. These may include, for example, the perception of an individual invitation to an event, improved customer loyalty, recommendations of the cultural offering and the company to friends and acquaintances, and the intention to accept future invitations from the sponsor, among others.

Company Output
The output for the corporate sponsor results from the positive psychological and behavioral effects among the target groups. This will less often be a clearly attributable economic success (e.g., increased sales), but rather the improvement of communication performance (e.g., improvements in brand awareness, in certain image dimensions, economic advantages through customer loyalty and recommendations), among others.

The success chain of arts and cultural sponsorship is an impact model that illustrates the **cause-and-effect relationships** among the target groups in arts and cultural sponsorship. However, these cause-and-effect relationships do not occur automatically. Rather, attention must be paid to which factors must be present in the chain links in order for the desired positive effect for the sponsor to occur.

The chain of effectiveness is particularly influenced by so-called **moderating factors**. These should be understood as "disturbing factors" that prevent the cause-and-effect relationship among the target groups from developing as desired. For example, **internal moderating factors** include a lack of professionalism in the planning and implementation of arts and cultural sponsorship by the corporate sponsor, insufficient internal cooperation with other communications departments, resistance among internal target groups to arts and cultural sponsorship, and much more. Also, and especially, **external moderating factors** influence the cause-and-effect relationship in the chain of effectiveness. This may be due to a general rejection of corporate sponsorship's involvement in culture, insufficient cooperation with the sponsored parties, poor implementation of arts and cultural sponsorships by the cultural institution, and much more. Particular attention must be paid to these moderators in order to achieve a positive effect through the company's arts and cultural sponsorship.

The introductory chapter illustrates, on the one hand, the diversity with which **arts and cultural sponsorship can be used as a communication tool by corporate sponsors**. On the other hand, it has also become clear that some fundamental elements must be considered when using arts and cultural sponsorship. The success chain can serve as a conceptual framework for arts and cultural sponsorship. How arts and cultural sponsorship can be used to communicate one's own achievements to the public is demonstrated in the following case study using the example of Alfred Kärcher SE & Co KG.

1.4.1 Case Study: Arts and Cultural Sponsorship by Alfred Kärcher SE & Co. KG

Initial Situation

Alfred Kärcher SE & Co. KG, a Swabian family business headquartered in Winnenden (Germany), is considered the world's leading cleaning specialist. In 2023, the corporate sponsor achieved sales of EUR 3.29 billion with 16,000 employees in 82 countries. In addition to high-pressure cleaners, the product range also includes blasting systems, vacuum cleaners, as well as sweepers and scrubber-driers. Therefore, the focus in traditional communication is primarily on product communication. Kärcher is involved in a variety of areas including sports, society, and the environment, but is particularly distinguished by its unique form of arts and cultural sponsorship.

Role of Arts and Cultural Sponsorship

For over 40 years, the cleaning equipment manufacturer has been committed to the preservation of historic monuments and buildings around the world free of charge. By providing equipment and professional cleaning experts, more than 150 projects have already been cleaned in a restorative manner. Some of the most famous "Kärchered" historic monuments include the Brandenburg Gate, the London Eye, the Christ the Redeemer statue in Rio de Janeiro, the Statue of Liberty in New York, and the monument to the American presidents at Mount Rushmore. In an outstanding way, the corporate sponsor succeeds in using its cultural engagement to present the features, functions, and advantages of its products. In doing so, the cleaning specialist demonstrates a special sensitivity for product affinity and the communication of brand trust. The sponsorship cleverly demonstrates to the public—and thus simultaneously to potential customers—the quality of Kärcher products at significant historical monuments, illustrating to customers the product's potential for their own applications at home. Thus, by supporting monument preservation, Kärcher deliberately uses its high-profile cultural engagement as public relations and target group communication.

Model Project for Monument-Appropriate Cleaning at Aachen Cathedral as an Example

An exemplary project is the cleaning of Aachen Cathedral in cooperation with the German UNESCO Commission (DUK) (see Fig. 1.4).

The restoration of the monuments is carried out in collaboration with experts, monument conservators, and restorers, creating additional synergies and enabling the acquisition of new expertise and ideas for the further development of proprietary products and cleaning methods. In this way, arts and cultural sponsorship also promotes internal processes related to innovation, research, and development.

2013: The DUK and Kärcher initiate a nationwide model project for the preservation of German cultural monuments. The basis of this collaboration is a public-private–private partnership agreement between the two parties. Kärcher's contribution is to provide and supply know-how, machines, and cleaning specialists. Furthermore, Kärcher, together with the project partners, is responsible for decisions regarding monument conservation. The timeline is as follows:

Fig. 1.4 The Charles and Hubertus Chapel of Aachen Cathedral

2014: Following a nationwide call for applications, 14 individual objects from nine World Heritage Sites apply on the topic of sustainability to an independent expert jury consisting of specialists in monument conservation, culture, and science. In the summer, test cleanings are carried out at three cultural monuments to determine the specific contamination of the building fabric and to identify a suitable cleaning method (see Fig. 1.5). In December, the 540-year-old Charles and Hubertus Chapel of Aachen Cathedral is named the winner of the competition.

2015: In May, cleaning work begins at Aachen Cathedral (see Fig. 1.6). In the first step, three hot-water high-pressure cleaners are used to remove biological growth from the masonry. In the main cleaning process, the method is switched to low-pressure particle blasting to clean the intricate stonework.

Fig. 1.5 Test cleaning using the low-pressure particle blasting method

Fig. 1.6 Start of the test phase at the Charles and Hubertus Chapel of Aachen Cathedral

In total, three Kärcher specialists work on this project every day over a period of eight weeks. At the same time, several educational workshops are launched to inspire children and young people about the World Heritage Site. In cooperation with the Inda-Gymnasium in Aachen, for example, students have the opportunity within such a workshop to have the cleaning methods explained to them up close by experts and to test the equipment themselves. In addition, the students produce a short film about their engagement with the World Heritage Site and its restoration, and develop their own ideas on how they can actively contribute to its preservation.

Objectives

In addition to the intended effects on economic indicators, Kärcher primarily pursues the following psychological objectives with its commitment in the field of arts and cultural sponsorship:

1. Cognitive Objectives

- Increase in brand awareness (through product presentation)
- Communicating the competence and application areas of the products
- Attracting attention
- Information about innovations

2. Affective Objectives

- Brand image management and experience profile
- Gaining sympathy (social engagement)
- Trust and acceptance among customers
- Employee motivation
- Employee identification

3. Conative Objectives

- Strengthening customer loyalty
- Establishing new contacts and maintaining existing relationships (with the German UNESCO Commission, among others)

In summary, Kärcher's primary objective is to contribute to society and to preserve culturally valuable historical monuments. As a positive side effect, corporate sponsorship can also showcase its product portfolio and convince existing and potential customers of its technology and expertise. The internal impact of these commitments should not be underestimated: on the one hand, they increase the motivation of individual employees who act as cleaning experts in the respective projects, and on the other, they create an opportunity for all employees worldwide to identify with the company.

Integration of Arts and Cultural Sponsorship into the Communication Mix

To integrate arts and cultural sponsorship into the company's communication mix, the communication tools are networked. For example, information about the engagement is presented on the Kärcher homepage and current projects are featured on the company's own social media pages. In addition, corporate sponsorship, in collaboration with its respective sponsorship partners, publishes reports on completed restoration projects, such as in the case of the cleaning of Aachen Cathedral or the Matsudagawa Dam in Japan.

In return for its high-profile cleaning campaigns, Kärcher receives classic PR as a benefit of the sponsorship. On the occasion of each project handover, especially for major cleaning operations, main press appointments are scheduled. In this way, Kärcher achieves consistent media presence, both locally and internationally.

For the company's 75th anniversary, arts and cultural sponsorship is prominently featured in a campaign that presents Kärcher as an efficient and effective cleaning solution for everyday and global cleaning challenges. In this cross-country anniversary campaign, which showcases the cleaning projects in before-and-after comparisons, the size and strength of the brand are illustrated (see Fig. 1.7). Tailored to the media consumption habits in each country, advertisements, posters, radio spots, point-of-sale (POS) promotions, and a dedicated online presence are launched. At the same time, a sweepstakes (online and in DIY stores) draws attention to the projects by offering the chance to win a trip to cleaning highlights such as the Space Needle in Seattle and Mount Rushmore in South Dakota.

Furthermore, arts and cultural sponsorship is also presented at the individual locations of the official Kärcher Centers. In the sales areas, videos of cleaning operations are played in the background, and the interior design, such as the sales counters, is decorated with the famous cleaning motifs. Since the concept of arts and cultural sponsorship at Kärcher provides an opportunity to emotionally charge the technical products, the company's trade fair stands are also designed in the same way.

Kärcher also uses arts and cultural sponsorship within internal communication. Through various channels, such as an app, newsletters, and the intranet, reports on

Fig. 1.7 Advertisements for cleaning projects in before-and-after comparison

individual cultural engagements are communicated to employees. An integrated like and comment function also promotes exchange with the internal stakeholder group. Arts and cultural sponsorship also plays a special role in the interior design of Kärcher's office buildings: photos of cleaning campaigns are displayed in employees' offices, beverage machines are printed with famous campaigns, and memories of cultural engagements are evoked in the auditorium as well.

Effects of Arts and Cultural Sponsorship

As part of performance evaluation, Kärcher measures the media impact of cleaning operations in terms of circulation, reach, and media equivalency values. For example, the cleaning of Mount Rushmore alone was covered in the USA by 750 television broadcasts and 450 newspaper articles. For documentation purposes, each project is also photographed by Kärcher itself, so that it can subsequently be used for internal and external communication purposes.

Conclusion

The example "Kärcher cleans the world" shows how a corporate sponsorship can strategically leverage its cultural engagement to present its own products and build an unparalleled corporate image and trust through its social commitment. As a result, the cleaning specialist achieves an extraordinary potential for differentiation compared to conventional cultural engagements of other corporate sponsorships. By integrating arts and cultural sponsorship into internal and external communication, the brand, which is otherwise defined by technical aspects, is emotionally charged. In this way, the sponsorship also generates a significant internal effect by fostering the company's innovative potential and employee identification, and the resulting corporate image also serves to recruit new employees.

Key Points

1. **Consider history:** Corporate cultural engagement has a long tradition, even if arts and cultural funding has not always been associated with the term arts and cultural sponsorship.
2. **Origin through patronage:** Arts and cultural sponsorship can also be traced back to the engagement of patrons, who, through their support of artists and cultural institutions, can be regarded as the first arts and cultural sponsors.
3. **Clarify terminology:** In practice, it is clear that in recent years a sometimes very diffuse understanding of the term sponsorship has developed. A clear definition must be established to avoid misunderstandings and to distinguish sponsorship from other forms of support.
4. **Understand sponsorship as a communication tool:** Arts and cultural sponsorship should be integrated into marketing and corporate communication.

5. **Note the special features of arts and cultural sponsorship:** Sponsorship in the cultural sector is a special form of support and communication by a company or organization to achieve specific effects. This means that arts and cultural sponsorship is clearly distinguishable from other forms, such as sports sponsorship.
6. **Goal-oriented partnership:** Sponsorship is ultimately an agreement between sponsor and sponsored party. From a corporate perspective, the achievement of marketing and corporate communication objectives should be the primary focus of sponsorship.
7. **Recognize image transfer as a key objective:** One of the main objectives of arts and cultural sponsorship is the image transfer between sponsor and sponsored party. This should be taken into account when selecting cultural partnerships.
8. **Ensure systematic planning:** The use of sponsorship should be based on a systematic planning and decision-making process with careful analysis, planning, implementation, and control. In addition, the implementation or activation of sponsorship requires further resources and expertise.
9. **Identify different types of sponsorship:** Arts and cultural sponsorship can be divided into three types: altruistic, promotion-oriented, and traditional sponsorship, into which one's own arts and cultural sponsorship strategy should be classified.
10. **Understand cause-and-effect relationships:** The success chain of arts and cultural sponsorship provides a conceptual framework that should be considered to understand the cause-and-effect relationships in arts and cultural sponsorship.

Forms of Cultural Sponsorship

2

Contents

2.1 Term of Arts and Cultural Funding and Arts and Cultural Sponsoring 22
2.2 Classifications of Arts and Cultural Sponsorship 24
2.3 Actors in the Process of Arts and Cultural Sponsorship 32
2.4 Arts and Cultural Sponsorship From a Marketing Perspective 34
2.5 Arts and Cultural Sponsorship From the Sponsors' Perspective 36
2.6 Arts and Cultural Sponsorship From the Perspective of the Sponsored 41

Abstract

The chapter first defines arts and cultural sponsorship and provides a classification according to different cultural sectors. A structured understanding of the various forms of arts and cultural sponsorship is conveyed by explaining the characteristics of cultural collaborations and illustrating them with examples. In addition, the three most important actors in the process of arts and cultural sponsorship are introduced: corporate sponsors, cultural institutions, and the media. Furthermore, in the process of arts and cultural sponsorship, it is important to distinguish between the perspectives of the sponsor and the sponsored, since sponsorship represents an instrument of marketing or communication for the corporate sponsor, while from the perspective of the sponsored it is a tool for resource acquisition as well as a measure of arts marketing. Both perspectives are presented and explored in greater depth in the following sections. The practical application of arts and cultural sponsorship is also illustrated through a case study of BMW's cultural engagement.

M. Bruhn and L. Pöllmann, *Arts and Cultural Sponsorship*,
https://doi.org/10.1007/978-3-658-50079-5_2

2.1 Term of Arts and Cultural Funding and Arts and Cultural Sponsoring

Since around the mid-1970s, in many countries, corporate sponsorships from various sectors have sought to differentiate themselves from competitors through the use of arts and cultural sponsorship as part of their marketing and corporate communications. Although art and culture have developed into a significant leisure sector in recent years, **expenditures in the area of arts and cultural sponsorship** remained almost constant from 2006 to 2014 (ZAW, 2015).

For years, numerous studies have predicted a considerable upswing for arts and cultural sponsorship, which, however, has only slowly become apparent in the **sponsorship investments of corporate sponsors** in recent years (Heinze, 2008; Pilot Checkpoint, 2008). During the global economic crisis, investments in arts and cultural sponsorship stagnated, but since 2013 a slight increase has been observed. Although approximately 60.4% of corporate sponsors are involved in art and arts and cultural sponsorship, on average only 18.5% of the total sponsorship budget is allocated to art and arts and cultural sponsorship, whereas 43% is invested in sports sponsorship (Bagusat, 2013). The development of public expenditures by the federal and state governments also shows slowly increasing investments in the cultural sector. While there was a significant increase from EUR 7.47 billion to EUR 8.21 billion between 1995 and 2000, expenditures remained largely constant at EUR 8.15 billion until 2007 and only jumped to EUR 9.13 billion in 2009. In 2020, public cultural expenditures had already reached EUR 14.5 billion (SÄBL, 2022, p. 19). These were further increased by additional funding programs in response to the challenges posed by the COVID-19 pandemic (see in detail Chap. 3).

Although there are no reliable figures on the scope of **private arts and cultural funding** in Germany, the Kulturkreis der deutschen Wirtschaft (German Business Culture Circle) assumes that the contribution of foundations to culture amounts to about EUR 125 million and that corporate sponsors spend around EUR 350 million annually on arts and cultural sponsorship (Kulturkreis der deutschen Wirtschaft im BDI e. V., 2016b). The institutes of the Sparkassen-Finanzgruppe alone invest over EUR 100 million each year in arts and cultural funding (SÄBL, 2022, p. 27). Since, in addition to financial contributions, in-kind and service contributions must also be considered, it can be assumed that the total sum of arts and cultural sponsorship in Germany now exceeds the estimated EUR 350 million.

The starting point for an analysis of the opportunities and risks of arts and cultural sponsorship is the **establishment of a uniform conceptual understanding**. This is especially important because arts and cultural funding and arts and cultural sponsorship are often not clearly distinguishable in practice due to the diverse motives of sponsors.

It is often assumed that **traditional arts and cultural funding** by private individuals and corporate sponsors is motivated by altruistic reasons. This is because corporate sponsors often have a decades-long tradition of arts and cultural funding, originating from the role of (founding) entrepreneurs who acted as patrons (e.g., Robert Bosch, Gottlieb Daimler, Friedrich Krupp, Herbert Quandt).

Today, patron-like and selfless arts and cultural funding by corporate sponsors is rarely observed. It is undisputed that corporate sponsors, through traditional arts and cultural funding, also achieve **effects with regard to corporate culture and communication**—whether intentionally, deliberately, or unintentionally. The practice of arts and cultural funding also shows that many corporate sponsors combine altruistic and commercial motives, making it useful to **develop a typology of corporate sponsors acting as cultural supporters**. Figure 2.1 illustrates that corporate sponsors engaged in the cultural sector can be divided into the types of altruistic patrons, patron sponsors, and classical sponsors. It should be noted that the possibilities for selfless arts and cultural funding fundamentally depend on corporate governance. As a result, owner-managed corporate sponsors can more easily allocate funding than those whose management is accountable to supervisory boards or shareholders.

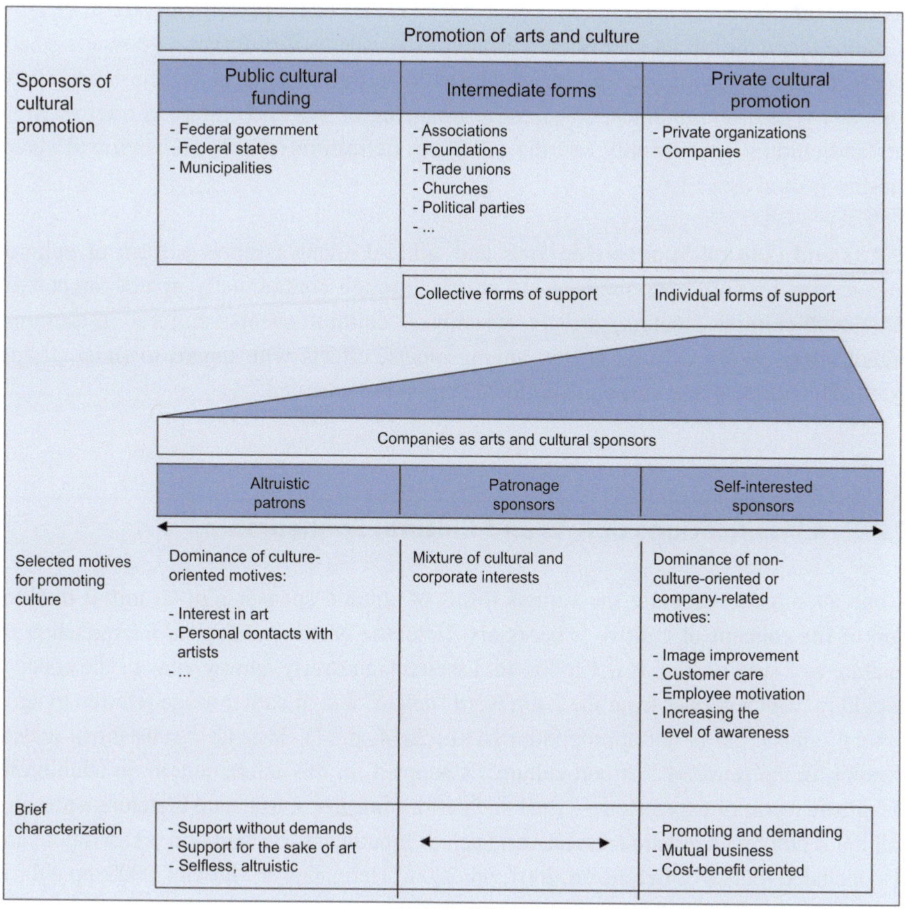

Fig. 2.1 Typology of corporate sponsors as cultural supporters. (Source: Fischer, 1989, p. 15)

The effects of the **combination of cultural and communication policy objectives** as well as the overlap between patronage and arts and cultural sponsorship are also evident in the divergent self-perceptions of different corporate sponsors regarding their cultural engagement. For example, Deutsche Bank has been committed to cultural and social causes since its founding 135 years ago. With the establishment of an art collection in 1979/1980 and the founding of several foundations and non-profit limited liability companies in the 1990s, the basis was created for a long-term, strategically oriented social commitment. In addition to altruistic activities through foundations, such as the Deutsche Bank Foundation established in 2005, which selflessly supports various cultural projects, especially for children, adolescents, and young adults, Deutsche Bank is also involved in classical arts and cultural sponsorship. Among the best-known arts and cultural sponsorship projects are the 2004-supported exhibition "MoMA in Berlin," the "Deutsche Buchpreis" (German Book Prize) sponsored since 2014, and the scholarship program of the "Akademie Musiktheater heute" (Academy for Contemporary Musical Theater) foundation (Münch, 2006; Deutsche Bank AG, 2008a; Deutsche Bank Stiftung, 2023a, b).

Since the visitor to an event is not aware of the effects of different corporate engagements, in the following, regardless of the stated self-perception of the corporate sponsors, any type of communication-effective financing of arts and culture is referred to as arts and cultural sponsorship, and the following **definition of arts and cultural sponsorship** is used as a basis:

▶ **Arts and Cultural Sponsorship** Arts and cultural sponsorship is a form of cultural engagement by corporate sponsors, in which, through contractually agreed support of individual cultural creators, artistic ensembles, cultural events, cultural institutions, organizations in the cultural sector, among others, effects with regard to (internal and external) marketing and corporate communication are intended.

2.2 Classifications of Arts and Cultural Sponsorship

If one attempts to structure the various forms of cultural sponsorship, an **initial distinction of the concept of culture** is necessary. Here, the broad sociological interpretation of "culture as a way of life" is not followed. Likewise, an overly narrow view of the concept of culture, which derives from the Latin word "colere" and in earlier usage referred to agricultural cultivation, is not appropriate (SÄBL, 2014, p. 11). Instead, a substantive understanding in the sense of "art and culture" is adopted. In this interpretation, in addition to the artistic forms of expression—visual and performing arts, music, and literature—arts and cultural sectors with artistic connections, such as monument and tradition preservation, are also included (Schad & Berentzen, 2007, pp. 220 f.; Hermanns & Marwitz, 2008, pp. 88 f.).

An analysis of the frequency of use of the various forms of cultural sponsorship shows that **art sponsorship** predominates. Nevertheless, the broader term arts and cultural sponsorship is used in the following, as it has also become established in general usage (Hermanns & Marwitz, 2008, p. 88).

Figure 2.2 illustrates the **classification according to different cultural sectors** with a depiction of the diverse characteristics within the various sectors as well as possible forms of implementation.

Art and culture	Characteristics	Possible forms of presentation
Visual arts	Painting Sculpture Graphic design Architecture Photography Urban art Design	Special exhibitions in museums and galleries, financing of catalogs/posters and materials, restoration of art works
Performing arts	Opera Operetta Musical Cabaret Ballet Drama Dance	Financing of performances, tours and individual engagements
Music	Classical music Light music	Financing concerts and tours (orchestras, bands, choirs, soloists)
Literature	Books Magazines	Scholarships, sponsorships, readings
Media	Movies Television productions Scripts Video Multimedia	Competitions and financing of productions and scripts, video clips
Festivals	Music festivals Film festivals Theater festivals	Financing of infrastructure, production, performances, concerts and live broadcasts, video-on-demand, competitions
Cultural preservation and architecture	Preservation of historical monuments Preservation of local traditions	Financing of and competitions for art in architecture and restoration work

Fig. 2.2 classification of various art and arts and cultural sectors

For Germany, there is only sparse empirical information available on **arts and cultural funding by German corporate sponsorship**. The following **studies** should be mentioned in particular:

- Study on the scope of arts and cultural funding in the administrative district of Lüneburg. Survey of 40 cultural institutions and 66 corporate sponsors in a joint project of the Lüneburg district government, the Lüneburg-Wolfsburg and Stade Chambers of Industry and Commerce, and the Lüneburg-Stade Chamber of Crafts (Kulturkontakte, 2003).
- Study "Corporate Cultural Responsibility (CCR) Study 2006." Survey of 31 corporate sponsors to highlight the relationships and overlaps between corporate social responsibility (CSR), Corporate Cultural Responsibility, and arts and cultural sponsorship in practice (Causales Agency for Marketing & Kommunikation, 2006).
- Study on the social engagement of corporate sponsors, particularly in the areas of culture, sports, and other social fields. Survey of 541 corporate sponsors in Baden-Württemberg in 2007 (Wegner, 2007).
- Study "arts and cultural sponsorship Germany 2007." Survey of 32 cultural institutions on the forms of cooperation between culture and business based on existing sponsorship partnerships in Germany in 2007 (Causales Agency for Marketing & Kommunikation, 2007).
- Study by the European Sponsoring Exchange and the Agency for Art Communication in 2006 among 500 corporate sponsors in Germany (ESB (European Sponsoring Exchange) 2008).
- Study "Cultural Engagement of Corporate Sponsors—Integrated Part of Strategy?" by Roland Berger Strategy Consultants. Survey of 193 corporate sponsors from 2003 to 2004 on whether cultural engagement is part of corporate strategy and leads to competitive advantages (Heusser et al., 2008).
- Study "Sponsoring Trends 2008" by Bob Bomlitz Group GmbH and the Institute for Marketing at the University of the Federal Armed Forces Munich. The survey includes a total of 391 sponsors and analyzes, among other types of sponsorship, arts and cultural sponsorship (Bob Bomliz, Group, 2008).
- Study "Sponsor Visions 2008" by the market research institute Pilot Checkpoint in 2008 among 130 advertising corporate sponsors and 88 agencies on all types of sponsorship. The survey also includes information on the specific areas within each type of sponsorship (Pilot Checkpoint, 2008).
- Study "Arts and Cultural Sponsorship Market in Germany, Austria, Switzerland, and Luxembourg 2013" by the Society for Arts Marketing and Arts and Cultural Sponsorship Causales. A survey of 106 cultural providers from the four German-speaking countries regarding sponsorship partners, communication measures, and their own organizational structure (Causales Agency for Marketing & Kommunikation, 2013).
- Basic study "Sponsoring 2014" by the market and opinion research institute Ipsos provides insights and analyses into the entire German sponsorship market based on data from 1000 face-to-face interviews with the population (Ipsos GmbH, 2014a).

- Study “Sponsoring Trends 2012” by Prof. Dr. Ariane Bagusat, Professor of Sponsoring and Event Management at Ostfalia University of Applied Sciences. The online survey includes 430 questionnaires from the highest-revenue corporate sponsors in Germany and, like the 2010 study, examines trends in various forms of sponsorship (Bagusat, 2013).
- Basic study “Sponsoring 2014” by the market and opinion research institute Ipsos provides insights and analyses into the entire German sponsorship market based on data from 1000 face-to-face interviews with the population (Ipsos GmbH, 2014a).
- Study “Sponsor Visions 2014/15,” conducted by the ZHAW School of Management and Law (SML) and the Association for Sponsoring in Germany, Austria, and Switzerland (FASPO) on relevant data regarding the status and trends in the Swiss sponsorship market. In Switzerland, 400 marketing and sponsorship managers from 40 different industries were surveyed using an online questionnaire (ZHAW, 2015).
- Analysis of the development of private art and arts and cultural funding in the Federal Republic of Germany by Anna Weiland (Weiland, 2017).

For **Switzerland**, the Sponsor Visions study found that in 2021, 59% of the corporate sponsors surveyed were engaged as sponsors of cultural offerings. In 2012, the figure was 49%. The study also shows that the cultural expenditures of corporate sponsors remained stable even during the COVID-19 pandemic (ZHAW, 2022; Fischer & Schmidli, 2022).

When considering **engagements in cultural sectors** in which corporate sponsors are involved as part of arts and cultural sponsorship, it becomes apparent that, above all, art exhibitions in the fields of visual and performing arts (e.g., museums, plays, ballet performances) and musical events (musicals, operas, operettas) are supported (Posadowsky, 2007, pp. 354 f.). The greatest growth opportunities are seen by corporate sponsors particularly in the support of festivals and operas. One study shows that 76% of the advertising corporate sponsors and agencies surveyed attribute increasing importance to the sponsorship of festivals, and 64% to the sponsorship of operas (Pilot Checkpoint, 2008). Furthermore, a positive development is expected especially in film sponsorship (financing of productions, screenplays), music (rock/pop music), as well as visual arts (art exhibitions, museums) (Nielsen Sports (formerly Repucom), 2015a, p. 9). Both individual artists, cultural groups and organizations, as well as cultural events in various performance categories are sponsored, i.e., across the entire spectrum from “high art” to “everyday art” at the grassroots level.

When selecting sponsorships in the cultural sector—especially in comparison to sports sponsorship—some **specific features of arts and cultural sponsorship** must be considered: For example, the primary approach is to narrowly defined target groups, there is the possibility for the company to appear exclusively, and it is necessary for the corporate sponsor to engage substantively with cultural concerns.

An analysis of the **industry origin** of corporate sponsors engaged in arts and cultural funding shows across various studies that, above all, corporate sponsors from the financial services and insurance sectors are very active in arts and cultural sponsorship. In addition to sports sponsorship, in which 78.8% of sponsoring corporate sponsors are involved, the field of art and culture, with a sponsorship participation rate of 60.4%, is also clearly a focus for the financial and insurance sector (Bagusat, 2013; Causales Agency for Marketing & Kommunikation, 2013).

The extent of support for cultural associations, foundations, public budgets, individual artists, and in-house activities is highly industry-dependent. Studies on the **recipients of arts and cultural funding** show that, of all cultural sectors, museums, orchestras, and spoken and musical theater are primarily supported (Causales Agency for Marketing & Kommunikation, 2013). When examining various corporate engagements, it also becomes clear that a large proportion of sponsors additionally invest in the promotion of young talent. The reason for this distribution may be that supporting young artists demonstrates a greater sense of social responsibility, in order to elicit positive reactions from the public (Ackermann, 2008; Eick, 2008).

Finally, arts and cultural sponsorships can be differentiated according to their **local orientation**: A large proportion of corporate sponsorship is engaged in its immediate geographical environment (55.4%), while only 24.6% of cultural sponsors are active at the regional level and 2.3% internationally (Causales Agency for Marketing & Kommuniation, 2013). These data clearly show that corporate sponsorship, through its cultural activities, primarily aims to gain acceptance and sympathy in its immediate surroundings. For many cultural sponsors, the focus of their efforts is less on increasing brand awareness at the national level or promoting product sales, and more on the relationship between the sponsoring corporate entity and its stakeholders.

Regardless of the specific design of cultural sponsorships, the eight **forms of arts and cultural sponsorship** shown in Fig. 2.3 are distinguished:

1. **Type of sponsorship contribution:** In addition to financial resources, contributions in kind, such as equipment or services (e.g., technical support, transportation services), are also offered as sponsorship contributions.
2. **Type of consideration:** The beneficiaries themselves provide active sponsorship benefits as part of the sponsorship, or leave it to the corporate sponsor to achieve communicative effects through the sponsorship.
3. **Type of beneficiary:** In broad terms, in addition to the artists themselves, cultural institutions (organizations) or projects (events, competitions, initiatives) can also be supported.
4. **Institution-based and project-based sponsorship:** With regard to the support of institutions, a distinction can also be made between sponsoring a cultural institution in general and supporting a specific project. For example, a theater or arts festival may receive a sum for general use (institution-based). The sponsorship contribution could also be earmarked for the realization of a specific artistic offering, an education project, or for new construction (project-based).

Delimitation features	Forms	Examples
Type of sponsorship	Financial resources Material resources Services	Contributions to artists (grants, exhibition fees), publication support, subsidies for productions Provision of working materials for artists, premises for exhibitions, infrastructure Technical and commercial advice for art events, provision of insurance and transportation services
Type of consideration	Active consideration Passive tolerance	Sponsored parties themselves take on advertising for the sponsor (Rihanna for Puma) Sponsored parties behave passively, sponsors draw attention to sponsorships (press releases)
Type of beneficiary	Cultural institutions Cultural projects Artists	Announcements of art prizes (Sparkasse) for established or up-and-coming artists Sponsorship of cultural institutions without project reference, e.g. opera houses, festivals (Deutsche Telekom)
Commitment of resources	Institutional sponsorship Project-based sponsorship	Targeted promotion of art events (concerts, performances) or cultural objects (monument protection) Promotion of a festival (as an institution) Promotion of an education project (project-related)
Intermediary bodies	Single-level sponsorship Multi-level sponsorship	Sponsorship of an art museum for the printing of a catalog (direct, single-stage sponsorship) Sponsorship of an art prize (multi-stage - the money is awarded to artists by a jury)
Performance level of the sponsored party	"Elite art/culture" Popular art/culture Mass art/culture	Promotion of concert series (Audi), poetry readings Promotion of pop events (Radio FFH)
Initiator of the sponsorship	Self-initiated sponsoring Third-party initiated sponsoring	Announcement of company-specific cultural awards (BMW Welt Jazz Award) Companies participate in sponsorships of cultural institutions (opera houses) or events (Salzburg Festival - Audi)
Number of sponsors	Exclusive sponsoring Cooperative sponsoring	Companies sponsor events on their own (Beyoncé tour with American Express) Several sponsors participate in the sponsorship (Schleswig-Holstein Festival with Provinzial and others)

Fig. 2.3 Forms of cultural sponsorship

5. **Single-stage versus multi-stage sponsorship:** This distinction can be made based on possible intermediaries of sponsorship contributions. If a sponsorship engagement supports a cultural institution that uses the funds to finance art prizes, this constitutes a two- or multi-stage form of arts and cultural sponsorship. In the case of supporting art prizes, this can also be referred to as indirect arts and cultural sponsorship, since the corporate sponsor does not select the cultural creators directly as recipients of a contribution, as is the case, for example, with the German Book Prize (sponsor Deutsche Bank) or the competition "Jugend musiziert" (sponsor Sparkassen Verband). In both competitions, a jury decides on the award winners and thus on the recipients of the sponsorship funds.
6. **Performance level of the beneficiary:** For larger corporate sponsors, the focus is often on supporting classical "high culture." However, popular or mass art can also be the subject of support.
7. **Initiator of the sponsorship:** As the initiator of a sponsorship, the corporate sponsor develops and implements its own ideas (self-initiated sponsorship) or participates in external sponsorship offers (externally initiated sponsorship).
8. **Number of sponsors:** If only a single sponsor is involved, this is referred to as exclusive sponsorship. If several corporate sponsors are involved, these are forms of cooperative sponsorship.

The abundance of opportunities for cultural engagement through corporate sponsorship is illustrated by the following **examples of arts and cultural sponsorships** in Germany:

- **Audi AG** has been sponsoring various major music festivals for many years, such as the Salzburg Festival, which it has supported for 25 years. In addition, Audi AG supports the Audi Wind Philharmonic, founded in 1962, which is made up of employees of Audi AG and gives its own concerts every year in numerous German cities as well as abroad. Furthermore, in 2007, the corporate sponsorship established the Audi Youth Choir Academy to give young singers the opportunity to sing professionally at a very high artistic level in a choir. The Audi Youth Choir Academy also actively participates in the "Audi Summer Concerts," where the role of the car manufacturer goes beyond that of a traditional sponsor and the corporate sponsorship acts as the organizer (Audi AG, 2023).
- At **Deutsche Telekom AG**, arts and cultural sponsorship is also an integral part of the company philosophy. For example, since 2005, the corporate sponsorship has organized the "International Ludwig van Beethoven Competition for Piano" in Bonn to support talented young pianists. In addition, Deutsche Telekom launches its own musical events, such as live events with well-known contemporary artists under the "Electronic Beats" program series or the "Telekom Street Gigs." With the latter, the corporate sponsorship aims especially to appeal to the younger generation and organizes concerts by well-known bands at unusual locations (e.g., on a parking deck or in a quarry) (Deutsche Telekom AG, 2023a, 2023b, 2023c).

- The technology group **Siemens AG** is a member of the Working Group for Arts and Cultural Sponsorship (AKS), an association of 65 corporate sponsors that have firmly anchored ongoing sponsorship engagement in the cultural sector within their corporate culture. As part of the Salzburg Festival, Siemens has been one of the main sponsors since 1999. In cooperation with Deutsche Grammophon, the company organizes and streams concerts from the Siemens Villa. It also supports young talent as a sponsor of the ARD Music Prize (Siemens AG, 2023).
- The insurance group **Allianz AG** merged its cultural foundation with its environmental foundation in 2022 to form the Allianz Foundation. The foundation's goal is to support initiatives with a civil society, ecological, cultural, and artistic background in Europe and the Mediterranean region (Allianz Foundation, 2022). In 2022, for example, the foundation realized the theater streaming project "Architecture of Ruined Body" in cooperation with theater festivals, theaters, and individual artists. The project "Art to Claim act" aimed to raise awareness of the consequences of climate change through artistic actions (Allianz Foundation, 2022).
- The corporate sponsorship **Hugo Boss AG** has had a long-standing collaboration with the Solomon R. Guggenheim Museum and, together with the museum, has awarded the Hugo Boss Prize annually since 1996 to international artists for their life's work (Hugo Boss AG, 2023; Guggenheim Foundation, 2023).
- **Landesbank Baden-Württemberg** (LBBW) sponsors the Kunstmuseum Stuttgart to maintain the Otto Dix collection, the National Theater Mannheim, and the Stuttgart State Opera. In addition, LBBW acts as a partner of the International Bach Academy and supports the Semperoper Dresden—even beyond Baden-Württemberg (Landesbank Baden-Württemberg, 2023).
- The Swiss retail company **Migros** has established a special institution called Migros-Kulturprozent, which supports the areas of culture, society, education, leisure, and business. Funded by the revenues of the cooperatives and the Migros Cooperative Association, this commitment by Migros makes an important contribution to the Swiss cultural landscape, aiming to provide the population with broad access to culture and education. In addition to numerous own projects, various initiatives have been supported and promoted. As a result, a sustainable "culture of arts and cultural funding" has developed (Altdorfer et al., 2014; Migros Cooperative Association, 2023a, see also Chap. 8).
- The chemical company **BASF SE** is active in the vicinity of its Ludwigshafen site by promoting regional young talent in the fields of art and culture and supporting the preservation and maintenance of cultural monuments of national and international significance around the Ludwigshafen site. BASF also supports, for example, the street art project Muralu, the Festival of German Film, and the Enjoy Jazz Festival (BASF SE, 2023).

Despite the wide range of possibilities for cultural engagement, in **practice, arts and cultural sponsorship** focuses on the initiation and financing of artistic events. In

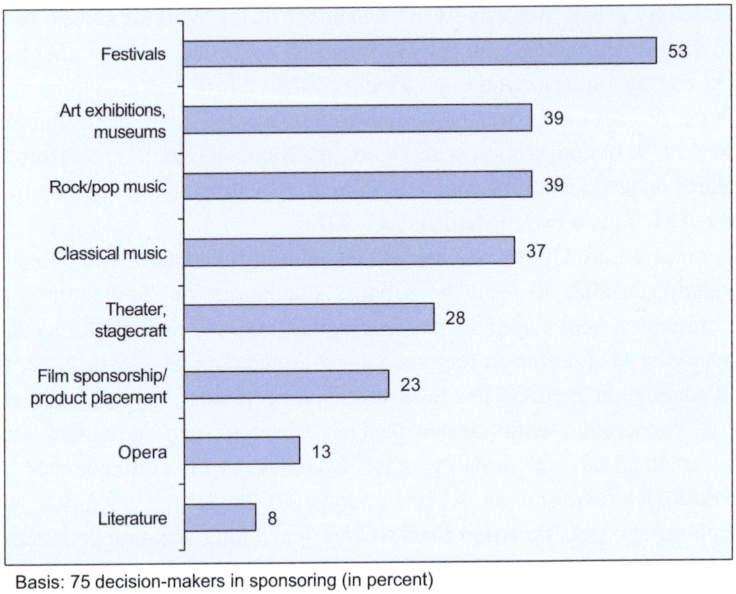

Fig. 2.4 Support of cultural sectors by corporate sponsorship in Germany. (Source: Nielsen Sports (formerly Repucom) 2015a)

particular, the areas of festivals, visual arts, and events in the rock/pop music sector are frequently chosen by corporate sponsors, with activities concentrating on supporting concerts and exhibitions (Nielsen Sports (formerly Repucom), 2015a). The reason for this is that such events achieve the highest number of target group contacts, and with international line-ups or art, they can also reach an international audience.

Figure 2.4 shows the extent of **arts and cultural funding in different cultural sectors**. Compared to 1997, sponsorship of music events in the rock and pop sector has increased significantly, but is highly dependent on the availability of large events (Bob Bomliz Group, 2008; Pilot Checkpoint, 2008; Nielsen Sports (formerly Repucom), 2015a). In addition, 28% of those responsible assume that the area of rock and pop music will continue to gain in importance in the future (Nielsen Sports (formerly Repucom), 2015a). This assessment is also supported by a current forecast on the development of the live music market in Germany, which, after the setbacks caused by the COVID-19 pandemic, had already largely recovered by 2023 (PWC Germany, 2023, p. 136).

2.3 Actors in the Process of Arts and Cultural Sponsorship

In the present analysis, arts and cultural sponsorship is not reduced to just the two actors, sponsor and sponsored party. For an understanding of the prerequisites for a successful sponsorship cooperation as well as the mechanisms of arts and cultural sponsorship, the perspective of the other **players in the arts and cultural sponsorship process** is indispensable, as will be shown below.

The **emergence and spread** of sponsorship in Germany is embedded in a general trend to increasingly utilize the leisure interests of the population for marketing and corporate communication purposes. This becomes particularly evident when analyzing the interests and network of relationships among the main participants in sponsorship. The **"Magic Triangle" of sponsorship** shown in Fig. 2.5 explains the emergence of sponsorships (Bruhn, 1987, p. 47).

1. **Cultural creators and cultural institutions** are interested in fulfilling their tasks, which require financial expenditures. Sponsorship opens up additional sources of funding and resources. Fulfilling these tasks is associated with events such as performances and artistic works, which, due to audience interest, generate media effects.
2. **Business** is constantly searching for new ways to engage with its target groups. By using sponsorship as an integral part of communication, corporate sponsorship has the opportunity to positively enhance the image of the brand or company, thanks to the environment perceived as positive by the audience. The need to seek innovative forms of communication is further intensified by changes on the part of communication recipients. Phenomena such as the general information overload of consumers (Kroeber-Riel & Gröppel-Klein, 2019), declining interest in media advertising, and zapping (ZAW, 2013; Bruhn, 2014) make it clear that communication success can no longer be guaranteed solely through the use of conventional communication instruments.
3. **Media** (electronic and print media) are guided by ratings and reach. They broadcast—either for a fee or free of charge—events that appeal to a broad audience. Media

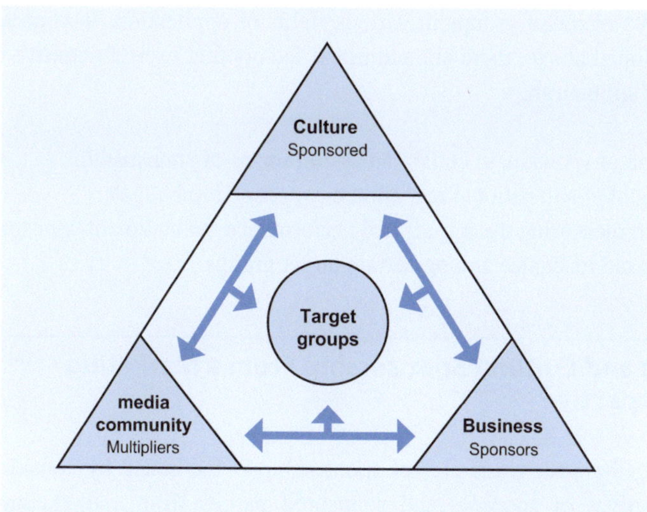

Fig. 2.5 The "Magic Triangle" of arts and cultural sponsorship

providers use these events created by cultural actors to reach their own target groups (readers, listeners, or viewers) and to distinguish themselves from media competitors. The media landscape has been radically transformed by the internet and social media. With the strong differentiation of channels and the establishment of social media, individual media outlets have lost power. For years, it was a major challenge to motivate media to report on the sponsorship activities of corporate sponsors. The willingness to do so was and remains limited for two reasons: First, the information that a corporate sponsor is supporting an art project generally lacks significant news value. Second, there is a risk of a cannibalization effect through such reporting, as media outlets also seek to win sponsors as advertising clients. However, if they report on a sponsorship engagement free of charge, this could lead to corporate sponsorship communication budgets being shifted in favor of sponsorship and at the expense of media advertising.

Today, coverage by high-reach media remains an important element in sponsorship impact planning. However, dependence on individual media outlets is lower. In addition, information about a sponsorship engagement is now disseminated by up to five **media actors**, into which the media sector can be divided:

- The "classic" news media.
- Newer media actors such as bloggers and influencers.
- Cultural institutions' own media channels (e.g., social media presence).
- Sponsors' own media channels (reach through corporate media activities).
- Individual social media profiles of target groups or visitors to cultural events, both public (e.g., via Instagram, TikTok) and in private chats (e.g., Signal, WhatsApp).

Based on these overlapping interests, sponsorship offers the opportunity to engage the leisure interests of target groups in various fields of application. In contrast to the tendencies mentioned above, there are additional factors that exert a **negative influence on the spread of sponsorship**:

- Proliferation of sponsors in certain areas and forms of sponsorship.
- Effects of global and national recession on sponsorship budgets.
- Problems in measuring the impact and performance evaluation of sponsorship.
- Resistance and reactance among certain target groups.

2.4 Arts and Cultural Sponsorship From a Marketing Perspective

Understanding the basic principles of sponsorship is facilitated by considering the different perspectives of sponsors and sponsored parties from a marketing standpoint. Figure 2.6 illustrates the **interrelationships of sponsorship** from the viewpoint of sponsors and sponsored parties.

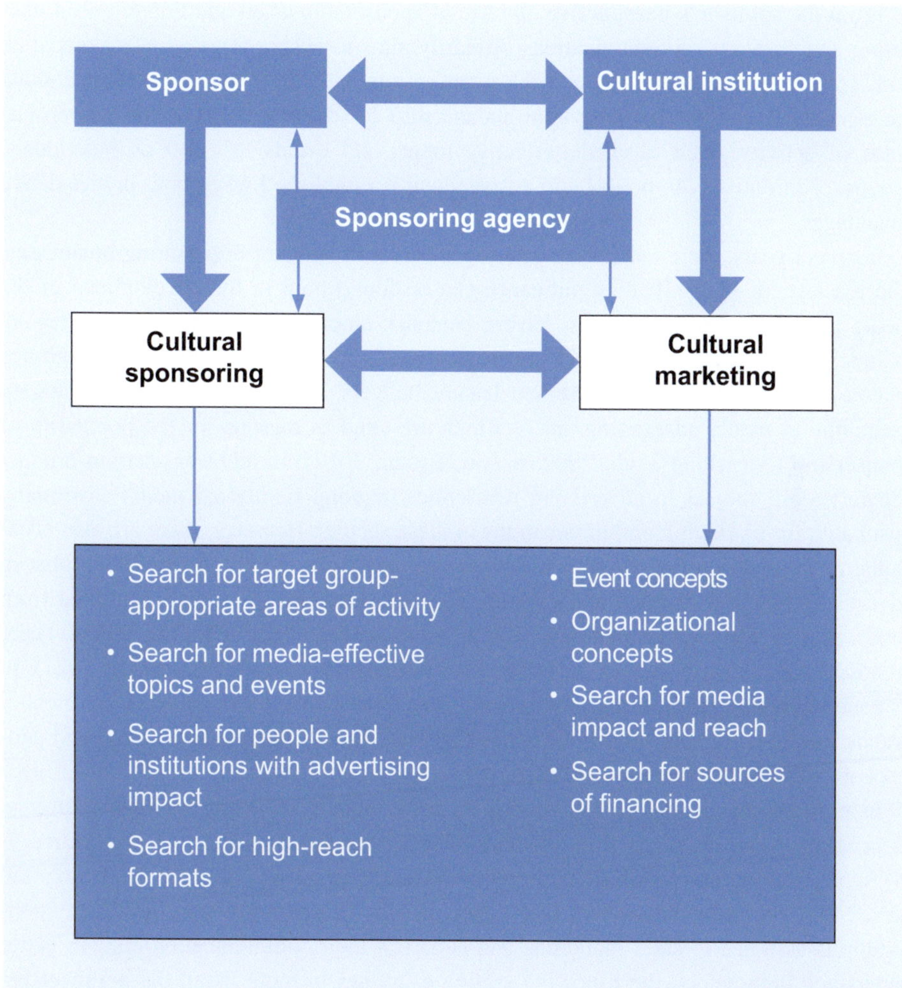

Fig. 2.6 Sponsorship from the perspective of sponsors and sponsored parties. (Source: Bruhn, 2018a, p. 19)

From the **perspective of the sponsored parties**, a professional approach involves engaging in arts marketing. Cultural institutions and artists seek to systematically improve and enhance the appeal of their offerings through marketing. This includes, for example, planning target group-oriented measures, developing event concepts, seeking media resonance, and providing innovative communication platforms. For the sponsored parties, sponsorship represents an opportunity to tap into additional sources of funding as part of their procurement marketing.

In recent years, numerous cultural institutions have increasingly adopted marketing principles to achieve their own objectives. **Arts marketing** has further developed in Germany and is already being practiced professionally by many theaters, museums, and festival organizers (Pöllmann, 2021a).

From the **sponsor's perspective**, the use of sponsorship as an additional tool in marketing and corporate communications primarily aims to ensure targeted communication with specific audiences. Based on the given communication situation, it is becoming increasingly important for corporate sponsorship to identify target group-appropriate areas of activity, such as media-effective topics and events, as well as individuals, groups, or initiatives. A sponsorship arrangement is established when both parties derive advantages.

In recent years, there has been a growing **interest in sponsorship among businesses**. The reasons for this shift in significance can be found both in the development of the media market and in changes in leisure behavior among the population. Key factors include rising costs for traditional advertising media, the ability to reach target groups in non-commercial settings, increased leisure budgets, and growing resistance among the public to media advertising, all of which are cited as reasons for the popularity of sponsorship (Nieschlag et al., 2002, p. 586; Bruhn, 2012). In addition, certain product categories are subject to advertising restrictions, making traditional media advertising unsuitable for marketing communications in these sectors. However, there are also occasional restrictions on the use of sponsorship: for example, since January 2022, tobacco advertising has been banned in Germany. Tobacco companies are also prohibited from sponsoring events or activities that have a "cross-border effect" (BMEL, 2020). There are also various restrictions on advertising for alcoholic beverages (Bundestag, 2021). In its code of conduct, the German Advertising Standards Council recommends that alcohol brands refrain from sponsorship activities that "are directly related to children and adolescents" (Deutscher Werberat, 2019, p. 10).

In practice, the forms of sponsorship in communications work are highly diverse. In general, it can be stated that arts and cultural sponsorship, from the perspective of the sponsored cultural institutions, is primarily assigned to procurement marketing and serves as a financing instrument (see Chap. 3). On the sponsors' side, however, sponsorship is assigned to sales marketing and is part of their communication mix. To better understand both actors, the following section examines in more detail the **perspectives of sponsors and sponsored parties**.

2.5 Arts and Cultural Sponsorship From the Sponsors' Perspective

To begin with, it is useful from the sponsor's perspective to differentiate between various manifestations. The following criteria illustrate the different **forms of sponsorship** (see Fig. 2.7):

- Type of sponsor
- Number of sponsors
- Type of sponsorship contribution

Differentiation features	Forms	Examples
Type of sponsorship	In cash	Contributions to cultural organizations and artists
	Material resources	Provision of instruments, event technology, catering
	Service	Provision of know-how, insurance, shuttle service
Number of sponsors	Exclusive sponsorship	Company is the sole sponsor, e.g. for art institutions or cultural productions
	Co-sponsorship	Several companies participate, e.g. at a festival
Type of sponsor	Performance sponsors	Equipping artists (endorsement), provision of material resources
	Companies as sponsors	Company as a whole sponsors projects, e.g. Siemens, DHL
	Foundations as sponsors	Corporate foundations support projects, e.g. Robert Bosch, Allianz
	Media as sponsors	Media are involved as organizers, e.g. Die Zeit, Radio eins and ARD
Initiator of the sponsorship	Third-party sponsorship	Cultural organizations or ensembles offer certain sponsorships
	Self-initiated sponsorship	Company is the sole initiator and exclusive user of the sponsorship
Variety of sponsorship	Concentrated sponsorship	Sponsorship is only used in one area, e.g. music festivals
	Differentiated sponsoring	Sponsorship is used in different areas, e.g. sport, culture and the environment
Type of use	Isolated sponsoring	Sponsoring is used separately from other communication instruments
	Integrated sponsoring	Sponsoring is used in conjunction with various communication instruments

Fig. 2.7 Forms of sponsorship from the sponsors' perspective. (Source: Bruhn, 2018a, p. 25)

- Initiator of the sponsorship
- Diversity of sponsorship
- Type of utilization

Type of Sponsor

In classical sponsoring, corporate sponsors market products or services that often have no relation to the execution of the sponsored party's cultural activities. These corporate sponsors use sponsorship solely as a communication tool. In contrast, there are also sponsors who have a direct, performance-related interest in the execution of the events they sponsor:

1. **Performance sponsors** (corporate sponsorship with a connection in terms of content)
   - Product sponsors are corporate sponsors who have an inherent interest in the execution of a cultural organization's activities through their offered products (for example, manufacturers of musical instruments, lighting and sound technology, or materials used in art productions),
   - Service sponsors are corporate sponsors who provide specific services necessary for the events (e.g., transportation, insurance of artworks).
2. **Corporate sponsorship as sponsors** (corporate sponsorship without a connection in terms of content)
   - Corporate sponsors whose service portfolio has no direct connection to the sponsored area and who use sponsorship solely as a communication tool (e.g., banks, breweries, credit card companies).
   - Corporate sponsors who also expect positive influences on their own service portfolio through sponsorship (e.g., influence of art on product design, furnishing office spaces with art objects).
3. **Foundations as sponsors**
   - Non-corporate foundations established solely for the purpose of financially supporting cultural institutions and cultural professionals (e.g., Aachener J.S. Bach Foundation, Arte Musica—Foundation for Art and Culture, Berlin Masters Foundation).
   - Corporate foundations (e.g., Allianz Foundation, Volkswagen Foundation, Robert Bosch Foundation, Fritz Thyssen Foundation, Daimler and Benz Foundation, Alfried Krupp von Bohlen und Halbach Foundation).
4. **Media as sponsors**
   - Media outlets that act as organizers (e.g., DIE ZEIT as organizer of conferences, author talks, panel discussions, exhibitions, and award ceremonies).
   - Media outlets involved in dissemination (e.g., SWR or Deutschlandradio Kultur as media partners of the Stuttgart State Opera or BR Klassik as media partner of the Bayreuth Festival).

Number of sponsors

Depending on the number of sponsors involved, their position relative to co-sponsors is determined. In addition to the dominance of individual sponsors (exclusive sponsors), it is also possible for a large number of additional sponsors to participate (co-sponsors):

1. **Exclusive sponsorship**
   - The sponsor appears as the sole sponsor at the event.
   - The sponsor's name is incorporated into the event (title sponsorship).
2. **Co-sponsorship**
   - Several sponsors (either a predetermined or unlimited number) participate in a sponsorship with a non-compete clause (i.e., only one co-sponsor per industry is accepted).
   - Participation of sponsors without a non-compete clause (i.e., any corporate sponsor is accepted under the given conditions).

While sponsorship collaborations with cultural institutions often involve few and frequently exclusive sponsorships, festivals are generally supported by numerous sponsors simultaneously, thereby broadening the financial base.

Type of Sponsorship Contribution

Sponsors have various options for supporting the sponsored party. Most commonly, a specific sponsorship amount, relevant material resources, or services are provided, or there is a transfer of know-how as part of sponsorships:

1. **Money**
   - One-time monetary payment.
   - Ongoing, regular payments.
2. **Material resources**
   - Provision of the sponsor's products (e.g., vehicles, computers, instruments).
   - Catering at events.
3. **Services and know-how**
   - Sponsor assumes administrative tasks (e.g., invitations, logistics).
   - Provision of services necessary for the execution of a cultural offering (e.g., hotel rooms, event venues).
   - Transfer of know-how through consulting services (e.g., legal advice, support in setting up a multimedia communication system).
   - Provision of employees for a limited period (secondments, corporate volunteering).

Initiator of Sponsorship

Depending on who initiates the sponsorship event, a distinction can be made between externally and self-initiated sponsorship:

1. **Externally initiated sponsorship** is characterized by corporate sponsors participating in externally offered sponsorships, e.g., from associations, clubs, organizations, or consultants. However, as the number of sponsors increases, as is often the case with music festivals, it becomes less attractive for a corporate sponsor to appear as just one among many sponsors.
2. **Self-initiated sponsorship** is characterized by sponsorships being developed and implemented internally within the company, such as competitions, proprietary cultural events, or the establishment of a company's own cultural foundation.

Diversity of Sponsorship

Depending on the scope and intensity of the sponsorship commitment, corporate sponsorships are either limited to specific sponsorships (concentrated sponsorship) or are active as sponsors in various areas (differentiated sponsorship):

1. **Concentrated sponsorship** is characterized by a corporate sponsorship focusing on a single area of support (culture, sports, social/environment, media) and entering into one or more sponsorships within this area.
2. **Differentiated sponsorship** is characterized by corporate sponsorships employing several forms of sponsorship in parallel, such as cultural and sports sponsorship.

Type of Utilization

Depending on the type of utilization of sponsorship, isolated and integrated sponsorship can be distinguished:

1. **Isolated sponsorship** occurs when a corporate sponsorship uses the instrument of sponsorship without linking it in terms of content, form, or timing with other communication instruments.
2. **Integrated sponsorship** is characterized by sponsorship being used in combination with other communication instruments on the basis of content, formal, and/or temporal integration, in order to convey a consistent corporate image.

An overview and examples of the various forms of sponsorship from the sponsors' perspective are shown in Fig. 2.7.

Based on the criteria of the diversity of sponsorship and the professionalism (in terms of written planning, coordination with other communication instruments, and performance evaluation) with which it is conducted by corporate sponsorships, four **types of sponsorship** can be distinguished on the basis of the results of a corporate survey (Hermanns 2001, pp. 3 f.). According to this, 23.7% of the sponsors surveyed are among the **sponsorship professionals**, who are particularly characterized by a highly planned approach to sponsorship and make above-average use of sports and media sponsorship.

The **big spenders** (21.8%) allocate about a quarter of their communication budget to sponsorship and are active in all types of sponsorship with above-average frequency. About one third of sponsors are **sports-oriented sponsors**. They plan their activities less professionally, and one third of these corporate sponsorships do not conduct any performance evaluations. In terms of professionalism, behind the sports-oriented sponsors are the **arts-oriented sponsors** (21.8%), who, in addition to cultural activities, are also increasingly involved in social sponsorship. Notably, this group allocates a large share of their sponsorship expenditures (79%) directly to the sponsored party.

2.6 Arts and Cultural Sponsorship From the Perspective of the Sponsored

In addition to these various forms of sponsorship from the sponsors' perspective, different manifestations can also be identified from the perspective of the sponsored. The following criteria are used for **classification**:

- Type of sponsored individuals/groups
- Performance level of the sponsored
- Type of sponsored organization
- Type of sponsored event
- Type of consideration provided by the sponsored

Type of Sponsored Individuals/Groups

The range of sponsored parties extends from individuals or communities who pursue their activities professionally, e.g., professional musicians or artists, to groups or ensembles who view the supported activities merely as a hobby, such as amateur orchestras. Overall, three **basic types** can be distinguished with regard to the type of supported individuals or groups:

1. **Professionals:** Individuals or groups who earn their living, for example, through cultural services and products and, based on their profession, seek to open up additional sources of income.
2. **Semi-professionals:** Individuals or groups who earn part of their income, for example, through artistic engagement and intend to create additional income and more freedom for their artistic activities through sponsorship. Since self-employed artists often have to manage with modest fees—the average annual income for beginners registered with the Artists' Social Insurance Fund was €17,495 (gross) in 2022 (Künstlersozialkasse 2023)—it is not uncommon for artists to have a second so-called "bread-and-butter job."

3. **Amateurs:** Individuals or groups who have a steady income from their profession and intend to cover part of the expenses of their artistic engagement through sponsors (e.g., equipment, travel). Amateurs pursue their activities at different performance levels (e.g., from hobby artists with small local exhibitions to bands and DJs with significant social media reach).

Performance Category of the Sponsored Party

The degree of professionalization is generally closely linked to the corresponding performance category. Cultural activities are either broadly based—with little emphasis on performance incentives—or are more performance-oriented. Accordingly, three different **performance categories** can be distinguished:

1. **Grassroots Level:** Individuals and groups who pursue their cultural activities in their leisure time at a comparatively low level of performance (e.g., amateur musicians, amateur painters).
2. **Performance Level:** Individuals and groups who participate in competitions and public performances as part of their respective activities, with organizations generally being more tightly structured (e.g., performance competitions in the arts).
3. **Elite Level:** Individuals and groups who achieve nationally and internationally competitive top performances in their respective fields (e.g., professional musicians).

These three performance categories are not strictly separated from one another. Rather, they illustrate the **career path of many professional cultural practitioners**. For example, in 2021, nearly 1.37 million music students were registered at the 933 music schools affiliated with the Association of German Music Schools (VdM, 2023). Some of these individuals, who initially belong to the grassroots level, participate annually in competitions such as the German music competition “Jugend musiziert” (Youth makes music) and thus move up to the performance level. Successful award winners in these competitions often choose to pursue university studies in their instrumental field, thereby remaining permanently at the performance level. Again, a portion of these professional musicians make it to the elite level. Corporate sponsorships that also support the grassroots level in their cultural engagement—such as the Sparkassen- und Giroverband as the main sponsor of “Jugend musiziert”—can thus establish early ties with young talents and foster their careers.

Various examples of performance categories in cultural fields are listed in Fig. 2.8.

Type of Sponsored Organization

Only in exceptional cases do individuals directly seek sponsors. This does not apply to groups organized as associations, federations, foundations, or other non-commercial institutions. In these cases, the organizations systematically take on the task of finding sponsors. Four different **types of organizations** interested in arts and cultural sponsorship can be distinguished:

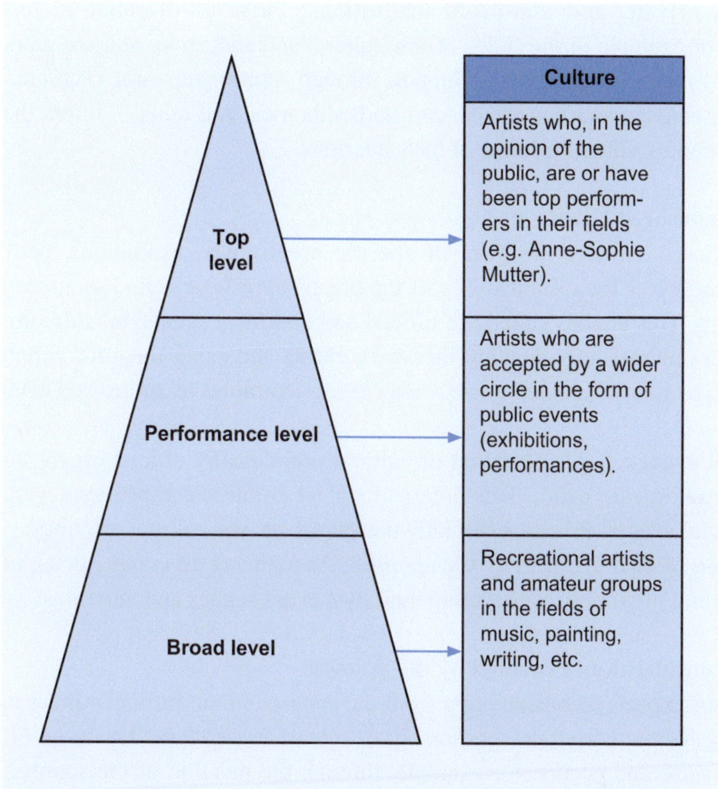

Fig. 2.8 Performance categories in sponsorship. (Source: Bruhn, 2018a, p. 27)

1. **Federations:** Organizations authorized to conduct national and international events and to confer honors, etc. (e.g., German Museums Association, German Music Council, German Cultural Council, Cultural Policy Society).
2. **Associations:** Groups formed to fulfill cultural, social, scientific, or similar purposes. A defining feature of associations is that they predominantly operate on a non-profit basis and often rely on financial contributions from public and private donors (e.g., local cultural associations).
3. **Foundations:** Institutions established to support specific areas of activity as defined by their purpose. In Germany, foundations are particularly common in the promotion of science and education. Sponsors have the opportunity to contribute to the foundation's capital through their involvement or to support individual projects such as events. In the cultural sector, foundations are also often used to protect historic buildings and prevent their sale. However, these foundations do not always have the necessary resources for the preservation and maintenance of the buildings and are therefore dependent on additional income from sponsors.

4. **Public, private, and non-profit institutions:** These fulfill public or private mandates, for example in the fields of art, culture, and education, and are predominantly funded by government grants. Support through sponsorship—for example, for theaters, museums, opera houses, concert halls, libraries, and others—offers the opportunity to improve the fulfillment of their missions.

Type of Sponsored Event

Sponsorships often take the form of specific events (e.g., exhibitions, performances, competitions). It is the responsibility of the organizer or host to find sponsors to finance these events. This applies equally to official and unofficial events. In addition, corporate sponsors are increasingly creating their own events and using them for communication purposes. The following three formats are cited as **examples of sponsored events**:

1. **Official events:** Implementation of cultural programs by official organizations (e.g., Salzburg Festival), national and international art or music competitions.
2. **Unofficial events:** Private, especially non-profit, art and cultural offerings.
3. **Creation of own projects by the sponsor:** Announcing art competitions, implementing cultural programs, constructing their own event venues and museums.

Type of Consideration Provided by the Sponsee

The sponsor expects a consideration from the sponsee in the form of (direct or indirect) advertising for the corporate sponsorship or one of its services. This type of consideration is diverse and occurs, for example, through the mention of the sponsor's logo or name at cultural events. When sponsoring events, the sponsor will generally seek to utilize the available advertising media (e.g., event posters, tickets, sales booths) during the event. If sponsorship takes the form of acquiring designations, these titles are used as part of classic marketing and corporate communications. Furthermore, it is important to consider involving the sponsored individuals or groups themselves in the communication process.

Overall, the following three **benefits provided by the sponsee** are conceivable (for a detailed discussion of sponsorship benefits, see Chap. 10):

1. **Advertising during an event**
   - **Person-related advertising:** Sponsees, such as musicians or artists, wear clothing or use products of the sponsor in a way that attracts public attention. In contrast to sports sponsorship, wearing sponsor logos on clothing is uncommon in the cultural sector. However, it is possible for cultural professionals to be equipped with clothing or products from the sponsor, and for the sponsor to highlight this equipment. In addition, collaborations between sponsors and cultural professionals in product development can often be observed. For example, in 2008, pianist Lang Lang designed a sneaker for the Adidas brand, which was sold as a special edition and presented with a concert by the pianist at the Berlin Adidas Store.

- **Advertising at the event location:** References to the sponsors are made through various advertising media such as tickets, posters, flags, or videos, as well as on various devices (e.g., transport vehicles, beverage carts, technical equipment).

2. **Use of designations in marketing and corporate communications**
   - **Official titles:** Sponsors receive permission to use official titles, such as "Official Logistics Partner" or "Sponsor of a Season," which are awarded by the cultural institution, as part of their communications.
   - **Title sponsorship:** The sponsor's name is included in the announcement of the event, such as Telekom Electronic Beats, Hugo Boss Prize.
   - **Licensing:** The sponsee grants licenses for certain emblems or symbols, which are used on packaging or other advertising materials, such as the designation "Official Festival Wine."
3. **Use of sponsees in marketing and corporate communications**
   - **Individuals:** Cultural figures are used, for example, in media advertising or in sales promotion activities (product presenters).
   - **Groups:** Sponsored artist groups, bands, orchestras, and others are, for example, integrated into print advertising.
   - **Objects:** Paintings, restored objects, etc., are sponsored and highlighted in print advertising or public private relations work.

A summary overview of various **forms of sponsorship from the perspective of the sponsees** is provided in Fig. 2.9.

The following section uses the BMW Group's cultural engagement to illustrate the understanding of arts and cultural sponsorship that the company has defined for itself, as well as the objectives and funding priorities it pursues.

2.6.1 Case Study: The BMW Group's Cultural Engagement

Initial Situation

The **BMW Group** is one of the world's largest automobile manufacturers and brings together the brands BMW, Mini, and Rolls-Royce. In 2022, the group employed nearly 150,000 people. Production in 2022 amounted to around 2.4 million automobiles and over 215,000 motorcycles. With a revenue volume of around EUR 142 billion, the BMW Group is a member of the DAX-40 corporate sponsorship.

The **company's cultural engagement** began in 1971 with a commissioned work for Gerhard Richter. Today, the BMW Group is active worldwide as a cultural sponsor. Thomas Girst, Global Head of Cultural Engagement at the BMW Group, locates the company's cultural engagement within "Corporate Citizenship" (Bunk, 2003), whereby numerous partnerships can also serve as a platform for customer acquisition and retention and contribute to positive brand positioning. In contrast to instrumentalizing cultural professionals for a company's marketing activities, the BMW Group sees itself, in its

Delimitation features	Forms	Examples
Type of consideration from the sponsored party	Integration into the media reach of the cultural sector or cultural professionals	Logo integration on posters, mention in social media communication
	Use of predicates	Title sponsorship, licenses, official awards
	Use of the sponsored event in the sponsor's corporate communications	Use of motifs from cultural events for own communication, artists as testimonials
Type of sponsored artists or institutions	Professional	Recognition of professional musicians with well-endowed prizes
	Semi-professionals	Promotion of full-time cultural professionals
	Amateurs and amateur groups	Promotion of amateur musicians and recreational artists
Performance level	Top level	Promotion of top ensembles
	Performance level	Promotion of established cultural institutions
	Popular level Clubs	Promotion of amateur groups
Type of sponsored organization	Associations Foundations	Support for regional cultural associations
	Public and non-profit organizations	Promotion of official associations (e.g. Tonkünstlerverband)
	Private sector organizations	Promotion of cultural foundations
		Promotion of state theaters and museums
		Cooperation with private music festivals
Type of sponsored event	Official events	Promotion of national and international cultural competitions
	Creation of own projects by the sponsor	Behind-the-scenes events
		Exhibitions by artists and concerts on the sponsor's premises

Fig. 2.9 Forms of sponsorship from the perspective of the sponsees. (Source: Bruhn, 2018a, p. 30)

perception of "corporate social responsibility (CSR)", as giving something back to the society in which it is economically successful (see also Labaronne, 2022, p. 1). This is implemented through numerous long-term partnerships with cultural institutions, with which the corporate sponsorship maintains active exchange.

Objectives and Target Groups

Thomas Girst, as the person responsible, sees the general **objective of corporate arts and cultural funding** as strengthening the reputation, visibility, and image of the company and its brands, whereby "contentious and controversial" aspects are not excluded. "It should enable the acquisition of knowledge and, in terms of what it supports culturally, should not be reduced to hollow, acclamatory bling-bling, show effects, and marketing events" (Girst, 2022, p. 103).

The **communicative objective** of the BMW Group's cultural engagement lies in generating public visibility and fostering a positive reputation for the company and its individual brands. This objective is derived from the realization that corporate sponsorship, as a "license to exist," also requires societal acceptance. If corporate sponsorship is not desired by society at large, this impedes its market activities. For this reason, the BMW Group's cultural engagement is directed not only at potential customers and at fostering loyalty among existing buyers, but also at society as a whole. In addition to customers and the general public, employees at more than 30 production sites worldwide are also a target group for these sponsorship activities.

These three target groups are not mutually exclusive, and thus, individual sponsorship projects can address several of them simultaneously. For example, the "Opera for All" format, in which public private-viewing opera events are held in Berlin and Munich for over 40,000 people, is aimed at the general public (see Fig. 2.10). Afterwards, there is a reception reserved for selected stakeholders.

By engaging at the world's most important art fairs, BMW directly addresses the target group for its core business, as these events attract an audience with the purchasing power required for the BMW Group's offerings.

Strategy of Cultural Work

The BMW Group's self-concept as a **supporter and partner**—as opposed to a mere sponsor—is also reflected in the implementation of its collaborations: rather than focusing solely on monetary transactions, the emphasis is on interactions through the provision of know-how, access to networks, and knowledge transfer.

For example, Maximilian Schöberl, Head of Corporate Communications and Governmental Affairs at the BMW Group, and Thomas Girst both serve on the board of Spielmotor München e. V. As Germany's oldest public-private partnership, the association is a prime example of collaboration between public and corporate arts and cultural funding. Spielmotor München e. V. was founded in 1979 to bring multicultural offerings to Munich. While the BMW Group actively supports the association's board work, it refrains from all content-related decisions and is not represented on any jury that awards prize money or honors.

Fig. 2.10 BMW-sponsored cultural event "Staatsoper für alle" 2014. (© BMW Group)

Other partnerships also demonstrate the reciprocal exchange between cultural practitioners and corporate sponsorship: for example, artist Olafur Eliasson developed the 16th BMW Art Car, in which the car's exterior was replaced by a fragile skin of ice (see Fig. 2.11). The basis for Eliasson's artistic work was a hydrogen-powered race car developed by BMW to achieve speed records while striving for forward-looking environmental compatibility (BMW, 2008). Norbert Reithofer, who was Chairman of the Board of Management of BMW AG at the time of Eliasson's premiere, commented on the three-year collaboration with the artist: "During his 'Art Car Project,' Olafur Eliasson sought intensive exchange with our engineers and designers over several years. As part of our

Fig. 2.11 BMW H2R Project: Olafur Eliasson's installation "Your mobile expectations" 2007 at the Pinakothek der Moderne, Munich. (© BMW Group/Olafur Eliasson)

long-term commitment to the arts, this challenging dialogue went far beyond the boundaries of purely cultural sponsorship." (BMW, 2008).

After more than 50 years of cultural engagement, the BMW Group has now established 100 long-term initiatives in numerous cultural fields. The **strategic orientation of the company's cultural work** focuses on the following four **core areas**:

- Modern and contemporary art,
- Classical music, sound, and jazz,
- Architecture and design,
- Culture within the company.

In addition, **film festivals** are supported, and there are collaborations typical for an automotive brand, such as **product placement** in TV shows and films—for example, through the integration of BMW in the feature film "Mission: Impossible—Fallout."

Implementation and Measures

The BMW Group enters into contracts with its partners for a term of three years. Due to the current general increase in costs, the **cultural budget**, which amounts to a double-digit million sum, had to be increased. As a result, the BMW Group's cultural engagement faces not only external competition for attention, but also internal competition regarding how budgets are allocated most effectively.

Those responsible for the BMW Group's cultural engagement receive around 2000 **sponsorship and cooperation requests** annually. The majority cannot be considered due to existing long-term partnerships. However, all requests are reviewed, and existing partnerships are occasionally replaced by new sponsorship collaborations after contracts expire. Requests are not evaluated based on personal preferences or the personal affinities of the company's management, but are assessed according to strategic considerations and criteria. Selection criteria include whether potential partners align with the BMW Group's values and can be reconciled with existing sponsorship priorities. In addition, individual artists and exhibitions are excluded from funding. Individual artists are supported indirectly through art prizes. Exceptions are commissioned works, such as the BMW Art Cars.

As part of its sponsorships, the company offers more than just financial support. For example, the BMW Group's corporate identity experts advised a consortium of museums on their umbrella brand strategy and the strategic positioning of the individual museum brands.

The BMW Group's international network can also be more valuable to cultural practitioners than financial resources—for example, when winners of a music competition supported by BMW are given concert opportunities at festivals that are also BMW Group cultural partners.

The BMW Group's cultural work can be illustrated by the following **examples** from the aforementioned sponsorship areas:

Modern and Contemporary Art

This sponsorship area includes, for example, the BMW Art Cars—automobiles designed by artists (see Olafur Eliasson example above)—or the Preis der Nationalgalerie, which was established in 2000 and has been awarded with BMW as a partner since 2006.

Classical Music, Sound, and Jazz

Since 1997, the free "Opera for All" format has been held in cooperation with the Bavarian State Opera in Munich and, more recently, with the Staatsoper Unter den Linden in Berlin. In London, BMW Classics has also offered a low-threshold open-air opera experience in collaboration with the London Symphony Orchestra since 2012. In addition, jazz concerts are supported worldwide—for example, the Gere Jazz Festival Villany in Hungary, the JZ Festival Shanghai in China, the Leipziger Jazztage in Germany, or the Seoul Jazz Festival in South Korea.

Architecture and Design

The claim to leadership as an innovative automotive brand is underscored by commissioning internationally renowned architects for the construction of office buildings, production facilities, and museums. For example, in 1973, Karl Schwanzer designed the company headquarters in Munich, and in 2005, architect Zaha Hadid designed a BMW factory in Leipzig (see Fig. 2.12).

Culture within the Company

Internal arts and cultural funding has played a significant role since the beginning of the company's cultural engagement. Due to stricter compliance regulations, the possibilities are now more limited than at the start of the sponsorship. Nevertheless, employees can

Fig. 2.12 BMW Factory Leipzig by Zaha Hadid. (© BMW Group)

still, for example, receive discounts for sponsored events. In addition, the company supports its own choir, Dixieland band, and chamber orchestra through its own culture and sports foundation.

All cooperation partners refer to the BMW Group's commitment in their communications, for example through logo integration or by mentioning the BMW Group in press releases and online publications. Furthermore, corporate sponsorship supports communication through publications on its own channels (e.g., social media) as well as through paid reach (e.g., when announcing events).

Evaluation

For cultural manager Thomas Girst, successful cultural engagement is characterized by enabling other people to access a cultural event "and thus to the peak achievements of which people are capable, and to the acquisition of knowledge" (Bühler, 2020, p. 17). The aim is also to lower the threshold for engaging with high culture. His aspiration for the BMW Group is: "We only open a door; we do not come between the viewer and the artwork or the listener and the orchestra. The subtlety of our presence is a testament to the confidence of the sponsoring company." (Bühler, 2020, p. 17). Such a subtle presence is possible for the company because the BMW logo itself is much better known than the trademarks of the sponsored institutions.

For the specific **evaluation of individual measures**, media or advertising equivalency analyses are conducted. These analyses capture the reach of coverage surrounding the cultural engagement and calculate its media value. This includes both third-party coverage and the reach generated through the company's own channels. In this way, it is possible to determine what reach was achieved in which media through the engagement, and to what extent the measures are worthwhile compared to booking paid advertising.

In addition to the economic analysis, a qualitative review is also conducted to assess which narratives are generated by media coverage and how these support the BMW Group's brand positioning. Information on the quantity and quality of generated leads is also important for the BMW Group's marketing department, provided that contact data was collected during events.

Key Points

1. **Leverage cultural engagement for marketing and communication:** Arts and cultural sponsorship is to be understood as contractually agreed support for cultural creators, intended to have effects on (internal and external) marketing and corporate communication.
2. **Arts and cultural sponsorship offers a broad spectrum:** As cooperation partners on the culture side, various cultural sectors such as visual arts, performing arts, music, literature, media, festivals, and cultural preservation are possible.

3. **Support for specific cultural sectors:** Despite the diverse possibilities of cultural engagement, in practice, arts and cultural sponsorship focuses on supporting artistic events, especially in the areas of festivals, visual arts, and rock/pop music events.
4. **Prioritize local engagement:** Corporate sponsorships are predominantly focused on their immediate local environment. Regional and international engagements are much less common. This can be explained by the fact that corporate sponsorships are mainly active in their procurement markets (e.g., as an employer branding measure) and their sales markets.
5. **Identify different forms of cultural sponsorship:** When considering forms of sponsorship, distinctions should be made according to the type of sponsor contribution, type of consideration, type of beneficiary, institution-based or project-based sponsorship, single-stage and multi-stage sponsorship, performance class of the beneficiary, initiator of the sponsorship, and the number of sponsors involved.
6. **Identify key players in the cultural sponsorship process:** It should be noted that corporate sponsors, cultural institutions, and media play a central role in arts and cultural sponsorship.
7. **Understand the dynamics of the "magic triangle":** Corporate sponsors, cultural institutions, and media organizations often have different objectives. Therefore, the risk of cooperation conflicts must be taken into account.
8. **Consider different forms from the sponsors' perspective:** When considering the forms of arts and cultural sponsorship, the type of sponsor, the number and diversity of sponsors, and the type of sponsor contribution should be distinguished.
9. **Include the perspective of sponsored cultural creators:** From the perspective of cultural partners, the type of sponsored individuals/groups, organizations, events, and the type of consideration should be taken into account.
10. **Use arts and cultural sponsorship for marketing and resource acquisition:** It should be noted that corporate sponsorship does not only provide financial support to cultural institutions. Sponsorship also supports the marketing of cultural institutions through the professional alignment of activities with their target groups and the implementation of communication measures offered as sponsorship benefits.

Classification of Arts and Cultural Sponsorship in the Financing of Arts and Culture

3

Contents

3.1 Fundamentals and Instruments of Financing Arts and Culture 54
3.2 Public Private Arts and Cultural Funding 57
3.3 Donation System and Fundraising... 65
3.4 Arts and Cultural Sponsorship as a Form of Private Third-Party Funding 74
3.5 Own Revenues in Distinction to Arts and Cultural Sponsorship...................... 76
3.6 Crowdfunding as a Form of Arts and Cultural Sponsorship 80

Abstract

From the perspective of the sponsored parties, arts and cultural sponsorship is an element within the funding mix. This mix consists of various financing instruments, which can be divided into primary and secondary operating income. In addition to public funding from the federal government, states, and municipalities, financing instruments also include private third-party funds such as donations and own revenues. The relevance of each financing instrument depends on the objectives and sponsorship of the cultural institutions. In addition to various practical examples, the strategy and approach of the Gewandhaus Orchestra Leipzig are presented in detail as a case study.

M. Bruhn and L. Pöllmann, *Arts and Cultural Sponsorship*,
https://doi.org/10.1007/978-3-658-50079-5_3

3.1 Fundamentals and Instruments of Financing Arts and Culture

For a better understanding of the perspective of the sponsored parties, it is necessary to situate arts and cultural sponsorship within the context of financing arts and culture. This is essential in order to comprehend both the opportunities and constraints faced by the sponsored parties in the context of scientific analysis or practical cooperation. The **prerequisites and possibilities of financing arts and culture** for individual cultural actors or cultural institutions vary significantly depending on the assigned legal sector, economic objectives, and the respective legal form (Gerlach-March & Pöllmann, 2019, p. 2):

- **Legal sector:** Numerous cultural institutions are primarily financed by the state and are under public or municipal ownership. They are thus assigned to the public sector. In contrast, there are cultural enterprises under private ownership.
- **Economic objectives:** The economic orientation of cultural institutions can generally be divided into a non-profit sector and a for-profit sector. Public and non-profit cultural enterprises do not pursue profit motives. However, the profit orientation of private commercial cultural enterprises does not necessarily equate to a goal of profit maximization. In the private commercial sector, there are indeed cultural enterprises whose main objective is to operate on a cost-covering basis. They are neither non-profit nor publicly owned. Therefore, they are assigned to the for-profit sector, such as smaller clubs. In contrast, professional private cultural enterprises such as commercial cinema chains, musicals, the art market, the book market, or the music industry can be assumed to have a stronger profit interest.
- **Legal form:** The chosen legal form of a cultural institution also influences the financing options and the practical design of a sponsorship cooperation. It is important to distinguish, for example, whether a cultural institution is organized as a municipal enterprise, a limited liability company, a (non-profit) association, a foundation, or in another form. For instance, the design and management of budget plans and the accounting of sponsorship income is simpler in a limited liability company than in a municipal enterprise or an association.

This structure of the cultural landscape is summarized by the **three-sector model** (see Fig. 3.1) (Weckerle & Söndermann, 2004). Based on the criteria mentioned above, it assigns artists, cultural professionals, and cultural institutions to the three sectors of state, economy, and civil society:

- **State:** Public and thus non-profit cultural actors are assigned to the state. These include, for example, public theaters, orchestras, memorial sites, and numerous museums.
- **Economy:** The private sector encompasses all for-profit cultural enterprises and includes industries such as the music industry, book market, art market, film industry, and others.

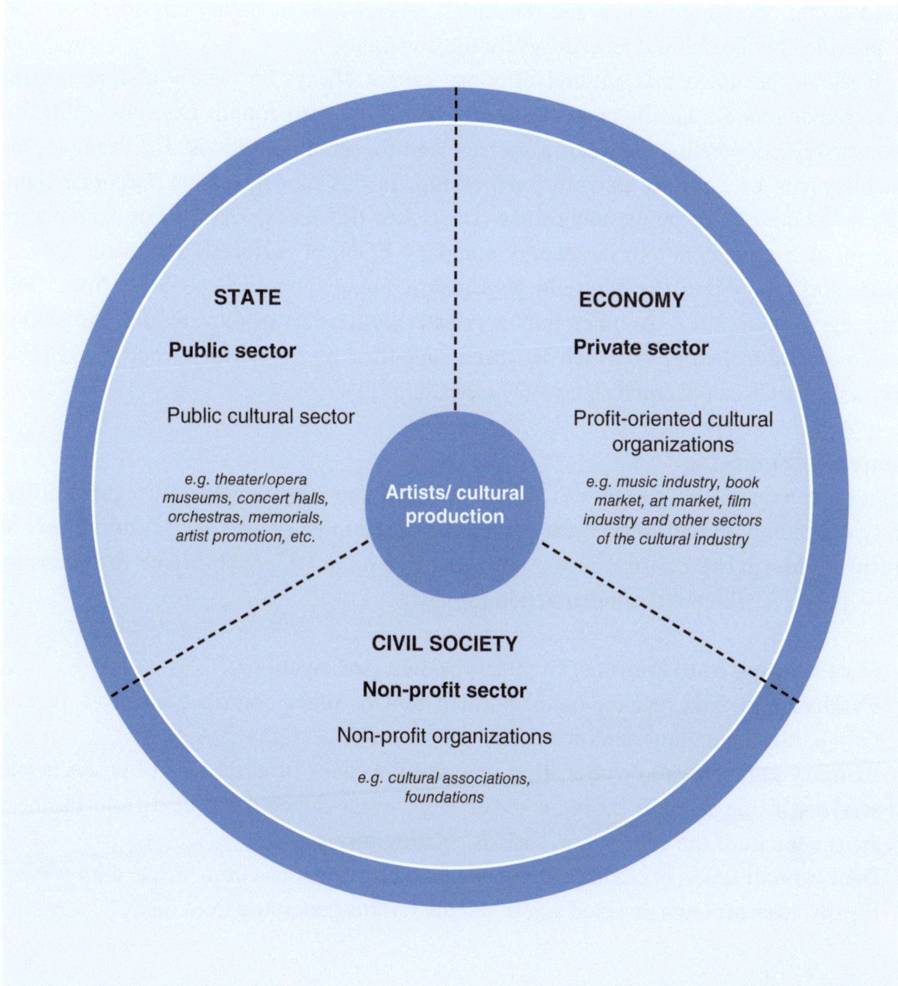

Fig. 3.1 Structure of the cultural sector according to the three-sector model. (Source: Weckerle & Söndermann, 2004)

- **Civil society:** The non-profit sector, in which civil society is engaged through non-profit cultural associations and foundations, is also referred to as the **intermediary sector**.

In principle, sponsorship cooperations take place in all three sectors. Since **sponsorship income** is treated as **operating income** for tax purposes by cultural enterprises, collaboration with the private sector is sometimes easier for sponsors. This is because the public and non-profit sectors are only permitted to generate operating income up to a certain limit. If the maximum allowable income is exceeded, sponsorship amounts are generally divided into operating income and donations, whereby no monetary consideration may be provided by the cultural enterprises for the donations.

It should be noted that cultural offerings cannot always be clearly assigned to the three-sector model, and in practice, hybrid forms are also found. One possibility for sponsorship cooperation between a sponsor and the public sector is, for example, the establishment of a **public private partnership**. In this model, private corporate sponsors collaborate with public authorities (Deutscher Bundestag, 2006). For example, as part of such a cooperation, the energy company EON, in partnership with the City of Düsseldorf, supported the Museum Kunstpalast Foundation in Düsseldorf from 1998 until the end of 2017. Another public private partnership is the cultural association Spielmotor München e. V., which has been supported by the BMW Group in cooperation with the City of Munich since 1979 (see Chap. 11).

Sources of Financing

Cultural enterprises have access to various financing options, which are weighted differently depending on their placement within one of the three sectors. The **funding mix of cultural enterprises** consists of the following five pillars (Gerlach-March & Pöllmann, 2019, pp. 4 f.), which are summarized in Fig. 3.2:

1. **State funding contributions:** Grants, subsidies, participations.
2. **Fundraising:** Non-revenue-based participation or other contributions from private third parties: donations, endowments.
3. **Primary and secondary operating income:** Revenues from the sale of products and services in the cultural business sector (e.g., event tickets), but also from business areas not part of the core sector, such as catering services.
4. **Debt capital:** Loans or credits and revenue-based participations from private third parties.
5. **Equity capital:** Own invested assets and the returns generated from them.

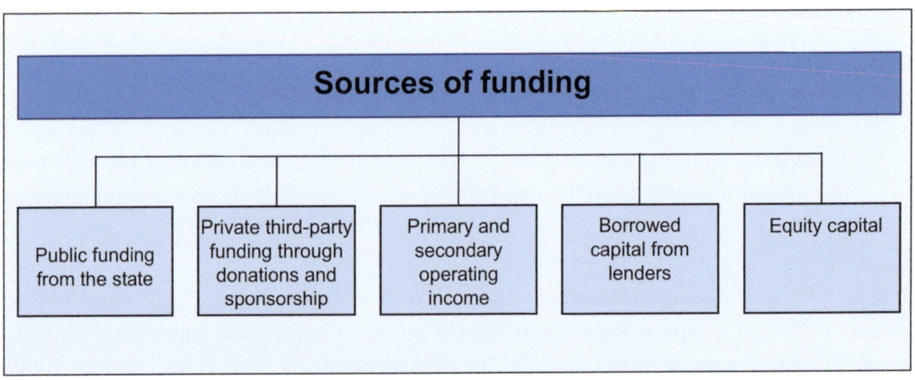

Fig. 3.2 Sources of financing arts and cultural

It should be noted that the term **fundraising** is defined more narrowly in German literature than in the Anglo-American context (Greenfield, 2002; Ciconte & Jacob, 2009, pp. 177 ff.; Urselmann, 2023). While in the USA fundraising is generally understood as the acquisition of financial resources, in German usage fundraising predominantly refers only to the solicitation of donations. Arts and cultural sponsorship is therefore considered part of fundraising in the Anglo-American understanding. Taking into account the five pillars of financing arts and cultural, there are several possible ways to classify sponsorship: If a company's cultural engagement is primarily supportive in nature and the sponsorship benefits are mainly symbolic (e.g., limited to discreet logo placement), it can be subsumed under fundraising. However, if the cultural enterprise provides the sponsor with a consideration commensurate with the sponsorship (for example, in the form of media contacts, licenses, etc.), sponsorship is to be assigned to secondary operating income. Since arts and cultural sponsorship usually involves an exchange of mutual services combined with the sponsor's support motive, sponsorship revenues can also be characterized as **private third-party funds**.

The particularly significant **financing instruments of cultural enterprises**—public private funding, donations, arts and cultural sponsorship, own revenues, and the acquisition form "crowdfunding"—are explained in more detail below.

3.2 Public Private Arts and Cultural Funding

State arts and cultural funding is an important factor in supporting the cultural landscape in many countries such as Germany, Austria, and Switzerland. In international comparison, however, **state financing of arts and culture** is not a given. For example, in 2022 the budget of the National Endowment for the Arts in the USA was 180 million USD (around 170 million EUR) (NEA, 2023), which is only a fraction of the more than 3 billion EUR in federal arts and cultural funding in Germany.

If one looks at **public cultural expenditure over time**, in 2020 a total of 14.5 billion EUR was spent on culture in Germany by the federal government, the states, and municipalities, which is 15.6% more than in the previous year. Public cultural expenditure increased by 55.1% over the past ten years. In 2010, the total public arts and cultural funding in Germany was still 9.4 billion EUR (SÄBL, 2022, p. 19). However, this comparatively high level of cultural expenditure in 2020 is not guaranteed for future budget years, as the significant increase in cultural spending in recent years is due to government aid measures to compensate for the effects of the COVID-19 pandemic. These measures include, for example, the "Neustart Kultur" (Restart Culture) funding program, which the federal government launched in 2020 and endowed with one billion EUR (Staatsministerin für Kultur & Medien, 2021). For comparison: In the ten-year period between 2005 and 2015, cultural expenditure increased by 30.5%. The strong participation of the federal government in aid programs has also changed the distribution of cultural expenditure, as a comparison of the current figures from 2020 with the cultural expenditure from 2015 in Fig. 3.3 shows (SÄBL, 2018, 2022).

In 2020, public cultural expenditure amounted to 0.43% of gross domestic product and averaged 174.51 EUR per inhabitant. It should be noted that per capita expenditure on arts and cultural funding varies depending on place of residence: In 2020, expenditure per inhabitant was 249.64 EUR in Berlin, while in Rhineland-Palatinate it was only 71.63 EUR (see Fig. 3.4).

Moreover, not all residents benefit equally from cultural expenditure. Rather, this depends on the individual **demand for subsidized cultural offerings**, as can be illustrated by the example of public theaters: In the 2019/2020 season, public theaters in

Share	Cultural expenditure 2015	Cultural expenditure 2020
Absolute expenditure	EUR 10.4 billion	EUR 14.5 billion
Share of total expenditure of public budgets	1,73 %	1,89 %
Share of the municipalities	44,9 %	39,1 %
Share of the federal states (territorial states and city states)	40,3 %	38,6 %
Federal share	14,8 %	22,4 %

Fig. 3.3 Five-year comparison of public cultural expenditure in Germany

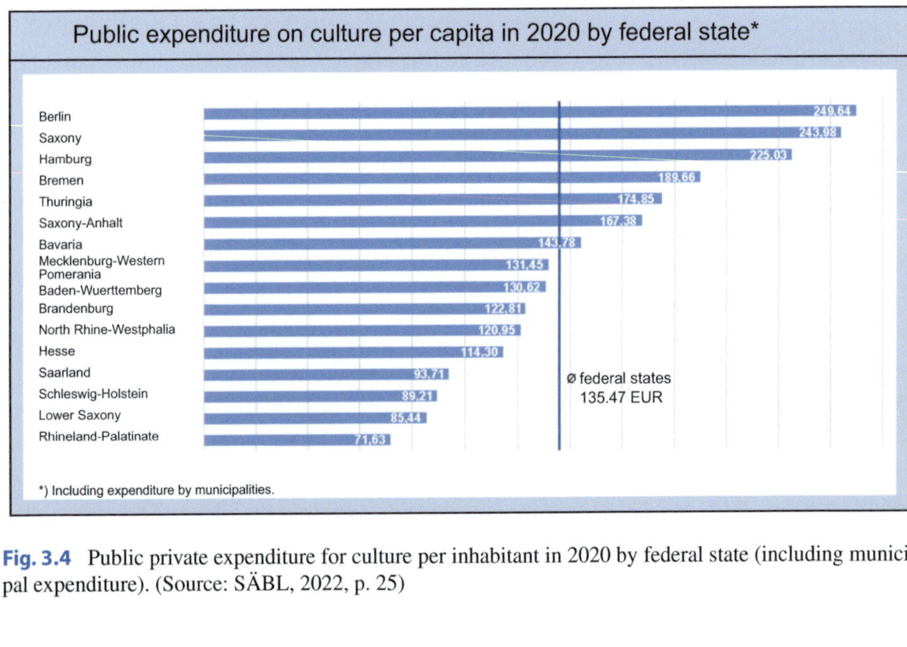

Fig. 3.4 Public private expenditure for culture per inhabitant in 2020 by federal state (including municipal expenditure). (Source: SÄBL, 2022, p. 25)

Germany recorded around 13.85 million visits—significantly fewer than in the previous season due to the COVID-19 pandemic, when around 20.35 million visits were counted. In the 2019/2020 season, the theaters received a total of around 2.83 billion EUR in public private allocations and grants. This resulted in an operating subsidy of 208.87 EUR per theater visit. Statistically, this means that a visitor to a single theater performance receives more state transfer payments than an average resident receives in annual cultural expenditure. However, the operating subsidy in the 2019/2020 season was also above average due to the pandemic. For comparison: In the 2018/2019 season, the subsidy per ticket was still 141.15 EUR (DBV, 2022).

Development and Distribution of Public Cultural Expenditure by Sector

An analysis of public cultural expenditure by sector shows that the areas of theater and music, with 4.6 billion EUR, receive the largest share of arts and cultural funding. This sector accounts for 31.4% of all public cultural expenditure.

The comparatively large area of "other cultural activities" encompasses a wide variety of expenditures. This includes funding for film promotion, support for the culture of expellees, folklore and local history, municipal spending on local heritage preservation, as well as numerous COVID-19 relief measures (SÄBL, 2022, p. 46). This area therefore cannot be clearly separated from the other sectors, as, for example, expenditures for monument preservation and the financing of museums of local and regional history could also be assigned to the promotion of folklore and local history. The five-year comparison (see Fig. 3.5) shows the impact of COVID-19 relief on the distribution of cultural expenditure. Due to the relief programs, the share of expenditure in the area of other cultural activities grew from 14.3% in 2015 to 21.6% in 2020, now ranking second. In

Divisions	2015		2020	
	%	EUR billion	%	EUR billion
Theater and music	35,4	3,7	31,4	4,6
Museums, collections, exhibitions	18,3	1,9	18,7	2,7
Libraries	14,4	1,5	12,1	1,8
Other cultural activities	14,3	1,5	21,6	3,1
Public art colleges	5,2	0,5	4,5	0,6
Monument preservation and protection	4,8	0,5	4,5	0,6
Cultural affairs abroad	5,3	0,6	4,8	0,7
Cultural administration	2,3	0,2	2,5	0,4

Fig. 3.5 Development and distribution of public cultural expenditure by sector in a five-year comparison

previous years, museums, collections, and exhibitions received the second largest share of public funding, and it can be assumed that the shares will shift again after the relief programs expire.

Comparison of Cultural Expenditure in Germany, Austria, and Switzerland

A comparison of public cultural expenditure in Germany, Austria, and Switzerland shows that the share of cultural expenditure in public budgets is highest in Germany at 1.89% (see Fig. 3.6): In 2020, public cultural expenditure in Germany totaled 14.5 billion EUR, compared to 2.93 billion EUR in Austria and 3.01 billion EUR or 2.97 billion CHF in Switzerland. In relation to economic strength, however, cultural expenditure in Austria was higher than in Germany and Switzerland.

It should be noted that the data from the three countries serve as a guide but do not allow for an exact comparison, as the calculation of cultural expenditure is based on different methods.

When considering the **distribution of cultural expenditure among government bodies**—federal government, states (or cantons in Switzerland), and municipalities—clear differences can be observed between the three countries. While in Germany and Switzerland the largest share of expenditure is borne by the municipalities, in Austria it is the states (see Fig. 3.7). The federal government also plays a significantly stronger role in Austria than in Germany and Switzerland. The share of federal expenditure in Switzerland has remained largely stable in recent years, fluctuating between 10.3% (2011) and 11.2% (2019) from 2010 to 2020. The 22.4% in Germany, on the other hand, as already mentioned above, is above average and attributable to the COVID-19 relief measures.

Differences are also evident with regard to **per capita expenditure on arts and cultural funding** in the three countries: Here, Switzerland ranks first with the equivalent

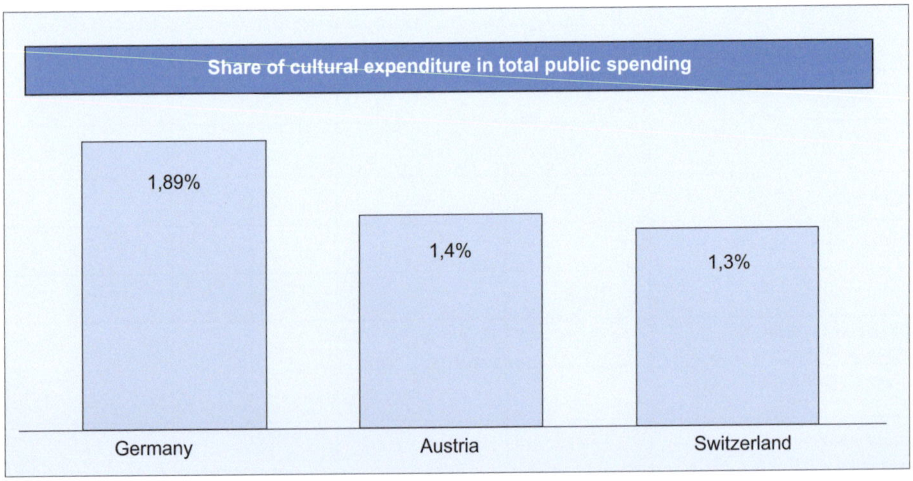

Fig. 3.6 Share of cultural expenditure in total public spending

Cultural expenditure 2020			
Share	**Germany**	**Austria**	**Switzerland**
Total expenditure	EUR 14.5 billion	EUR 2.93 billion	EUR 3.01 billion (2.97 billion Swiss francs)
Share of total expenditure in public budgets	1,89 %	1,4%	1,3%
Share of municipalities	39,1%	26,5%	48,3%
Share of federal states (areas and city states) and cantons (CH)	38,6%	37,2%	40,5%
Share of the federal	22,4%	36,2%	11,1%
government Expenditure per inhabitant	EUR 174.51	EUR 328.00	EUR 347.26 (343 francs)
Share of GDP	0,43%	0,77%	0,43%

Fig. 3.7 Comparison of cultural expenditure in Germany, Austria, and Switzerland. (Sources: SÄBL, 2022; BfS, 2022; Statistik Austria, 2022, p. 161)

of 347.26 EUR per inhabitant (343 CHF). Austria spends an average of 328.00 EUR per capita, and Germany, as already shown above, 174.41 EUR per capita.

In addition to the national expenditure on arts and cultural funding shown, it should be mentioned that at the European level, funding is also allocated to cultural institutions and cultural projects. The **EU cultural funding program** "Creative Europe Culture" has been supporting transnational cultural projects since May 2021 with a budget of 804 million EUR (Dietzmann, 2022, p. 38). The funding program runs for seven years and is already the fourth funding period for cultural projects in the EU.

Justification of Arts and Cultural Funding

The legitimacy of cultural expenditures is based on various arguments and patterns of justification that guide cultural policy (Scheytt, 2008; Klein, 2009; Bendixen, 2010; Gottschalk, 2016). From a **cultural policy perspective**, arts and cultural funding is primarily intended to protect cultural heritage and enable the cultural education of the population.

From a **macroeconomic perspective**, the necessary cultural goods would not be available in sufficient quality and quantity due to "market failure." This can be attributed, for example, to the fact that the production of many desired cultural offerings is so costly that the resulting sales prices would exclude large segments of society: With an average operating subsidy of over 200 EUR per theater ticket, school visits would no longer be possible and cultural offerings would be accessible only to high earners. At the same time, production costs can only be reduced to a limited extent, since especially performing arts offerings (music, theater, opera, dance) are services and the necessary personnel input cannot be rationalized. In fact, production costs continuously increase due to rising wages and fees.

In order for cultural offerings to be available nationwide—not just in metropolitan areas and large cities, and to all income groups—government subsidies are necessary. Furthermore, it can be assumed that the diversity of artistic work would be significantly reduced if only those productions with high demand were realized. While market demand is a central criterion in the private sector, subsidized cultural institutions can more easily experiment with new formats that may not generate sufficient (in the economic sense) demand.

In addition to these cultural and educational policy considerations, there are also arguments for arts and cultural funding from an **economic policy perspective**, since a high-quality cultural landscape enhances a location as a place to live. The consideration of culture as a location factor is also reflected in the funding efforts of sponsors, who seek to create cultural offerings at their own sites and provide access for their employees.

Furthermore, reference should be made to the so-called **indirect profitability**. Visitors to attractive cultural offerings generate revenue through travel, accommodation, restaurant visits, shopping, and similar activities. As a result, major events create an indirect benefit, and public subsidies are, in a sense, partially refinanced. This also increases the quality of life in the region.

Based on the arguments presented and the three-sector model, it becomes clear that actors in the cultural market operate under unequal conditions, as not all cultural institutions benefit equally from public spending. Thus, economic pressures in the private sector are more existential than in the public cultural sector. This also results in a varying degree of urgency for a **multidimensional concept of financing arts and culture** and the acquisition of sponsors.

For sponsors, arts and cultural funding policy is relevant because cultural engagement often leads to the creation of new, additional cultural offerings, and sponsors wish to present themselves as enablers of these offerings. On the one hand, there is a critical view of the risk that public-private funding may be reduced in the case of successful sponsorship cooperation. On the other hand, so-called **"matching funds"** can provide an incentive, whereby cultural institutions receive additional public funds depending on the amount of private funding they raise.

Direct and Indirect Cultural Funding

After reviewing the key figures for financing arts and culture, the following section presents the framework conditions for public arts and cultural funding. Two main **forms of cultural support** can be distinguished (Gerlach-March & Pöllmann, 2019, pp. 13 f.):

- **Indirect cultural funding** results from a waiver of tax revenues and the creation of legal frameworks that facilitate the management of cultural institutions. This includes, for example, culture-friendly laws on building regulations, noise protection, monument protection, fixed book pricing, or copyright regulations.
  For the nonprofit sector, the ability to issue donation receipts to supporters is particularly advantageous. This provides donors with an additional incentive to make a

donation, as they can claim it as "tax-deductible" and thus reduce their tax burden proportionally.

A key indirect tax law benefit arises from the reduced value added tax rate in Germany of 7% instead of 19% on cultural products and services such as admission tickets, artworks, sound recordings, or books. Unlike directly paid subsidies or tax relief for non-profit institutions, the reduced value added tax rate benefits cultural enterprises from all three sectors. Thus, for example, tickets for privately run rock festivals or the sale of artworks in for-profit galleries are also supported by the reduced value added tax rate.

However, some details must be considered, as illustrated by the example of the art trade: The aim of the reduced value added tax rate is to promote new artworks, not the trading of art. To avoid indirectly promoting speculation in art objects, the reduced value added tax rate can only be applied to the initial sale between artist and collector. If an artwork is resold to a third party, the full value added tax rate applies.

Indirect funding can also be utilized by corporate sponsors who organize their own cultural events as part of their cultural engagement, such as the Bayer AG Startfestival (see the case study in Chap. 8). However, it is crucial that a cultural offering is recognized as such by the tax authorities. For example, the events of the Berlin techno club Berghain were only recognized as cultural services by the Berlin-Brandenburg tax court in 2016 after a legal challenge (Pöllmann, 2021b).

- **Direct arts funding** includes all grants and subsidies paid to cultural institutions or sponsors of cultural projects. In addition, public-private sponsorship of a cultural institution can also be classified as direct funding. The scope of direct arts and cultural funding has already been illustrated using selected statistical data. With regard to direct funding, a distinction can be made between institutional and project-based funding, as explained below.

Institutional Funding and Project Sponsorship

If a cultural organization is funded as an entire institution and not just for individual projects, this is referred to as **institutional funding**. This funding approach is linked to the goal of preserving the institution as such, which is why this type of funding is generally long-term. It provides basic financing that ensures the financial security of the beneficiary institutions. However, it is granted relatively rarely. Admission to institutional funding is only possible for a cultural organization if another organization leaves the funding scheme. This procedure is also known as the **"bus principle"**: the bus is full and there is only room when someone gets off. However, the Federal Audit Office has also critically noted that repeated individual grants to a recipient can repeatedly result in "as it were-institutional funding" (Der Präsident des Bundesrechnungshofes, 2016, p. 24; Deutscher Bundestag, 2011, p. 12).

Cultural organizations that benefit from **institutional funding in Germany** include, for example, the Prussian Cultural Heritage Foundation, the Klassikstiftung Weimar, the German National Library, the German Historical Museum Berlin, the Bayreuth Festival, and many others.

Project sponsorship is awarded for projects that are limited in time and scope. These do not necessarily have to involve the realization of cultural offerings. Project sponsorship can also be used to finance construction projects, digitization measures, or research projects. Project funding is often awarded on the basis of funding guidelines, for which cultural organizations can apply with their own projects. This is intended to specifically promote cultural policy priorities, such as ecologically sustainable cultural productions or international cooperation between cultural organizations.

Types of Financing

A complete coverage of all costs of a cultural institution, the so-called **full financing**, is rare. Even in heavily subsidized theaters, the institution's own revenue share still amounts to 15.8% (in the 2019/2020 season, see DBV, 2022). More common is a **partial financing** of institutions and projects. This, in turn, can be differentiated as follows (Gerlach-March & Pöllmann, 2019, p. 16):

- With **proportionate financing**, a percentage of the costs is covered by the state, usually with an upper limit set. As a result, additional sources of funding must be secured alongside public funds—for example, by attracting sponsorship contributions. Furthermore, this is also intended to motivate careful resource management and economic action.
- With **shortfall financing**, on the other hand, the state compensates funding gaps up to a maximum limit. This provides applicants with a certain degree of planning security and reduces the risk of financial loss, for example, if fewer tickets are sold at the box office than expected or a sponsor withdraws. On the other hand, this form of risk coverage also reduces the incentive for economic action, since efforts to acquire more funds may simply lead to a reduction in state funding.
- **Fixed amount financing** guarantees the cultural institution a fixed sum, which is generally not adjusted based on the final accounts or depending on the proof of use of funds. Compared to proportionate and shortfall financing, fixed amount financing involves less accounting effort. However, a problematic aspect is that fixed amount financing is often paid only after submission of the final accounts, which can lead to liquidity gaps for cultural institutions. For the financial planning of a cultural institution, fixed amount financing most closely resembles income from arts and cultural sponsorship, since in both cases a fixed amount is guaranteed that can be reliably planned with.

These explanations show that public private arts and cultural funding takes place at various governmental levels and can be differentiated into different forms and types of financing. Fig. 3.8 summarizes the funding systematics graphically.

In addition to government bodies such as cultural offices, ministries of culture (at the state level), or the Federal Government Commissioner for Culture and the Media (at the

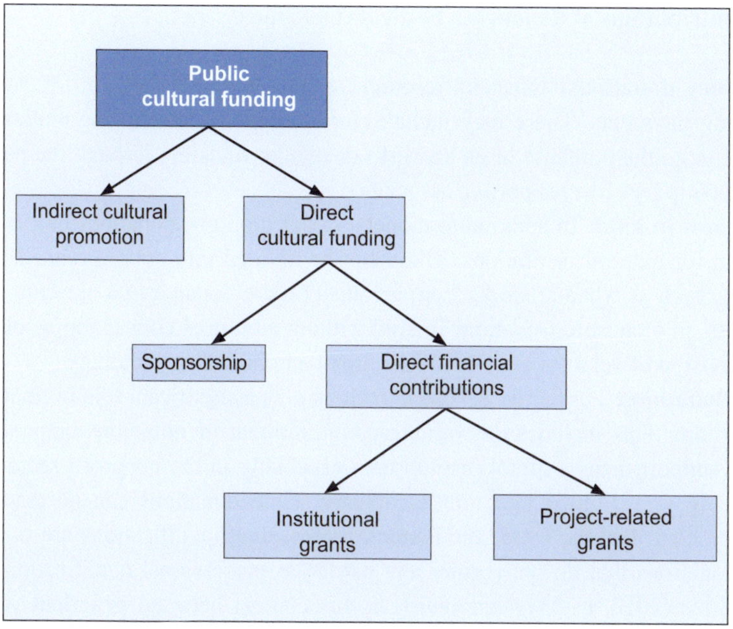

Fig. 3.8 Systematics of public arts and cultural funding

federal level), public private funding is also distributed through intermediary organizations, such as the German Federal Cultural Foundation. The development of expertise regarding the various public funding opportunities and calls for proposals, as well as the preparation of applications, presents significant challenges for cultural institutions.

In addition to the possibilities of public funding, further financing instruments are also available, such as donation marketing and fundraising.

3.3 Donation System and Fundraising

Donations are voluntary contributions to third parties for which there are no direct sponsorship benefits in return. In museums and other cultural institutions, containers are often placed at the entrance to solicit monetary donations from visitors. However, this form of collecting small amounts through impulse donations should not be understood as part of donation marketing. Rather, **donations as an instrument of financing arts and culture** involve a planned management process consisting of analysis, goal setting, strategy definition, fundraising instruments, and final controlling (Urselmann, 2018, pp. 424 f.). Donation marketing thus relies on the systematic acquisition of contributions to support the financing of a cultural institution.

The **contributions of donors** can be divided into three types:

- **Monetary donations:** Financial resources are provided in the form of one-time or recurring payments. These may include, for example, funds for the realization of a project (e.g., the purchase of an artwork) or regular transfers through the payment of membership fees to a supporting association.
- **Donations in kind:** In addition to monetary contributions, donations in kind are also relevant for cultural institutions. These can be divided into culture-related donations in kind, such as when artworks from a collection are donated to a museum or instruments to an orchestra. Donations in kind without a cultural connection would include the provision of vehicles or IT hardware, up to and including buildings.
- **Time donations:** Furthermore, time donations play a significant role in financing arts and culture. This includes the voluntary commitment of numerous helpers, without whose support many cultural institutions—especially in the nonprofit sector—would have only very limited operational capacity. Time donations can be distinguished between contributions where the donor's professional qualifications are utilized and time donations that do not require any particular professional qualification. Leißner and Stolze (2016, p. 834) distinguish in this context between **practical volunteers** and **professional volunteers**. For example, a lawyer who is a member of a cultural association may provide pro bono legal advice as a time donation. She could also help with the cake sale at the annual summer festival. Both contributions are important for the association, but if one were to attempt to calculate a monetary equivalent for the time donations received, different, market-appropriate hourly rates would be used as the basis for calculation depending on the type of contribution.

In principle, donations are a valuable way to secure additional resources for a cultural organization. However, in the practice of cultural management, challenges repeatedly arise in dealing with received donations, which in some cases can even lead to their **rejection and reactance towards donations**. This is illustrated by three (anonymized but real) examples relating to the aforementioned donation categories:

- **Example: monetary donations:** Several years ago, the friends' association of an orchestra collected a considerable sum from donations and membership fees. The orchestra management was pleased with the money, as it was urgently needed for the modernization of chairs and music stands. However, the association's board had little interest in investing the money in such infrastructure. Instead, they wanted to use the funds to pay the fee of an internationally renowned soloist, so that a concert event with the orchestra and the soloist could be realized. Even though support associations are fundamentally tasked with generating resources for a cultural organization, as this example shows, this does not automatically lead to the same objectives regarding the intended use of funds as those pursued by the institution's management.

- **Example: donations in kind:** The donation of items is not always as selfless as it sometimes appears. This becomes particularly clear when the cultural organization commits to using or handling the donations in kind. For example, donors may attempt to transfer the costs of preserving artworks to a cultural institution by donating them. Donors may also wish to obligate a museum or exhibition venue to display an artwork, rather than storing it in the depot or only exhibiting it during special exhibitions. If cultural organizations accept such obligations, donations in kind come with additional costs and less flexibility in program planning.
- **Example: time donations:** Volunteer helpers in cultural institutions often take on tasks that do not require formal professional training. However, this does not mean that the individuals are always sufficiently qualified for the tasks they assume. Just because almost everyone now owns a digital camera does not mean that everyone can naturally handle the photographic documentation of an event. Someone may enthusiastically take on the task of documenting the premiere party of a new play, but then deliver only unprofessional photos. The result is that the communications team cannot use the photos for marketing, and sponsors are annoyed by the poor documentation of the event. Since not every cultural association can afford professional photographers, volunteers are often used for similar tasks. However, if the price is an unprofessional public image of a cultural brand, cultural management must consider whether the time donation is truly an advantage.

These three practical examples show that donations must always be assessed according to their actual benefit and any associated costs.

Motives of Donors and Distinction From Sponsorship

Since corporate sponsors, like private individuals, can also act as donors, a clear distinction from arts and cultural sponsorship is not always easy. Donors are generally assumed to act altruistically, that is, selflessly and with consideration for others (Urselmann, 2018, pp. 132 f.). Corporate sponsors differ from sponsors in that sponsorship is essentially characterized by a reciprocal business arrangement.

It becomes more difficult to distinguish between donations from private individuals and sponsorship by corporate sponsors when corporate sponsors provide financial **support for the private engagement of their employees**. For example, Deutsche Bank supports the time and monetary donations of its employees by donating money to the organizations supported by employees or granting employees time off for their engagement. According to its own figures, in 2021 around 15,500 Deutsche Bank employees (18% of the workforce) contributed approximately 133,000 hours of volunteer work to various charitable organizations. In 2021, Deutsche Bank invested 7.4 million EUR through matching donations, salary-based programs, and other fundraising campaigns (Deutsche Bank, 2023c).

The **motives of donors** are diverse. The motive of helping others can be seen as clearly altruistic. This often results from personal involvement. The fact that a large proportion of Germans donate for this reason is evident from the fact that funds for humanitarian aid have for years represented the category with the highest donation volume (GfK and Deutscher Spendenrat, 2022, pp. 20 f.; 2021a, p. 21; 2021b, p. 24). However, there are also motives that pursue a personal benefit. For example, membership in a friends' association to be part of a community and make contacts, or the hope of enhancing one's own reputation through being perceived as a philanthropist. The desire for active participation in cultural activities or to influence a cultural organization can also be cited as examples. Since these are not direct monetary sponsorship benefits, these motives do not contradict the definition of a donation. Even the material benefit of tax savings does not change the classification as a donation—after all, this form of benefit is explicitly anchored as a motivator in legislation. Donation activities, however, enter a "gray area" when donors receive additional monetary sponsorship benefits beyond the donation receipt, such as exclusive invitations or free tickets to events. Donors may be granted a pre-purchase right for sought-after tickets. However, if they do not have to pay for tickets that are otherwise available for sale, it is no longer considered a donation.

From an **information economics perspective**, donations are classified as so-called trust goods. This means that donors must trust the cultural organization to use the contributions for the stated purpose. This issue arises primarily for monetary and in-kind donations, but less so for time donations. For this reason, donors expect information and transparency regarding the use and application of donations. Without a basic level of trust in the cultural organization, donations are not possible (unless donors are pursuing another goal). In addition, donors expect to be thanked for their commitment. Especially when building a circle of regular donors, practical fundraising shows that this always involves relationship building, which is why fundraising is also referred to as "friend-raising." However, this term is sometimes criticized, as efforts to initiate friendships from a professional position, especially with the actual aim of gaining these friends as donors, are seen as unprofessional. It therefore seems more appropriate to understand **fundraising as an element of relationship marketing** (Bruhn, 2022) for a cultural organization. For even if it is not about friends in the strict sense, relationship work with fans, volunteers, and other supporters plays a decisive role.

Donor Pyramid as a Model for Target Group Segmentation

To do justice to the importance of relationship work, donation marketing is based on a model of target group segmentation that has become established under the name **donor pyramid** (Ciconte & Jacob, 2009, p. 102; Haibach, 2012, pp. 219 f.; Urselmann, 2018, p. 18; Gerlach-March & Pöllmann, 2019, p. 66). The general, broad public is the target of communication efforts by cultural organizations, as interested parties and potential visitors are reached, some of whom become donors (see Fig. 3.9). New or first-time donors represent the first of five donor categories. The goal of fundraising is to motivate first-time donors to donate repeatedly and ultimately become regular donors. People who have supported a cultural organization as donors over a long period can be asked to make larger donations, for example through invitations to special charity events. At the top are

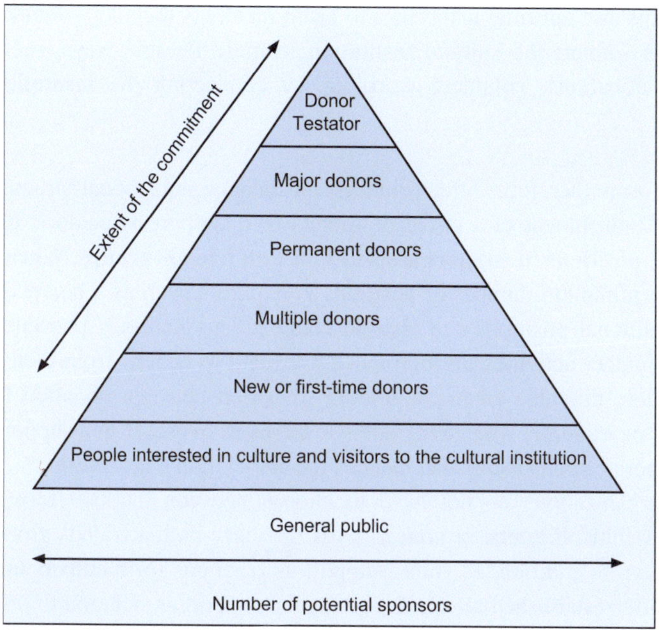

Fig. 3.9 Stages of a donor pyramid. (Source: Gerlach-March & Pöllmann, 2019, p. 66)

benefactors and testators, who bequeath particularly large sums to an institution through legacy donations.

Support Associations and Circles of Friends

To organize donors and supporters of cultural institutions, many cultural organizations establish support associations or circles of friends. The **characteristics and organizational structures** of these two forms can be described as follows:

- **Support associations** are generally structured organizations with a clear hierarchy, formal membership requirements, and regular meetings. They are often founded with the goal of raising funds for cultural institutions and have defined objectives set out in their statutes. In many cases, the association's purpose is also recognized as charitable, allowing support associations to issue tax-deductible donation receipts. As registered associations, support associations, unlike circles of friends, are independent legal entities. Members of support associations are usually required to pay regular contributions, either through annual membership fees or donations for specific projects.
- **Friends groups**, on the other hand, are less formal networks of individuals who share a common interest in supporting a cultural institution. They may not have specific requirements for membership or regular meetings, but instead rely on personal

relationships and informal gatherings to bring members together. Members of friends groups can support the cultural institution in more flexible ways, such as through monetary donations, volunteer work, or by connecting the institution with new networks.

The two forms therefore differ primarily in their organizational structure and legal status. The establishment of a circle of friends or a support association often requires filling several **positions in support associations and friends groups**. When founding an association, a minimum number of positions is required, such as a board or a treasurer. However, additional positions can also be created. This makes it possible to organize members' volunteer activities through these roles and to benefit from their professional expertise. Often, this also creates a smooth transition between donation behavior and sponsorship, for example, when a tax advisor serves as treasurer in a support association and their corporate sponsorship also handles the association's tax returns.

Cultural organizations do not have to choose between the two forms. There are numerous museums, theaters, or concert halls that have both a friends group and a support association. In addition, a "young support association" for members up to about 30 years old is often established alongside the regular support association to provide special support for the next generation of patrons.

The following section uses the **example of the Festspielhaus Baden-Baden** to show how private individuals and sponsors are organized as supporters through the institutions of the friends group and the support association, and what benefits are offered to them.

Example: Festspielhaus Baden-Baden

The Festspielhaus Baden-Baden is distinguished by its particularly diverse structure for attracting private third-party funding. The supporting organization is the Festspielhaus Baden-Baden Cultural Foundation, established in 2000. The concert hall of the Festspielhaus has 2500 seats, making it one of the largest venues for classical music in Europe. In addition to a business circle as a support network, the funding institutions also include a support circle for private individuals and a circle of friends organized as an association.

Support Circle

The support circle does not operate as an independent legal entity. It is understood as an association of culture enthusiasts who support the Festspielhaus with individual donations. Members of the support circle receive exclusive advance booking rights for all events, access to an exclusive club lounge, the opportunity to participate in rehearsals, music seminars, and cultural trips, as well as invitations to gatherings "in front of and behind the scenes" of the Festspielhaus.

Members of the support circle are divided into nine categories depending on their contributions to the Festspielhaus (Festspielhaus Baden-Baden, 2023a):

- Patrons: contributions from one million EUR
- Diamond: divided into annual donations from 250,000 or from 100,000 EUR
- Tanzanite: from 75,000 EUR annual donation
- Emerald: from 50,000 EUR annual donation
- Ruby: from 25,000 EUR annual donation
- Sapphire: from 15,000 EUR annual donation
- Platinum: from 10,000 EUR annual donation
- Gold: from 5000 EUR annual donation
- Silver: from 2500 EUR annual donation

An analysis of the supporters shows that the support circle is made up predominantly of private individuals, with most supporters being (married) couples (as of January 2023). In addition, several foundations are among the supporters. Sponsors in the classic sense are not represented in the support circle, as they are part of the partner or business circle.

Friends Group
The friends group is a non-profit association and was founded in 1995. It has over 1500 members (as of January 2023). Members include private individuals as well as corporate sponsors. The annual membership fee includes (Festspielhaus Baden-Baden, 2023b):

- Individual members: 520 EUR
- Couples: 780 EUR
- Corporate sponsorship: 1500 EUR
- Junior individual members: 120 EUR
- Junior couples: 180 EUR

Membership goes far beyond supporting the Festspielhaus, as members benefit from numerous **privileges**, including:

- A dedicated newsletter for members of the circle of friends.
- A dedicated service hotline for ticket bookings, reservations, etc.
- Advance booking rights for tickets to Festspielhaus events.
- Priority placement on waiting lists for sold-out concerts.
- Invitations to exclusive artist receptions.
- Backstage tours of the Festspielhaus operations.
- Invitations to attend rehearsals.
- Participation in cultural trips to other opera houses and concert halls.
- Workshops on musical topics.
- Invitation to the “Intendant’s Salon”—a discussion event with the artistic director and managing director.
- Invitation to the “Circle of Friends Festival”—an exclusive event for association members. ◀

Measures and Campaigns

The sponsorship benefits shown in the example of the Festspielhaus Baden-Baden serve as incentives for joining one of the organizational forms. However, the associated membership fees are only part of the income. In addition, the friends' and supporters' organizations initiate **donation campaigns** to acquire further funds for the institution. These campaigns are usually limited in time and are used to finance a specific project. They are aimed at the members of the supporting organizations as well as the interested public and also serve to attract first-time donors.

Fundraising campaigns can be distinguished according to various characteristics.

- **Type of donation:** Fundraising campaigns can first be classified according to the type of donation sought. Usually, monetary donations are requested, but campaigns to solicit in-kind or time donations are also possible. For example, in March 2022, the monument protection organization "World Heritage Watch" launched a donation appeal asking for packaging materials for Ukrainian museums. This was intended to help Ukrainian museums and galleries secure cultural assets.
- **Media channel:** Another way to differentiate is by the media used, for example, whether it is an online campaign or crowdfunding campaign, or whether it is conducted through personal direct solicitation of donors.
- **Schedule:** Campaigns can also be classified by timing and duration, e.g., annual campaign, Christmas campaign, short-term campaign (e.g., for the purchase of an artwork), or long-term campaign (e.g., for multi-year construction projects such as the Humboldt Forum Berlin).
- **Target groups:** Donation campaigns can be targeted at specific audience segments, e.g., new donors, major donors, legacy donors, individuals, corporate sponsorship, etc.
- **Purpose:** The specific purpose of a campaign can also be used for classification, especially since similar purposes are often observed. These include, for example, campaigns for the purchase of instruments or works of art, for the financing of operating resources (e.g., purchase of a new lighting system), or the financing of new buildings or renovations.

Example: Campaigns for Chair Sponsorships

A form of donation campaign popular among cultural institutions is the **concept of chair sponsorships**. In this concept, a donor is asked to "sponsor" a chair. This can be a physical seat in a theater or venue, or a metaphorical "chair" representing a specific program or project. In return, the donor's name is displayed on a plaque or sign associated with the chair, sometimes also on the cultural institution's website.

Fig. 3.10 shows examples of prices and durations for chair sponsorships at selected German cultural institutions. Often, a volume discount is granted when multiple sponsorships are taken on.

Chair sponsorships are aimed equally at individuals and corporate sponsors. For corporate sponsors, they offer the opportunity to gain visibility at cultural events quickly and easily. However, the reach of this measure is limited to those who actually sit in the sponsored chairs.

An **analysis of the chair sponsorships** at the Naturtheater Grötzingen (n=239) in January 2023, for example, shows that the chair sponsors consisted of 54% individuals, 6% groups (e.g., graduating classes, church congregations), and 40% corporate sponsors. This illustrates that chair sponsorships are used by many corporate sponsors as a sponsorship measure—often with a clearly promotional intent, for example, by displaying the company's website address on the chair instead of the company name. Since in this example a service is provided by the company in exchange for a promotional consideration, this measure does fulfill the essential characteristics of arts and cultural sponsorship. Nevertheless, it should be distinguished from a professional sponsorship cooperation, as it is largely left to chance whether relevant target groups are reached. ◀

Cultural institution	Price	Duration
BKA Theater Berlin	200 EUR	Unlimited duration
Elbphilharmonie Hamburg	1,000–2,000 EUR	5 years
Schwäbisch Hall open-air theater	500 EUR	at least 10 years
Gärtnerplatz Theater Munich	100–1,000 EUR	min. 10 years
Gewandhausorchester Leipzig	Depending on seating quality 300-800 EUR	2 years
Konzerthaus Berlin	300-1,000 EUR	5 years
Kronberg Academy	2.000 EUR	5 years
Grötzingen Nature Theater	150 EUR	Unlimited duration
Oldenburgisches Staatstheater	500 EUR	min. 10 years
Pfefferbergtheater Berlin	200 EUR (private individuals) 300 EUR (companies)	Unlimited duration
Renitenz Theater Stuttgart	250 EUR (private individuals) 500 EUR (companies)	Unlimited duration
Sandkorntheater Dresden	300 EUR	Unlimited duration

Fig. 3.10 Selection of examples of prices and durations for chair sponsorships (as of January 2023)

3.4 Arts and Cultural Sponsorship as a Form of Private Third-Party Funding

Collaboration with sponsors represents another pillar in the funding mix for cultural organizations. Like fundraising, sponsorship serves to acquire financial resources, in-kind contributions, and services. However, in contrast to donations, sponsorship involves offering a monetary equivalent in return for the resources obtained, which necessitates the **provision of extensive communication services** that can be offered to sponsors during cooperation negotiations. For this reason, the use of sponsorship as a financing instrument is closely linked to the professional marketing management of the cultural institution.

The **importance of sponsorship in the funding mix** varies among different cultural institutions and depends on the types of financing used as well as the attractiveness of a cultural institution for cooperation. For cultural organizations that do not receive government funding, the funding mix is limited to donations, sponsorship, and own revenues. Since these organizations often do not operate on a non-profit basis, this also makes fundraising more difficult. Thus, the importance of sponsorship for these institutions is generally greater than for cultural organizations that receive government funding. However, this importance can only be realized in practice if the cultural organization can also offer sufficient attractiveness to sponsors, for example through a strong image and wide media reach.

The decision to **integrate sponsorship into the funding mix** initially involves investments for cultural organizations. For example, it can be calculated that with a monthly salary for a sponsorship manager of EUR 4000 (gross) plus employer contributions, workplace costs, work equipment, and other personnel expenses, at least EUR 60,000 in sponsorship services must be raised per year for sponsorship to begin to become economically efficient.

Example: Sponsorship income of various cultural institutions

As an example of the amounts of sponsorship funds raised, the following cites the 2019 Sponsorship Report (see tables on pages 79 ff.), which shows the sponsorship income of the cultural institutions Stiftung Preußischer Kulturbesitz, Deutsche Akademie Rom Villa Massimo, Filmförderungsanstalt (FFA), Stiftung Deutsches Historisches Museum, and Stiftung Jüdisches Museum Berlin (BMI, 2019). The report is published as part of anti-corruption efforts and summarizes sponsorship services for the years 2017 and 2018. Donation income is also published, but is not shown here. When considering the comparatively high amounts for the Stiftung Preußischer Kulturbesitz, it should be noted that this foundation encompasses numerous cultural institutions. For example, the Staatliche Museen Berlin (a total of 15 collections and four research institutes) are also included.

Stiftung Preußischer Kulturbesitz

Sponsorship income 2017 and 2018 of the Stiftung Preußischer Kulturbesitz:

Sponsor	Sponsorship amount	Purpose of the sponsorship	Type of sponsorship
Riyadh	1.394.593,00 EUR	Project support for the Museum of Islamic Art	Cash contribution
Bayer AG, Leverkusen	200.000,00 EUR	Project support for the SPK	Cash contribution
Bertelsmann SE & Co KGaA, Gutersloh	200.000,00 EUR	Project support for the SPK	Cash contribution
Daimler AG, Stuttgart	100.000,00 EUR	Project support for the SPK	Cash contribution
Deutsche Bank AG, Frankfurt am Main	300.000,00 EUR	Project support for the SPK EUR	Cash contribution
Deutscher Sparkassen & Giroverband Berlin; Landesbank Berlin/Berliner Sparkasse; Feuersozietat Berlin Brandenburg	740.000,00 EUR	Project support for the State Museums	Cash contribution
Linde AG, Munich	200.000,00 EUR	Project support from SPK	Cash contribution
KPMG AG, Berlin	200.000,00 EUR	Project support from SPK	Cash contribution
SAP SE, Walldorf	200.000,00 EUR	Project support from SPK	Cash contribution
Siemens AG, Munich	250.000,00 EUR	Project support from SPK	Cash contribution
The Robert Ho Family Foundation, Hong Kong	180.000,00 EUR	Support for the special exhibition "Faces of China" at the National Museums in Berlin	Cash contribution
Vattenfall Europe Warme, Berlin	25.000,00 EUR	Support for the educational project "Alchimistenkuche" of the National Museums in Berlin	Cash contribution
Wurth Group/Kunzelsau	2.200.000,00 EUR	Project support of the SPK	Cash contribution
Radio Paradiso R.H.B. Radiohaus Berlin GmbH	24.000,00 EUR	Promotion of the annual tickets of the National Museums in Berlin	Sachleistung: Radiospot
Verlag Der Tagesspiegel GmbH, Berlin	35.080,00 EUR	Promotion of the exhibition "Moving Times"	In-kind service: Advertisements
Verlag Der Tagesspiegel GmbH, Berlin	18.360,00 EUR	Promotion of the "Hello World" exhibition	In-kind service: Advertisements
Verlag Der Tagesspiegel GmbH, Berlin	35.284,00 EUR	Promotion of the exhibition "Alchemy"	In-kind service: Advertisements
Verlag Der Tagesspiegel GmbH, Berlin	35.284,00 EUR	Promotion of the exhibition "China and Egypt. Cradles of the world"	In-kind service: Advertisements
GCM Go City Media GmbH, Berlin	8.002,00 EUR	Promotion of the exhibition "Alchemy"	In-kind service: Advertisements
GCM Go City Media GmbH, Berlin	8.226,00 EUR	Promotion of the exhibition "China and Egypt. Cradles of the World"	In-kind service: Advertisements
GCM Go City Media GmbH, Berlin	6.162,00 EUR	Promotion of the exhibition "Faces of China"	In-kind service: Advertisements
National Geographic	11.000,00 EUR	Promotion of the exhibition "Moving Times"	Benefit in kind: Advertisements
National Geographic	6.300,00 EUR	Promotion of the exhibition "China and Egypt. Cradles of the World"	Contribution in kind Reportage, Promotion of the exhibition
With pleasure Hielscher and Turkowski GbR	6.375,00 EUR	Promotion of the exhibition "Alchemy"	Contribution in kind: Advertising services
Sum:	**6.383.666,00 EUR**		

Deutsche Akademie Rom Villa Massimo

Sponsorship income 2017–2018 of the Deutsche Akademie Rom Villa Massimo:

Sponsor	Sponsorship amount	Purpose of the sponsorship	Type of sponsorship
German Savings Banks and Giro Association, Berlin	82,000.00 EUR	Event for the presentation of Villa Massimo and its scholarship holders on 7.12.2017	Financial contribution

Filmförderungsanstalt (FFA)

Sponsorship income 2017 and 2018 of the Filmförderungsanstalt (FFA):

Sponsor	Sponsorship amount	Purpose of the sponsorship	Type of sponsorship
Bayerische Motorenwerke AG, Munich	8,016.23 EUR	Evening event Branchentiger 2017	Cash benefit
Bayerische Motorenwerke AG, Munich	6,762.67 EUR	Anniversary celebration "50 years Filmforderungsanstalt" 2018	Cash benefit

Stiftung Deutsches Historisches Museum

Sponsorship income 2017 and 2018 of the Stiftung Deutsches Historisches Museum:

Sponsor	Sponsorship amount	Purpose of the sponsorship	Type of sponsorship
Axel Springer Foundation, Berlin	10,000.00 EUR	Catalog Picture of the time	Cash benefit

Stiftung Jüdisches Museum Berlin

Sponsorship income 2017 and 2018 of the Stiftung Jüdisches Museum Berlin:

Sponsor	Sponsorship amount	Purpose of the sponsorship	Type of sponsorship
Evonik Industries AG, Essen	240,000.00 EUR	Main support for the chamber music week "intonations" in 2017 and 2018	Cash contribution
expofair GmbH, Berlin	8,550.00 EUR	Support for the 2018 New Year's reception	Contribution in kind

◀

3.5 Own Revenues in Distinction to Arts and Cultural Sponsorship

Arts and cultural sponsorship as a financing instrument is discussed **in distinction to own revenues**. Therefore, own revenues are only briefly introduced in this chapter. The points of contact with sponsorship, which arise in the concrete design of sponsorship benefits, are highlighted.

The **own revenues of cultural institutions** can be divided into primary and secondary operating income (Gerlach-March & Pöllmann, 2019, pp. 97 f.). **Primary operating income** includes revenues from core business, i.e., artistic offerings. These are predominantly income from ticket sales and exploitation rights. **Secondary operating income**, on the other hand, is generated through additional services and products. These include, for example:

- Income from catering services,
- Cloakroom fees,
- Sales of programs and catalogues,
- Revenue from renting out spaces,
- Sales of merchandising products.

The **importance of own revenues** fundamentally varies depending on the sponsorship and financial objectives of a cultural institution. While in public cultural institutions the share of own revenues in total income is often low, it constitutes the main source of income for private cultural institutions. For example, public theaters in Germany recorded a box office result of 15.8% in the 2019/2020 season. For comparison: before the COVID-19 pandemic, in the 2018/2019 season, it was 17.7%. For the 2019/2020 season, this means that on average, 39.26 EUR in income was generated per visit, and, as shown above, 208.87 EUR or 84.2% per visit was publicly subsidized (DBV, 2022). Private cultural providers have to compensate for the lack of public funds by increasing their own revenues, relying more heavily on the sale of catering services, merchandising, or rentals.

Sponsorship collaborations often influence the **weighting of own revenues** of cultural institutions. If a sponsor receives tickets to an event as a consideration, these are removed from regular sales, thereby reducing the share of own revenues. Additional services and thus secondary income are also related to the design of arts and cultural sponsorship measures and cannot always be clearly separated. For example, it is common for catering in cultural institutions to be offered by a tenant or licensee. A catering license is particularly attractive at larger festivals, as significant sales can be achieved in a short period of time. The beverage license can be sold to a beverage company, which also appears as a sponsor of the festival and advertises itself on the festival grounds and in festival media. For example, the brewery Warsteiner is the main sponsor and "beverage partner" of the German music festivals "Rock am Ring" and "Rock im Park." In addition to beverage sales, the beer brand is also present as a sponsor through its own band contest for newcomer bands and a 400-square-meter exhibition area. There is also an interface with merchandising through the production of a special edition of festival beer cans (see Fig. 3.11).

Another **interface between arts and cultural sponsorship and secondary income** arises when additional services can only be offered through a sponsorship collaboration. This is the case, for example, when a car brand presents itself at a cultural event with a shuttle service. The car brand pays as a sponsor for the opportunity to offer a shuttle service and covers the costs of its implementation. The cultural institution, in turn, can sell a contingent of high-priced "VIP tickets," whose holders are entitled to use the shuttle service. Other sponsorship benefits, such as promotional gifts or entertainment offerings at music festivals, also have an indirect impact on operating income. The added value resulting from sponsorship benefits for visitors enables a higher ticket price.

The weighting of the funding pillars discussed in this chapter varies according to sector, sponsorship, and economic orientation of cultural institutions. As an example of a publicly funded theater that uses all of the mentioned types of financing (public private funding, private third-party funds, own revenues), the following presents a summary of the annual report of Theater Basel for the 2021/2022 season (Theater Basel, 2022).

Fig. 3.11 Rock am Ring and Rock im Park—2022 Festival Edition Warsteiner

Example: Types of financing at Theater Basel

In the 2021/2022 season, Theater Basel employed 429 permanent staff and 468 temporary staff. A total of 572 performances were realized, which attracted 148,155 visits and achieved an occupancy rate of 61.4%. It should be noted that some performances had to be canceled due to the pandemic. In addition to the in-house performances, guided tours were conducted with 152 groups and a total of 3533 participants.

The breakdown of income (see Fig. 3.12) shows that within own revenues, most income is generated from ticket sales (80.5%). In the overall view, however, it becomes clear that own revenues cover only 14.8% of costs. The largest share of expenses is covered by the public private sector. Private third-party funds, acquired through sponsorship and donations, account for 3.6% of the theater's financing (see Fig. 3.13). ◀

Own revenue		
Type of own revenue	Absolute total	Share of own revenue
Income from ticket sales (primary)	6,659,092 CHF	80,5 %
Result from external guest performances (primary)	181,203 CHF	2,2 %
Income from checkroom fees (secondary)	499,201 CHF	6,0 %
Program booklets and advertisements (secondary)	64,771 CHF	0,8 %
Contributions	291,600 CHF	3,5 %
Sales, rental and personnel services (secondary)	285,540 CHF	3,5 %
Other income (secondary)	289,031 CHF	3,5 %
Total own income	**8,270,438 CHF**	**100,0 %**

Fig. 3.12 Breakdown of own revenues at Theater Basel in the 2021/2022 season. (Source: Theater Basel, 2022)

Financing			
Type of financing	**Composition of the type of financing**	**Absolute total**	**Share of total financing**
Own revenue	Primary and secondary income	8,270,438 CHF	14,8 %
Private third-party funding	Sponsoring and donations	1,995,953 CHF	3,6 %
Public funding	Grant from the Canton of Basel-Stadt	43,573,529 CHF	78,2 %
	Subsidy Canton Basel-Landschaft	1,875,000 CHF	3,4 %
Total funding		**55,714,920 CHF**	**100,0 %**

Fig. 3.13 Breakdown of the financing of Theater Basel in the 2021/2022 season. (Source: Theater Basel, 2022)

3.6 Crowdfunding as a Form of Arts and Cultural Sponsorship

Crowdfunding is a comparatively new financing instrument and also has links to arts and cultural sponsorship. **Crowdfunding** refers to raising funds via online channels with the aim of obtaining a predefined sum for the realization of a project through many small contributions. In return for their contributions, participants in a campaign receive non-material or monetary sponsorship benefits. The sponsorship benefits can be freely designed. Thus, the classification of crowdfunding within the above-mentioned financing instruments depends on the type of sponsorship benefits, which are shown below.

The principle of achieving a larger funding amount through many small contributions underlies almost all donation campaigns. In addition to the type of media usage and the extensive design of sponsorship benefits, crowdfunding campaigns are particularly distinguished by the defined "funding threshold," as illustrated by the **characteristics of crowdfunding**:

- **Distribution media:** Crowdfunding is associated with the principle of crowdsourcing (Howe, 2006, 2008), in which the participation of many people enables complex tasks (e.g., Wikipedia as a crowdsourcing encyclopedia). It emerged with the establishment of social media and relies on the viral communication effects of digital media. This expands the reach of potential donors. Each project has its own blog, which typically provides updates on the project's progress and the funding already achieved.
- **Funding threshold:** Crowdfunding campaigns are initiated to realize a specific project. The goal is not to collect as much money as possible with an open-ended objective. If the funding threshold is not reached and the project is therefore not implemented, the donors receive their contributions back. Participation is thus low-risk, as repurposing the funds is not intended. To ensure this, crowdfunding platforms act as trustees.
- **Trust principle:** The crowdfunding platforms act as intermediaries between the donors and the cultural institution. They collect and manage the incoming funds as trustees until the end of the campaign period. If the funding threshold is reached or exceeded, the money is paid out to the cultural institution. However, if the minimum goal is not reached, the funds are returned.
- **Sponsorship benefits:** While donation campaigns ensure that no monetary sponsorship benefits are provided, crowdfunding campaigns often feature a very flexible design of sponsorship benefits, ranging from an idealistic "thank you" to the purchase of artworks or access to exclusive events.

Main Forms of Crowdfunding

Crowdfunding campaigns can be differentiated according to the **type of sponsorship benefits** into three main forms (Hemer, 2011; Sixt, 2014, p. 101):

- **Reward-based crowdfunding:** One of the most common types of campaigns is reward-based crowdfunding, in which supporters fund a cultural project from which they subsequently benefit. This form can also be compared to a pre-sale. For example, this form is popular among musicians to pre-finance the studio production of an album and then provide the supporters with the result as a CD, MP3, or stream link.
- **Donation-based crowdfunding:** If, on the other hand, there is no monetary reward and supporters receive "only" thanks or symbolic gestures, it is considered a donation.
- **Crowdinvesting:** If supporters intend to achieve a financial gain with their contributions, it is an investment and a bet on the project's success. The goal is to obtain a profit distribution. This form of participation is comparable to the use of venture capital. Crowdinvesting can be further divided into **equity-based crowdfunding**, in which supporters acquire a long-term stake in the project or enterprise. Alternatively, the **lending-based crowdfunding** model can be used, in which supporters participate as lenders based on a defined interest rate.

While reward-based and donation-based crowdfunding are frequently used, often in combination, for smaller cultural projects, crowdinvesting campaigns are rarely found in the cultural sector.

Crowdfunding Platforms

Most crowdfunding campaigns are carried out with the help of crowdfunding platforms. These platforms are structured according to the principles of social media blog networks or e-commerce shops. Cultural projects can create their own profile on the platforms and provide information about their project with texts, photos, and videos. In addition, the key figures of a project are displayed transparently on the homepage. These include:

- Funding goal or funding threshold (minimum amount that must be reached).
- Duration.
- Number of supporters.
- Current amount transferred.
- Time of project realization (if the funding goal is reached).

The most important function of the profiles is a shop system where various sponsorship benefits can be purchased. Relevant **crowdfunding platforms for cultural organizations** include Startnext, crowdfunding.at (for Austria), Indiegogo, or Kickstarter. While these platforms serve the function of pre-financing cultural projects, in recent years the principle of direct transactions between cultural creators and their fans has also become established for the distribution of existing cultural goods. The development of e-commerce offerings has led to strong growth in **direct-to-consumer sales (D2C)**. Here, corporate sponsors use their own online shops to bypass distribution partners such as department stores, supermarkets, Amazon, etc., and can thus also retain the distribution margin.

Direct-to-consumer sales or **direct-to-fan sales** can also be observed in the cultural sector. Platforms such as Patreon enable cultural creators to sell directly to increase their own revenues without relying on partners such as publishers or music labels. However, when using platforms, cultural creators remain dependent on them, which entails risks, as the case of PledgeMusic shows: The service was founded in 2009 and enabled musicians to pre-finance studio productions through crowdfunding campaigns. However, when PledgeMusic filed for bankruptcy in 2019, not all musicians received the money they were entitled to. An alternative to using crowdfunding platforms is therefore to design your own website that provides information about a project and offers transaction options for supporters. Since this involves significantly more effort and additional costs, a dedicated crowdfunding website is only worthwhile for complex and long-term projects, as was the case, for example, with the new construction of the Städel Museum in Frankfurt.

The design of sponsorship benefits for a crowdfunding campaign and their evaluation from the perspective of financing arts and culture will be illustrated below using the **example of a Startnext campaign** for a short film.

Example: Crowdfunding Campaign for the Film Project "NICHTS"

Jana and Sofia Münster sought supporters for their short film project "NICHTS" via the crowdfunding platform Startnext from January 10 to February 17, 2023. A minimum funding threshold of 5000 EUR was specified. In their justification for why the project should be supported, the filmmakers explained: "With your support, you help young female filmmakers realize a film with a philosophical background, which so far has not been represented in the film and media industry. (…)" (Startnext, 2023). Thus, they appealed to altruistic motives and primarily addressed donors. However, the offered sponsorship benefits could be assigned to all three funding pillars, as shown in Fig. 3.14.

The listing and categorization of the sponsorship benefits show that **crowdfunding cannot be assigned to a single financing instrument**. Since participation by public bodies is uncommon, and thus no public-private funding is raised through crowdfunding campaigns, these campaigns usually consist of private third-party funds and own revenues. However, as the example illustrates, the classification of some sponsorship benefits as arts and cultural sponsorship must be made with reservations. Although the film project "NICHTS" offers the category "main sponsor," the sponsorship cooperation outlined here differs in several respects from professional sponsorship management:

- It is unusual for a sponsorship concept to provide for an unlimited number of main sponsors.
- The target groups of the film are described rather vaguely as "young adults searching for identity, the meaning of life, and the things that really matter" (Startnext,

2023). This makes it difficult for the sponsor to assess whether there is sufficient overlap with their own target group.

- No detailed information is provided about the distribution of the film, making it difficult to predict the number of contacts achieved and thus to economically evaluate the invested sponsorship amount.

These points of criticism did not stand in the way of the campaign's success: The filmmakers were able to reach their funding goal. By the end of the campaign on February 17, 2023, a total of 8909 EUR had been transferred to the project by 60 supporters, including two "main sponsors." ◀

The classifications of arts and cultural sponsorship within the financing of arts and culture have shown that cultural organizations finance themselves through the use of multiple instruments. The sometimes complex funding mix involves not only visitors, but also interested patrons, corporate sponsorship, and the state. The discussion of the various financing instruments made it clear that arts and cultural sponsorship cannot always be clearly delineated, as there are numerous **overlaps and interrelationships between the various instruments** and sponsorship.

Title	Price	Availability	Classification in the financing mix
Free support	Self-selectable	Unlimited	Donation
Link to the finished film	15,- EUR	Unlimited	Own revenue (primary)
2 tickets to the premiere	100,- EUR	5	Own revenue (primary)
Virtual thank you (thanks by e-mail)	5,- EUR	Unlimited	Donation
Link to the finished film and signed film poster	35,- EUR	20	Own revenue (primary and secondary)
Link to the film and name in the credits	45,- EUR	20	Own revenue (primary) and donation
Meet & Greet with the filmmakers	150,- EUR	10	Own revenue (secondary)
Main sponsor (logo in the credits of the film)	1000,- EUR	Unlimited	Sponsoring

Fig. 3.14 Sponsorship benefits of the crowdfunding campaign "NICHTS" (2023)

Moreover, in practice, sponsorship is sometimes interpreted very broadly, leading to forms of support being attributed to sponsorship that, strictly speaking, are donations or at least not professionally planned communication measures. In such cases, arts and cultural sponsorship is misunderstood as an almost arbitrary communication measure, and the importance of professional marketing communication by the cooperation partners is underestimated. However, in order to successfully use arts and cultural sponsorship in the funding mix of a cultural institution, it is important that **cultural organizations understand sponsorship** as an instrument of marketing and corporate communication as a means of support.

Finally, the following case study of the **Gewandhausorchester Leipzig** illustrates the use of arts and cultural sponsorship as a financing instrument from the perspective of a cultural organization. The cooperation strategy and the sponsorship benefits offered are presented.

3.6.1 Case Study Gewandhausorchester: Arts and Cultural Sponsorship from the Perspective of an Orchestra

The Orchestra and the Initial Situation for Arts and Cultural Sponsorship

The **Gewandhausorchester** originated from the concert society "Das Große Concert," founded in 1743 by Leipzig entrepreneurs, and is the oldest civic symphony orchestra in the world. The orchestra received its name when it moved into the clothmakers' guild hall in 1781, which became its first concert hall. This civic founding history is also reflected in the Gewandhaus's sponsorship activities, in which Leipzig's business community is engaged in supporting the concert hall.

The orchestra performs around 300 concerts and events annually at its three Leipzig venues: as the concert orchestra of the Gewandhaus, as the orchestra of the Leipzig Opera, and as an ensemble that performs the Bach cantatas weekly in the St. Thomas Church together with the Thomanerchor. With its approximately 185 musicians (see Fig. 3.15), the symphony orchestra is one of the largest professional orchestras in the world (Gewandhausorchester, 2023a, b).

The orchestra's artistic trademark is a characteristically warm and dark sound that clearly distinguishes it from many other major orchestras. Since 2018, the artistic direction of the symphony orchestra has been held by conductor Andris Nelson as "Gewandhauskapellmeister."

Administratively, the Gewandhausorchester is part of the Gewandhaus zu Leipzig as a **municipal enterprise of the City of Leipzig**. The subsidies from the City of Leipzig ensure stable operations and cover fixed costs. For additional special projects such as open-air concerts, costly tours, outstanding soloists, special festivals, music education projects, etc., further financial resources are necessary. To access these additional resources, arts and cultural sponsorship was integrated into the Gewandhausorchester's funding mix.

The Gewandhaus management saw the risk that, without the aforementioned special projects and the necessary additional resources, it would no longer be possible in the

Fig. 3.15 Full financing of the open-air concert "Klassik airleben" in Leipzig's Rosental through sponsorship income. (Photo: Eric Kemnitz)

future to guarantee artistically excellent operations at a world-class level (with top conductors, star soloists, and a varied program).

Objectives of Sponsorship

With its strategy, the Gewandhaus pursues several **objectives of arts and cultural sponsorship**. First, the aim is to secure stable and predictable financial resources in order to expand the scope for action beyond the basic public funding. In addition to financial resources, a transfer of knowledge between the institution and its business partners is also desired, to provide the concert hall operation with new management impulses.

Furthermore, through sponsorship, the orchestra pursues its own **marketing and communication objectives**. Collaboration with globally operating sponsors such as DHL and Porsche serves the goal of further increasing the **Gewandhausorchester brand**'s recognition.

In addition, the orchestra aims to strengthen the legitimacy of the concert hall among the region's business community and thus also gain the advocacy of the business sector for the orchestra. For the cultural institution, which depends on public funds, one of the **image objectives** is to avoid the perception of the Gewandhausorchester as a "petitioner" to the public sector. Instead, the aim is to use sponsorship activities to achieve

positioning as an innovative concert hall capable of generating alternative sources of revenue on its own.

The Gewandhaus management also recognized the long-term potential that arises from contacts with sponsors beyond a specific cooperation. Thus, the expansion and strengthening of the network in Leipzig and the region are also defined as general objectives of sponsorship.

Target Groups and Target Group Acceptance

The **main target group** of the Gewandhaus Orchestra is an educated, culturally interested bourgeoisie in Leipzig. According to the Sinus Milieus, it can be classified into the conservative-upscale milieu, the post-materialist milieu, and the traditional milieu. The secondary target groups are found in the nostalgic-bourgeois milieu, the adaptive-pragmatic milieu, and the performer milieu.

For the orchestra's sponsors, particularly affluent and value-oriented contacts within the main target groups are of interest. For sponsors who wish to support their B2C communication through their engagement, the purchasing power of the target group is a decisive criterion. For increasing brand awareness among sponsors, both main and secondary target groups are of similar interest.

Sponsorship Acceptance

Due to the bourgeois founding and development history of the Gewandhaus Orchestra, **audience acceptance** of sponsorship efforts is largely present. The necessity of acquiring third-party funding to supplement public funds is communicated in an understandable way and is understood by the audience. Sponsorship partnerships are viewed critically when the cooperating corporate sponsorship has a negative effect on a particular reference group in the city of Leipzig in the course of its business activities, such as through noise or odor pollution. Such factors can lead to increased sensitivity and critical engagement with the respective corporate sponsorship, up to and including public protest, which can also impact the sponsorship partnership.

Strategic Orientation of Arts and Cultural Sponsorship

The sponsors of the Gewandhaus Orchestra are organized in a so-called **Sponsors Club**. This is divided and staffed according to the extent of the commitment as follows (as of 2023) (see Fig. 3.16):

- **Global Partner:** DHL
- **Premium Partner:** B&B Media GmbH, EnBW, LVV (Leipziger Versorgungs- und Verkehrsgesellschaft mbH), Leipziger Volkszeitung, Porsche Leipzig GmbH, Sparkasse Leipzig

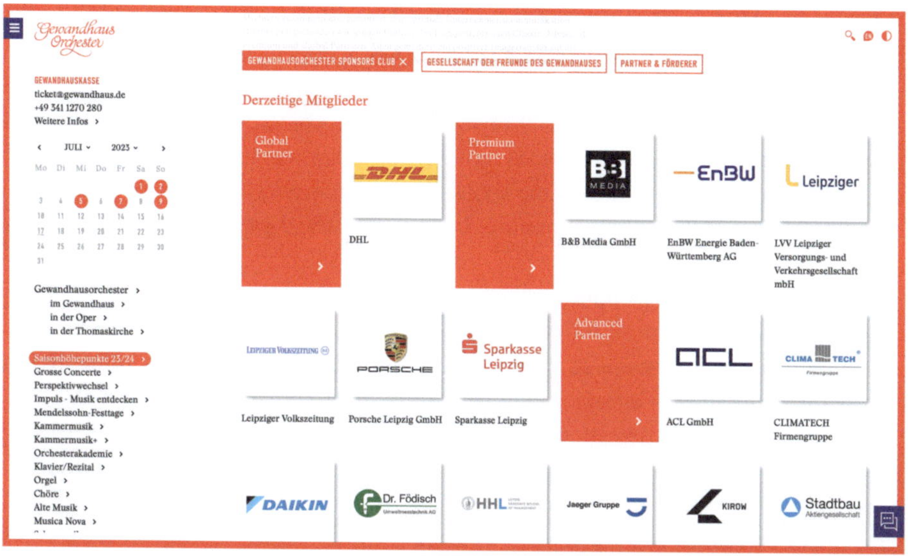

Fig. 3.16 Presentation of the Sponsors Club on the Gewandhaus Orchestra website

- **Advanced Partner:** ACL GmbH, Climatech Group, Dr. Födisch Umweltmesstechnik AG, HHL Leipzig Graduate School of Management, Jaeger Group, Techne Kirow GmbH, Leipziger Stadtbau AG, Margon Brunnen GmbH, Neue ZWL Zahnradwerk Leipzig GmbH, Reum & Schwarze, Rotkäppchen-Mumm Sektkellereien GmbH, VNG AG, Wagnermeyer Group

In addition, the Sponsors Club includes 51 corporate sponsors in the **Classic Partner** category, including Amazon, KPMG, Leipziger Messe, PwC, and many more.

The **strategic orientation of the Sponsors Club** aims to stabilize and increase pool sponsorship revenues by expanding value and enlarging the membership of the Sponsors Club. In addition, there is an intention to increase project sponsorship revenues.

No industries are categorically excluded from joining the Sponsors Club. However, corporate sponsors that pose a risk to the brand image of the Gewandhaus Orchestra or to public relations are generally not considered for partnership.

Internal Organization of Sponsorship

From 2005 to 2023, sponsorship was managed by the **department** of **marketing/sales/fundraising**. Since May 2023, responsibility has been with the newly established **fundraising department**. The acquisition of corporate sponsors as well as sponsorship inquiries from corporate sponsors to the Gewandhaus Orchestra are discussed and decided between the head of fundraising and the management.

In the **practical implementation of partnerships**, it is sometimes considered challenging to find a suitable mode of cooperation when the Gewandhaus Orchestra, as a medium-sized cultural enterprise, collaborates with a global corporation or a local small business. In such cases, very different organizational processes, corporate cultures, legal forms, etc., must be taken into account in the sponsorship partnership. Particularly challenging are partnerships in which the sponsor's commitment is decided "top-down" by management, but the company structure, budget, or staff capacity are not available to actually activate the partnership.

The **implementation of sponsorship partnerships** is carried out independently by Gewandhaus management, from acquisition to execution to evaluation—without external sponsorship agencies. Large corporate sponsors, on the other hand, often engage international sponsorship agencies on a permanent or project basis, which are responsible for activation, project creation, and implementation. This intermediary role between two partners can lead to misunderstandings, which may pose a risk to the partnership.

Selection of Sponsors

The **acquisition of sponsorship partners** and the response to sponsorship inquiries from corporate sponsors are handled exclusively by the fundraising department and management.

Sponsorship contracts with clearly defined services and sponsorship benefits (including tax assessment) have been and continue to be concluded with partners. During negotiations, it is made transparently clear from the outset that sponsors' decisions are excluded from artistic decisions.

The **duration of the contracts** varies depending on the partner, the type of support, and the subject of funding (institution or individual project). In pool sponsorship, the duration is usually one year or one season, with the option of automatic contract renewal.

Services and Sponsorship Benefits

The Gewandhausorchester primarily requests **monetary contributions** from sponsors, as these can be used more flexibly in the resource and financial planning of the cultural organization. In some partnerships, **goods and services** are also provided, which represent a financial saving or advantage for the Gewandhaus. This includes, for example, the use of the media reach of media partners.

The **sponsorship benefits** that sponsors receive from the orchestra include:

- Brand rights (the opportunity to publicly present themselves as a sponsor in association with the Gewandhausorchester),
- Advertising presence within the Gewandhausorchester's media, e.g., in program booklets, on the website, on advertising media (flyers, posters, etc.) (see Figs. 3.17 and 3.18),
- Concert tickets as well as purchase options for highly sought-after tickets,
- Product placement (see, for example, the placement of Porsche sports cars in front of the stage during the open-air concert "Klassik airleben" in Fig. 3.15),

Gewandhaus Orchester

SPONSORS CLUB

Das Gewandhausorchester dankt herzlich für die freundliche und großzügige Unterstützung der Saison 2023/2024.

GLOBAL PARTNER

PREMIUM PARTNER

ADVANCED PARTNER

CLASSIC PARTNER

Amazon · ARCADIA Investment GmbH · Area9 Lyceum GmbH · ARTIS – Personal für Kunst und Kultur GmbH · B.A.C. Bau- und Anlagenconsult GmbH · Baumlink GmbH · BE-terna GmbH · Bosch Sicherheitssysteme GmbH · E. Breuninger GmbH & Co. · CMS Hasche Sigle Rechtsanwälte Steuerberater · commlab GmbH · DauHerkert GmbH · Dr. med. Peter Dietel · Farben Schultze GmbH & Co. KG · firm – Training & Seminare GbR · Fischer Analysen Instrumente GmbH · Flughafen Leipzig/Halle GmbH · fröscher GmbH und Co. KG · Goldschmidt Holding GmbH · Gossler, Gobert & Wolters Gruppe · GP Günter Papenburg Unternehmensgruppe · IMPERICON · Jolig Automobil Handels GmbH · Kältepunkt Plus GmbH · Kieback&Peter GmbH & Co. KG · Konsum Leipzig eG · KPMG AG Wirtschaftsprüfungsgesellschaft · Krostitzer Brauerei · KSW GmbH · Lecos GmbH · Leipziger Messe GmbH · NEL GmbH · N+P Informationssysteme GmbH · Dr. Arend Oetker · PETERSEN HARDRAHT PRUGGMAYER Rechtsanwälte Steuerberater · pmhLE GmbH · POMMER Spezialbetonbau GmbH · PwC · Reinwald GmbH · Scheid Rechtsanwälte · Stölting Kleine Service GmbH S&P Ingenieure + Architekten · TAS AG · Gerhard D. Wempe GmbH & Co. KG, Filiale Leipzig Wendt & Kühn KG

Fig. 3.17 Presentation of sponsors in the Gewandhausorchester's season program

Im großen Stil

Felix Mendelssohn Bartholdy
5. Sinfonie d-Moll
MWV N 15
(»Reformations-Sinfonie«)
—
Felix Mendelssohn Bartholdy
Sinfonie-Kantate
»Lobgesang« op. 52
MWV A 18

VERHAGELT

Dass Felix, der Glückliche, auch herbe Rückschläge zu verkraften hatte, vergisst man leicht angesichts seiner alles überstrahlenden Erfolge. Besonders bittere Erfahrungen bescherte ihm die *Reformationssinfonie*, bestimmt zur Feier des 300. Jahrestags des Augsburger Bekenntnisses 1830. Doch nichts lief nach Plan. Mendelssohn geriet in Verzug, bekam weder in Augsburg noch in Berlin die erhoffte Aufführungsgelegenheit und eine potenzielle Leipziger Premiere wurde ebenfalls vereitelt. Am Festtag tönte zwar Luthers *Ein feste Burg* landauf landab von allen Dächern – Mendelssohns »Kirchensinfonie«, die in eine Apotheose dieses Chorals mündet, war nirgends zu hören. In Paris verweigerten Musiker ihre Mitwirkung. Noch die verspätete Uraufführung in der Singakademie war von Enttäuschung überschattet und machte Mendelssohns Berliner Stellenaussichten zunichte. *Fast immer stürmt oder gewittert es*, registrierte der Rezensent und traf nicht nur die Musik. Es blieb die einzige Aufführung unter Mendelssohns Leitung. Er ließ das Werk nicht drucken, ja hätte es am liebsten verbrannt.

78

SONNENSEITE

10 Jahre später erhielt Mendelssohn – mittlerweile ans Gewandhaus berufen – den prestigeträchtigsten Auftrag, den die Stadt Leipzig zu vergeben hatte: die musikalische Gestaltung der mit immensem Aufwand begangenen Gutenberg-Feier des Jahres 1840. Stattliche 208 Druckerpressen, über 116 Buch- und Musikalienhandlungen sowie 23 Buchdruckereien hatte Leipzig damals vorzuweisen und nahm 400 Jahre Buchdruckerkunst zum Anlass für eine gigantische Selbstinszenierung des stolzen Bürgertums. Mendelssohn krönte die Festtage mit seiner *Symphonie-Cantate nach Worten der heiligen Schrift*, dem *Lobgesang*. Was Beethoven in der Neunten vorgeführt und Mendelssohn in der *Reformationssinfonie* instrumental erprobt hatte, erfüllt sich. Alle zur Verfügung stehenden musikalischen Mittel werden aufgeboten, um der Leitidee Ausdruck zu verleihen, die Mendelssohn mit Worten des 150. Psalms zelebriert: *Alles, was Odem hat, lobe den Herrn!*

ALLZEITHOCH

Du verstehst schon, erläuterte er seinem Freund Carl Klingemann, *dass erst die Instrumente auf ihre Art loben, und dann der Chor und die einzelnen Stimmen. Die Instrumentalsätze, die drei Sätzen einer Sinfonie entsprechen, verkünden das Grundthema vom ersten Ton an […], indem eigentlich alle Stücke auf die Worte »Alles was Odem hat…« komponiert sind.* Am Nachmittag des 25. Juni 1840 wurde die Sinfonie-Kantate in der überfüllten Thomaskirche von 500 Sängern und Instrumentalisten uraufgeführt. Mendelssohn liebte sie sehr, revidierte und publizierte sie rasch und führte sie so häufig auf, wie kein anderes seiner sinfonischen Werke.

DO/FR/SO
21./22./24. SEP 2023
20/20/11 UHR
GROSSER SAAL

Gewandhausorchester
MDR-Rundfunkchor
Andris Nelsons
Christiane Karg, *Sopran*
Elsa Benoit, *Sopran*
Werner Güra, *Tenor*

Konzerteinführung mit Ann-Katrin Zimmermann um 19.15 Uhr (DO/FR) und 10.15 Uhr (SO) im Schumann-Eck

Normalpreis: 80/61/49/37/23/6 EUR
FLEX-Preis: 88/67/54/41/25/7 EUR
Ermäßigung für Berechtigte

SERIE I/1
SONNTAGS-ANRECHT II/1

Präsentiert von

Sparkasse Leipzig

79

Fig. 3.18 Example of the integration of a program sponsor in the Gewandhausorchester's season program

- Use of Gewandhaus premises for sponsor events,
- Exclusive experiences at the Gewandhaus that cannot be purchased (e.g., "behind the scenes" events),
- Industry exclusivity.

Among the most popular and frequently requested sponsorship benefits are advertising presence, use of the premises, and access to exclusive experiences at the Gewandhaus.

Impact and Evaluation

The **impact of sponsorship** can be considered from both a financial perspective and a marketing perspective. The sponsorship funds raised account for an average of 6% of the Gewandhaus's total budget, corresponding to approximately 2.1 million EUR in sponsorship income.

For the **Gewandhausorchester brand**, cooperation with sponsors is seen as a logical continuation of the orchestra's civic founding and development history. As a result, the brand is coherently enhanced by these partnerships and perceived as progressive, business-minded, and solution-oriented. The large network created by the Gewandhausorchester's pool sponsorship also fosters a perception of civic and entrepreneurial legitimacy for the cultural institution. The orchestra considers this particularly important and necessary for cultural organizations.

Sponsor companies individually and to varying degrees—depending on the measures implemented—conduct an **evaluation of their sponsorship engagements**. The sponsors are supported by the orchestra in evaluating their activities. Where advertising contacts are measurable, these are made available to the sponsors, for example in online marketing in the form of click numbers, page impressions, likes, etc.

In addition, discussions are held during a partnership and after the completion of projects to evaluate the impact of the measures and the organizational processes.

Key Points

1. **Understand funding mix:** Ideally, the financing of cultural organizations should utilize various sources such as public and private funding, donations, sponsorship, and own revenues.
2. **Differentiate types of sponsorship and objectives:** The differences between public-law, private-commercial, and private non-profit cultural organizations in terms of their sponsorship and economic objectives must be taken into account.
3. **Understand public arts and cultural funding:** A distinction must be made between direct funding through the sponsorship of cultural organizations and financial grants, and indirect funding through tax reductions.

4. **Recognize the responsibilities of state bodies:** The different responsibilities of the federal government, states, and municipalities in arts and cultural funding must be considered, with municipalities in Germany bearing the largest share.
5. **Understand fundraising concepts:** Fundraising is to be distinguished from sponsorship as donation marketing, since no monetary consideration is expected for donations.
6. **Differentiate forms of donations:** Donations are to be classified into monetary donations, donations in kind, and time donations.
7. **Support the institutionalization of donations:** By establishing support associations and friends' groups, donors can be organized to create long-term ties to cultural institutions.
8. **Differentiate own revenues:** In financial planning, a distinction must be made between primary revenues from the sale of core services such as tickets and secondary revenues from the sale of additional services.
9. **Understand crowdfunding as an alternative financing method:** The possibility of raising a predefined sum for the realization of a project through many small contributions via online channels should be considered as a source of financing.
10. **Consider sponsorship benefits in crowdfunding:** The classification of crowdfunding as donations, sponsorship, or own revenues depends on the services offered.

Management Process of Arts and Cultural Sponsorship and Arts and Cultural Sponsorship Canvas

4

Contents

4.1 Phases of a Management Process for Arts and Cultural Sponsorship 94
4.2 Areas of Action of an Arts and Cultural Sponsorship Canvas 97

Abstract

The planning and implementation of arts and cultural sponsorship projects is based on a management process that begins with an analysis of the initial situation and ends with the evaluation of the activities carried out. For the practical planning of this process, the use of a Business Model Canvas is helpful, as it thematically consolidates the key areas of a cultural sponsorship concept and supports decision-making with guiding questions. This chapter first provides an overview of the individual phases in the arts and cultural sponsorship management process. Subsequently, the arts and cultural sponsorship canvas is explained along with its fields of action, and guiding questions are defined for each field.

Supplementary Information The online version contains supplementary material available at https://doi.org/10.1007/978-3-658-50079-5_4.

M. Bruhn and L. Pöllmann, *Arts and Cultural Sponsorship*,
https://doi.org/10.1007/978-3-658-50079-5_4

4.1 Phases of a Management Process for Arts and Cultural Sponsorship

From a corporate perspective, arts and cultural sponsorship is an instrument of marketing and corporate communication. If a corporate sponsorship decides to integrate arts and cultural sponsorship into the communication mix, the multitude of available action options requires similar planning considerations as, for example, the use of classic communication instruments such as media advertising, sales promotion, or public private relations. The basis for the disposition and implementation of arts and cultural sponsorship is the **planning process for arts and cultural sponsorship** shown in Fig. 4.1. It consists of the following **management phases** that must be taken into account when developing a cultural sponsorship concept:

1. Situation analysis
As with any management concept, the process begins with an analysis of the initial conditions. This involves examining both the internal and external situation of the company, identifying current strengths and weaknesses as well as opportunities and risks. The result of a situation analysis is the identification of the problem.

2. Definition of the objectives of arts and cultural sponsorship
Based on the analysis results, objectives can be derived for corporate sponsorship in general and for arts and cultural sponsorship in particular. These objectives must be formulated in operational terms, based on the requirements for setting objectives.

3. Identification of the target groups
Corporate objectives are always related to specific target groups. Since the measures of arts and cultural sponsorship can differ significantly depending on the chosen target groups, it is essential to define concrete target groups before implementing sponsorship activities.

4. Definition of the arts and cultural sponsorship strategy and philosophy
The arts and cultural sponsorship strategy is closely linked to a company's brand strategy. The brand strategy, in turn, is guided by the company's values, which are fundamental to the cultural sponsorship philosophy. When developing an arts and cultural sponsorship strategy, it is important to align the objectives and target groups of arts and cultural sponsorship with the company's strategic orientation.

5. Budget calculation for arts and cultural sponsorship
Budget calculation is influenced both by the overall budget for marketing communication and by the selection of potential cooperation partners. In addition, effects and synergies with other communication instruments and further sponsorship activities must be taken into account when calculating the budget, since cultural sponsorship measures are ideally complemented by additional communication activities.

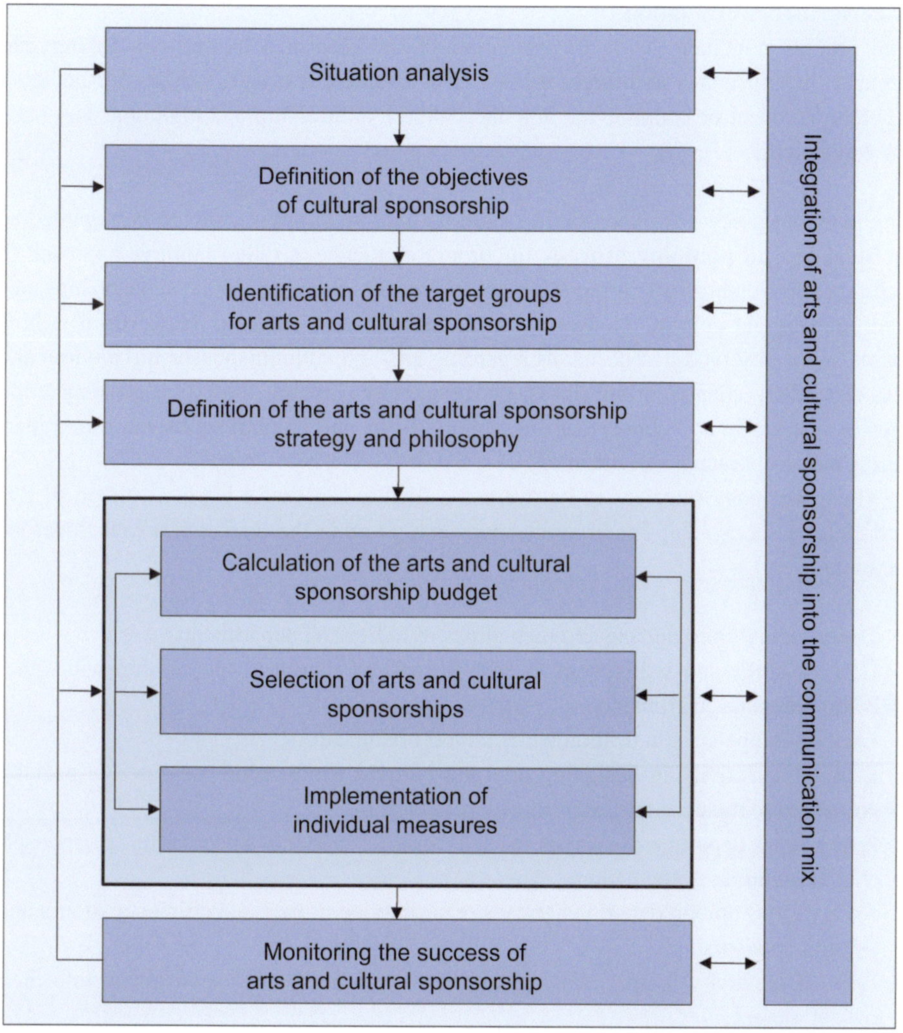

Fig. 4.1 Planning process for arts and cultural sponsorship from a corporate perspective. (Source: Bruhn, 2018a, p. 238)

6. Selection of sponsorships

In the next step, suitable cooperation partners such as cultural institutions or cultural projects and artists are selected for collaboration. For this, the selection and decision criteria must be defined in detail from the company's perspective.

7. Implementation of individual measures

After agreeing on the design of the sponsorship cooperation, the individual measures are implemented by the corporate sponsorship, the cultural partner, and other third parties, such as marketing and media agencies.

8. Performance evaluation

The process concludes with an evaluation of the measures carried out, taking into account the objectives and target groups. This step thus provides a basis for deciding whether to repeat or continue the arts and cultural sponsorship and highlights any need for adjustments.

The planning process for sponsorship, with its individual phases, should be regarded as an **ideal-typical planning process**. In corporate practice, a rather intuitive approach to defining sponsorships was often observed in the past. Some corporate sponsorships carried out arts and cultural sponsorship without long-term planning. However, it is now increasingly observed that decisions regarding arts and cultural sponsorship are less and less shaped by chance, arbitrariness, or spontaneity. Instead, there is a growing trend toward systematic and conceptual integration of arts and cultural sponsorship into marketing and corporate communication.

There are many **barriers** to be overcome for the successful implementation of arts and cultural sponsorship in corporate sponsorship and in the market. These include, for example:

- Departmental thinking and silo mentalities of individual departments,
- Lack of skills and willingness to network arts and cultural sponsorship with other communication instruments,
- Lack of competence in dealing with cultural organizations,
- Lack of sensitivity in designing arts and cultural sponsorship measures (especially compared to the possibilities in sports sponsorship),
- Fear among departments of cuts to their "classic" budgets when additional sponsorship commitments are made,
- Reservations among department heads regarding the impact and efficiency of arts and cultural sponsorship,
- Lack of creativity in specialist departments when integrating sponsorship into their own strategies,
- Concerns among subordinate departments that the executive board cannot be won over for new and innovative commitments,
- Lack of professionalism in the communicative use of sponsorships.

If the use of sponsorship within marketing and corporate communication is to help achieve the desired communication objectives, it is necessary to overcome the barriers mentioned and to plan a sponsorship commitment carefully and integrate it systematically into the communication mix. However, this approach must not lead to neglecting the creative component in the development of a sponsorship concept, since successful sponsorships often thrive on an innovative idea. It is particularly important to maintain the right balance between systematic planning and allowing creative freedom.

4.2 Areas of Action of an Arts and Cultural Sponsorship Canvas

The development of an arts and cultural sponsorship concept is based on extensive marketing data and is usually not developed by a single person, but by a team that may also include external partners such as agencies. To support practical teamwork, a special **arts and cultural sponsorship canvas** is presented, which can serve as a basis for workshops to develop an arts and cultural sponsorship strategy and a holistic concept.

Canvas models have become known through the Business Model Canvas by Alexander Osterwalder and Yves Pigneur (Osterwalder & Pigneur, 2011) and are suitable as a structuring tool for carrying out various phases of brainstorming and other idea generation instruments. A canvas is a two-dimensional graphical **arrangement of action fields** for a specific task. In this way, topics are defined that need to be addressed as part of the task. These include, for example, internal analyses, consideration of the competition, ideas for specific measures, the definition of evaluation instruments, etc. For this publication, the authors have developed an arts and cultural sponsorship canvas that encompasses both the theoretical components of the cultural sponsorship process and empirical experience in planning and implementing cultural sponsorship collaborations. The canvas has been revised and further developed through practical applications.

For each action field, several **guiding questions** are defined, which are to be answered during a workshop. The advantage of a canvas is that it enables associations and leaps of thought while still automatically creating an order among the individual results. This order is predetermined by the structure of the canvas and can subsequently be transferred into a classic concept and documented in writing.

The practical **use of the Canvas** involves a moderator guiding the discussion of the various action areas and questions, with the sought-after answers being written on sticky notes (Post-its) and placed in the respective fields. For this purpose, it is recommended to project the Canvas onto a large wall or to print it in large format (see Fig. 4.2).

A print file can be found at the following link and can be used as a basis for practical work: Appendix (Electronic Supplementary Material).

The **process of a sponsorship workshop** can proceed as follows: After assembling a team tasked with developing a concept for arts and cultural sponsorship and appointing a moderator, a kick-off meeting is held in which the objectives and approach are explained. This is usually followed by several workshop phases in which the Canvas is used. Once the workshop phases are completed, the results documented on the Canvas can be written up. In addition, for all operational tasks, responsibilities as well as binding timelines and budgets must be agreed upon. The assignment of temporal milestones and the regulation of responsibilities are not explicitly addressed in the Canvas shown below.

It should also be noted that the Canvas is suitable for developing a **briefing for cooperation with an agency**. In this case, the Canvas is not used to answer all questions

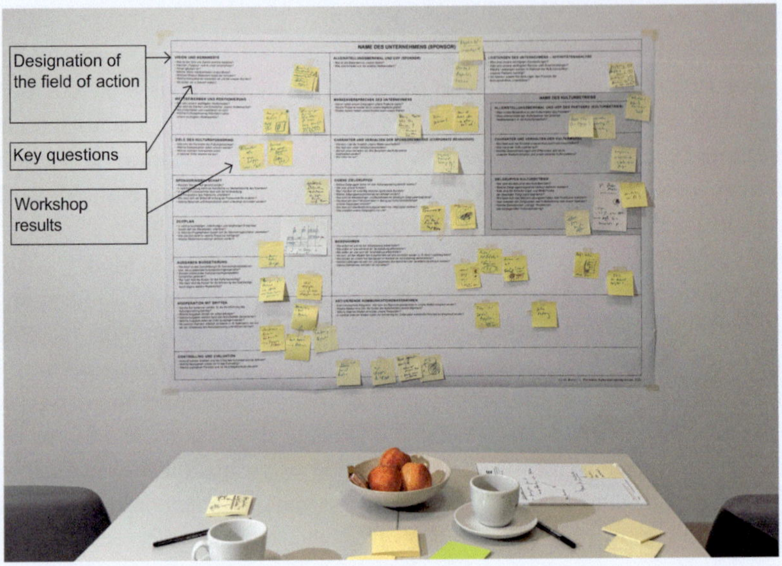

Fig. 4.2 Use of the Canvas model in a sponsorship workshop

independently, but rather to define the general strategy and then formulate relevant questions that are passed on to an agency as a task.

Those action areas that need to be addressed from the perspective of cultural organizations are also suitable for use in **negotiations with cultural institutions**, in order to request essential information and requirements regarding a collaboration, such as the characteristics of the audience, the identity of the cultural brand, or the planned communication channels and their reach.

Action Areas

A total of 18 **action areas** have been defined for the arts and cultural sponsorship Canvas:

1. Vision, core values, and purpose
2. Competitors and positioning
3. Objectives of arts and cultural sponsorship
4. Sponsoring message
5. Unique selling proposition (USP) and USP of the sponsor
6. Unique selling proposition (USP) and USP of the cultural partner
7. Target groups of the sponsor
8. Target groups of the cultural organization
9. Company services—affinities
10. Individual measures

11. Activating communication measures
12. Brand promise of the company
13. Budgeting
14. Timeline
15. Character and behavior of the sponsor's own brand
16. Character and behavior of the cultural brand (sponsored party)
17. Cooperation with third parties
18. Controlling and evaluation

If we consider the **relationships between the action areas**, these do not form a strict hierarchy within the Canvas. On the contrary, working on several areas in parallel and moving between them is encouraged. Nevertheless, there are logical sequences in the processing of the action areas, and their arrangement is not arbitrary (see Fig. 4.3): For example, questions about vision, core values, and objectives should be addressed before deciding on relevant partners. The definition of target groups is clarified before the development of concrete measures, and the actual need for cooperation with third parties depends on the measures to be implemented.

Below, the individual **action areas and guiding questions** are briefly explained and named for practical workshop work. A presentation of the arts and cultural sponsorship Canvas, including the respective guiding questions, is available for download at the link mentioned above. More detailed information and practical examples for the individual action areas are provided in Chaps. 5 to 11.

Section 1: Vision, Core Values, and Purpose

The **vision** of a company describes a desired future state. It should be understood as a statement that provides insight into a fundamental strategy. The vision should be ambitious but also achievable. It reflects the company's desired future image.

The **core values**, on the other hand, summarize the fundamental beliefs, principles, and ethical standards that shape a company's behavior and culture. They are the non-negotiable principles that define how corporate sponsorship operates and how it interacts with customers, employees, and society or the general public.

Vision and core values are to be understood as supporting inspiration and identification in leadership. Closely linked to vision and core values is the purpose (see, e.g., Reichertz, 2019; Baetzgen, 2022) of a company, i.e., the question of what the corporate sponsorship stands for and what the meaning and purpose of the company is.

With vision, core values, and purpose, a company communicates as clear a picture as possible of the future it wants to shape through its activities and services. These are therefore important factors for brand positioning and image building. The compatibility of a company's vision, core values, and purpose (as a potential sponsor) with those of a cultural organization is a key prerequisite for arts and cultural sponsorship to be perceived as credible by the target groups.

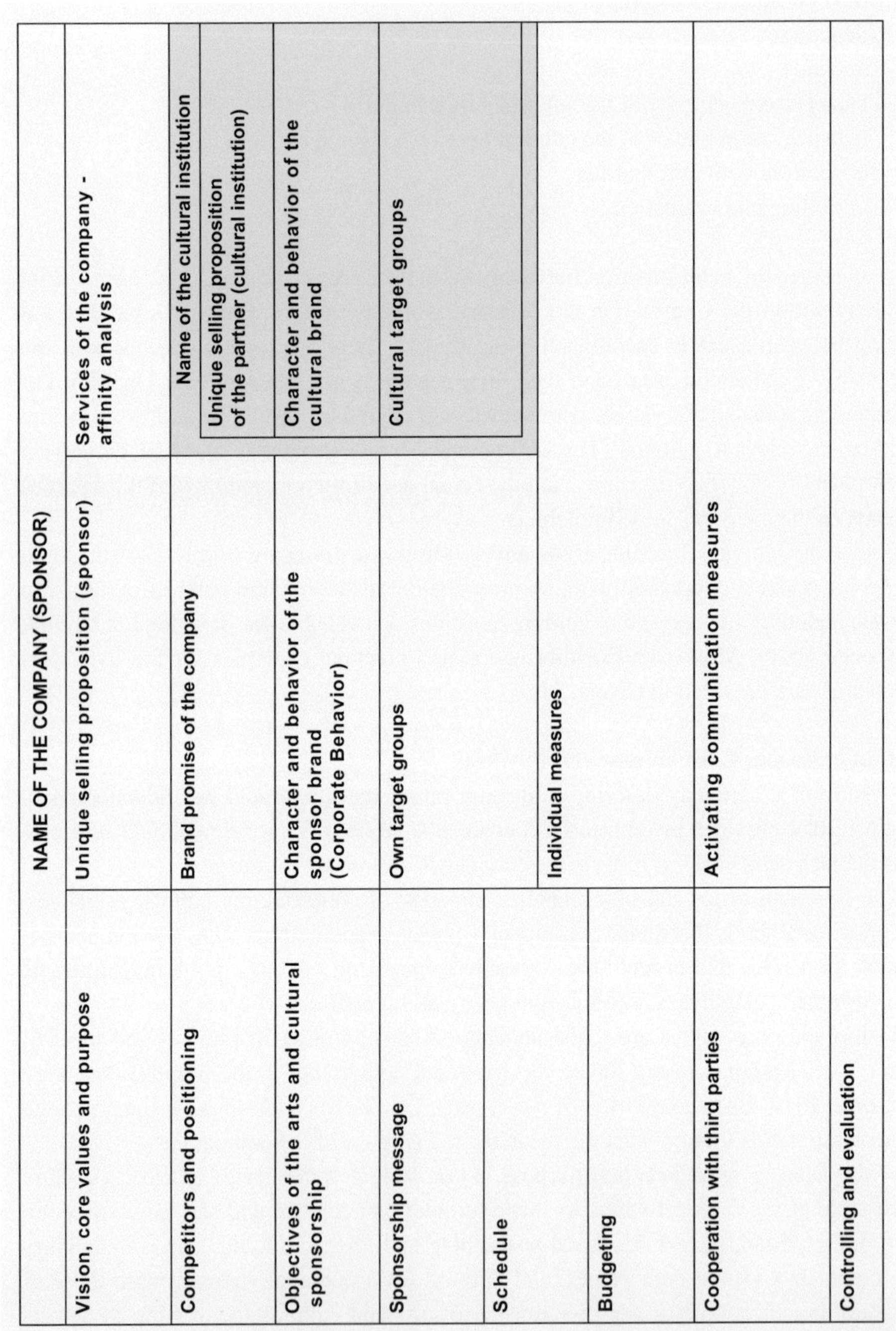

Fig. 4.3 Action areas of the arts and cultural sponsorship Canvas

Guiding Questions

- What is the objective of our actions?
- What purpose does our corporate sponsorship represent?
- What do we believe in?
- Which values does our brand represent?
- What mission statement have we formulated?
- What associations do we want our customers to have?
- Where do we want to be in the future?

Section 2: Competitors and Positioning

Corporate sponsorships are generally not monopolists in their market, but rather compete with other competitors. This makes **positioning** necessary in order to differentiate and highlight the advantages of one's own offering. The aforementioned options for establishing a unique selling proposition are used for this purpose. The use of arts and cultural sponsorship is also intended to strengthen or improve a company's **positioning in relation to competitors**. Therefore, it is important to analyze the strategies and measures of arts and cultural sponsorship employed by competitors. This helps, on the one hand, to assess the intended positioning of other corporate sponsorships and, on the other hand, provides valuable insights for selecting one's own sponsorship activities.

Guiding Questions

- Who are our most important competitors?
- What are the strengths and weaknesses of our competitors?
- How do they present and stage themselves?
- Which cultural sponsorship activities do our key competitors use?

Section 3: Objectives of Arts and Cultural Sponsorship

The analysis of the initial situation and the desired positioning of the company lead to objectives that are to be achieved through arts and cultural sponsorship. These **objectives of arts and cultural sponsorship** must also be determined with regard to the company's general marketing and communication goals. It is important that the defined objectives are specific enough to be subsequently reviewed and to evaluate the success of the arts and cultural sponsorship. Furthermore, they should be formulated specifically for sponsorship and should be achievable through the sponsorship activities. Since sponsorship is to be integrated into the company's communication mix and other communication instruments are used in parallel to sponsorship, a direct causality of individual measures—such as regarding a brand's image change—is not always possible.

The **core objectives** can be formulated more generally, for example, that arts and cultural sponsorship should support image transfer in favor of certain brand values. In addition, concrete sponsorship objectives should be defined, such as reach, measured by the number of contacts to whom the sponsorship message is to be communicated. Specific sales targets, if products are sold as part of the sponsorship, can also be set as sponsorship objectives, but these are rarely observed.

Guiding Questions

- What are the core objectives of arts and cultural sponsorship?
- What number of contacts is being targeted?
- What other key performance indicators can be achieved, and to what extent?

Section 4: Sponsoring Message

Arts and cultural sponsorship is a communication instrument and serves to convey specific messages in marketing communication. The **communication message** represents the communicative operationalization of the brand promise. Taking into account the framework provided by the cultural partner, the identity, values, and advantages of the company's offerings should be communicated. It is therefore important to consider which narrative should be used for the cultural sponsorship project—which story can be told specifically and how the sponsoring message can be operationalized.

If the cultural event allows, the staging of the sponsoring message can also be structured as dramaturgy from the audience's perspective. For this purpose, the visitor process is broken down into individual steps using the **technique of event blueprinting** (Pöllmann, 2021a, p. 139) (e.g., arrival at the venue, cloakroom, access to event areas, etc.), and for each step, it is clarified how the sponsor can accompany the audience in order to communicate the sponsoring message at specific touchpoints. It is important to ensure that the staging is not too intrusive and that the core benefit of the cultural offering always takes precedence over the sponsorship communication, in order to avoid reactance.

In general, when **defining the sponsoring message**, it is also advisable to clarify which messages should *not* be communicated. In this context, it is helpful to review one's own staging for the potential of possible misunderstandings. For example, a sponsor who values "innovative" and "ecologically sustainable" can present themselves at a cultural event by supporting the visitor process for guests. This support can be provided through service-oriented innovations that have a lower CO_2 consumption than alternative means (e.g., in shuttle service, catering, energy generation, etc.). The sponsoring message would be, in essence, that sustainable living does not mean doing without, and can be combined with leisure value—thanks to the sponsor's innovative ideas. The prerequisite for such measures, however, is that the innovations used also match the sponsor's expertise and do not appear arbitrary, as otherwise accusations of merely superficial ecological sustainability or **"green washing"** could quickly arise.

Guiding Questions

- Which narrative can be used? Are there alternatives?
- How does the story relate to the sponsor's brand identity?
- Into which process steps can the event be divided from the audience's perspective?
- How can the message be conveyed along the process steps?
- Which messages and associations should absolutely be avoided?

Section 5: Unique Selling Proposition of the Sponsor

The **unique selling proposition (USP)** of the company is a special benefit that a product or service offers to customers and that distinguishes it from other competitors. It contains the core argument for the question of why a company's offering should be purchased.

The strategic **differentiation from competitors** can be achieved in various ways. Essentially, there are several categories that, either alone or in combination, can form a company's unique selling proposition (USP):

1. **Product or service quality:** Corporate sponsorships can set themselves apart from the competition by offering superior quality in their products or services compared to their competitors.
2. **Price:** A unique selling proposition can be achieved through price if a corporate sponsorship offers its services at the lowest price on the market (price leadership). Differentiation can also be achieved through a particularly high price, for example in the case of luxury goods.
3. **User experience:** Corporate sponsorships can distinguish themselves from competitors through exceptional user-friendliness, if the experience customers have when using the services is particularly positive.
4. **Unique features:** Corporate sponsorships can differentiate themselves through special additional features such as design elements or extra functions.
5. **Customer service:** A special unique selling proposition, which is gaining importance especially in e-commerce, is the quality of the customer service offered, which can differ significantly from competitors based on criteria such as response speed, friendliness, helpfulness, goodwill, etc.
6. **Brand image:** Corporate sponsorships can differentiate themselves by establishing a strong brand and a unique brand image, which provides customers with additional symbolic value beyond the actual product.

Guiding Questions

- What is special about our brand?
- What sets us apart from other competitors?
- Is this point of differentiation or unique selling proposition also perceived by customers?
- Is the unique selling proposition relevant to purchasing decisions?
- How sustainable is our unique selling proposition?

Section 6: Unique Selling Proposition of the Cultural Partner

The questions regarding the special profile and the USP are not only to be answered for the corporate sponsorship, but also with regard to the **unique selling proposition of the cultural partner**. The quality of a cultural sponsorship partnership is characterized by the fact that the corporate sponsorship and the cultural brand are a credible match. If the cooperation is decided solely based on the image or target group of the cultural institution, there is a risk that a corporate sponsorship, through a cultural sponsorship initiative, moves too far away from its own positioning and the cooperation does not appear authentic.

Therefore, the concept must address what makes the cultural partner special and why this particular partner was chosen for a cultural sponsorship cooperation.

Guiding Questions

- What is special about the partner's cultural brand?
- What distinguishes the cultural partner from other competitors in the cultural landscape?
- Who are the main competitors of the cultural partner?
- Is the point of differentiation or unique selling proposition also perceived by the public and by specific target groups?

Sections 7 and 8: Target Groups of the Sponsor and the Cultural Institution

As already shown in the so-called "magic triangle" of sponsorship (corporate sponsorship—cultural institution—media), a sponsorship strategy must always be aligned with the target groups of the sponsor. The particular challenge is that the sponsor's own target group matches that of the cooperating cultural institution. Therefore, the canvas considers not only the sponsor's own target group, but also that of the cultural institution. Through **target group analysis and description**, it must be ensured that the sponsorship activities are relevant from the perspective of the target groups and that the company's messages are understood. This means that the associations that an arts and cultural sponsorship is intended to evoke must align with the sponsor's intentions. For example, a corporate sponsorship that wants to position itself as "traditional" and "experienced" might cooperate with an established art history museum. However, this collaboration could, through poor staging, also evoke associations such as "conservative" and "lacking in innovation" among certain target groups.

Considering the target groups is also important for the additional **activation of the arts and cultural sponsorship** through further communication measures. To implement this efficiently, knowledge of the media usage behavior of the target groups is indispensable.

Finally, the **expectations** and possible **reactances** towards a cultural sponsorship commitment must also be weighed. Attitudes towards arts and cultural sponsorship and the role of sponsors vary greatly across different sectors. For example, it is generally easier to present oneself as a sponsor in the pop culture sector than in classical cultural fields. The role of target groups is discussed in more detail in Sect. 7.2.

Guiding Questions for the Sponsor's Target Groups

- Which target groups should be reached with the arts and cultural sponsorship?
- Who are our customers?
- Whom do we want to reach in the future (potential customers)?
- Which target group segments can be defined?
- What are the requirements and needs of the respective target group segments?

- How can the leisure behavior of our target groups in relation to cultural events be explained?
- How can the media usage behavior of the target groups be explained?
- What do the target groups of the cultural institution expect from us?

Guiding Questions for the Target Groups of the Cultural Institution

- Who are the visitors of the cultural institution?
- Which target group segments can be defined?
- What are the requirements and needs of the respective target group segments?
- How can the media usage behavior of the audience be explained?
- What do our target groups expect from a sponsor?
- What sensitivities and, if applicable, reactances exist towards arts and cultural sponsorship?

Section 9: Company Services—Affinity Analysis

Another area of action that examines the **fit between corporate sponsorship and cultural institution** within the framework of an affinity analysis focuses on the core services of the company. The core services and competencies of the company must be identified. In addition, it is necessary—usually in discussion with representatives of the cultural institution—to determine which products and services are needed for cultural production. This helps to decide where the sponsor can support the cultural institution with its expertise, thereby making the cooperation particularly credible. Often, the question of competence fit is already answered by sponsorship requests from the cultural institutions.

However, a fit does not always have to be created through the direct alignment of the sponsor's core services and the production conditions of the cultural institution. The alignment of working methods and the culture of the sponsor and the cultural institution can also form a basis for cooperation from which both sides benefit, for example by conducting joint workshops that provide insights into each other's techniques and approaches to project management.

Guiding Questions

- What are our most important core services?
- What are our most important service and additional offerings?
- Which services are needed for our partner's cultural production?
- Where can our core services support the process of cultural production?

Section 10: Individual Measures

In the area of **individual measures of arts and cultural sponsorship**, specific actions, forms of brand mention, etc. are defined, which are derived from the preceding fields. The measures also determine the desired sponsorship benefits for the cultural partner. In addition to standard benefits such as logo integration or the right to officially call oneself a partner of the cultural institution, creative and company-specific measures can also be developed here. The guiding questions do not refer to other instruments of the sponsor, but only to measures that are directly coordinated with the cooperating cultural institution. Further communication measures are covered in the field "activating communication measures."

Since numerous steps precede the planning of measures, such as analysis, goal setting, and strategic considerations (e.g., defining the sponsorship message), this area of action is addressed later in the workshop process. However, it can already be used as an "idea garage" at the beginning, since ideas for individual measures often arise earlier during the workshops and can then be collected in this canvas field.

Guiding Questions

- How do we want to present ourselves before the event?
- How do we want to present ourselves during the event?
- How do we want to present ourselves after the event?
- Where can we be referenced in the media of the cultural institution (e.g., through logo integration)?
- How can we demonstrate our core competence in the context of the event?
- What services can we provide to the visitors of the event?
- Which measures do we want to avoid?

Section 11: Activating Communication Measures

Arts and cultural sponsorship is not limited to the measures of the specific cooperation with the cultural institution. Rather, the aim is to enhance the impact of arts and cultural sponsorship through **additional communication activities** in order to achieve synergistic effects in a company's communication mix. Thus, within the framework of the arts and cultural sponsorship canvas, it must be clarified which additional external media can be used. This question is based on the results of the media usage analysis of the sponsor's target groups.

Guiding Questions

- Integration of arts and cultural sponsorship into the company's communication mix: How can the sponsorship cooperation be integrated into our media?
- Which media are already covered through the channels of the cultural institution?
- Which external media reach our target groups?
- In which external media should additional reach be purchased to activate the target groups?

Section 12: Company Brand Promise

A **brand promise** is a commitment that a corporate sponsorship makes to its customers and stakeholders, outlining what they can expect when interacting with the corporate sponsorship. The brand promise is a key element of a company's brand strategy and an important factor in building trust and thus brand loyalty. It should be meaningful, relevant, and unique, reflecting the company's distinctive identity and value proposition.

Thus, the formulation of the brand promise is directly related to the above-mentioned areas of action: vision, core values, purpose, and the unique selling proposition (USP). The brand promise provides a concrete answer to the question of what relevance the company's products or services have for its customers. This means that a problem is assumed on the part of the customer that they want to solve. The company's products or services are intended to help solve precisely this problem.

As the canvas process continues, the question arises as to how a cultural cooperation could **interpret the brand promise** or convey it through metaphors. Here is an example: If a financial services provider such as a bank or insurance company distributes eucalyptus candies to guests at a classical concert in the fall, this initially seems to have little to do with their actual service. Nevertheless, it is a simple measure to show guests that the company has thought ahead on their behalf to reduce disruptive coughing during the concert. The real message lies in demonstrating a forward-thinking character, which is also relevant for financial products. This example illustrates how a cultural sponsorship measure can make a relatively abstract and initially arbitrary-sounding brand promise such as "We think about your future!" tangible in practice.

Guiding Questions

- What is the specific brand promise regarding our products or services?
- Is this brand promise perceived as such by current and potential customers?
- Why should our target groups buy our products and why do our target groups buy our services?
- What purchase barriers exist for the target groups?
- Which problems are solved by our offerings?
- What advantages do our customers have through our brand?

Section 13: Budgeting

The available **budget** provides a crucial framework for the possibilities of arts and cultural sponsorship, which is why questions about financial resources are of particular relevance in workshops on sponsorship strategy (see Sect. 9.3). Essentially, there are two options for **cost planning**: Either the scope for specific measures is derived based on an overall budget, or the costs for desired measures are collected in this field in order to determine the budget requirements for arts and cultural sponsorship.

Guiding Questions

- What is the total budget for sponsorship collaborations or the planned sponsorship project
- Will revenues be generated during the sponsorship collaboration?
- What are the costs for the arts and cultural sponsorship?
- What are the costs for activating the sponsorship through own additional media work?

Section 14: Timeline

The **timeline for a sponsorship collaboration** can vary depending on the scope and type of partnership. However, some typical elements of a timeline can be defined, which are also helpful when setting milestones (see Fig. 4.4). These include:

1. **Initial Contact:** This is the first contact between the corporate sponsor and the cultural institution, in which one of the two parties signals interest in a collaboration.
2. **Proposal:** The corporate sponsor or the cultural institution submits a proposal outlining the terms of the partnership, including possible services and sponsorship benefits.

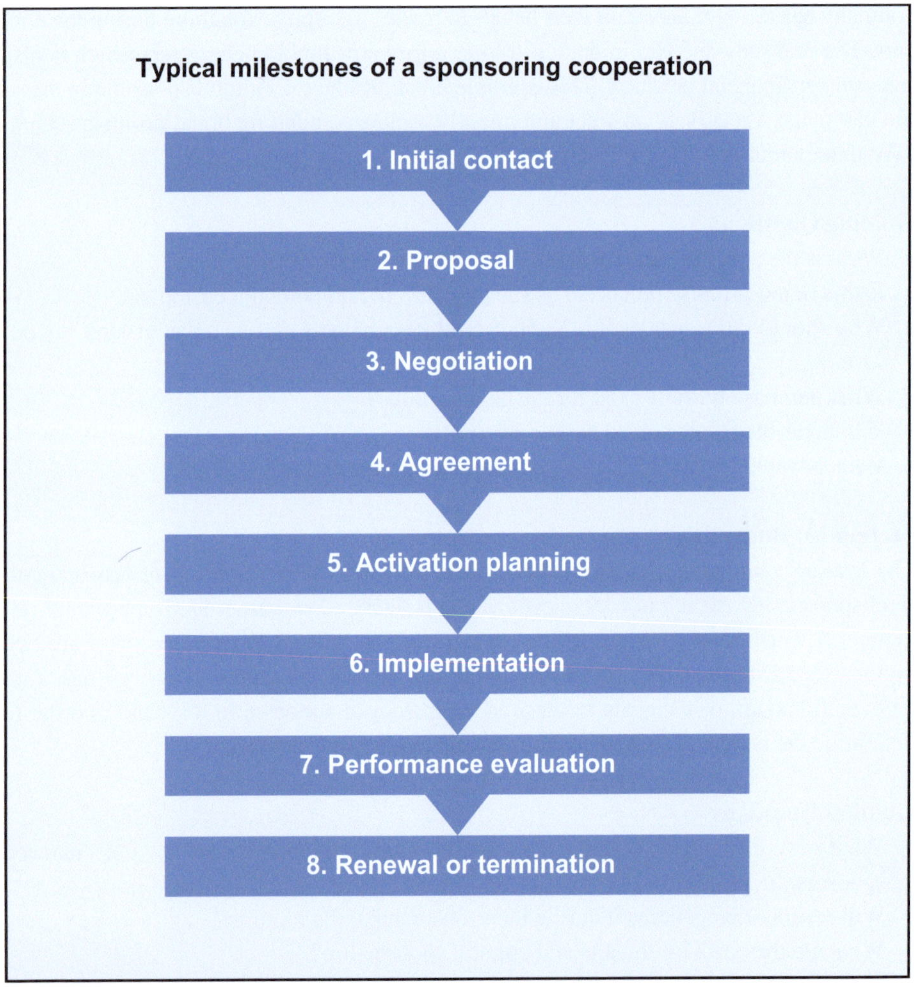

Fig. 4.4 Chronology of typical milestones in a sponsorship collaboration

When cultural institutions make inquiries, various "sponsorship packages" are often offered at this stage (see Chap. 10).

3. **Negotiation:** The corporate sponsor and the cultural institution negotiate the terms of the partnership, including the duration of the sponsorship as well as the services to be provided and sponsorship benefits.
4. **Agreement:** Once the terms of the partnership have been agreed upon, both parties sign a formal agreement (contract or letter of intent).
5. **Activation Planning:** The sponsor and the sponsored cultural institution work together to plan the activation of the sponsorship. The planning covers a longer period and is only partially suitable as a milestone for scheduling. Depending on the complexity of the measures, it makes sense to define various milestones here.
6. **Implementation:** The sponsored activity of the cultural institution (e.g., event) is carried out. This is when the agreed services are provided by the cultural institution to the corporate sponsor.
7. **Performance Evaluation:** Both parties monitor the performance of the sponsorship and assess the effectiveness of its implementation.
8. **Renewal or Termination:** Once the services and sponsorship benefits have been delivered, the collaboration is evaluated based on the performance assessment and the nature of the cooperation, and a joint decision is made on whether to end or continue the partnership.

Guiding Questions

- Into which short-term, medium-term, and long-term events can the collaboration be divided?
- Into which project phases can the sponsorship activities be divided?
- How much time is available for each phase?
- Which milestones can be defined?

Sections 15 and 16: Character and Behavior of the Own Brand (Sponsor) and the Cultural Brand (Sponsored)

A company's behavior refers to the actions, decisions, and strategies it undertakes in the course of its business activities and its interactions with stakeholders. It can be defined as the way in which a corporate sponsor behaves and the impact it has on its stakeholders and society.

There are various fundamental categories of **corporate behaviors**, such as:

1. **Ethical behavior** involves adhering to moral principles and standards of conduct accepted by society, such as honesty, integrity, and fairness. Ethical behavior requires that the corporate sponsor acts in the best interests of its stakeholders, i.e., its customers, employees, and the general public.
2. **Socially responsible behavior** means that the corporate sponsor considers the impact of its actions on the environment and society. This includes initiatives such as reducing

CO_2 emissions, supporting local communities, ensuring fair working conditions, or a voluntary commitment to support the UN Sustainable Development Goals (United Nations, 2023).
3. **Corporate governance behavior** describes the way in which a corporate sponsor is managed and directed, including the relationships between management, shareholders, and other stakeholders. This includes establishing policies and procedures to ensure accountability, transparency, and ethical conduct.
4. **Customer-oriented behavior** means placing the needs and interests of customers at the center of business activities. This includes providing high-quality products and services, professional customer service, and ensuring customer satisfaction through additional services, goodwill arrangements, etc.
5. **Innovative behavior** encompasses the ability to develop and implement new ideas and solutions to meet changing market demands. This includes investing in research and development, introducing new technologies, and fostering a culture of creativity and entrepreneurship.

Based on these categories, different areas of behavior can be identified, which can be summarized at an abstract level into characteristics. When abstracting, it can be helpful to use **polarity profiles** as a basis. In this way, the behavior of a company as well as a cultural institution—and thus the target specification for customer or visitor contact staff at cultural sponsorship events—can be determined using the following (and other) poles:

- Friendly—Unfriendly
- Emotional—Rational
- Introverted—Extroverted
- Competent—Incompetent
- Creative—Uncreative
- Conservative—Progressive

Guiding Questions: Behavior in Corporate Sponsorship (Sponsor)
- How can we describe the tone of our brand?
- How can our behavior be described?
- How should our behavior be described by visitors to the cultural event?
- How do we present ourselves?

Guiding Questions: Behavior of Cultural Partner (Sponsored Party)
- How can the tone of our cultural partner be described?
- How does our cultural partner present themselves?
- What overlaps and differences exist between our brand behavior and that of our cultural partner?

Section 17: Cooperation with Third Parties

The implementation of sponsorship activities requires the expertise of various areas of brand communication, such as public relations, advertising, social media communication, or event marketing. Especially in practical implementation, support from third parties is usually enlisted, for example, in the creation of layouts related to sponsorship or in recruiting service staff for sponsor presence at an event. It is therefore necessary to clarify which tasks in the implementation of a sponsorship concept can be carried out internally ("in-house"), which are handled by the cooperating cultural institution, and which are outsourced to third parties. It should be noted that the number of outsourced tasks increases the interfaces within the sponsorship organization. This must be taken into account in the structural and process organization of sponsorship project management.

Guiding Questions

- What competencies are required for the implementation of arts and cultural sponsorship?
- Which tasks can be handled internally?
- Which tasks are taken on by the cultural institution?
- Which tasks should be outsourced to third parties?
- With which partners do we already have experience (e.g., agencies) who can support the implementation of arts and cultural sponsorship?

Section 18: Controlling and Evaluation

Decisions regarding the **implementation of controlling** form the conclusion of the cultural sponsorship concept, which is why this area of action is located at the end of the canvas. Controlling and evaluation (see Chap. 11) serve to assess the sponsorship activities. This area is therefore directly related to the objectives. Criteria and key performance indicators must be defined that can answer whether the goals of arts and cultural sponsorship have been achieved.

Guiding Questions

- Based on which criteria is the success of arts and cultural sponsorship defined?
- Which key performance indicators do we use for controlling?
- Which qualitative factors are relevant for performance evaluation?

The arts and cultural sponsorship canvas is a suitable tool for structuring the development of a sponsorship concept. When **critically evaluating** the canvas model, several points should be considered. **On the positive side**, the model is very clear, easy to understand, and quickly grasped. It also enables discussions about different strategies, and various perspectives from company departments can be incorporated. **On the negative side**, it can be noted that the highly simplified representation may not always do justice to the complexity of the situations on the part of the company and the cultural institution.

Factors may also be overlooked, as it is often a snapshot based on numerous assumptions. Corresponding future developments should be anticipated.

Overall, however, the cultural sponsorship canvas has proven itself many times over and is a tool that can be used effectively in practice.

Key Points

1. **Implement a holistic management process:** A cultural sponsorship concept should be developed based on a holistic management process.
2. **Apply elements of the management process:** For the management process of sponsorship, situation analysis, goal definition, identification of target groups, strategy definition, budget calculation, selection of cooperation partners, implementation of measures, and performance evaluation must be considered.
3. **Use canvas models effectively:** For joint workshops, canvas models should be used as a supporting tool to structure information in graphical form.
4. **Ensure alignment on vision and values:** It must be ensured that there is sufficient alignment between the vision, values, and purpose of both partners to guarantee the credibility of the cooperation.
5. **Clearly define milestones:** The typical milestones of a sponsorship cooperation, including initial contact, proposal of cooperation, negotiation, agreement, activation planning, implementation, performance evaluation, as well as renewal or termination, should be defined in advance.
6. **Identify involved actors:** The various actors, including the sponsor, the cultural institution, and supporting service providers, must be identified. In addition, it should be planned which tasks will be carried out in-house and which can be outsourced to third parties.
7. **Plan sponsorship communication:** The behavior and appearance of the sponsor and the cultural institution should be analyzed in order to plan the character and tone of the sponsorship communication during an event.
8. **Conduct competitive analysis:** The sponsorship activities of competitors should be analyzed to support decisions regarding one's own sponsorship strategy and to gain insights into their strategic brand positioning.
9. **Anticipate target group reactions:** Possible reactions of target groups to planned sponsorship activities should be considered in order to stage the desired image objectives with the appropriate communicative codes.
10. **Apply budgeting methods:** For budget calculation, the top-down method should be applied to derive design options from a fixed budget, or, based on a calculation of the costs of individual measures, to create the necessary total budget.

Situation Analysis in Arts and Cultural Sponsorship

5

Contents

5.1 Relevance of a Situation Analysis in Arts and Cultural Sponsorship 113
5.2 Internal Analysis 115
5.3 External Analysis 120

Abstract

The management process of cultural sponsorship projects begins with an assessment of communication-relevant facts. This analytical activity examines, internally, the existing resources and prerequisites for a cultural sponsorship project, as well as, externally, the situation of cooperation partners, competitors, and the general framework conditions. This chapter explains the various areas and methods of a situation analysis that are conducted as part of the management process of arts and cultural sponsorship.

5.1 Relevance of a Situation Analysis in Arts and Cultural Sponsorship

The process of a cultural sponsorship project is designed as a systematic management process. Thus, at its outset stands the **situation analysis** with a comprehensive internal and external analysis. This is of particular relevance because various stakeholders with differing interests are involved in arts and cultural sponsorship, all of whom influence the course and success of the arts and cultural sponsorship. This results in numerous interfaces that are challenging for the organization of arts and cultural sponsorship, for

M. Bruhn and L. Pöllmann, *Arts and Cultural Sponsorship*,
https://doi.org/10.1007/978-3-658-50079-5_5

example, in the collaboration between sponsor, cultural institution, supporting marketing agencies, and other third parties who act as suppliers to implement individual measures. The aim of the analysis from an organizational perspective is to conduct a systematic situation analysis so that planning can be structured to ensure the project is carried out as effectively and efficiently as possible.

Furthermore, the reaction of a cultural institution's audience to the cooperation, as well as the public, private, and media perception of a cultural sponsorship project, is significant. For this reason, the analysis not only focuses on avoiding wasted coverage, but also aims to anticipate possible reputational damage from ill-considered and inappropriate measures at an early stage.

To achieve this, a well-founded **self-image** should be developed with the help of the sponsorship analysis, which assists in the selection of suitable cultural partners. The various target group segments are defined, including their attitudes and expectations, in order to understand them from a marketing perspective. In addition, the analysis provides insights into the market and competitive situation, enabling decisions to be made from a comprehensive perspective.

In summary, the following definition of sponsorship analysis is applied in the present context:

▶ **Sponsorship analysis** A sponsorship analysis comprises a situation analysis of communication-relevant facts with the aim of revealing strengths and weaknesses as well as identifying opportunities and risks associated with a planned cultural sponsorship cooperation. The analysis is conducted by collecting and evaluating internal and external data. Based on this, the central issues to be addressed are identified.

The result of a situation analysis is therefore the **identification of key issues** that need to be addressed in the further planning process. Examples of such issues include the following questions:

- Which cultural partners best fit our brand values?
- Can we adequately leverage our competencies in products and services with the partner?
- Are there opportunities for hospitality to maintain relationships with our key clients?
- Are our cultural engagements perceived as credible and authentic by our internal and external target groups?
- Are the potential cultural partners willing to explore new and creative approaches to arts and cultural sponsorship with us?

These and similar questions arise in a systematic situation analysis that addresses both the internal and external situation.

5.2 Internal Analysis

The **internal sponsoring analysis** helps to assess the initial situation in corporate sponsorship, the marketing needs of the cooperation, and the available resources. In principle, it is a **strengths-weaknesses analysis**. Since in arts and cultural sponsorship, general and long-term positioning goals often take precedence over short-term sales targets, the first step is to determine one's own positioning based on the desired and actual image. Closely linked to this is the definition of the company's unique selling proposition (see Chap. 5) and the question of how this can be strengthened and communicated through the sponsorship cooperation.

The intended process of arts and cultural sponsorship can be viewed from the **perspective of branding**. The branding process described by Esch (Esch, 2014, p. 98), which also underlies the creation of cultural brands (Pöllmann, 2021a, p. 33), can be expanded to include cooperation with a cultural institution (see Fig. 5.1). In this context, the brand identity of the company as a potential sponsor is first defined based on its own vision, core values, and unique selling proposition. This is primarily an internal view of one's own corporate sponsorship. In this step, the relevant strengths and weaknesses are identified, which set the framework for how the corporate sponsorship could be positioned. The subsequent strategic decision on positioning is then made taking into account the competitive situation. For operational implementation within the framework of brand management, cultural partners are then identified whose image supports the intended positioning. Thus, arts and cultural sponsorship shows parallels to the co-branding strategy (Bruhn, 2024) and leads to the necessity that, in addition to one's own analysis, the image of the cooperation partners must also be examined, as will be shown.

The determination of the desired positioning to be achieved through arts and cultural sponsorship can be defined on the basis of a multidimensional **polarity profile** (see also the discussion of the character and behavior of the sponsor brand in Sect. 4.2). Here, the results of the analysis of one's own brand identity are mapped, and then the intended change is specified. The profile dimensions shown in Fig. 5.2 are only examples and can be adapted depending on one's own core values. In a further step, the results of the image analysis of potential cultural partners are compared with the positioning objectives.

The **polarity analysis** is suitable not only for comparing one's own company with a potential cultural partner, but can also be used to evaluate possible cultural creators or artistically independent offerings that align with the company's sponsorship concept. This can contribute to the planning of the artistic programming of self-initiated cultural offerings.

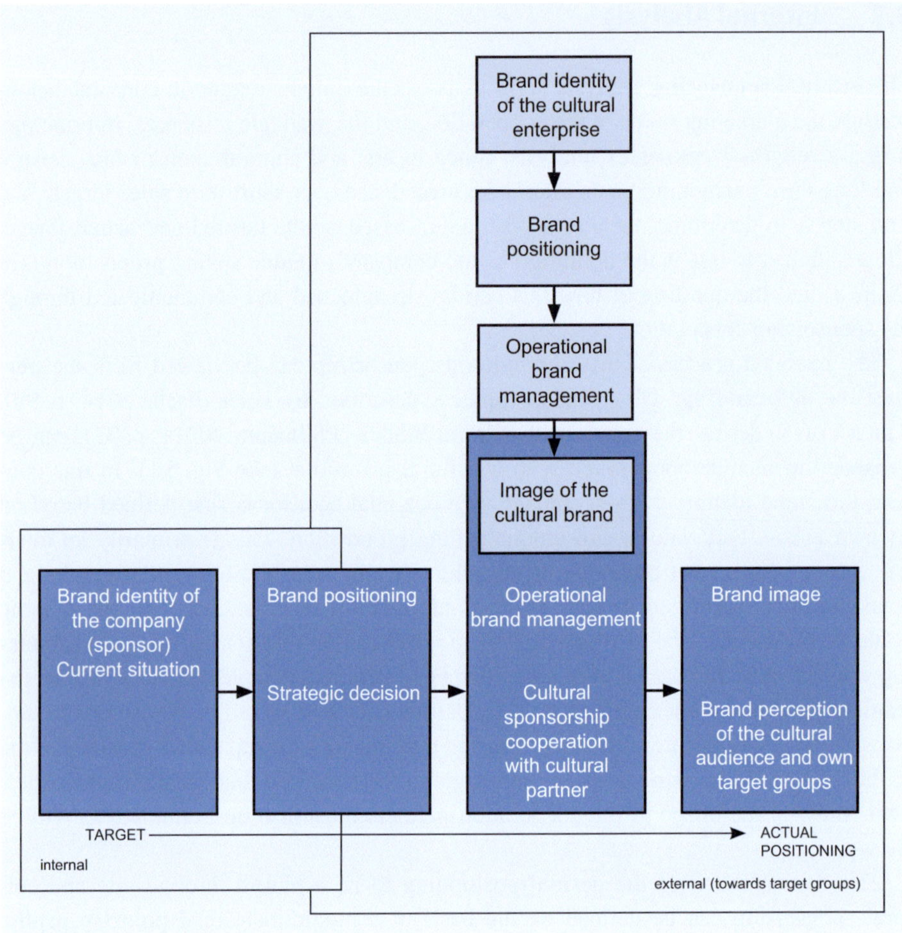

Fig. 5.1 Branding process in arts and cultural sponsorship

The focus of an internal analysis is a **resource analysis**. Arts and cultural sponsorship is essentially the result of a **"make-or-buy decision"**. This is because the sponsor cooperates in order to use a cultural offering for its communication objectives that it cannot create itself—or only at disproportionate expense. After all, corporate sponsorship's cultural engagement is not limited to cooperation with cultural institutions, but also includes the realization of cultural offerings under its own management, such as the museums of entrepreneur and art collector Reinhold Würth with their more than 18,500 works of art.

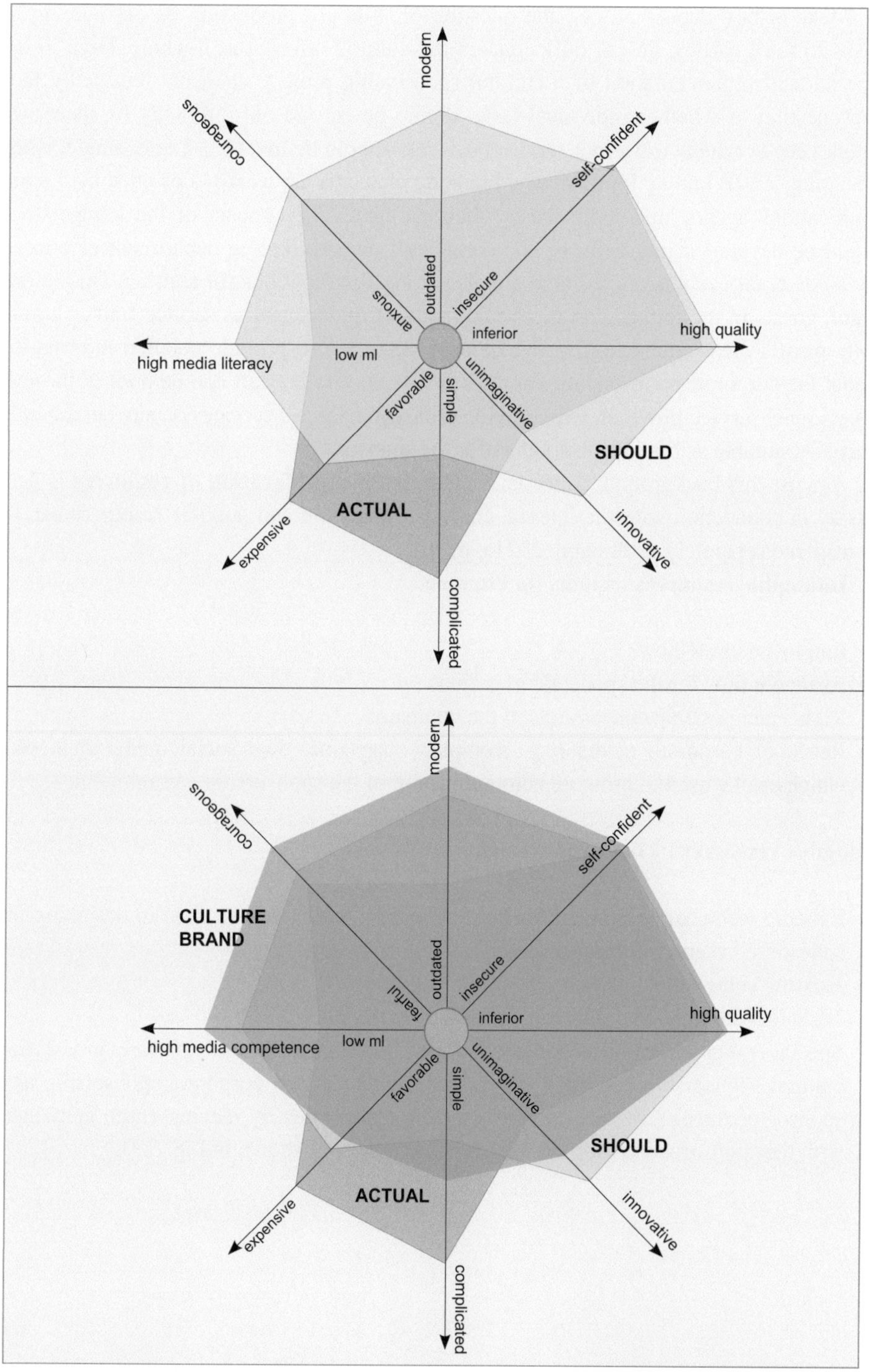

Fig. 5.2 Polarity profile for positioning (top) and comparison with the cooperating cultural brand (bottom)

Make-or-buy decisions, i.e., the question of in-house production or outsourcing of tasks to third parties, do not only concern the cultural offering as a whole. Even in the operational implementation of a cultural sponsorship project, sponsors repeatedly face the question of whether individual tasks should be carried out internally by their own employees or whether external service providers should be involved. For example, when designing a VIP lounge for sponsors, branding elements are usually designed by a communications agency and produced by their partners. The concept of the lounge itself could be developed internally by the company's own marketing department or created by an external event agency. There are also at least two options for staffing: On the one hand, guests in the lounge can meet employees of the sponsor as service staff, who not only have a clear connection to the sponsor but can also provide detailed information about the corporate sponsorship. On the other hand, service staff can be booked through a personnel service provider, who provide professional guest services on site but are only partially suitable as brand ambassadors for the sponsor.

Against this background, it becomes clear that a **consideration of resources** is necessary in connection with the internal analysis. Intangible and tangible resources can be considered separately (Pöllmann, 2021a, p. 79).

Intangible resources include, for example:

- Employee know-how,
- Available time for the sponsorship project,
- Rights and possible concessions of the company,
- Reach of corporate media (e.g., company magazine, own social media channels), which can be used to promote communication of the sponsorship commitment.

Tangible resources include, for example:

- Existing technical equipment for holding events, which can be used in designing the sponsor's presence at a cultural event.
- Existing vehicle fleet, which can support logistics.
- Technical devices for producing advertising materials.
- Special equipment of the company that can showcase the brand's performance during cultural sponsorship activities (for example, DB Cargo's corporate sponsorship as a sponsor of music festivals demonstrated its capabilities by placing cargo containers with the sponsor's branding on the festival grounds, as shown in Fig. 5.3).

Fig. 5.3 Staging the sponsor with its own resources using the example of DB Cargo

5.3 External Analysis

Once the internal analysis is complete, the **external influencing factors** must be examined. In addition to a general external analysis, particular attention should be paid to a careful examination of the cooperating cultural institution. In principle, this is an **opportunity-risk analysis**, i.e., an analysis of which influencing factors could give rise to opportunities or risks.

5.3.1 Cultural Organization-Related Analysis

The cultural organization, as a cooperation partner and the most important stakeholder in a cultural sponsorship project, must also be analyzed. This is generally done even before a potential partner is selected. However, some important aspects, such as the type, organization, and dynamics of the collaboration, can only be determined in more detail once the cooperation is already underway. The areas analyzed with regard to the cultural organization include, in particular:

- **Cooperation design potential:** Determination of content overlaps between sponsor and cultural institution (see also affinity analysis in Sect. 8.2), scope of communication opportunities.
- **Organization:** Description of the management and sponsorship structures on the part of the cultural institution, definition of the number and type of interfaces that arise in the structural and operational organization of the project, and the resulting communication and coordination effort.
- **Audience:** Assessment of the openness, tolerance, or, if applicable, reactance of the target groups of the cultural institution towards arts and cultural sponsorship in general and corporate sponsorship as a potential sponsor in particular, as well as the possibility of integrating the audience as active participants in sponsorship activities.

In an external analysis, the focus is on **risk analysis**. A risk analysis is a systematic examination and evaluation of potential risks and uncertainties associated with the implementation of arts and cultural sponsorship. The aim of this analysis is to identify and prioritize possible risks in order to minimize them and facilitate decision-making.

A **systematic risk analysis** generally comprises three steps: identification, assessment, and monitoring:

1. **Identification:** In the first step, all potential risks associated with a cultural sponsorship project are identified. The main focus is on the reactions of the audience and the general (media) public to the activities of the cultural organization as well as to the fact that the cultural organization is cooperating with the sponsor.

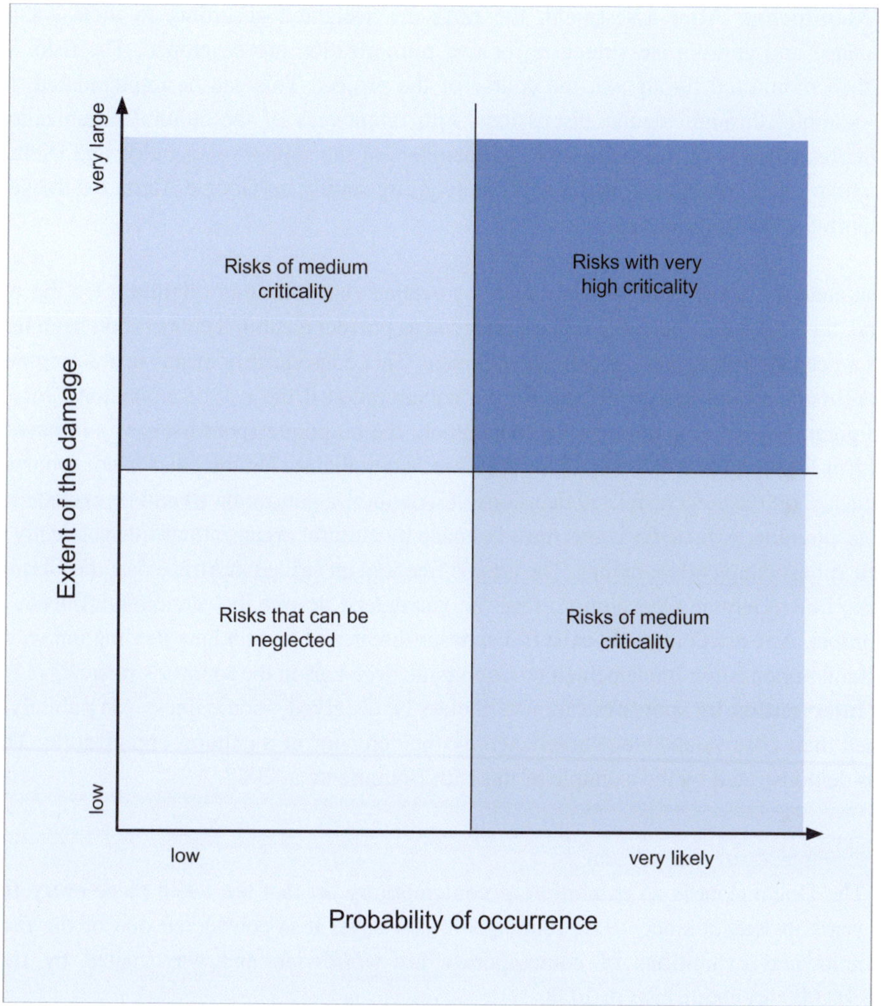

Fig. 5.4 Risk analysis of cultural sponsorship projects

2. **Assessment:** In the next step, each identified risk is assessed and positioned using a risk matrix (see Fig. 5.4). The risks are evaluated based on the predicted probability of occurrence and the estimated extent of damage. Risks with a low probability of occurrence and minor impact on the corporate sponsorship (or the cultural organization) can be neglected. The risk analysis is particularly useful for identifying risks that, due to a high probability of occurrence and significant potential damage, require countermeasures or force the sponsor to seek alternatives.

3. **Monitoring:** After assessment, the risks are weighted according to their significance and appropriate strategies for risk minimization are developed. The risks are then monitored throughout the course of the project. This can be implemented, for example, through regular discussions with employees of the cultural organization, representatives of the audience (e.g., members of the support association and friends' circle), and continuous media analysis (e.g., by setting up Google Alerts for the supported cultural project).

Risk analysis can present sponsors with a so-called **risk handling dilemma**: On the one hand, the analysis of potential risks is intended to prevent a cultural cooperation from having a negative impact on the company's image. This consequently means that a corporate sponsorship would have to refrain from a collaboration if the risk of reputational loss is too great. Even during an ongoing cooperation, the corporate sponsorship would have to act if it is recognized that dangerous risks are materializing. On the other hand, sponsors' influence on the content-related decisions of a cultural organization should be excluded as far as possible. Artistic decisions must be made by cultural organizations independently of their sponsorship collaborations. The artistic freedom enshrined in Article 5 of the German Basic Law (German Constitution) must be guaranteed despite the economic influence of sponsors. A restriction would exist if a sponsor threatened to withdraw funding unless the cultural organization implemented programmatic decisions in the sponsor's interest.

Intervention by sponsors can nevertheless be observed—sometimes even publicly—when their core values are counteracted by the behavior of a cultural organization. This was demonstrated by the example of the 15th Documenta in 2022.

Example: Documenta Kassel

The Documenta is an exhibition of contemporary art that has taken place every five years in Kassel since 1955, running for 100 days. It is considered one of the most renowned exhibitions of contemporary art worldwide and was visited by over 700,000 art enthusiasts in 2022.

When, in June 2022, an artwork with anti-Semitic imagery was discovered, criticism of the Documenta management dominated the public and private perception of the cultural event. The sponsors of the Documenta also voiced criticism of the incidents: For example, the German Savings Banks and Giro Association (DSGV) told Handelsblatt: "The events of recent weeks have caused significant damage to the Documenta and its supporters. Anti-Semitic depictions are unacceptable. (…) The very fact that these could be shown at all has raised fundamental questions about the perception of responsibilities by those in charge and the way the Documenta institutions have dealt with the problems that have arisen." (Handelsblatt, 2022) The Sparkassen Finanzgruppe supported the Documenta as a main sponsor with a six-figure sum (Documenta Fifteen, 2022). The continuation of the cooperation was linked by the corporate sponsorship to the demand for "forceful changes" in the organization of the exhibition (Kunstforum,

Fig. 5.5 Media coverage (screenshots) of sponsor demands in response to criticism of Documenta 2022

2022; Deutschlandfunk Kultur, 2022). Volkswagen, as the second main sponsor of the Documenta, also criticized the organization of the art exhibition. The sponsors' demands were picked up by the German Press Agency and distributed via their news ticker, resulting in widespread media coverage (see Fig. 5.5). ◀

The example of Documenta illustrates a case of **crisis communication** as a reaction to the imminent loss of image for the sponsor in an ongoing sponsorship. In other cases, however, cooperation between the cultural organization and the sponsor does not even take place because the risk appears too great. For example, the director of a renowned theater decided to integrate a vending machine from a well-known soft drink manufacturer into the stage design. The theater's marketing department approached the soft drink manufacturer as a potential sponsor. However, the company declined, fearing public and private criticism. Although the idea for the sponsorship arose from the artistic decision and the stage design was conceived before the sponsorship idea, the audience would not have been aware of this chronology, and thus irritation and a loss of image for the sponsor would have been likely. The theater production ultimately had to be realized without the sponsor. Nevertheless, the vending machine remained on stage, and the corporate sponsorship thus received free exposure for its brand.

5.3.2 Market, Competition, and Environment Analysis

The external analysis can also be conducted in a broader sense. This includes, on the one hand, market and competition analysis, which focuses on the behavior of competitors. On the other hand, it is recommended to consider important developments in the global environment, as these can have an impact on the planning and design of cultural sponsorship projects.

Market and Competitive Analysis

Knowledge of the **market and competitive situation** is assumed for any existing corporate sponsorship and is generally not collected as part of the narrower sponsorship analysis. Typically, information on the following factors, for example, is gathered as part of the market and competitive analysis:

- Market size and market growth (market potential),
- Number and size of competitors,
- Strengths and weaknesses of competitors,
- Own market share and market share of key competitors.

However, some information that is not collected in the classic market and competitive analysis is nevertheless relevant for the **sponsorship analysis**. This includes the evaluation of competitors' sponsorship behavior (see Sect. 4.2) and the identification of other sponsors of the cooperating cultural institution. This leads, for example, to the following **questions** for the analysis:

With Regard to Our Own Arts and Cultural Sponsorship Engagements

- Which corporate sponsors support the cultural institutions that we also sponsor?
- Do the other sponsors fit with our communication strategy?
- What advantages or disadvantages (opportunities and risks) can be identified based on the other sponsors?

Since so-called **"industry exclusivity"** is usually agreed upon with cultural organizations, it can be assumed that no direct competitors will appear as co-sponsors of the cultural partner. The sponsorship activities of competitors must be considered separately.

With Regard to Competitors

- Who are our most important competitors?
- Which cultural sectors are supported by our competitors?

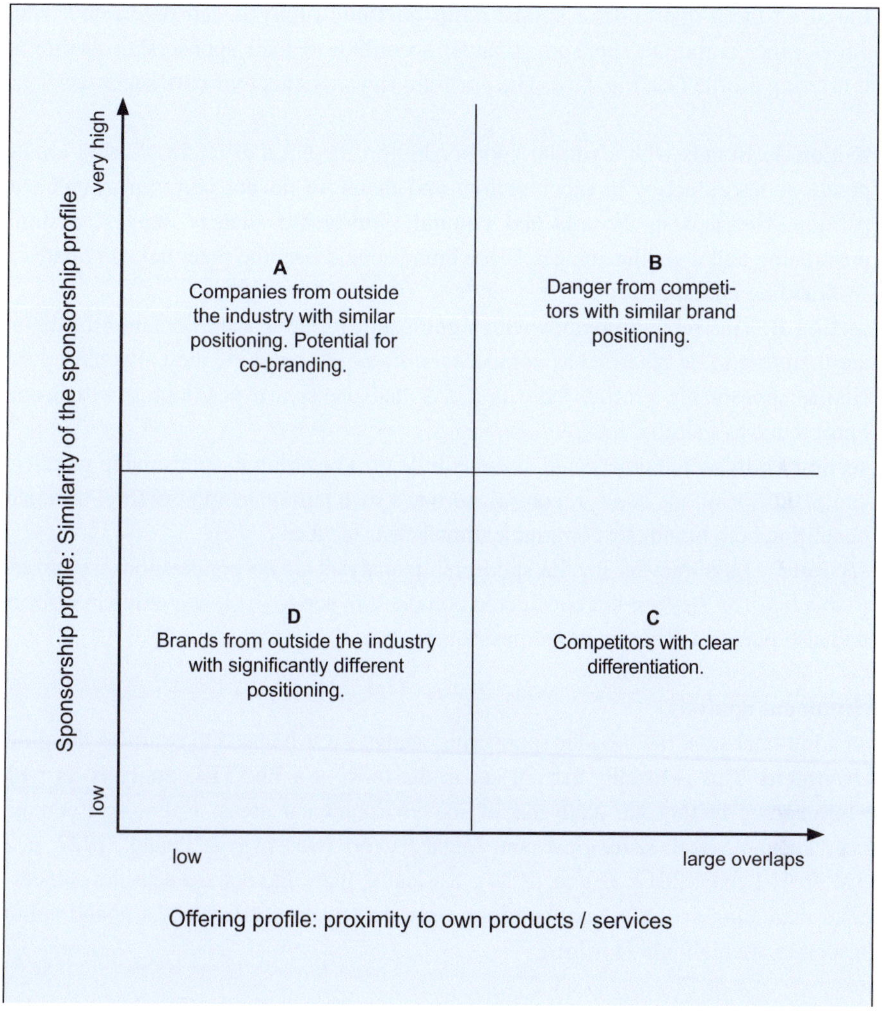

Fig. 5.6 sponsorship portfolio analysis

- Which specific cultural offerings and cultural institutions are supported by our competitors?
- Which brand positioning objectives of the competitors can be derived from their sponsorship engagements?
- What significance does this have for the positioning objectives and sponsorship collaborations we have selected?

Based on these questions, a **sponsorship portfolio analysis** can be created, which classifies other corporate sponsors (brands) according to their sponsorship profile and their offering profile (see Fig. 5.6). The portfolio shown yields four **core sections**:

- **section A:** Brands with a similar sponsorship profile but a different offering are corporate sponsors active in other sectors and therefore do not represent direct competition. Overlaps in the arts and cultural sponsorship strategy suggest a similar positioning and a similar image. These brands could become potential candidates for co-branding initiatives.
- **section B:** This refers to brands with significant overlap in their content offering and are therefore to be regarded as competitors. If, as in section A, they also have a very similar sponsorship profile, there is a risk that one's own positioning will become blurred due to a similar image.
- **section C:** If, on the other hand, there is little or no overlap in sponsorship practice, a competitor positions itself in contrast to one's own corporate sponsorship, ultimately benefiting both brands by communicating a clear identity.
- **section D:** Less relevant for the sponsorship analysis are corporate sponsors assigned to this field, as they are not considered competitors due to the low overlap in offerings and also pursue a different brand positioning.

environment analysis
In an additional step, the broader sponsoring analysis can be used to examine the **global environment**. This is usually carried out in the form of a **PESTEL analysis**, in which the influencing factors are analyzed in six environmental areas: **P**olitical, **E**conomic, **S**ocial, **T**echnological, **E**cological, and **L**egal Factors (Boseman & Phatak, 1989, p. 26; Welge & Al-Lahan, 2012; Bruhn, 2024). Basically, these factors are also the subject of general marketing analysis, and therefore, only the specific features of arts and cultural sponsorship are highlighted below:

- **Political influencing factors:** This area includes factors determined by political institutions or the state. Specifically, this means legislation, regulations, etc. at the federal, state, and municipal levels.
- **Economic influencing factors:** Overall economic development has a particular impact on decisions regarding arts and cultural sponsorship, for example, in that the forecasted market development influences the budget planning of communication policy and cooperation opportunities. Trends such as recession, inflation, etc. affect both the financial situation of corporate sponsors and their willingness to engage in cultural sponsorship, as well as the available net household income of consumers, thereby also reducing the opportunities to participate in paid leisure activities (such as cultural events).
- **Sociocultural influencing factors:** Sociocultural or societal factors include social changes such as shifting norms and values, which require that the content and type

of communication as well as the design of cultural sponsorship measures be aligned accordingly. Communication trends, such as design principles in social networks, must also be considered as sociocultural factors.

- **Technological influencing factors:** Technological developments must also be taken into account in the analysis, as new communication channels and technologies (e.g., augmented reality, virtual reality, mixed reality) create additional opportunities for sponsorship communication. Furthermore, innovations in information and communication technologies often lead to new analytical tools that can be helpful in sponsorship evaluation. Technology developments also offer potential in the organization and implementation of sponsorship projects—for example, through the use of environmentally sustainable materials or production processes, or the application of artificial intelligence.
- **Ecological influencing factors:** Corporate sponsors, the state, the population, and others are challenged to address ecological issues. This includes CO_2 reduction, resource conservation, and many other aspects. Thus, arts and cultural sponsorship projects must also be examined more intensively in the future with regard to sustainability.
- **Legal influencing factors:** Arts and cultural sponsorship is subject to a diverse legal framework. This includes, for example, the tax law treatment of sponsorship as well as public cultural funding practices, among others (see Chap. 3), which have an impact on arts and cultural sponsorship.

A situation analysis is often carried out using the **SWOT analysis** method. In this process, the results of the various analyses presented are summarized in a specific form. The SWOT analysis is a tool for examining the strengths, weaknesses, opportunities, and threats of a company (Welge & Al-Laham, 2012, p. 289; Bruhn, 2024). The acronym SWOT stands for **Strengths, Weaknesses, Opportunities, and Threats.** A SWOT analysis supports the goal-setting process of arts and cultural sponsorship by sorting the preceding analysis results into these four areas. Strengths and weaknesses primarily refer to the internal perspective, while opportunities and threats relate to the external perspective. In principle, the four sections of analysis automatically yield a series of logical objectives: strengths should be expanded, weaknesses addressed, opportunities seized, and strategies and measures defined for risks in order to avoid or respond to them.

Key Points

1. **Consider internal and external analysis:** The management process of arts and cultural sponsorship begins with a systematic and comprehensive analysis, which is to be distinguished into internal and external analysis.
2. **Conduct situation analysis:** To capture relevant communication-related facts, a situation analysis must be conducted, serving as the basis for further decisions in the cultural sponsorship process.

3. **Define brand identity:** The target positioning of arts and cultural sponsorship must be based on the determination of its own brand identity through an internal analysis.
4. **Align positioning:** The sponsor's positioning should be compared with the image of the cultural partner using a polarity profile.
5. **Conduct resource analysis:** Intangible and tangible resources must be analyzed to decide which tasks can be performed internally and which can be outsourced.
6. **Analyze cultural partners:** The design potential of the cooperation, the organizational structure, and the audience of the cultural partners must be determined.
7. **Conduct risk analysis:** Potential risks must be identified and assessed based on the extent of damage and the probability of occurrence.
8. **Use the sponsoring portfolio matrix:** The sponsoring portfolio matrix should be used to segment competitor behavior based on similarities in product and service offerings as well as overlaps in sponsoring activities.
9. **Conduct global environment analysis:** The global analysis should be divided into political, economic, sociocultural, technological, ecological, and legal influencing factors.
10. **Conduct SWOT analysis:** The analysis results should be summarized in a SWOT analysis by categorizing the collected information into strengths, weaknesses, opportunities, and threats.

Goals and Target Groups of Arts and Cultural Sponsorship

6

Contents

6.1 Defining the Goals and Motives of Arts and Cultural Sponsorship 130
6.2 Target Group Planning in Arts and Cultural Sponsorship 135

Abstract

As part of the situation analysis, a strengths-weaknesses as well as opportunities-threats analysis is conducted for engagement in arts and cultural sponsorship. The results of this sponsorship analysis lead to a more precise definition of objectives for arts and cultural sponsorship as an instrument of marketing and corporate communication in the next step. The design of economic and psychological objectives depends on which type of support the corporate sponsorship is assigned to. The formulation of objectives takes into account specific target groups. In this context, target group analysis is supported by the consideration of consumer typologies and can be supplemented by the development of persona models. This chapter outlines the possibilities for formulating objectives and planning target groups for arts and cultural sponsorship. In addition, the case study of Pandion AG illustrates the practical implementation of arts and cultural sponsorship for different target group segments.

M. Bruhn and L. Pöllmann, *Arts and Cultural Sponsorship*,
https://doi.org/10.1007/978-3-658-50079-5_6

6.1 Defining the Goals and Motives of Arts and Cultural Sponsorship

Due to the frequent blending of altruistic and communication policy motives in cultural activities, the corporate objectives of arts and cultural sponsorship are often not clearly identifiable. In this context, it is useful to distinguish between **owner-managed and manager-led corporate sponsorship**. Independent entrepreneurs are more emotionally committed and driven by egoistic motives, as they are not accountable to other authorities but instead manage their own money and determine its use themselves. Employed managers, on the other hand, are accountable to the supervisory board and shareholders for their decisions and must therefore rationally legitimize them. Achieving a benefit for the corporate sponsorship takes absolute priority in their decision-making.

Regardless of whether the motives are self-serving or charitable, it must be assumed that the **goals of cultural sponsorship** cannot be directly derived from the marketing and advertising objectives of corporate sponsorship. Rather, it is necessary for corporate sponsorship — in contrast to the field of sports sponsorship — to engage substantively with the areas of art and culture. This substantive engagement with arts and cultural sponsorship rarely takes place at the level of products or brands. Instead, it occurs at the level of the entire company.

As part of a **substantive engagement of the company with arts and cultural sponsorship** regarding the significance of art and culture within marketing and corporate communication, questions of corporate identity must be addressed. The aim is to define the framework for all marketing and corporate communication by establishing the corporate philosophy, corporate culture, and the desired corporate image. If a corporate sponsor succeeds in defining its own identity, it has not only established its corporate purpose but also determined its stance toward its most important target groups and the form of self-presentation in the societal context. Thus, defining corporate identity is also associated with a specific form of **society-oriented marketing**, in which art and culture play important roles (Pundt et al., 2007; Frohne et al., 2015).

Depending on the corporate identity, **arts and cultural sponsorship** is viewed **as an element of corporate communication** to document the philosophy, culture, and thus the identity both internally and externally. For example, the BMW Group derives the focus of its "Cultural Communication" from its corporate self-concept, in line with corporate values, and considers intercultural dialogue as a means to foster an identity-shaping corporate culture (BMW AG, 2016b).

According to a survey of 193 corporate sponsors in Germany, Switzerland, and Austria, **corporate sponsors engaged in culture** can be divided into the following three **basic types** based on their general motivational aspects (Heusser et al., 2008, pp. 22 ff.):

1. The **commercial type**: Corporate sponsors of this type display a strong commercial and communicative orientation in their cultural engagement. Social responsibility and personal aspects of management or the company founder play a subordinate role. For these

corporate sponsors, arts and cultural sponsorship primarily serves targeted communication and network strengthening. However, this type of company is relatively rare.
2. The **patronal type**: Corporate sponsors of this type feel committed to cultural achievement in line with company tradition, and the cultural competence of the founders or management is usually highly developed. Here, particular importance is attached to inward-facing employee motivation. Commercial and communicative goals are less significant for these corporate sponsors.
3. The **Good Citizen type**: Corporate sponsors of this type primarily fulfill social responsibility through their arts and cultural sponsorship and especially pursue a positive image transfer. Accordingly, a positive impact of cultural activities on employer attractiveness and investor attitudes is considered important. This type of company is the most common in practice.

Comparing these **basic types across the three countries**, it is noticeable that in Switzerland, the patronal and Good Citizen types are predominant. In Germany, alongside the Good Citizen type, the commercial type is most frequently found, while in Austria, most corporate sponsors can be assigned to the patronal type. While in Swiss corporate sponsorship, art lovers often make decisions about cultural engagement, in Germany, commercial and communicative goals are more central to sponsorship decisions. For Austrian corporate sponsors, the commitment of board members or managing directors and employee orientation are decisive (Heusser et al., 2008, pp. 23 ff.).

Against the backdrop of the increasing importance of relationship- and customer loyalty-oriented measures, the goals of arts and cultural sponsorship are also based on the **success chain of relationship marketing**, as presented in Chap. 1 (Bruhn, 2006, pp. 343 f.; 2015, p. 516). Depending on the focus of cultural activities, overarching marketing goals such as customer satisfaction and customer loyalty may be pursued directly, or the realization of preliminary communication goals, such as awareness and image, may take precedence.

Economic Goals of Arts and Cultural Sponsorship

A direct link between cultural support measures and economic sponsorship goals can rarely be established and is likely sought by corporate sponsors only in exceptional cases. For example, in a study, only about 12% indicated direct sales targets and 22% medium- and long-term sales effects as objectives of their cultural sponsorship activities (Nielsen Sports (formerly Repucom) 2015b, p. 4). The economic effect may become apparent through advertising by the sponsored artist or organization for the company's products, resulting in higher sales. However, the immediate effect is usually difficult to prove.

Psychological Goals of Arts and Cultural Sponsorship

According to the chain of effectiveness of relationship marketing, psychological goals are preliminary, pre-economic objectives. Based on the tripartite division from psychology and behavioral sciences, psychological goals can be categorized into cognitive goals (concerning knowledge), affective goals (concerning evaluation), and conative goals (concerning behavior and behavioral intentions).

Cognitive Goals

Due to the relatively low media resonance of most cultural events, increasing **awareness** in arts and cultural sponsorship does not have the same significance as in sports sponsorship. An exception is the support of tours by well-known pop and rock stars, which can expect large live audiences and national media interest. For Deutsche Telekom, music sponsorship is an essential part of brand communication. For this reason, the telecommunications provider has sponsored various national and international music stars on their tours for many years, including bands such as Linkin Park, Depeche Mode, Snow Patrol, or artists like Katy Perry and Robbie Williams. The focus here is on the brand promise “Experience what connects,” or internationally, “Life is for sharing.” As an accompanying measure, products and services are offered at the individual events to provide fans with a unique experience with their stars (Deutsche Telekom AG, 2016e, 2023a, b).

The fact that public and private attention can also be gained through the promotion of classical music is demonstrated by BMW’s involvement in the annually held and multiple award-winning event “Opera for All” in cooperation with the Bavarian State Opera since 1997. Since 2007, the event “Staatsoper für alle” has also been held in Berlin in collaboration with the Staatsoper Unter den Linden. In 2012, the format was internationalized in London with the London Symphony Orchestra under the title “BMW LSO Open Air Classics.” All events are live and free of charge (BMW AG, 2015, 2023a; see also the case study on BMW Group’s cultural engagement in Chap. 11).

Affective Objectives

Arts and cultural sponsorship is particularly suitable for **image management**, by seeking to transfer positively associated image attributes to the sponsor as a whole company. The focus is not on the development and building of new brands, but rather on maintaining established brands and a desired external corporate image. To achieve this goal, cultural sponsors in most cases aim to transfer the existing image of an external object of opinion, such as a musical or artistic genre or a musician or artist, to their own corporate sponsorship. Often, it is **positive image attributes** of art, such as innovation, creativity, exclusivity, or sensuality, that a sponsor wishes to transfer to its corporate sponsorship or a brand. Against the backdrop of increasingly interchangeable products and services, corporate sponsorships also seek, through the support of artists, to transfer their individuality and the uniqueness of their works to their own corporate sponsorship.

Beyond this image transfer, sponsors of cultural activities also benefit from the act of sponsoring itself. The effect of arts and cultural sponsorship lies in the fact that corporate sponsors are perceived by target groups as supporters of social causes, resulting in a **gain in sympathy**. Unlike image transfer, the focus here is particularly on the assignment of denotative characteristics (e.g., sense of responsibility, social commitment). It is not the image of an external person or event that is important, but rather the cultural engagement itself, which is exercised at a specific time and under certain environmental conditions (Causales Agentur für marketing & communication, 2006, pp. 6 ff.; Pundt et al., 2007; Unkelbach & Nill, 2014; Neßler et al., 2015). The central message in such a perspective is the information "corporate sponsorship supports culture," which is associated with certain "collective" image dimensions (Colbert et al., 2005; Posadowsky, 2007, pp. 350 ff.; Unkelbach and Nill, 2014; Frohne et al., 2015, pp. 5 ff.). If corporate sponsors increase their reputation through arts and cultural sponsorship, it can be assumed that these corporate sponsors will also benefit from this reputation, for example, in the recruitment of new employees, access to financing opportunities, and negotiations with stakeholders (Schwaiger, 2008, p. 120; Frohne et al., 2015, pp. 5 ff., pp. 26 ff.).

The promotion of cultural activities also has positive effects on **employee motivation**, as corporate sponsors support cultural activities that interest their employees or actively involve them, for example through the establishment of company clubs. In addition, arts and cultural sponsorship offers an opportunity to improve **employee satisfaction, loyalty, and willingness to recommend**. Employees who place particular value on a company's social commitment and image are especially positively influenced. Arts and cultural sponsorship increases a company's attractiveness as an employer and thus also proves to be a competitive advantage in HR policy. In this sense, corporate cultural engagement also emerges as a **location factor** and an element of local attachment (Schwaiger & Bury, 2003; Causales Agentur für Marketing & Kommunikation, 2016a).

Conative Objectives

Corporate sponsors are increasingly discovering opportunities to use arts and cultural sponsorship as a component of relationship-oriented marketing and to specifically promote **customer satisfaction and loyalty** through cultural activities. For example, the Vienna-based art insurance company Barta & Partner, as exclusive sponsor of the "Salzburg World Fine Art," offered its clients advice and information in the areas of all risk management and art insurance in a 150-square-meter exhibition lounge. Electronic databases such as "artprice" or "The Art Loss Register" were available in the lounge. Art historians and art experts answered questions about the international art market or specifically Austrian topics (Barta & Partner, 2016). The Swiss insurance company Mobiliar, as main sponsor of the Zurich Zoo, offers its customers discounts on admission prices (Mobiliar, 2016). As main sponsor of Art Basel, UBS welcomes clients and art-interested potential clients in its VIP lounge and organizes special events for clients, opinion leaders, and employees (Handelszeitung.ch, 2016; Kobel, 2019).

The reasons for this development are easy to understand, as the diversity of cultural engagements offers the opportunity to specifically promote the **quality of relationships** with different target groups at different levels. The focus is usually on demanding, elite target groups who play an outstanding role as "top clients," partners in business-to-business transactions, or opinion leaders. The high level and sophisticated atmosphere of many cultural events (e.g., vernissages or the openings and previews of art exhibitions or concert series) provide a valuable setting for maintaining personal contacts and fostering dialogue with these target groups. What is special here is that these occasions cannot typically be booked or purchased in the traditional sense, but that the corporate sponsor can create this exclusive opportunity as part of the arts and cultural sponsorship agreement. Personal conversations can be held with opinion leaders, during which the company's views and interests can also be presented. At the same time, there is the opportunity to learn the perspectives of the conversation partners and to draw one's own future conclusions from them.

The advantage of **relationship management through arts and cultural sponsorship** lies above all in the fact that, for example, a highly educated audience that cannot be reached through sports sponsorship can be addressed with minimal wastage. The risk of appearing self-promotional is also lower at cultural events, as sponsors generally act more discreetly than in sports sponsorship. However, relationship management in arts and cultural sponsorship is not limited to upscale target groups. Even through less elaborate side events as part of mass and popular art events, distances between other (less profitable) customer segments and the corporate sponsor are reduced, and the loyalty of these customers to the corporate sponsor is positively influenced.

Results of Empirical Studies on the Objectives in Arts and Cultural Sponsorship
When conducting empirical studies on the **corporate motives for arts and cultural sponsorship**, it must be taken into account that these are publicly stated reasons. It can be assumed that in many cases rational motives as well as the subsequent legitimation of decisions play a role, and that the responses are subject to social desirability bias (Rothe, 2001, p. 78). In this sense, survey effects—caused by public-private scrutiny—cannot be ruled out. However, a fundamental analysis of corporate surveys over time shows that the reasons for cultural engagement are increasingly closely linked to communication and corporate objectives, while altruistic motives such as social responsibility are losing significance (Posadowsky, 2007; Schad & Berentzen, 2007; Schwaiger, 2008).

A comparison of the stated objectives of corporate sponsorships that describe their cultural activities either as arts and cultural sponsorship or as arts and cultural funding is particularly interesting. Here it becomes apparent that in studies of the **motives for arts and cultural sponsorship**, almost all motives are primarily related to communication, and hardly at all to the promotion of culture. Important or very important reasons cited include increasing brand awareness, image cultivation, and contact with the target group. Corporate identity and employee motivation are considered less important, while social motives are in most cases completely neglected (ZHAW, 2015, p. 41). For corporate sponsorships that refer to their activities as **arts and cultural funding**, however, social motives are the main focus. Other important reasons mentioned include personal motives and image cultivation. Customer care, employee motivation, and tax or financial motives play only a subordinate role for these corporate sponsors (Schwaiger, 2008; Kulturkreis der deutschen Wirtschaft im BDI e. V., 2010, p. 12; Frohne et al., 2015, pp. 25 f.).

A study by the European School of Management ESCP Berlin examined the **effects of arts and cultural sponsorship on corporate image** using the examples of the corporate sponsors Audi and BMW. The results show that participants who were aware of a company's cultural engagement attributed a higher level of social responsibility to the company than those who were not informed about the arts and cultural sponsorship (Jacob & Schnurbein, 2004). These studies also clearly indicate that the only objective regularly pursued by both groups of corporate sponsors is image cultivation. A comparable result was found in a study of an Austrian Urban Art Forms music festival in 2010. Through sponsorship, the corporate sponsors were able to achieve higher brand awareness among festival visitors (Rothmair, 2010).

A study by Schwaiger (2006) investigated the **long-term effects of sponsorship**. No general statements could be made regarding the lasting impact on the public. However, in certain segments, such as high-income target groups, a sustainable increase in reputation was achieved through arts and cultural sponsorship. A study on the economic significance of the Beethoven Festival for the city of Bonn and the surrounding region concluded that there was an almost twofold **multiplier effect** of direct returns to the city, as well as a multiplier of 4.15 for the region's corporate sponsors. This refers to the **indirect profitability** of cultural events. Furthermore, the city of Bonn was able to sustainably improve its image as a cultural location by creating networks with corporate sponsors and cultural institutions (DHPG Dr. Harzem & Partner KG, 2010).

Corporate sponsors engaged in the promotion of art and culture have neither been tempted into a "forced" subsequent rationalization of their cultural engagement, nor—at the other extreme—have they cited excessively selfless and overly honorable motives when, in fact, a clear image benefit is also achieved. While it is undisputed that arts and cultural sponsorship can hardly achieve ultimate behavioral effects, it is equally undisputed that it facilitates the company's economic activities.

6.2 Target Group Planning in Arts and Cultural Sponsorship

The **definition of the target groups of arts and cultural sponsorship** forms the basis for a targeted selection of sponsorships in the cultural sector. Especially in arts and cultural sponsorship, the precise identification of the target groups to be addressed is a significant determinant of successful sponsorships. Only by tailoring the approach to the specific characteristics of the respective target groups is it possible to generate the desired image effects.

First, it is important to point out some specific features in addressing target groups within the framework of arts and cultural sponsorship. According to the **type of target group approach**, two types can be distinguished:

1. **Collective target group approach**: Target groups are informed about the company's cultural engagement through mass communication channels (e.g., posters).
2. **Individual target group approach**: Through arts and cultural sponsorship, personal communication with the target individuals or groups is sought. This can be achieved, for example, through personal invitations to the sponsored cultural events.

In many corporate sponsorship efforts—especially in the area of sports sponsorship—the collective target group approach via mass media is the primary focus. In contrast, for cultural sponsorships, the **individual target group approach in arts and cultural sponsorship**, combined with the use of third-party or self-initiated events as part of event marketing, is of significantly greater importance. By individually addressing the target groups, scatter losses, which are common when using other communication instruments, are avoided. In this sense, arts and cultural sponsorship represents an exceptionally precise or target-person-specific communication instrument. However, target group analysis in arts and cultural sponsorship should not be reduced to minimizing scatter losses within given target group potentials. Fig. 6.1 shows that arts and cultural sponsorship offers the opportunity to tap into two **target group potentials**:

1. Target Group Potential I—Acquisition Strategy

The first target group potential refers to the original audience of the sponsored event, which is addressed through an acquisition strategy. For example, in 2022, the Ruhr Piano Festival recorded a total of 27,000 visitors. The festival was supported by RWE as the main sponsor. This allowed RWE to present itself at a total of 63 events in 24 cities during the festival (Klavier-Festival-Ruhr, 2022). An even greater reach was achieved by the Hurricane

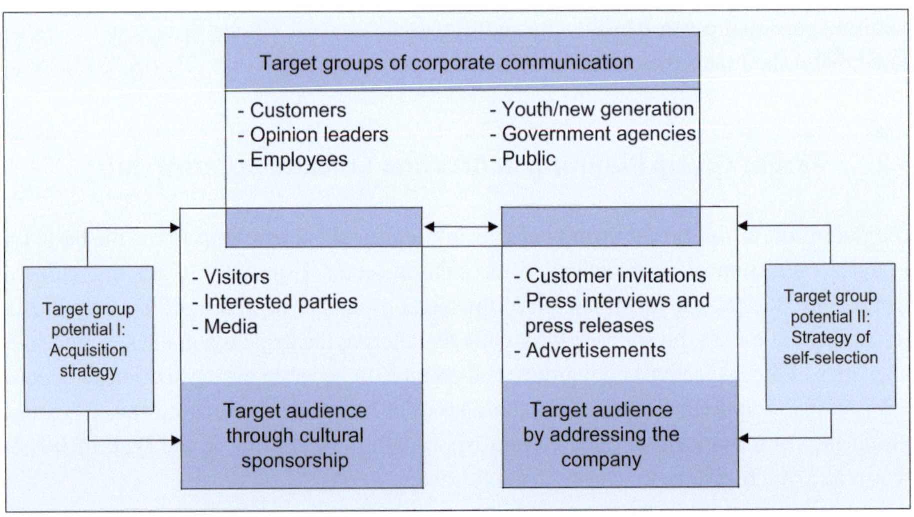

Fig. 6.1 Target group potentials in arts and cultural sponsorship. (*Source* Bruhn, 2018a, p. 245)

Festival 2022 in Scheeßel, with around 78,000 visitors, enabling high contact values for event sponsors such as Beck's and Hornbach (Hurricane, 2022; HBPeople, 2022).

Target group overlaps arise, for example, when visitors to an exhibition or recipients of media coverage also belong to the relevant target groups of marketing and corporate communications.

2. Target Group Potential II — Strategy of Self-Selection

Target group potential II consists of that group which is addressed and made aware of the sponsorship by the sponsoring corporate sponsorship itself — preferably directly — within the framework of a strategy of self-selection. This occurs, for example, in the form of invitations to business partners and customers, as well as through references in press releases and advertisements relating to the company's arts and cultural sponsorship. Overlaps between target groups are based on the fact that recipients are addressed both through selection and as part of general marketing and corporate communications.

In contrast to sports sponsorship, which addresses broader target groups and places greater importance on the strategy of acquisition, in arts and cultural sponsorship the strategy of addressing target groups as individually as possible within a selection strategy is of greater significance. Since, in the case of target group potential II, the corporate sponsorship itself undertakes the development of target groups through the strategy of self-selection, arts and cultural sponsorship can be described as a **target group medium** in the context of advertising media selection. It is therefore important to first determine how the audience of cultural institutions is composed according to sociodemographic criteria and which media this target group uses to obtain information about cultural events and exhibitions. Figures 6.2, 6.3, and 6.4 show the results of a recent survey on the composition and media usage behavior of people interested in culture.

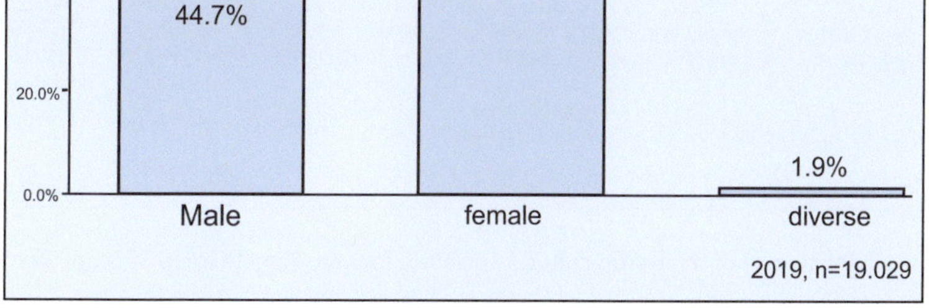

Fig. 6.2 Gender distribution of the Berlin cultural audience. (*Source* Target Group, 2020, p. 12)

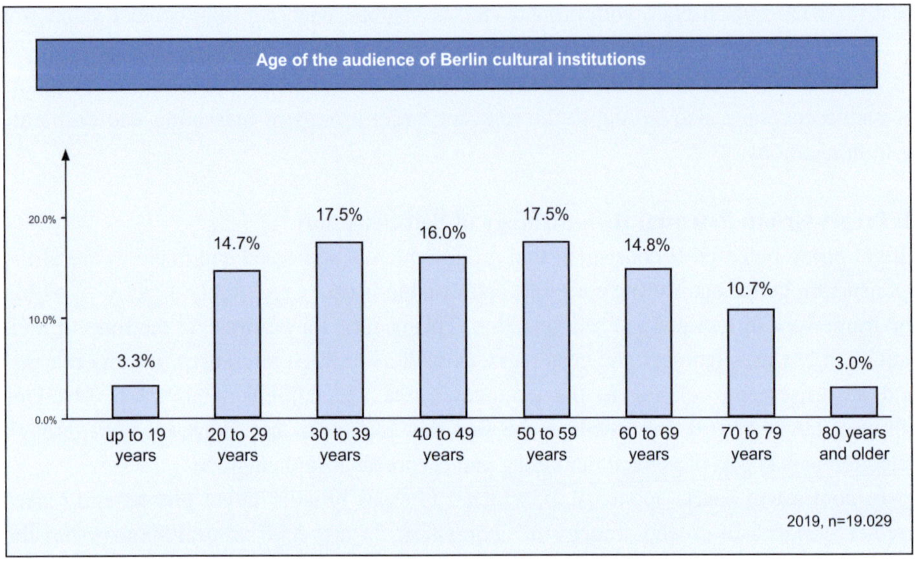

Fig. 6.3 Age distribution of the Berlin cultural audience. (*Source* Target Group 2020, p. 14)

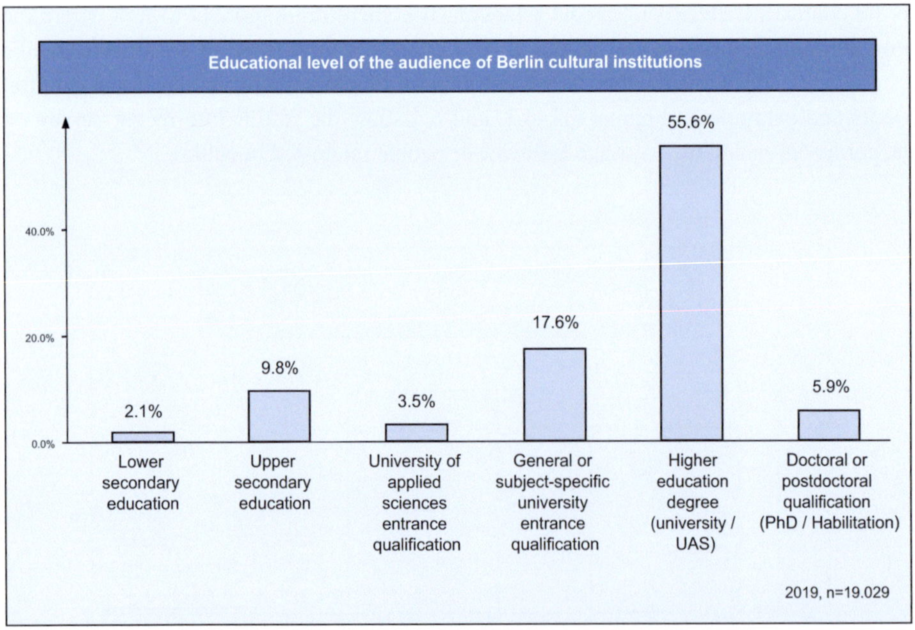

Fig. 6.4 Educational level of the Berlin cultural audience. (*Source* Target Group 2020, p. 19)

Empirical Data on the Cultural Audience

The research project Kulmon (culture monitoring) has been surveying various cultural institutions in Berlin since 2008 and provides extensive statistical data on the Berlin cultural audience. The project is not limited to a single cultural institution or sector, but examines numerous cultural organizations and offerings from the fields of opera, ballet, spoken theater, museums, and memorial sites. The data are collected through personal interviews on site with individuals aged ten and older. Several survey days are conducted to avoid distortions—for example, due to visits by school classes. To provide an understanding of the audience for classical cultural offerings, selected results from the 2019 study are presented below. In the survey year, 19,029 interviews were conducted. This makes the survey one of the most comprehensive cultural audience studies in the German-speaking world (Target Group, 2020).

The results show that, on average, the cultural organizations studied were visited by slightly more women than men (see Fig. 6.2). Overall, 46% of visitors are over 50 years old (see Fig. 6.3). The **average age** does, however, vary depending on the sector—for example, the average age at opera events is significantly higher than among visitors to festivals, museums, and memorial sites. It should be noted that the survey was conducted among individual visitors. Thus, the age group under 19 would be significantly larger if visits by school classes were taken into account. The **educational level** of the cultural audience is above average compared to society as a whole: 61.4% of respondents have a university degree (see Fig. 6.4). The findings on gender distribution, average age, and educational level are typical for classical cultural offerings and are also frequently observed in other studies on cultural audiences (Pöllmann, 2013, pp. 167 ff.; Föhl & Nübel, 2016, pp. 225 ff.). Initial studies on digital cultural audiences suggest that these characteristics also apply to digital audiences of cultural organizations (Duyster & Pöllmann, 2023).

The question of **information behavior** shows that the most important source for the audience is recommendations from friends and acquaintances (28.8%), followed by the website or blog of a cultural institution (see Fig. 6.5). Friends and acquaintances are often cited as an important source of information about cultural and leisure offerings. This can be explained by the fact that cultural offerings are classified as experience goods (Pöllmann, 2021a, pp. 22 f.). This means that the quality of the cultural offering can only be assessed after it has been experienced. The audience therefore takes a risk when purchasing tickets and can only decide after attending whether the ticket purchase was worthwhile. If the event attended is not one for which prior experience exists (e.g., attending a concert by a favorite orchestra), visitors rely on trustworthy recommendations and signals.

A particular problem is the question of available **target group data** with regard to a specific cultural sponsorship project. Sufficiently up-to-date information about the target groups reached through cultural sponsorship (e.g., socioeconomic visitor structure,

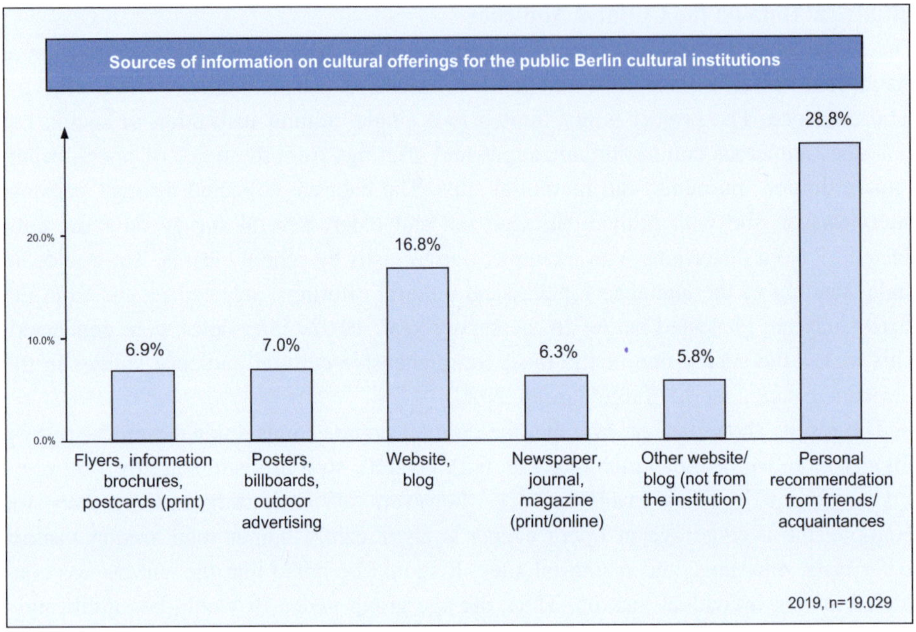

Fig. 6.5 Information behavior of the Berlin cultural audience. (*Source* Target Group, 2020, p. 22)

media coverage reach data) is rarely available. In contrast, target group data on the audience reached through the company's own communications are generally available (e.g., customer addresses, media and advertising reach).

For the efficient design of a sponsorship cooperation, it is therefore important that sponsors and cultural organizations agree on similar **models for target group definition**. These models enable a mutual understanding of the respective target groups and clarify overlaps or reach potentials. If the audience of a cultural organization is described using a model that the sponsor also uses for its target group definition, the sponsor can very quickly decide whether a sponsorship aligns with its marketing objectives. An absolute match between the audience of a cultural organization and the sponsor's target groups is not required. The audience can also represent a potential customer base in a target market that the corporate sponsorship aims to tap into through its engagement in arts and cultural sponsorship.

Common models for target group definition include **consumer typologies** and **persona models**. Both models are illustrated below using established examples.

Example of Consumer Typology: Sinus Milieus

The **Sinus Milieus** are a consumer typology developed by the German Sinus Institute in Heidelberg, based on a comprehensive social science study. It divides the population into different groups that differ in their lifestyles, values, and consumption habits. The milieus are generally characterized by a combination of features such as level of education, occupation, income, lifestyle, cultural interests, and political attitudes. The individual milieus are classified according to two dimensions:

- **Social status**, which is defined primarily by income and education, assigns the milieus to the lower, middle, or upper class.
- **Basic orientation** differentiates the milieus according to their attitudes. Depending on whether the attitude is more conservative or progressive, the basic orientation is divided into three areas: tradition, modernization, and reorientation.

In total, this classification results in ten milieus for society in Germany, as shown in Fig. 6.6. These milieus can be grouped into four categories: **Leading Milieus, Future Milieus, Modern Mainstream, and Traditional Mainstream**. The individual milieus are briefly described below (Sinus Institute, 2023) (see Fig. 6.7).

The milieus shown in Fig. 6.7 refer to the entire market in Germany. Since cultural institutions, unlike internationally operating corporations, mainly address a regionally limited audience, it should be noted that the size of the various milieus depends on the location. Furthermore, the milieus differ when comparing different countries, as illustrated by Figs. 6.8 and 6.9 using the example of the Sinus Milieus in Austria and Switzerland.

The **advantage of using consumer typologies** lies in the fact that extensive market research data is available for each milieu. Based on data on information behavior and media usage, for example, media strategies can be developed. However, it should be noted that, in order to reliably assign target groups to a consumer typology, it is usually necessary to collect one's own market research data (e.g., customer or audience surveys).

Persona Models

While milieu models describe larger groups, persona models define individual **example persons**. These are fictional individuals, but they represent a real (sub-)target group.

Persona models are popular because they are more vivid than the comparatively abstract milieus. In workshops or when developing measures, decisions can always be specifically reflected upon in terms of possible reactions of the persona. The prerequisite for this is that a persona is characterized in detail and understood by everyone involved in sponsorship planning. The level of detail used to describe a persona is not standardized. The following **characteristics of personas** are frequently used (Pöllmann, 2021a, p. 72):

- Name,
- Demographic data,
- Occupation and position,
- Personal values,
- Lifestyle,
- Personal goals,
- Challenges,

Sinus milieus	Brief description
Leading milieus	
Conservative-Upscale milieu	The old structural conservative elite: classic ethics of responsibility and success as well as claims to exclusivity and status; desire for order and balance; self-image as a "rock in the surf" of postmodern arbitrariness; erosion of the social leadership role.
Post-material milieu	Committed-sovereign educational elite with post-material roots: self-determination and self-development as well as orientation towards the common good; advocates of post-growth, sustainability, non-discriminatory conditions and diversity; self-image as a social corrective.
Performer milieu	The efficiency-oriented and progress-optimistic performance elite: global economic and liberal thinking; overall social perspective based on personal responsibility; self-image as style and consumption pioneers; high affinity for technology and digital.
Future milieus	
Expeditive milieu	The ambitious creative bohemians: urban, hip, digital, cosmopolitan and networked; in search of new frontiers and unconventional experiences, solutions and successes; strong self-expression skills, self-image as a postmodern elite.
Neo-Ecological milieu	Progressive realists: optimism and a spirit of optimism combined with a pronounced awareness of the planetary challenges; Self-image as a changemaker and initiator of global transformation; Open to new syntheses of values: Disruption and pragmatism, success and sustainability, party and protest; sustainable lifestyle without an ideology of sacrifice.
Modern Mainstream	
Adaptive-Pragmatic Center	The modern mainstream: willingness to adapt and perform, utilitarian thinking, but also a desire for fun and entertainment; strong need for anchoring and belonging; growing dissatisfaction and insecurity due to social developments; self-image as flexible pragmatists.
Consumer-Hedonist milieu	The (lower) middle, focused on consumption and entertainment: having fun in the here and now; self-image as cool lifestyle mainstream; strong need for recognition; professional adaptation vs. leisure escapism; increasingly annoyed by the dictates of sustainability and political correctness.
Precarious milieu	The lower class striving for orientation and participation: Belonging and keeping up with the standard of living of the broad middle class - but accumulation of social disadvantages and exclusion; feeling of being left behind, bitterness and resentment; self-image as a sturdy bruiser.
Traditional Mainstream	
Nostalgic middle-class milieu	The harmony-oriented (lower) middle: Desire for secure circumstances and an appropriate status; self-image as middle of society, but growing excessive demands and fears of relegation; felt loss of learned rules and certainties; longing for the old days.
Traditional milieu	The security and order-loving older generation: stuck in the small-town world or traditional working-class culture; undemanding adaptation to necessities; increasing acceptance of the new sustainability norm; self-image as righteous little people.

Fig. 6.6 Characteristics of the Sinus Milieus. (*Source* Sinus Institute, 2023)

- Media usage behavior,
- Leisure behavior,
- General consumption behavior and preferred brands,
- Experience (and thus also expectations),
- Personal quote.

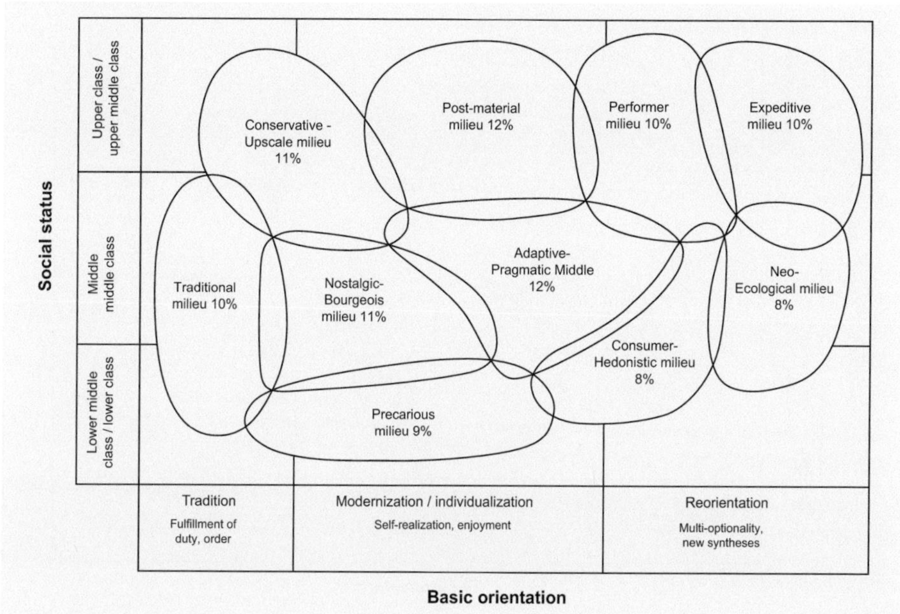

Fig. 6.7 Sinus Milieus 2022 in Germany. (*Source* Sinus Institute, 2023)

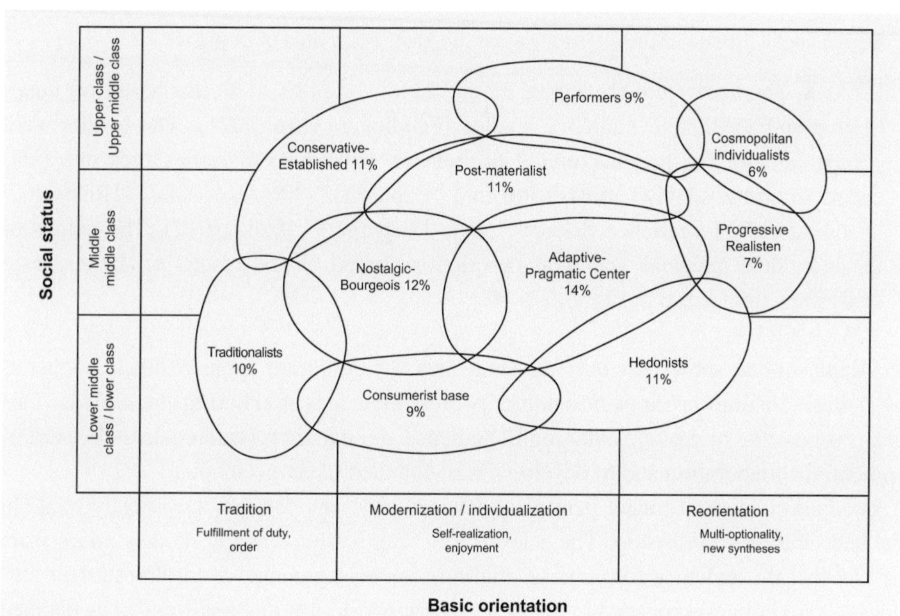

Fig. 6.8 Sinus Milieus 2022 in Austria. (*Source* Integral, 2022)

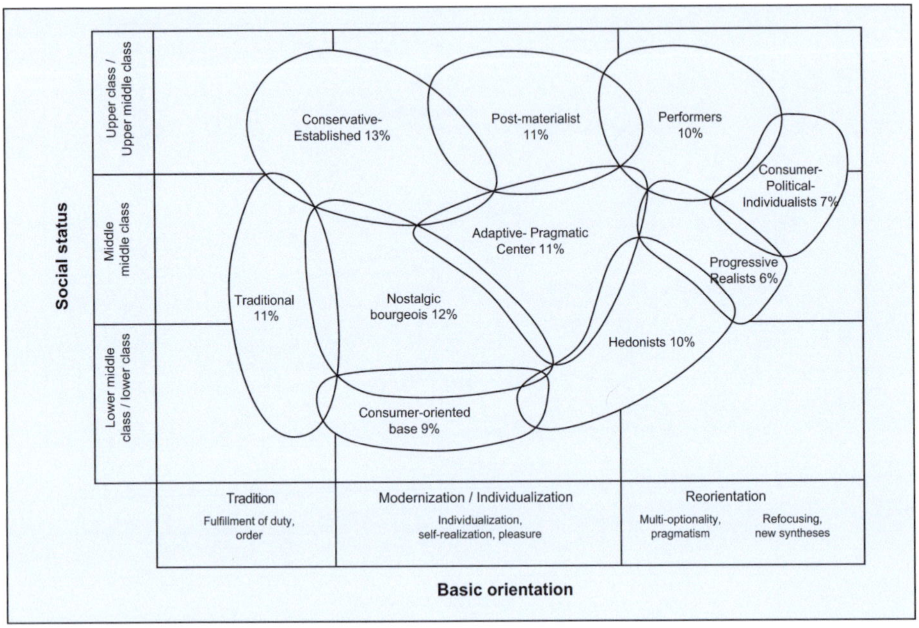

Fig. 6.9 Sinus Milieus 2019 in Switzerland. (*Source* Integral, 2019)

Example of a Persona Model: Personae of the State Museums of Berlin

In 2018, personae were developed at the State Museums of Berlin based on quantitative and qualitative audience studies (Fendius & Otte, 2021). The results were compared with the persona model of John H. Falk, who classifies museum audiences according to **visit motivation** into "Explorers," "Professionals," "Hobbyists," "Facilitators," "Experience Seekers," and "Rechargers" (Falk, 2012). The names of the individual personae and their descriptions based on the results of the audience study are summarized in Fig. 6.10. ◀

The explanations show that it is advantageous for corporate sponsorship if cooperating cultural institutions already conduct **professional arts marketing** themselves. This makes it possible to provide meaningful audience and market research data at the start of a potential collaboration and to develop a well-founded target group plan.

In addition, **custom target group models** can be developed that specifically relate to arts and cultural sponsorship. The relevance of sponsorship-specific models arises from the fact that the audience for cultural offerings can be segmented according to their attitudes toward cultural sponsorship measures, allowing for different measures to be planned for the various segments. A **sponsorship-specific target group model** could, for example, divide the audience of a cultural institution along two dimensions (see Fig. 6.11):

Persona designation	Description
Explorers	Curiosity-driven visitors with a generic interest in the museum's content. They expect to find something that attracts their attention. Personal quote: "I just like new impressions, generally getting into things, whether it's art or history or something else. If I have half an hour, my eyes might linger on something, then I'll stay there longer." Demographic characteristics: • Male, 54 years old, professional, university degree, Germany or • Female, 52 years old, professional, university degree, Berlin/abroad • Accompaniment: mostly with partner or friends and acquaintances
Professonals/Hobbyists	Visitors who feel a close connection between the museum content and their profession or passion. Their visits are usually motivated by the desire to achieve a specific content-related goal. Personal quote: "Museums have actually interested me since childhood. And now it's almost indispensable for me. I'm basically interested in pictorial history: What is being told there?" Demographic characteristics: • Male, 55 years old, employed, university degree, Germany or • Female, 60 years old, retired, university degree, Berlin • Accompaniment: mostly alone or with a partner
Facilitators	Socially motivated visitors who focus their visit primarily on enabling others to experience and learn in their accompanying social group. Personal quote: "I regularly go to the Picture Gallery with schoolchildren. We call it a 'private children's academy'. I come from Kreuzberg, where many children don't have the opportunity to go to museums. They are totally interested and want a lot - they need stories and background." Demographic characteristics: • Male, 54 years old, professional, university degree, Germany or • Female, 52 years old, professional, university degree, Berlin/abroad • Accompaniment: mostly with partner or friends and acquaintances
Experience Seekers	Visitors who are motivated to visit because they see the museum as an important place. Their satisfaction is primarily based on the mere fact that "I've been there" and done that. Personal quote: "When I go to a city, I'm always interested in the museums. And then I like to see the paintings in the original. The exhibition at the Gemäldegalerie with the great architecture and lighting looks like choreography!" Demographic characteristics: • Male, 54 years old, professional, university degree, Germany or • Female, 52 years old, professional, university degree, Berlin/abroad • Accompaniment: mostly with partner or friends and acquaintances
Rechargers	Visitors who are primarily looking for a contemplative, spiritual and/or relaxing experience. They see the museum as a refuge from the working world and a place where they can see inspiring and beautiful things. Personal quote: "I always find art interesting when it surprises me and opens up new perspectives and points of view. So this classic picture: large rooms with large pictures, in the middle a lonely bench where someone sits and looks at the pictures. I wanted to clear my head, so it was a good opportunity to just go there." Demographic characteristics: • Female, 38 years old, professional, university degree, abroad or • Male, 70 years old, retired, university degree, Germany • Companion: usually alone or with partner

Fig. 6.10 Personae of the State Museums of Berlin. (*Source* Fendius & Otte, 2021, pp. 6 f. and pp. 38 f.)

1. Attitude toward arts and cultural sponsorship
2. Interest in the sponsor

Based on this division, several segments emerge for which the sponsor's likely optimal behavior can be determined. In some cases, sponsorship-specific **Visitor Journeys** can also be designed, so that appreciative and sponsor-interested visitors are given access

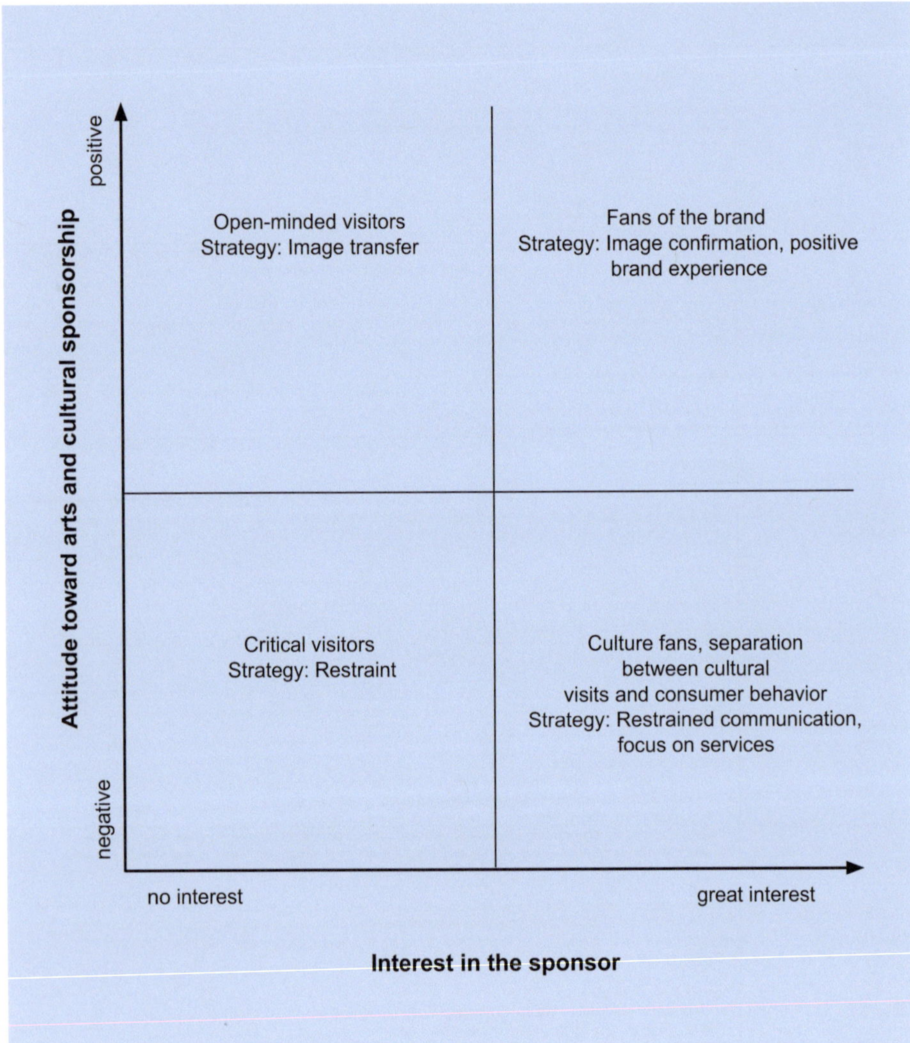

Fig. 6.11 Example of a cultural sponsorship-specific audience segmentation

to the sponsor's VIP areas and benefit directly from the sponsor's involvement. Contact with visitors who are more critical of arts and cultural sponsorship, on the other hand, can be planned more cautiously.

The following **case study of Pandion AG** provides insight into the implementation of cultural sponsorship projects. With its arts and cultural sponsorship, Pandion AG addresses different target groups, as its measures are aimed on the one hand at politics, authorities, and internal target groups, but on the other hand also explicitly seek to reach the general public in the neighborhoods where it is engaged.

6.2.1 Case Study: Concept of Arts and Cultural Sponsorship at Pandion AG

Initial Situation

Pandion AG is an owner-managed real estate company that has been involved since 2002 in the development, realization, and marketing of high-quality residential and commercial projects.

The **starting point for Pandion's cultural engagement** was the awareness that, as a project developer, the corporate sponsorship shapes cities with its residential and office construction projects, and thus **bears responsibility for the urban community**. In view of the increasing densification of major cities and the fact that cultural creators are finding it increasingly difficult to secure suitable spaces for their projects, the corporate sponsorship decided not to leave vacant existing buildings unused. Temporary spaces are provided free of charge to socio-cultural organizations that are not needed during the construction planning phase. In this way, Pandion AG enables the creation of meeting places in neighborhoods, supports district management, contributes to the community, and engages with local residents in the neighborhoods.

Objectives and Target Groups of Arts and Cultural Sponsorship and Sponsorship

The **main objective of the engagement** is to foster neighborhood relations and long-term, sustainable **neighborhood design**, in order to strengthen trust in the corporate sponsorship both externally and internally. The long-standing engagement and public-private presence of Pandion AG reinforce the image goal of being a credible and trustworthy company. At the same time, the cultural sponsorship projects counteract prejudices against the real estate sector and make less well-known aspects of a real estate developer's work visible both to the public and within the company.

In addition, Pandion aims to increase the **visibility of the company** in the relevant district and to raise awareness of the location of each construction project. This generates additional reach and underscores its positioning as a city shaper and enabler. Taking on local responsibility for the site is intended to have a positive impact and foster acceptance among decision-makers in politics and administration.

Employer branding objectives are also pursued through arts and cultural sponsorship: The engagement highlights Pandion as an attractive employer, as these interim uses offer great potential to promote identification with Pandion as an employer. According to Pandion, the corporate sponsorship is seen within the industry as a driver and pioneer in the field of interim use.

Based on the objectives mentioned, three main **target groups** of the cultural sponsorship measures can be identified:

- The **neighborhood** of the respective construction sites: By promoting art, culture, and social initiatives, Pandion appears in new media contexts and gains recognition in target group segments that the corporate sponsorship would otherwise find difficult to reach with conventional measures.
- Decision-makers from **politics and administration**, who are among the key stakeholders in the development projects.
- **Employees** of the company, to strengthen Pandion as an employer brand.

Strategic Orientation of Arts and Cultural Sponsorship

The **strategic orientation in arts and cultural sponsorship** at Pandion is to provide free, temporary spaces for organizations that foster a sense of community at construction sites. This is understood as part of the company's social engagement and responsibility within the framework of its sustainability management. This strategy is based on the principles of the **Corporate Sustainability Reporting Directive (CSRD)**, which came into force in the European Union in January 2023. The CSRD directive requires corporate sponsorship to provide comprehensive reporting on environmental, social, and governance aspects in order to promote sustainable investment. The CSRD directive will play an increasingly important role for investors, real estate buyers, and tenants in the future when purchasing and renting real estate.

In addition, in 2021 Pandion, together with other project developers and the BFW (Federal Association of Independent Real Estate and Housing Companies) Berlin/Brandenburg e. V., founded the **Transiträume Berlin e. V. Association**. This association is a joint initiative of the real estate and creative industries, serving as a central contact point that brings together interested users and owners of vacant spaces. Through the association's website, inquiries can be made and viewing appointments arranged.

Selection of Sponsorships

For the allocation of interim uses, the submitted concepts are reviewed according to the following **selection and evaluation criteria**:

- Originality, substantive strength, and creativity (all social and cultural fields are possible),
- Participation of neighborhood communities (residents, associations, businesses, schools, daycare centers),
- Consideration of local social, cultural, educational, and integrative needs in the neighborhood,
- Consideration of space requirements and proportionality of building improvements in relation to the duration of use,
- Expected media coverage and reach,

- Degree of establishment of the users,
- Personnel and financial resources of the users,
- Planned duration of use.

Anchoring in Corporate Sponsorship

The review and selection of possible usage concepts is the responsibility of the **Corporate Communications Department** together with the branch manager of the respective location and the board of Pandion. Regular meetings serve for consultation and decision-making based on the above-mentioned selection and evaluation criteria. Corporate Communications oversees and communicates the collaboration, while (if necessary) the construction management and administration support the project.

In the **selection of usage concepts** to be implemented as a cultural sponsorship project, it is fundamentally important to consider the associated costs, the duration for which the existing building or space is available for interim use, the available infrastructure (location and transport connections, condition of sanitary facilities, electronics, heating), and any requirements regarding monument protection and fire safety. In a careful **review process**, all factors are taken into account in order to make a decision based on a balanced cost-benefit analysis. The weighing and resolution of these matters is the responsibility of the branch manager and the board.

For collaboration with users, a **transfer or usage agreement** is concluded. The term depends on the construction processes and can range from seven days to several years. Components of the agreement include:

- General information about the usage,
- General information about the building or space,
- Regulations for joint events,
- Photography rights,
- Regulations for mutual communication.

Measures for Implementing the Sponsorship

The art projects are implemented by the sponsored organizations, predominantly **independently** and based on the submitted concepts, with support from Pandion. The measures can be divided into on-site events and activities as well as accompanying communication measures.

In the provided spaces, vernissages and finissages (organized by the creative users) are usually held (see Figs. 6.12 and 6.13), as well as joint networking events with the creative users within the real estate and creative industries. In addition, guided tours are offered by the sponsored parties for Pandion employees.

The **accompanying communication measures** generally include posters (see Fig. 6.14), flyers, postcards from the users, and social media posts. These media are supplemented by coordinated press relations, which are supported by Corporate Communications and the respective branch managers of Pandion.

Fig. 6.12 Light installation by the artist Djeff in the exhibition Once only Once in the premises of Pandion AG

Fig. 6.13 Sculpture by the artist Djeff in the exhibition Once only Once sponsored by Pandion AG

Integration of Sponsorship into Overall Communication

The interim use projects are presented in the annual company brochure, the internal annual meeting, the company magazine, the company website, the digital communication of new construction projects, e.g., in the form of news articles, in social media posts,

Fig. 6.14 Poster announcement for the art exhibition Berlin Bishkek Art Weeks sponsored by Pandion. (Photo: Louise Amelie, Graphics & Edit: Studio KOA Berlin)

on the window films and construction fences of the usage properties, as well as at sales events. The commitment to interim use is communicated across locations, but there is no substantive linkage between the individual projects.

Coordination with Other Departments

For the most part, the measures are planned and implemented in the Corporate Communications Department. Measures that are directly visible at the usage property or at new construction projects are coordinated with the branch, project development, and project management departments.

Budgeting and Costs

The sponsored parties receive the premises under conditions that also include incidental costs. Therefore, the sponsor Pandion incurs **external costs** in the form of covering incidental expenses (heating and electricity costs, water, cleaning services, maintenance costs) for operations. Otherwise, the sponsored parties do not receive any additional financial support, as this is indirectly granted in the form of rent waivers and the assumption of incidental costs. The amount of incidental costs depends on the duration of use, the season, and the size of the usage property, and therefore varies greatly from project to project. In budget planning, **internal costs** in the form of personnel expenses in the Corporate Communications Department are also taken into account.

Effects and Performance Evaluation

There is no systematic measurement of impact or success. The success of the projects is determined by personal impressions during visits to events on site and based on conversations with network and business partners. In addition, media coverage of the projects is evaluated internally.

Key Points

1. **Consider different motives:** It should be noted that in arts and cultural sponsorship, different motives for cultural engagement may dominate between owner-managed and manager-led corporate sponsorship, based on their differing circumstances.
2. **Identify basic types of culturally engaged corporate sponsorship:** Various basic types of culturally engaged corporate sponsorship should be identified, including the commercial type, the patronal type, and the Good Citizen type.
3. **Consider economic and psychological objectives:** It should be taken into account that arts and cultural sponsorship pursues both economic objectives, such as increasing sales, and psychological objectives, such as changing the attitudes of target groups toward the sponsor's brand.
4. **Differentiate psychological objectives:** The psychological objectives of arts and cultural sponsorship can be differentiated into cognitive objectives such as increasing brand awareness, affective objectives such as image transfer, and conative objectives such as customer retention.
5. **Vary target group communication:** Target group communication in sponsorship collaborations should vary between collective and individual approaches, with the latter being of particular importance in arts and cultural sponsorship.
6. **Utilize audience studies:** Audience studies should be evaluated to understand that visitors to cultural institutions often rely on recommendations from friends and acquaintances, as cultural offerings are experience goods and require trustworthy information.
7. **Characterization of the audience for classical cultural offerings:** The audience for classical cultural offerings is often characterized by an above-average level of education and above-average income.
8. **Use models for target group description:** Established models for describing target groups should be used to support the coordination and planning of cultural sponsorship projects between sponsors and cultural organizations.

9. **Use the consumer typology Sinus Milieus:** Models such as the Sinus Milieus consumer typology should be used to describe the population structure based on the dimensions of social status and basic orientation.
10. **Apply persona models:** Persona models should be used to describe fictional example individuals whose characterization is based on market research data and on which further communication measures for addressing target groups can be based.

Strategy Development of Arts and Cultural Sponsorship

7

Contents

7.1 Strategy Dimensions of Arts and Cultural Sponsorship 155
7.2 Strategic Guidelines in Arts and Cultural Sponsorship and Arts and Cultural Sponsorship Philosophy.. 158
7.3 Types of Strategy in Arts and Cultural Sponsorship 162

Abstract

Corporate sponsors face the challenge of strategically deploying sponsorship engagements to achieve their communication objectives. This chapter outlines both the strategic dimensions and the types and forms of arts and cultural sponsorship. These form the basis for formulating sponsorship guidelines, which define the key points of an arts and cultural sponsorship strategy. The components involved in developing an arts and cultural sponsorship philosophy are also explained, as well as various manifestations such as mainstream, niche, and regional sponsorship. In addition to various practical examples, the strategy and approach of the DHL Group are presented in detail as a case study.

7.1 Strategy Dimensions of Arts and Cultural Sponsorship

The first **strategic fundamental decision** a company makes in arts and cultural sponsorship is the decision for or against engaging in sponsorship. In doing so, it must be examined to what extent the communication tool of sponsorship is integrated into the

M. Bruhn and L. Pöllmann, *Arts and Cultural Sponsorship*,
https://doi.org/10.1007/978-3-658-50079-5_7

company, marketing, or brand strategy, and whether it aligns with the image of the company and its products or services, as well as with the corporate culture. Strategic fundamental decisions must therefore always be made based on brand identity and the content associated with the concepts derived from it. Only after these conceptual preliminary considerations are the product- and brand-specific justifications for a sponsorship cooperation with a cultural institution provided.

The sponsorship strategy targeted by a corporate sponsorship includes, depending on communication objectives and numerous situational influencing factors, various substantive priorities in individual dimensions. The substantive **definitionof the sponsorship strategy** represents a complex planning problem in which several decisions must be made simultaneously. In defining the content of the sponsorship strategy, the framework conditions for the selection of sponsorships are established, with orientation towards various elements. The **dimensions of a sponsorship strategy** are illustrated in Fig. 7.1. They comprise the following seven dimensions:

- **Sponsoring subject:** The first step is to determine the reference subject that will appear publicly as the sponsor. The sponsoring subject may be the entire company, a product line, or individual product brands or service programs that become the communicative focus of a sponsorship engagement in culture.
- **Sponsorship target groups:** The next step is to define the target groups the company wishes to address (e.g., art-interested women aged between 25 and 50, key customers, opinion leaders). In principle, all target groups of corporate and marketing communication are eligible for arts and cultural sponsorship, i.e., both external target groups such as customers, suppliers, shareholders, and investors, as well as internal target groups such as employees.
- **Sponsoring message:** Next, the message to be communicated is defined. This may take the form of a core statement, a slogan, name, logo, or emblem. When defining the sponsoring message, it is important to note that both the content and design of the message are subject not only to company-specific restrictions but also to the framework conditions of arts and cultural sponsorship (e.g., integration into the aftermovie of a festival, restrictions on the placement of promotional messages on stage, restrictions on rights exploitation).
- **Sponsored party:** The determination of the sponsored party is made in terms of subject matter, personnel, and time (e.g., sponsoring an artist, a dance group, or a cultural event for three years).
- **Sponsorship measures:** Finally, the various instruments in the form of advertising media and materials for the engagement in arts and cultural sponsorship are defined (e.g., advertising in connection with announcements, outfitting cultural creators, merchandising items, sales promotion measures such as distributing product samples in "goody bags," personal invitations to the VIP lounge, etc.).

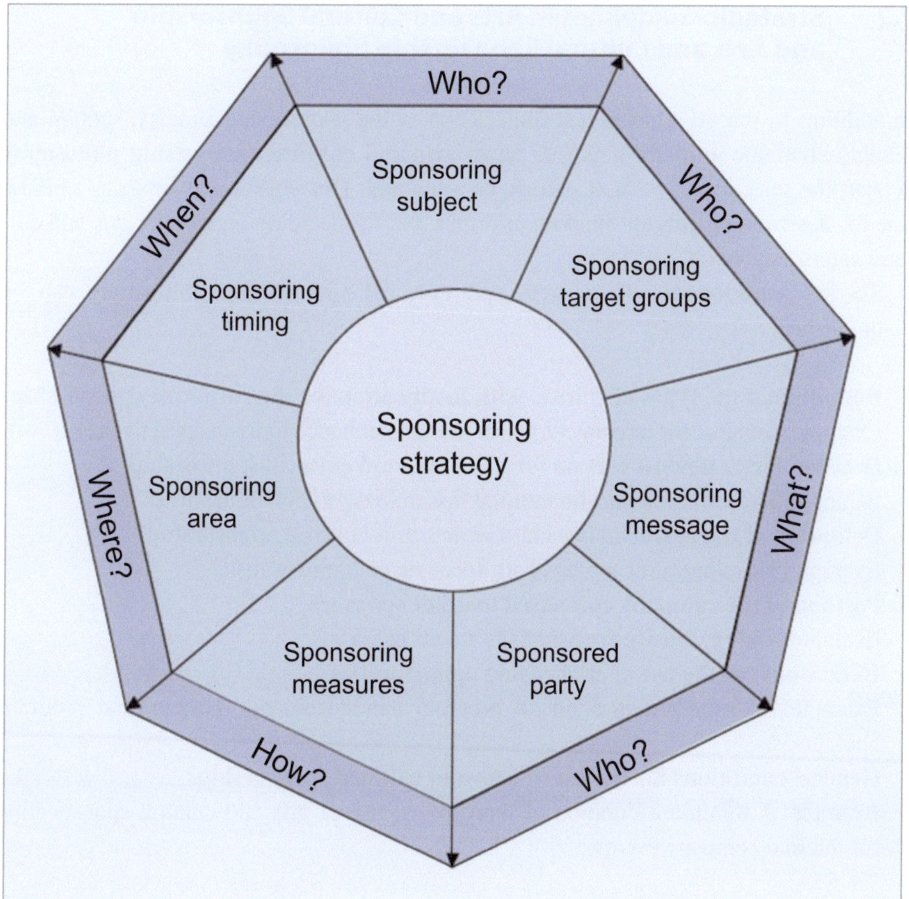

Fig. 7.1 Dimensions of a sponsorship strategy. (*Source* Bruhn, 2018a, p. 59)

- **Sponsoring area:** By deciding on the sponsoring area, a corporate sponsorship determines whether its sponsoring activities are primarily focused on the local, regional, national, or international cultural landscape and its actors.
- **Sponsorship timing:** This involves deciding on the temporal allocation of the sponsorship activity. Sponsorship timing, i.e., the determination of the timeframe and the intensity of the individual measures, is closely linked to the content of the message. For example, a comprehensive image campaign requires a different temporal design than measures for the launch of a new product. The duration of an engagement in arts and cultural sponsorship must therefore be contractually fixed.

7.2 Strategic Guidelines in Arts and Cultural Sponsorship and Arts and Cultural Sponsorship Philosophy

In addition to the aforementioned dimensions of the sponsorship strategy, written and binding **strategic guidelines** as well as an **arts and cultural sponsorship philosophy** support the selection of cultural areas to be promoted. This philosophy serves as a guideline for determining cultural funding priorities and for deciding on specific arts and cultural sponsorships.

Six key **components of an arts and cultural sponsorship philosophy** can be distinguished:

1. **Definition of the types of culture with justification for the corporate sponsorship**
   Example: Support for monument preservation to enhance tourism attractiveness.
2. **Decision for or against certain forms of arts and cultural sponsorship**
   Example: Exclusive support for cultural institutions, no individual artists.
3. **Definition of the performance class in arts and cultural sponsorship**
   Example: No support for top-level art, focus on emerging artists.
4. **Position of the company compared to other sponsors**
   Example: Only exclusive sponsorships are accepted.
5. **Conditions for the use of advertising opportunities**
   Example: Sponsor presence on all program announcements, posters, and program booklets.
6. **General conditions for the use of arts and cultural sponsorships**
   Example: A minimum duration of three years, use of arts and cultural sponsorships for internal company events.

The scope of guidelines or principles for arts and cultural sponsorships varies greatly in terms of content and level of detail. For example, the spray can manufacturer Montana Cans requires only documentation of the artwork by photos or video recordings as a condition for providing free spray cans to street artists (Montana Cans, 2016). The Migros Culture Percentage ("Migros-Kulturprozent"), on the other hand, provides a much more detailed guideline for those seeking sponsorship. As an example of strategic guidelines, key excerpts from the **Guideline for Funding Contributions to Cultural Projects** are quoted below (Migros-Genossenschafts-Bund, 2023b). It is helpful for applicant cultural organizations as well as decision-makers on the sponsor's side (Migros) that the guidelines not only specify what is funded, but also clearly communicate which projects are excluded from funding.

Example: Guidelines for culture funding contributions of the Migros Cooperative Association

General Provisions

1.1 With its culture funding contributions, Migros Culture Percentage supports outstanding cultural creation with substantial financial resources. The aim is to enable artists to enjoy artistic freedom and thus promote the diversity of cultural life in Switzerland.

1.2 The supported fields include visual arts, comics, film, jazz, classical music, cabaret, literature, pop, digital culture, dance, theater, as well as cross-disciplinary projects.

1.3 Supported are promising approaches and pilot projects that take artistic risks and receive little or no support from other funding institutions.

1.4 Our funding targets cultural creation that

- is contemporary (i.e., relevant to current discourse),
- aims to be implemented professionally,
- is distinctive (i.e., stands out in terms of content and quality),
- is or will soon be relevant to a broader audience,
- is guided by overarching social values such as diversity, integration, participation, and accessibility,
- actively shapes cultural life in Switzerland,
- is of supraregional significance or, as a regional pilot project, has the potential to become so,
- is innovative, i.e., is genuinely perceived as novel by audiences. (…)

1.9 Merely fulfilling the formal criteria is not sufficient to receive funding. The decisive factor is the quality of the project.

(…)

Migros Culture Percentage supports high-quality projects and initiatives in the following artistic creation phases:

- Ideation
- Diffusion

Funding Criteria in the Area of Ideation

In the area of ideation, activities that serve artistic idea development are supported. Projects from all artistic fields we support (see 1.2.) as well as cross-disciplinary projects are considered. Supported are projects at the beginning of the artistic creation process, where ideas are articulated, research is conducted, and experiments are undertaken. Both artists and organizations that support and disseminate culture are eligible to apply. (…)

Funding Criteria in the Area of Diffusion

In the area of diffusion, activities are supported that enable and promote the repeated presentation and supraregional dissemination of cultural creation to audiences. Projects from all artistic fields we support (see 1.2.) are considered. Supported are diffusion concepts and projects that pursue innovative presentation strategies, question the conditions of diffusion, and demonstrate engagement with changing media and art reception. Also supported are artistic endeavors that move beyond traditional disciplinary thinking, set a counterpoint to common diffusion formats, and place the exchange between artists and audiences at the center. Both artists and organizations that support and disseminate culture are eligible to apply. (…)

Exclusion Criteria in the Areas of Ideation and Diffusion
The following are not supported:

- Production costs
- Projects that have already been completed
- Applications submitted too late
- Infrastructure or operating costs
- Deficit guarantees
- Institutions abroad
- Performances abroad
- Translations
- Amateur culture
- Commercial projects
- Commissioned works
- Projects of a regional character (except pilot projects)
- Charity events
- Private and benefit events
- Fundraising campaigns
- Purchase of musical instruments or museum exhibits
- Installation of art in buildings
- Projects by schools, universities of applied sciences, or universities
- Projects created as bachelor's, master's, or diploma theses in an educational context
- Projects related to scientific research
- Didactic projects
- Requests for scholarships
- Monographic projects, especially monographic publications
- Non-contemporary directions in all fields (except classical music)
- Field-specific projects in photography, design, and architecture (without involvement of other fields)
- Services to be provided under subsidy agreements ◄

The so-called Migros-Kulturprozent (Culture Percentage) of the Migros Cooperative Association has a long tradition in Switzerland (since 1957) and demonstrates a highly professional approach in the strategic orientation of arts and cultural funding. Despite this positive example of corporate guidelines in arts and cultural sponsorship, the list should not obscure the fact that **written rules for arts and cultural funding** have not yet been adopted by all corporate sponsors. Since many corporate sponsors are active in numerous cultural fields and therefore run the risk of "spreading themselves too thin," it is advisable to set priorities in arts and cultural funding and sponsorship through thorough analysis.

The guidelines and the criteria derived from them also form the basis for a **checklist** that corporate sponsors use to select externally offered (third-party initiated) sponsorships. Fig. 7.2 shows an example of such a formalized procedure. In this decision matrix, for example, sponsorships are evaluated based on how well they can be justified internally and in the market, and to what extent the sponsorships are suitable for addressing various corporate target groups.

Evaluation criteria	Weighting factor	Point value (from 10 = very good to 1 = very bad)	Weighted score
How well does the sponsorship match the sponsorship strategy?			
Does the sponsorship reach the target groups?			
Can the sponsored party ensure that the sponsorship is carried out professionally?			
Do the main competitors carry out similar sponsorships?			
Is a medium to long-term commitment with the sponsored party possible?			
How is the expected media impact of the sponsorship to be assessed?			
Can the sponsorship be integrated within the company?			
Has the sponsorship achieved a dominant position as a sponsor?			
How is the price-performance ratio to be assessed?			
Sum of the weighted point values			

Fig. 7.2 Decision matrix for the selection of sponsorships

7.3 Types of Strategy in Arts and Cultural Sponsorship

The desired sponsorship objectives are achieved through **alignment with the company's communication strategy**. In this context, the strategy for arts and cultural sponsorship must first be brought into harmony with the company's fundamental communication objectives. It is necessary to analyze which communication problem the corporate sponsorship is expected to solve in the medium term and to what extent the use of arts and cultural sponsorship contributes to solving this problem. This may relate to updating a brand, launching a new product with specific image dimensions, addressing customer segments in a differentiated manner, profiling against competitors, and similar objectives.

According to the affinity concept (Waite, 1979; Bruhn, 2024; see also Sect. 8.2), various lines of connection are conceivable, which—as shown in Fig. 7.3—can serve as the basis for strategy development. A rough distinction can be made between the following **types of strategy in arts and cultural sponsorship**:

- **Performance profiling strategy**
  The prerequisite for pursuing a performance profiling strategy is the existence of a relationship between the sponsor's offering and the situation of the sponsored party. For example, the brand Boss, manufacturer of loop stations, acts as a sponsor at the German Beat Box Competition. The participants in the competition use Boss devices on stage, providing a virtuoso demonstration of the products' capabilities (see the

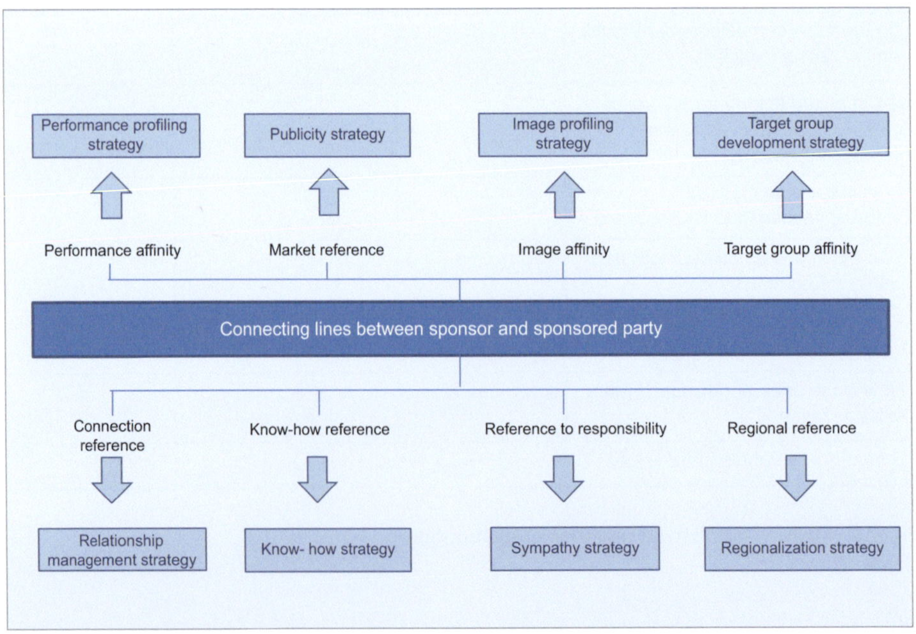

Fig. 7.3 Types of strategy in arts and cultural sponsorship based on the affinity concept. (*Source* adapted from Bruhn, 2018a, p. 226)

Beat Box Germany case study in Chap. 9). In addition, payment service providers such as PayPal frequently act as sponsors of festivals, as the advantages of cashless transactions can be experienced in practice at a festival (see Fig. 7.4). Often, the sponsorship cooperation means that the festival audience has no alternative but to use the payment service, since, for example, all transactions for drinks, catering, or merchandise are processed using NFC technology (Near Field Communication) and the payment service provider's software.

- **Awareness strategy**
  An awareness strategy aims to increase the recognition and acceptance of products or brands among customers and other market participants. This applies equally to existing products or brands as well as to new products. Consequently, this strategy focuses on the pure presentation of the product, company, or brand name. For example, music

Festival top-up station of the sponsor PayPal.

Presentation of the sponsor PayPal on a festival stage.

Fig. 7.4 PayPal as a festival sponsor and the provision of charging stations for NFC chips in festival wristbands

festivals are suitable for launching new beverage brands, as a large number of people can try the drinks in a short period of time, and the consumption situation is associated with the festival atmosphere. Automobile manufacturers repeatedly use cultural events to offer VIP shuttle services, thereby enabling selected target groups to experience the benefits of new vehicles.

Through creative staging, other products can also be made known through cultural collaborations. For example, the shower gel manufacturer Axe built the “Axe Festival Shower” at the Wacken Open Air rock festival, where festivalgoers could shower and were provided with “Axe Cool Metal Shower Gel” and towels (Wacken, 2023).

The presentation of new products is usually documented using multimedia, so that after the cultural sponsorship event, the content can be repurposed for social media.

- **Image profiling strategy**
  An image profiling strategy targets specific image dimensions of a brand or company, which are realized or reinforced in the minds of target groups through the sponsored areas. The profiling strategy can relate to various image dimensions of a brand. These are derived from the brand’s Unique Selling Proposition (USP) and may include factors such as sustainability, service, price, exclusivity, quality features, and more. For example, the science and technology company Merck supports numerous cultural activities in Darmstadt to position itself as a significant cultural sponsor in the region. Merck is the main sponsor and long-standing partner of the multi-day Schlossgrabenfest in Darmstadt (Merck, 2023).
- **Target group development strategy**
  A target group development strategy focuses on specific target groups, such as young people, whose engagement with a product or brand is additionally sought. This strategy is particularly suitable for cultural offerings that reach a clearly defined target group. While, for example, municipal museums often have a very broad target group orientation, sponsors can address much more specific target groups and thus reduce wastage by cooperating with techno clubs or a classical opera festival.
- **Relationship maintenance strategy**
  A relationship maintenance strategy focuses on establishing and maintaining contacts and relationships with relevant target groups with the aim of enhancing relationship management and customer loyalty. Cultural events are suitable for relationship management by inviting particularly important customers or business partners to the events and hosting them in VIP areas.
- **Know-how strategy**
  A know-how strategy is based on the fact that some corporate sponsors, due to their market activities, possess special know-how or particular internal capabilities to support specific sponsorship areas. The resources or potentials available in corporate sponsorship, i.e., personnel, products, or services, are used to actively support specific culture-related challenges. For example, a law firm might advise a cultural organization on legal matters, or a tax advisor’s office might assist a cultural association with accounting. Through their sponsorship commitments, corporate sponsors demonstrate

their special knowledge and skills externally, in order to make these known to a broader audience and to position themselves against the competition. This strategy is thus similar to the performance profiling strategy mentioned above. However, while performance profiling aims to communicate the company's core offering, the know-how strategy can also involve expertise that is not part of the company's direct service portfolio, such as the agile management competence of a start-up.

- **Sympathy strategy**
  Pursuing a sympathy strategy in sponsorship requires the existence of a sense of responsibility between a corporate sponsor and the sponsorship object. This involves the company's ethical obligation to address social or ecological problems and contribute to their solution. This can be seen, for example, in cultural partnerships with energy companies that produce green electricity, or in collaboration with environmental service providers that enable sustainable cultural productions. Compared to the strategy options presented so far, credibility is of particular importance in the sympathy strategy, as the company must fulfill the responsibility it has assumed. For the sponsoring corporate sponsor, it is necessary to credibly communicate to target groups which factual and personal motives are significant for its commitment. As credibility increases, so does the likelihood that corporate sponsors can build sympathy through their engagement and thus achieve positive communicative effects. Conversely, if there is a lack of "fit" between the sponsorship and the brand, product, or service, reactance may arise among the public and the company's target groups.
- **Regionalization strategy**
  When pursuing a regionalization strategy, the central prerequisite is that a regional connection between sponsor and sponsored party is recognizable. For many corporate sponsors, it is not the supraregional but the local or regional reach of a cultural sponsorship commitment that is important. This is derived, for example, from a sales market limited to the region, as is the case with municipal utilities, savings banks, or municipal real estate/construction companies.

Figure 7.5 provides a **summary of the types of strategy** and gives examples of the objectives pursued, how they should be designed, and which examples can be used as illustrations.

The individual types of strategy in arts and cultural sponsorship place different emphases and, in practice, often appear in mixed forms. Of fundamental strategic importance is whether corporate sponsorship as a sponsor focuses on regional, national, or international sponsorship engagements. Here, the **importance of company size for arts and cultural sponsorship** plays a role. Large companies are often more diverse, and more nationally and internationally involved. The significance of regionally limited sponsorships is often underestimated.

In particular, regionally limited sponsorship in culture is able to place messages precisely for target groups and minimize wastage. Such engagements are often underestimated. Its impact can be managed as precisely as in few other marketing disciplines.

Strategy types	Goals	Design	Examples
Performance profiling	Proof of competence and reputation for the sponsor's performance	Credible performance - accountability for the sponsored party's performance	Boss, PayPal
Publicity	Perception, awareness and acceptance	Massive sponsorship with high reach and intensive presence	Axe, beverage manufacturer
Image profiling	Image enhancement, credibility, positive customer attitude	Sponsorship design more as a cultural promoter than as use for commercial purposes	Merck
Target group development	Concentration on market participants with certain characteristics, customer acquisition	Concentrated use of funds in the living and cultural environment of said groups	Companies with a very specific target group with an affinity for culture
Relationship management	Establishing and expanding contacts, increased customer loyalty	Supporting the target groups in their private environment through presence and consumer offers	Companies with key account CRM or B2B activities (e.g. DHL)
Know-how	Proof of special know-how for the implementation of cultural events	Large part of sponsorship as a service, e.g. legal advice	Lawyers, tax consultants
Sympathy	Making known and acceptance of fundamental responsibility between sponsor and sponsored party	Sponsoring as a contribution to better fulfillment of social and climate policy goals of the sponsored party	Energy companies, environmental and climate service providers
Regionalization	Awareness of a regional connection between sponsor and sponsored party	Sponsorship contribution to solving regional or local issues, promotion of local cultural offerings	Companies with a strong local or regional focus such as municipal utilities, savings banks, etc.

Fig. 7.5 Summary presentation of different types of strategy in arts and cultural sponsorship

Sponsorship is also established and popular in the **communication mix of small and medium-sized corporate sponsorships**. Reaching selected target groups in a focused, emotional environment without disruption usually enables a higher contact quality compared to traditional communication instruments. Positive side effects, such as national reach beyond the region, are also possible and can be deliberately factored in depending on the design of the partnership.

In arts and cultural sponsorship with a regional character, aspects of **local affiliation** and internal **networking with employees** play a particularly important role. For sponsors involved in local or regional cultural work, the focus of engagement is less on increasing awareness or image transfer. For locally and regionally active corporate sponsorships, the main concern in most cases is **social engagement** and making a contribution to the community for people at the company location, i.e., the primary motivation is support. Especially for small and medium-sized corporate sponsorships, it is more or less part of their social responsibility to contribute to the cultural offerings, the cultural engagement of the population, or other topics in the region. Cultural associations in particular benefit from such engagement and are, to a large extent, dependent on it. Here, sponsorship is often practiced in connection with the civic or overall societal engagement of corporate sponsorships—also known as corporate social responsibility (CSR) (see, e.g., Asongu, 2007)—which is why it is sometimes referred to as **responsible sponsoring** (S20, 2021).

Regional (cultural) sponsorship offers numerous opportunities. The **advantages of regional sponsorship** include, in particular, the following arguments:

- It is concrete, personally tangible, and the sponsor can actively contribute ideas.
- It takes place in the immediate neighborhood and shows that the corporate sponsor also wants to be involved as a "good neighbor."
- It happens in front of employees, gives them the opportunity to participate, and therefore has a strong internal impact.
- It improves relationships with the people the regional sponsor deals with every day, whether customers, local media, politicians, or government representatives.
- It supports sponsors in recruiting employees for the corporate sponsor.

From a corporate perspective, the **credibility of sponsorship** is the most important success factor. A partnership is perceived as credible and positively evaluated by the public, especially when a cultural association or a municipal cultural institution and its sponsor are a good fit. This is the case, among other things, when the sponsor's target groups and products as well as its image match the cultural offering, the sponsor can demonstrate a regional connection to the cultural content or institution, and a medium- to long-term partnership is agreed upon.

Every corporate sponsor interested in sponsorship will, as part of its strategic considerations, think about which focus it wants to set within the above-mentioned types of strategy in arts and cultural sponsorship, and which engagement best aligns with its objectives. This does not always have to be the usual route of classic sponsorship of established and high-profile cultural "flagships," but can also be achieved through the **support of cultural niche offerings**. Such opportunities can be differentiated according to criteria such as scope (e.g., regional, supraregional, national, international), level of performance (amateur ensembles, professional cultural providers, stars), effort (large or small, over- or under-proportional), as well as restrictions (e.g., of a legal nature) (see Fig. 7.6).

In addition, the possibilities and **classic manifestations** of arts and cultural sponsorship can be distinguished as mainstream sponsorship and niche sponsorship:

Mainstream sponsorship

Mainstream engagement refers to collaborations with supraregional established cultural institutions, which generally appeal to broader target group segments and have greater media perception. These include, for example, cultural "flagships" such as state art museums, multi-genre venues, or large music festivals of various genres.

Such engagement is generally associated with considerable time and financial investment and relates to at least supraregional or national presence. Since these institutions often have a high proportion of cultural tourists in their audience segments, the communication objective of international presence can also be supported.

This form of arts and cultural sponsorship is mainly found among large companies that are involved with large communication budgets. These corporate sponsors often

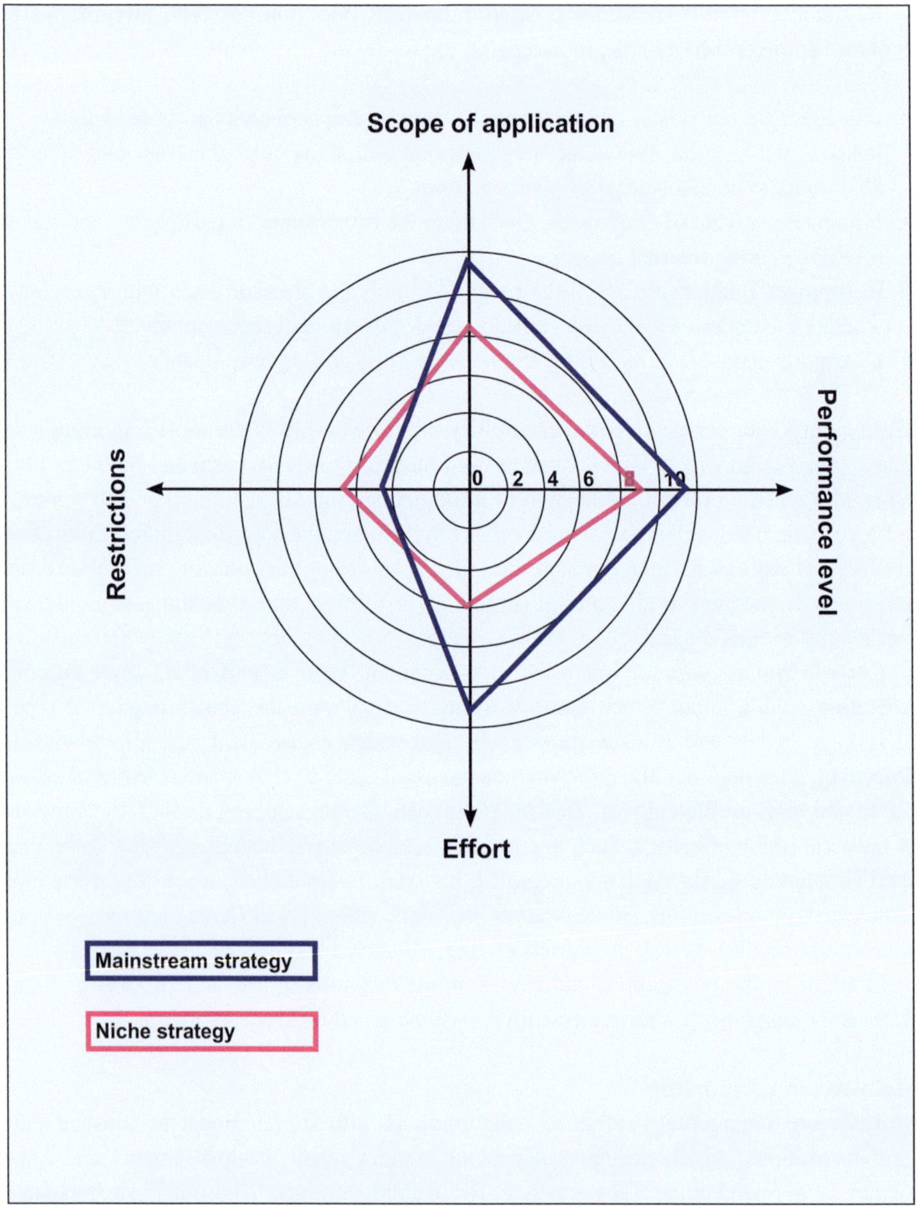

Fig. 7.6 Manifestations in arts and cultural sponsorship (exemplary presentation)

pursue strategies that are cross-border and use arts and cultural sponsorship as a marketing instrument very professionally, as can be seen, for example, from the main sponsors of the Salzburg Festival 2023 or the Bayreuth Festival (as of May 2023):

- Main sponsors of the Salzburg Festival 2023: Audi, Siemens, Rolex, BWT.
- Main sponsors of the Bayreuth Festival 2023: Commerzbank, American Express, PwC.

Niche Sponsorship

The examples shown illustrate that mainstream sponsorship is not equally suitable for all corporate sponsorships. Due to the high costs and broad target group definition, mainstream sponsorship can be too complex and inefficient for many corporate sponsorships. In contrast to mainstream sponsorship, **niche sponsorship** can also be considered, which focuses on target group segments that are less frequently addressed in mainstream sponsorship, such as children and adolescents. In addition, niche sponsorship can refer to engagements in cultural sectors that are also underrepresented in the mainstream, such as experimental new music, performance art, or amateur art.

A niche sponsorship is usually aimed at a narrower target group. This can be less of a disadvantage and more of an advantage, because with better information about the size and nature of the target group or audience, there is hardly any wasted coverage. After all, a niche sponsor is not just one among many, but can become more intensively involved and finds a greater **opportunity for co-creation and development** with the sponsored party.

In addition to more efficient use of reach, niche sponsorship is also suitable for stronger brand profiling, as the relationship between the cultural offering and the sponsor allows for more individual and unusual narratives in **sponsorship storytelling** than is often the case with mainstream sponsorship: The shuttle service of a premium car brand at an internationally established art event may underscore the brand's leadership in its industry, but it does not provide a new "story"; rather, it reinforces familiar images of a sponsorship engagement. Supporting young cultural creators, on the other hand, allows for the development of personal and individual stories that help the sponsor communicate a commitment to support authentically.

Example: "Jugend musiziert" (Youth makes music)

"Jugend musiziert" is the largest music competition in Germany. The competition was founded in 1963 and has so far recorded over one million participants. Jugend musiziert is organized at the regional, state, and federal levels. In various constellations (solo or ensemble categories), young people between the ages of eight and 22 compete, divided into eight age groups. Particularly good performance at the regional level leads to advancement to the state level, and with another very good performance, advancement to the federal level. Unlike sports competitions, Jugend musiziert does not have only one first place. The highest score of 25 points can (theoretically) be awarded any number of times, so that the musicians are not in direct competition with each other.

The Deutsche Sparkassen- und Giroverband (German Savings Banks and Giro Association), or the Sparkassen Finanzgruppe (Savings Banks Finance Group), has supported "Jugend musiziert" as the main sponsor since 1963. The sponsorship engagement includes financial support, the awarding of special prizes and scholarships, assistance in organizing concerts, and even financial services. For example, the Sparkassen Finance Group regularly awards the "Sparkassen Special Prize for Particularly Meritorious Achievements by a Family Ensemble," which is endowed with 5000 EUR.

The "Jugend musiziert" engagement falls under arts and cultural sponsorship and represents the largest area of support for the Sparkassen Finance Group. In total, the group supported arts and cultural projects amounting to 107 million EUR in 2021 (Deutscher Musikrat, 2023; DSVG, 2022). The nationwide engagement of the Sparkassen Finance Group is also implemented at the regional level through cultural sponsorship cooperations of municipal institutions with the organization of regional competitions. For example, the Bank Kreissparkasse Böblingen supports the local regional competition and regularly organizes concerts in its own premises with prize winners and young musicians. After the event, it is publicized by the Kreissparkasse's public relations work, including social media posts (see Fig. 7.7). ◀

The following provides insights into the **arts and cultural sponsorship strategy of the DHL Group**. The case study shows how the DHL Group creatively stages and communicates its core service as an international logistics provider through cultural engagement initiatives.

7.3.1 Case Study: Cultural Engagement of the DHL Group

Initial Situation

The **DHL Group** is a globally leading logistics group, employing around 600,000 people and generating over 94 billion EUR in revenue in 2022. The group's best-known brands are:

- DHL (the name derives from the founders Adrian Dalsey, Larry Hillblom, and Robert Lynn) is a service provider for parcel shipping, international express shipping, freight transport, supply chain management, and e-commerce solutions.
- Deutsche Post is Europe's leading postal and parcel service provider.

The DHL Group is divided into five **business divisions**. These include:

- Express (transport of urgent documents and goods),
- Global Forwarding, Freight (international freight forwarding services for air, sea, and land transport),
- Supply Chain (customized logistics services and supply chain solutions),

Fig. 7.7 Media utilization of the cultural engagement of Kreissparkasse Böblingen using the example of support for "Jugend musiziert"

- E-Commerce (domestic last-mile parcel deliveries),
- Post and Parcel Germany (transport, sorting, and delivery of documents and goods in Germany as well as export to the rest of the world). The Post and Parcel Germany division accounted for approximately 17.3% of the DHL Group's total revenue in 2022.

The group headquarters is located in Bonn, Germany, from where the marketing of the DHL Group as well as its arts and cultural sponsorship is organized.

The **cultural engagement of the DHL Group** did not start suddenly due to a single event, but has developed over many years. Two areas of cultural engagement can be distinguished: on the one hand, the support and realization of cultural offerings at the location of the group headquarters in Bonn; on the other hand, there are supraregional cultural partnerships in which DHL participates as a sponsor.

Depending on the target group and the regional reach of a measure, the group appears as DHL Group or as Deutsche Post (German postal service). Since the Deutsche Post brand is less well known internationally compared to the DHL Group, the DHL brand is generally used in communication for international cooperations.

Objectives and Target Groups

Arts and cultural sponsorship is understood by the DHL Group as an interactive communication tool. In this context, various **objectives of arts and cultural sponsorship** are pursued. For example, it supports the Group in engaging with different target groups and achieving a positive image transfer. The individual measures are aimed at creating experiences that evoke positive emotions—for instance, by giving the local community the opportunity to attend cultural events at the Post Tower, the company's headquarters in Bonn. About a quarter of all concerts of the Beethoven Festival sponsored by DHL, for example, take place in the Post Tower.

The **target groups of arts and cultural sponsorship** can be distinguished internally and externally, as well as geographically. Since DHL is a major employer in Bonn, the approximately 8000 employees and their families are part of the internal target group on site. At the same time, there is significant overlap with the regional external target group, the Bonn community. The Group sees itself as part of the city and thus aims to position itself as part of the local community and Bonn's cultural landscape. The many experiences created as touchpoints with corporate sponsorship at cultural events support the image goal of being a committed, responsible, and approachable company. The interactive staging through participatory activities and the emotionalization through cultural offerings enable a perception of the company that goes far beyond an association with the topic of transport.

On a supraregional and international level, the target groups are more narrowly defined. The image objectives are also broken down more specifically by submarket in order to make them more measurable as part of the evaluation. In the case of **supraregional and international cultural engagements**, the measures are more strongly aimed at customers and especially B2B partners, who are, for example, specifically invited to customer events.

Strategic Orientation

The DHL Group is a logistics expert. Therefore, as a strategic principle, it seeks to highlight this **performance competence** through arts and cultural sponsorship.

In the case of **regional engagement**, there is also a strong identification with the composer Ludwig van Beethoven, who was born in Bonn in 1770. Bonn positions itself as the city of Beethoven and celebrated the composer's 250th birthday in 2020 with numerous events. The DHL Group is also involved as a supporter of the Beethoven Festival, the Beethoven House, and other initiatives in preserving and communicating Beethoven's cultural heritage. For the DHL Group, the connection to Beethoven can also be argued beyond the regional link: Beethoven himself was a customer of the postal service—when the musician sent letters in the 18th century, the postal service had already existed for around 250 years. Moreover, Beethoven is regarded in music history as a disruptor due to his innovative creativity. The DHL Group also sees itself as a disruptor, continually transforming global transportation through logistical innovations, from the introduction of the postal system to the invention of express shipping, which is now part of everyday life as e-commerce.

A key **focus of the DHL Group's arts and cultural sponsorship** is the promotion of music. This support is not limited to Beethoven but extends well beyond the classical genre. Indie and electronic festivals as well as jazz concerts are also supported. In addition, the DHL Group sponsors literary events, a video art biennial, and various art projects, ranging from temporary exhibitions to art in architecture, such as the Mercurius by Marcus Lüpertz in front of the company headquarters or the light installation by the Breton artist Yann Kersalé at the Post Tower. However, an analysis of all cultural sponsorship projects shows a strategic focus on the music sector.

In principle, the DHL Group supports its partners through **sponsorship services** such as providing venues, logistics services, financial resources, consulting, and promoting the sponsored event. No influence is exerted on the content design. An exception was a traveling exhibition on the occasion of the major Beethoven anniversary in 2020. This was curated in cooperation with DHL and enabled interested parties worldwide to view particularly valuable exhibits, such as Beethoven's ear trumpet (see Fig. 7.8).

Selection of Sponsorships

The decision for or against an arts and cultural sponsorship depends in particular on the following **key questions**:

- Which target groups are reached through the engagement, and do these align with the target groups of the DHL Group?
- What image transfer is likely to be generated by the cooperation?

Fig. 7.8 Exhibition of Beethoven's ear trumpet as part of the DHL project "BTHVN on Tour"

- To what extent can the project be considered sustainable from economic, ecological, and social perspectives?
- What costs are associated with the project?

In addition, the **duration of a cooperation** or existing partnerships is important, as the DHL Group is interested in long-term collaboration with its partners. Thus, continuing a successful, existing engagement is more important than supporting short-term individual initiatives. This assessment is based on the consideration that the end of a partnership is always taken into account from the outset. It would be counterproductive if, after a short funding period, no new arts and cultural sponsorship were established and the Group were suddenly perceived by the public as an obstacle to culture rather than an enabler.

Potential partnerships are discussed, depending on the investment volume, with the DHL Group's Board or a **sponsorship decision-making committee**, taking into account the strategic orientation. For partnerships at the Bonn location, there is also regular exchange with other relevant cultural sponsors, in particular Deutsche Telekom, Sparkasse, and the municipal utilities. If a cultural project is already supported by another corporate sponsorship, this is not a criterion for exclusion for DHL Group's own involvement. There is a transparent dialogue among cultural sponsors regarding funding projects. This makes it more difficult for applicants to (rarely) attempt to play the partners off against each other by claiming that another corporate sponsor has already agreed to a partnership.

The **selection of a suitable partnership** for the DHL Group can be illustrated by the example of the Gewandhaus Orchestra in Leipzig (see also the case study on the Gewandhaus Orchestra in Chap. 3): The Gewandhaus Orchestra is one of the world's leading orchestras and provides the basis for a positive image transfer. In addition, the orchestra serves the strategic focus on music promotion. Through its many tours and orchestra trips, the Gewandhaus Orchestra also offers the opportunity to highlight the core competence of logistics, as transport services must be organized not only for the musicians but also for particularly valuable instruments. Furthermore, the partnership can also be justified by a local connection, as the DHL Group operates its largest global hub in Leipzig and is also a major employer there through its corporate sponsorship.

Measures for Implementing Sponsorships

The **measures of arts and cultural sponsorship** are not limited to brand presentation through logo integration on the media of cultural partners. Rather, actions are taken that either make the services of the DHL Group tangible or lead to a positive emotional experience. For example, at the Panama Openair, a "Panama Post Office" was set up. On site, the audience had the opportunity to send pre-stamped postcards, onto which photos of the visitors were printed.

At the Wacken Openair music festival, the DHL Group also presented itself with its own "Mail and Parcel Office" (see Figs. 7.9 and 7.10), where a limited edition Wacken

Fig. 7.9 DHL presentation with a post office branch at Wacken Openair 2023

Fig. 7.10 Interior view of the post office branch at Wacken Openair 2023

Fig. 7.11 Limited special edition stamp for Wacken Openair 2023

stamp was issued on site, which quickly became a collector's item among festivalgoers (see Fig. 7.11).

In addition to these event-specific measures, numerous other **corporate communications instruments** are also used, such as:

- Placement of advertisements in the publications of cultural partners,
- Production of films as promotional material for subsequent events,
- Accompanying events such as panel discussions, exhibition openings, exhibitions, concerts,
- Tours of the Post Tower Bonn (in connection with cultural events),
- Organization of prize draws (e.g., ticket raffles for concert tickets to sponsored events),
- Social media communication (in addition to the company's own posts, there are also collaborations with cultural partners, who publish posts as part of the cooperation on their own social media channels in their own corporate design).

For the **implementation of the measures**, agencies are occasionally used, with these being regarded as an "extended workbench." In principle, the aim is to implement as much as possible in-house. This applies in particular to all conceptual and creative tasks. Agencies and other external service providers are brought in for implementation, for example in the areas of event technology, event security, or advertising design.

Integration into Overall Communication

For the **activation of a cultural sponsorship project**, ideally the same amount is invested as the base costs for the partnership. All communication disciplines are also integrated into the partnerships in order to utilize both internal and external channels and to leverage the expertise of colleagues.

Examples of **measures** include:

- “Money-can’t-buy” activities (e.g., the opportunity to experience a performance on Beethoven’s viola at a customer event),
- Outdoor advertising through posters,
- Postcard campaigns,
- Social media communication on the company’s own channels,
- Announcements on the company’s own website,
- Placement of advertisements,
- Guerrilla communication (e.g., promotional activities in pubs),
- Publication of press releases,
- Dialogue marketing through invitations.

Evaluation

The measures carried out are comprehensively evaluated. This applies both to the company’s own activation measures and to the communication activities associated with the cultural project.

The following are evaluated, for example:

- People reached on site and through the various communication media,
- Number of responses from audience surveys,
- Number and quality of media coverage through press clippings,
- Social media metrics (e.g., reach, engagement, etc.),
- Number and quality of generated leads (e.g., through prize draws).

In addition to economic indicators, personal sentiment also plays an important role in evaluating a cultural sponsorship project. **The experience of those responsible for cultural sponsorship** at DHL Group shows that a good feeling after a project is usually reflected in the figures obtained.

Especially in Bonn, in addition to economic indicators, it is important to be perceived as an **authentic supporter**. This is achieved through long-standing personal relationships and by ensuring that not every form of support is subject to an obvious communicative exploitation logic. These relationships and effects within the city community are of great importance to DHL Group, but can only be measured to a limited extent with established evaluation tools. A holistic assessment of the commitment is therefore less about key figures and more about evaluation by expert panels. For example, in 2020 DHL Group (then still under the name Deutsche Post DHL Group) received the award "European Cultural Investor of the Year" after its cultural engagement was evaluated by a jury.

Key Points

1. **Create clarity about objectives:** The objectives of marketing and corporate communication must be clearly defined. The relevance and use of arts and cultural sponsorship should be examined in line with the objectives of marketing and corporate communication and assessed based on sponsorship guidelines.
2. **Consider decision dimensions:** All decision dimensions in arts and cultural sponsorship, such as subject, target groups, message, sponsored parties, measures, geographic area, and time aspect, must be considered as the foundation of a professional sponsorship concept.
3. **Actively seek out engagements:** Suitable sponsorship engagements should be actively sought and shaped. New sponsorship areas and forms can often offer better communicative competitive advantages than overcrowded, conventional sponsorship platforms.
4. **Monitor significance and trends:** The significance and trends of sponsorship types should be monitored in order to recognize and take into account the development of public interest in various leisure fields as well as the acceptance of different areas.
5. **Integrate and coordinate sponsorship:** Sponsorship should be developed as a central communication platform and integrated and coordinated with other communication and sales activities, with strategic priorities aligned to the corporate perspective and competition as appropriate.
6. **Consider other forms of sponsorship:** The use of other forms such as niche and regional sponsorship should be weighed in order to better achieve corporate and marketing objectives, rather than always taking the classic route via established cultural "flagships."
7. **Use arts and cultural sponsorship philosophy as a reference framework:** An arts and cultural sponsorship philosophy should serve as a reference framework for defining the individual elements of a sponsorship strategy. This framework includes, among other things, the determination of the supported arts and cultural sectors and the selection of the organizational framework.
8. **Clearly formulate principles:** Your own principles and guidelines for arts and cultural sponsorship should be formulated clearly and precisely to avoid scatter losses or misguided engagements, especially in view of limited resources.

9. **Use sponsorship in the communication mix:** Sponsorship should also be used in the communication mix of small and medium-sized corporate sponsorships to reach selected local and regional target groups more effectively in a manageable emotional environment than with traditional communication instruments.
10. **Regularly review sponsorship:** Sponsorship activities should be regularly reviewed and the cost-benefit ratio continuously evaluated in order to deploy key engagements efficiently and draw strategic conclusions.

Selection of Arts and Cultural Sponsorships

8

Contents

8.1 Levels of the Selection Decision . . . 181
8.2 Initial Selection of Arts and Cultural Sectors According to the Affinity Concept . . . 182
8.3 Detailed Selection by Cultural Offerings and Sectors . . . 186
8.4 Termination of Sponsorship Agreements . . . 188

Abstract

The selection of cultural sectors and specific cultural institutions with which a sponsorship cooperation is to be established involves both strategic and tactical decisions. This chapter first describes the strategic process of the initial selection of arts and cultural sponsorships, in which, according to the affinity concept, relationships between sponsor and sponsored party are analyzed at various levels. The subsequent detailed selection addresses specific questions for the development of selection criteria for a sponsorship. Finally, possible communication strategies for terminating sponsorships are also explained. In addition to various practical examples, the chapter also provides an in-depth discussion of the Bayer AG case study.

8.1 Levels of the Selection Decision

The decision for arts and cultural sponsorships follows a **multi-stage process**. Special importance is attached to the selection of the sponsored party. This takes place on two **levels** — the initial selection of the types of art or culture and the detailed selection of sponsorship forms:

M. Bruhn and L. Pöllmann, *Arts and Cultural Sponsorship*,
https://doi.org/10.1007/978-3-658-50079-5_8

1. The **initial selection** involves choosing the cultural sector. This concerns the decision regarding which arts and cultural sectors are suitable for corporate sponsorship, such as theater, music, or street art.
2. As part of the **detailed selection**, the choice of sponsorship forms is made. The focus here is on deciding the form of support within the respective art and cultural form. Possible options include sponsoring individual artists, cultural associations, ensembles, specific cultural institutions, or cultural events.

8.2 Initial Selection of Arts and Cultural Sectors According to the Affinity Concept

A central aspect in defining an arts and cultural sponsorship strategy is the selection of the arts and cultural sectors. It is advisable to first make an **initial selection** (a fundamental decision about which arts and cultural sectors are relevant for corporate sponsorship), in order to subsequently make a detailed selection and decision about a arts and cultural sponsorship (selection among alternative sponsorships within a cultural sector) based on this foundation and its results.

An important decision criterion in the initial selection of arts and cultural sectors to be supported is the question of the extent to which it is possible to identify **lines of connection** that make the cultural commitment plausible and credible to target groups and the public. These connections relate to the corporate sponsorship itself, its products, or the communication challenge. To answer this question, it is useful to proceed according to the **affinity concept**, which consists of analyzing correspondences between specific corporate and cultural characteristics in order to establish a "fit" between corporate sponsorship and cultural engagement.

For the lines of connection relevant to strategy planning and the resulting patterns of justification, the potential affinities and relationships shown in Fig. 8.1 are placed at the center. As the figure illustrates, the following six **forms of affinities** can be distinguished:

(1) Product Affinity

In the case of product affinity, there is a connection between the cultural engagement and the products or corporate services. An example of **direct product affinity** is the art supply retailer Boesner, which has been a sponsor of the Stuttgart Art Exhibition for many years. The exhibition is organized by the Association for the Promotion of Art in Stuttgart (Verein zur Förderung der Kunst Stuttgart). In November 2022, the exhibition was held for the 32nd time. Artists from all over Germany were invited to showcase their work on more than 320 square meters of exhibition space. The exhibition demonstrates the processing possibilities of the products offered by Boesner and thus has a strong connection to the sponsor's core services. In addition to Boesner, other sponsors include the brush manufacturer da Vinci and the paper brand Hahnemühle, both of which also exhibit a very high product affinity (Verein zur Förderung der Kunst Stuttgart, 2022).

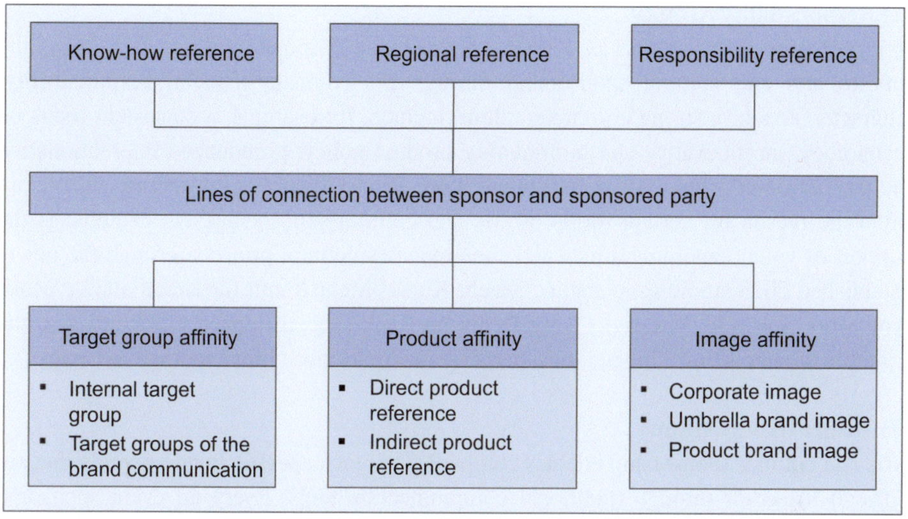

Fig. 8.1 Lines of connection and patterns of justification for corporate sponsorship in arts and cultural sponsorship. (*Source* Bruhn, 2018a, p. 253)

An **indirect product affinity** is exemplified by the "Partners in Preservation" program initiated by American Express in 2006, which supports the preservation of landmarks and monuments as well as tourism. Product affinity exists here because credit cards are typically used when traveling. Another example is the cooperation between the BMW Group and the Solomon R. Guggenheim Foundation, in which the corporate sponsorship supported several exhibitions and workshops under the title "BMW Guggenheim Lab." From 2011 to 2014, this mobile event series was held in New York, Berlin, and Mumbai. Through this cooperation, which was awarded the Kulturmarken-Award (cultural brand award) in 2012, BMW demonstrated its affinity for innovation and, in the mobile research lab, combined urban development, architecture, technology, design, and science. Another example is the cultural engagement of the Swabian family business Alfred Kärcher Vertriebs-GmbH. For over 40 years, the cleaning specialist has been committed to preserving historical monuments worldwide. As part of this project, Kärcher has already supported more than 150 restoration projects around the world, cleaning monuments such as the Brandenburg Gate in Berlin, the Statue of Liberty in New York, the Christ the Redeemer statue in Rio de Janeiro, and the London Eye in London free of charge. The corporate sponsorship thus not only provides financial support but also brings the know-how and commitment of its employees as well as the latest technological equipment to bear. Under the title "Kärcher Cleans the World," the product is ideally showcased through cultural sponsorship, thereby also fostering customer trust in the quality of the cleaning specialist (Schad & Berentzen, 2007; Alfred Kärcher Vertriebs-GmbH, 2016, 2023) (see also the Kärcher case study in Chap. 1).

(2) Responsibility Affinity

If a corporate sponsorship has a strongly developed corporate culture, this forms the link to arts and cultural sponsorship through the company's **social responsibility**. Characteristics of a strong corporate culture include, for example, a consistent focus on technology, an innovative and high-quality product policy, pronounced internationality, the promotion of young talent, and much more. These features of corporate culture are often the reason for certain forms of arts and cultural sponsorship. An example is the support of young emerging artists and contemporary cultural projects through the newly established 2023 studio scholarship "Macht Kunst! Mehr Raum für Kreativität" ("Make Art! More Space for Creativity") by Deutsche Bank (Social Impact, 2023; see also the example of support for "Jugend musiziert" by the Sparkassen Finanzgruppe in Chap. 7).

(3) Target Group Affinity

Arts and cultural sponsorship enables companies to reach **specific target groups** that are difficult to access through traditional communication tools. Every art event sponsored by a corporate sponsor is thus accompanied by invitations to selected customers. For example, the private bank Julius Bär has sponsored the Städel Museum in Frankfurt for many years and offers its clients and business partners exclusive event formats such as private tours outside regular opening hours. In addition to the Städel Museum, the private bank also supports other cultural institutions worldwide that enable targeted communication with select audiences in exclusive settings, such as Art Dubai, the Museu de Arte Moderno de Bogotá, the Museum of Contemporary Design and Applied Arts in Lausanne, or the Montreux Jazz Festival (Julius Bär, 2013, 2023). The aim of such exclusive offerings is, on the one hand, to achieve higher customer loyalty and, on the other, to foster more intensive contact with selected customer groups (Hermanns & Marwitz, 2008, p. 94). As part of the Instagram competition "Take the Wheel" by Mercedes, the corporate sponsor initially provided CLA model vehicles to popular photographers on Instagram. The artist whose artistic documentation of their journeys convinced the most followers was allowed to keep the CLA as a prize. This campaign not only generated increased sales of the featured model for the corporate sponsor but also reached the youngest age group in the company's history (Daimler AG, 2013; McDermott, 2014).

(4) Image Affinity

Arts and cultural sponsorship is associated with the attempt to transfer **positive image attributes** from the cultural and arts sectors to the corporate image. Although arts and cultural sponsorship offers fewer image attributes than sports sponsorship that allow for a direct transfer to corporate sponsors, brands, or products, many corporate sponsors nevertheless emphasize the connection of image as a justification for their cultural activities. For example, Air Canada, Mastercard, and SAP support the tours and performances of Cirque du Soleil (Cirque du Soleil, 2023).

Through such engagements, corporate sponsors seek an **image transfer** from successful ensembles, orchestras, or even rock and pop groups in order to transfer the positive image attributes to their own brand image. According to the phenomenon from "Gestalt theory" known as the **law of proximity**, recipients learn to perceive the similarity of image attributes when there is a lasting closeness between the sponsor and the sponsored party.

A survey on the image of selected classical and modern cultural sectors among 3000 people aged 14 and over, the results of which are shown in Fig. 8.2, found that both musicals and casting shows, comedy, as well as rock and pop music events are predominantly perceived as entertaining. The cultural sector of classical music is mainly seen as conservative, and exhibitions in museums and galleries are perceived as more quality-conscious (Ipsos GmbH, 2008).

(5) Know-how Reference

Various corporate sponsors possess specific know-how or special capabilities to support arts and cultural sectors. For example, the Swiss telecommunications company Swisscom supports events such as the Energy Live Sessions or the One FM Star Night by offering, in addition to classic product sponsorship, know-how in the form of creative mobile services (e.g., streaming services) (Swisscom AG, 2016a).

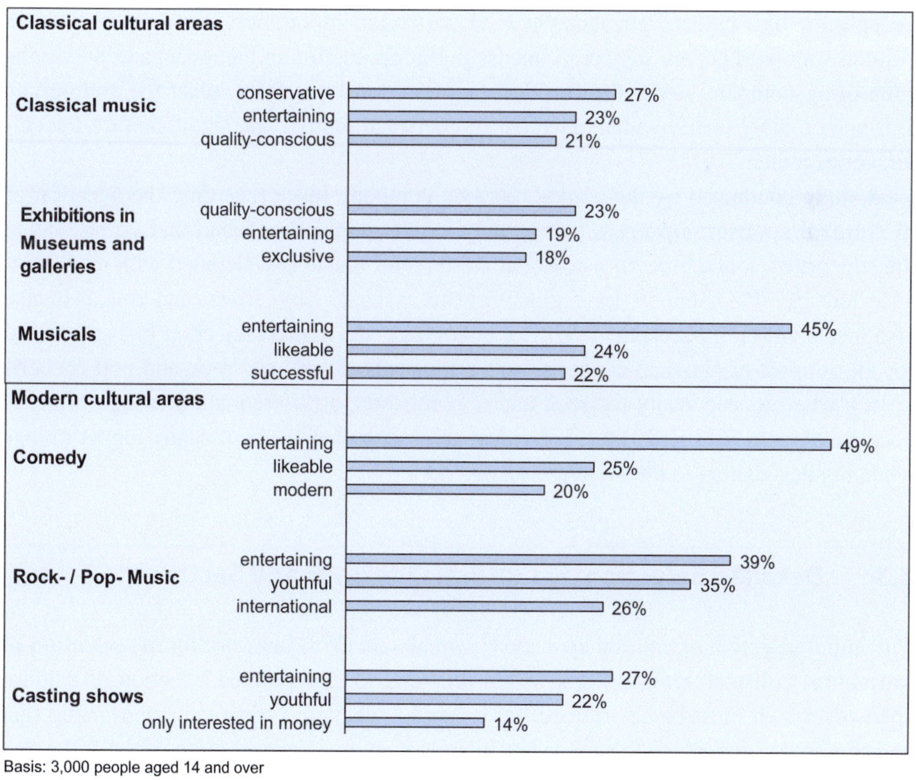

Fig. 8.2 Image of classical and modern cultural events. (*Source* Ipsos GmbH, 2008)

(6) Regional Reference

The rationale for supporting certain arts and cultural sectors is also provided by the presence of cultural activities in the region. As part of the **integration of the company into its geographical and social environment**, local arts and cultural sectors are therefore often supported. This corresponds to a regional strategy, as already described in Chap. 8. An example is the cultural engagement of the financial services provider HypoVereinsbank in the vicinity of its main location in Munich (HypoVereinsbank, 2016a), or the corporate sponsors DHL Group and Deutsche Telekom AG (2023d, e), both of which support cultural offerings at their main location in Bonn.

To select the arts and cultural sectors that a corporate sponsor wishes to support, a systematic evaluation of the different alternatives must be carried out. The affinity assessment should, if possible, be based on empirical information. In addition, it is advisable to establish a methodological **point evaluation procedure** in order to take various strategic influencing factors into account. The result is a ranking regarding the suitability of cultural sectors for corporate sponsorship, along with an argumentation aid explaining why certain arts and cultural sectors are particularly suitable for support.

In addition to the formal affinity assessment and the search for lines of connection between the area of support and the corporate sponsor, the issue of **credibility and acceptance** of a cultural engagement is of particular importance. Since many arts and cultural sponsorships are subject to intense public discussion in the media and within the sponsoring company itself, the corporate sponsor must carefully select the appropriate area and credibly justify which objective and personal motives are significant for the cultural engagement.

A study conducted by the market research company Ipsos regarding the **acceptance of cultural sponsorship areas** among the German population found that, in particular, the support of young emerging artists in culture and music is welcomed with an acceptance rate of 77%. Support for regional events, such as city, street, and folk festivals, also meets with high acceptance (72%). In contrast, the highest rejection rates are found for the support of classical concerts (40%), musicals (38%), and rock and pop concerts (37%), whereby especially for rock and pop concerts, a differentiation by age group is necessary (Ipsos GmbH, 2014a). Individual areas also receive significantly higher ratings when regular visitors to the event are surveyed.

8.3 Detailed Selection by Cultural Offerings and Sectors

The initial selection of cultural sponsorship areas sets the framework for the **selection of individual cultural sponsorships** within this area. In the detailed selection of cultural sponsorships, it must be determined, for example, whether a corporate sponsorship that has chosen to support the theater sector intends to support one or more of the following individuals, groups, or organizations:

- Cultural association
- Artist
- Ensemble
- Cultural institution
- Cultural event

The **decision criteria for the detailed selection,** especially for externally initiated sponsorships, are extremely diverse. Examples include:

- Unique selling proposition (USP) of the cultural brand,
- Visions and goals of the cultural brand,
- Achievements and successes of the cultural creators,
- Assessment and acceptance by the target groups,
- Awareness and favorability among the target groups,
- Management qualifications of the cultural organization or association,
- Public private relations work of the cultural organization,
- Media resonance,
- Previous experience with the cultural organization,
- Possibility of awarding titles, distinctions, licenses,
- Position of the sponsor compared to other sponsors,
- Industry exclusivity compared to other sponsors,
- Use of advertising opportunities and "sponsorship packages,"
- Duration of the cultural commitment and possibilities/necessities of contractual binding,
- Willingness of the institution or artist to participate in arts and cultural funding within the corporate sponsorship,
- Costs for the cultural sponsorship,
- Networking opportunities with other commitments,
- Controlling options for the commitment.

If, within the framework of arts and cultural sponsorship, specific events are shortlisted, the following **decision criteria for events** are of particular importance:

- Expected number of visitors to the event,
- Anticipated media presence at the event,
- Presence of the event on the internet/on social media,
- Expected television ratings and reach of the broadcast media,
- Expected sponsoring cost per mille (corresponds to the cost of 30 s on-screen time to reach 1000 viewer contacts),
- Expected advertising value of the event (corresponds to the amount a sponsor would have to spend on media advertising to achieve the same on-screen time as in the sponsorship),

- Participation of certain personalities and groups of people in the events,
- Possibility of awarding distinctions, licenses, and titles,
- Position of the sponsor compared to other corporate sponsorships with sponsorship commitments,
- Use of advertising opportunities before, during, and after the event,
- Costs for the preparation, execution, and follow-up of the sponsorship.

With regard to the **evaluation criteria for the allocation ofsponsorship funds**, the following criteria are highlighted based on various specialist articles and surveys of sponsoring corporate sponsorships (Bruhn & Wieland, 1988; Heusser et al., 2008; Causales Agentur für Marketing & Kommunikation, 2008, 2013):

- Cost-performance ratio,
- Image affinity,
- Credibility,
- Cultural achievement,
- Target group affinity,
- Media suitability,
- Audience interest,
- Product affinity,
- Exclusivity.

The detailed selection phase should also be methodically supported by the use of **point evaluation procedures**. Some corporate sponsorships already work with fixed scoring approaches in which their evaluation criteria are defined with weighting factors.

8.4 Termination of Sponsorship Agreements

Cultural sponsorship activities are often designed for the long term in order to achieve a sustainable image transfer and to lend the partnership the necessary authenticity through its multi-year duration. In addition, long-term cooperation is more efficient, as it involves lower transaction costs than frequent changes and the associated need to reconceptualize the collaboration. However, cultural sponsorship activities are also repeatedly terminated. Since the **termination of an arts and cultural sponsorship** can be of public interest and does not always proceed without conflict, this process should also be considered as an element of professional arts and cultural sponsorship. Therefore, the termination of sponsorship agreements should be regarded as an independent field of decision-making. In doing so, the causes and consequences of termination must be systematically considered, as well as the communicative handling of a termination strategy.

In this context, the literature and practice identify various situations that can be **causes for a termination of sponsorship agreements** (see Salzer, 2022, p. 88 for a detailed discussion):

- **Strategic realignment:** The partnership no longer fits the brand communication strategy or the company's overall strategy.
- **Insufficient value generation:** The KPIs (Key Performance Indicators) defined in the objectives were not met, for example, if the measured reach was too low.
- **Misconduct:** The sponsor is dissatisfied with the behavior of the cultural partner, for example, because they can no longer sufficiently identify with the cultural institution (see, for example, the case of Documenta 2022 in Chap. 6), or because the sponsored party has not adhered to contractual agreements (e.g., by violating exclusivity rights).
- **Financial difficulties:** Budgets are cut or shifted to other communication instruments.
- **Counteroffer from a competitor:** The sponsored party accepts a competitor's counteroffer, which cannot be outbid.
- **Economic crisis:** Already during the 2007 financial crisis, it became apparent that fewer corporate sponsors participated as sponsors, as financial resources were no longer available or corporate sponsorship wanted to be perceived as frugal.
- **Natural end:** Especially for projects with a defined conclusion and one-off events, a partnership often ends automatically.
- **Personnel changes:** A new appointment at the operational level or in higher-level management (e.g., head of marketing or executive management) can lead to a reassessment of existing partnerships, thereby questioning the effectiveness and efficiency of a cultural sponsorship commitment.
- **Inappropriate demands:** Cultural institutions also reassess their sponsorship benefits after the successful completion of a project or event. However, this reassessment can lead to disagreements between sponsor and cultural institution regarding the value of services and counter-services, resulting in new, excessive demands.
- **Dissatisfaction with the outcome of the sponsored project:** Content-related dissatisfaction is particularly critical when it touches on artistic freedom, as the sponsor could be accused of trying to influence artistic processes by withdrawing resources. However, the sponsor may, for example, be dissatisfied with the organization of an event if it is not professionally managed and thus sees the intended image transfer at risk.
- **Signaling to society:** A partnership with a cultural offering no longer aligns with societal norms—for example, following the attack on Ukraine in February 2022, many corporate sponsors reassessed their support for Russian cultural institutions. This can be perceived as a signal to society.
- **Lack of personnel:** Particularly complex sponsorship partnerships, such as global engagements or resource-intensive activities like VIP offerings, require trained personnel. If this is not sufficiently available, sponsorship activities can no longer be implemented.

- **Relevance of the topic:** If certain cultural offerings or cultural creators are no longer in demand by the target groups, sponsoring these offerings also loses significance for a corporate sponsor.
- **Closure of a cultural institution:** If ensembles disband or cultural institutions cease operations, the basis for a sponsorship partnership is lost.

The sponsorship partnership is usually governed by a sponsorship contract, which always specifies the duration of the collaboration. Even though this defines a (provisional) end for both parties, cultural institutions in particular often expect that a partnership will continue in a follow-up contract beyond the current contract period. The **communication of a termination** thus takes place in two ways:

- **Internal communication:** Within the relationship between sponsor and cultural institution, information about a termination or non-renewal of the contract should ideally be provided as early as possible to give the cultural institution more time to find a new partner. However, from the sponsor's perspective, several strategic options arise regarding the timing of this information. For example, in the case of a strained relationship between sponsor and sponsored party, the information about a termination may only be communicated shortly before the contract expires, as the sponsor fears that early disclosure could result in disadvantages due to the behavior of the cultural partner.
- **External communication:** In external communication, the sponsor decides whether and how the general public should be informed about the termination of a sponsorship. In addition, it must be decided whether the communication about the termination will be carried out jointly with the cultural partner, or whether sponsor and cultural institution will inform the public separately and individually. The manner of communication includes both a range of possible communication strategies and various communication channels, from a brief press release or short social media post to a joint press conference with the cultural institution.

The type and scope of communication fundamentally depend on the anticipated public or **media interest** in an expiring arts and cultural sponsorship. This interest can sometimes be considerable, as the loss of a main sponsor can quickly lead to significant, even existential, financial challenges for the cultural institution. If a cultural offering is thereby endangered or a cultural institution has to close, the sponsorship effect can turn into a reputational loss, since gratitude for a company's commitment also creates a specific set of expectations. If these are not met, corporate sponsors are sometimes accused of being responsible for the loss of cultural offerings.

For example, the conflict over the end of a cultural sponsorship activity by Commerzbank in Frankfurt am Main led to several press reports (see, among others, Riethmüller, 2022; Leclerc, 2023), and the corporate sponsor considered it necessary to publish a detailed statement in which the sponsor's criticism of the sponsored theater was also made clear (see an abridged version in Fig. 8.3). The background to this conflict was the situation that The English Theatre Frankfurt would likely have to vacate its current building due to the expiration of a funding measure. As a result, operations in their current form could not be maintained. The theater launched a petition to remain in this building, which collected over 27,000 signatures between October 2022 and September 2023 (as of September 2023), and is being discussed in the local cultural scene.

In literature and practice, various **communication strategies** can be observed that can be used to terminate a sponsorship (see in detail Salzer, 2022, pp. 101 ff.). These communication strategies depend on the relationship with the cultural institution, the actual reason for the decision to terminate, and the anticipated reaction of the target groups:

1. **Strategy of "phasing out":** With this strategy, the sponsor assumes that the termination of a cooperation will not attract particular public interest. Therefore, the end of the collaboration is not further commented on. In an expert survey, Salzer concludes that this strategy "should be regarded as the standard approach" (Salzer, 2022, p. 101).
2. **Strategy of content-based positioning:** The termination is justified by a change in the sponsor's strategic focus. This strategy is chosen because the sponsor sees a need to provide a justification, or because the sponsor wants to use the termination of a cooperation as an opportunity to communicate its positioning. For example, after seven years of partnership, the car brand Audi ended its collaboration with the international film festival Berlinale. In addition to endowing the Short Film Award, worth 20,000 EUR, the sponsorship included a shuttle service with 250 vehicles. The decision was explained to the media as a result of a new strategic focus and with reference to other sponsorship commitments: "We are constantly realigning our brand and reviewing our partnerships," said Audi spokesperson Brigitte Urban. The company now wants to focus more than before on the topics of digitalization, sustainability, and design. This apparently fits better for the group with the green technology festival "Greentech" or the start-up conference "Bits & Pretzels," which Audi now sponsors—and less so for the Berlinale (Perdoni & Peitz, 2020).
3. **Gratitude strategy:** The termination is used as an opportunity to express mutual thanks for the collaboration and to highlight the successfully realized cultural offerings. Public expressions of gratitude are not only communicated by the sponsor. A professional ending of a cooperation also includes thanks from the cultural institution, even if it is not happy about the end of a sponsorship agreement. The termination of the sponsorship of the Augsburg Philharmonic Orchestra by MAN Energy Solutions in 2021 was regrettable for the orchestra and a financial challenge, but nevertheless, the director André Bücker published his thanks at the end of the collaboration: "We are extremely grateful for the loyal support and excellent cooperation with MAN Energy Solutions in recent years." (Presse Augsburg, 2021).
4. **Strategy of factual information:** The termination is communicated without detailed justification, or the communication of the termination is left to the sponsored cultural

Press release

For business editors
September 16, 2022

Commerzbank offers the English Theatre Frankfurt an extension of its performance schedule until April 2023

- **Final concession to the theater management**
- **Commerzbank's sponsorship ends on April 15, 2023**
- **To date, there is no rental agreement between the new owner of the Gallileo Tower and the English Theatre**
- **Commerzbank has assumed rental and operating costs totaling around €9 million since 2003**

Commerzbank has offered the English Theatre Frankfurt (ETF) an extension of its sublease in the Gallileo high-rise building until April 15, 2023. The bank is thus saving the Frankfurt cultural institution from a premature end. The last performance of the musical "Sister Act" is scheduled for April 2.

Commerzbank had originally agreed in writing with the English Theatre that the bank's financial commitment and thus the sublease agreement between the bank and the theater would expire at the end of 2022. Although the theater management has been aware of this for seven years, it has still not found a new main sponsor or new premises. Instead, the ETF has expressed the expectation that it will continue to be able to use the existing premises free of charge. The current owner of the Gallileo high-rise building has not yet agreed to step in as direct landlord and thus guarantee the continued existence of the theater.

The English Theatre has been housed rent-free in Frankfurt's Gallileo high-rise since 2003. Although Commerzbank has only been a tenant in the Gallileo since 2013, it has assumed the rental and operating costs for the theater resulting from the rental agreement for the duration of the lease. The rental costs of the English Theatre borne by Commerzbank have accumulated over the years to around €9 million, which underlines Commerzbank's contribution to education and the promotion of culture in Frankfurt.

Commerzbank communicated its withdrawal from the Gallileo and from sponsoring the English Theatre several years in advance. The contract between the tenant Commerzbank and the subtenant English Theatre was due to expire without notice on December 31. will end in 2022. The theater management had been aware of this since the sublease agreement was concluded in 2015. Since then, Commerzbank has repeatedly advised the theater management to look for new premises and alternative financial backers or to consider concluding a lease agreement with the new owner. Commerzbank is still the tenant of the Gallileo high-rise until January 2024. However, before handing over the entire high-rise building to the owner, it must guarantee the return and dismantling modalities under the lease agreement so that the building can be handed over smoothly and with legal certainty. With the end of gaming operations in April 2023, this would still be possible for Commerzbank.

Notwithstanding the latest concession, Commerzbank has made it clear to the English Theatre that its financial commitment and the sublease agreement will definitely end on April 15, 2023. Whether the English Theatre can remain in the Gallileo high-rise building beyond April 15, 2023 is a matter to be clarified solely between the current owner and the English Theatre. In the event of an early agreement between the two parties, Commerzbank is prepared to withdraw early from the lease agreement with the owner for the part of the Gallileo high-rise building in which the theater is housed, so that a seamless direct lease by the English Theatre would be possible.

Fig. 8.3 Press release by Commerzbank AG on the termination of the arts and cultural sponsorship of the English Theatre

institution. In this case, the sponsor sees no relevant added value in leveraging the end of the collaboration for communication purposes.

5. **Strategy of announcing the successor sponsor:** If a smooth transition between sponsors is achieved, so that a cultural institution does not have to go without a partnership for an extended period, the termination of the previous partner can be mentioned when introducing the new sponsor. This can be combined with the gratitude strategy by acknowledging the previous commitment and directing media coverage to the new cooperation.
6. **Strategy of restrained information:** If a termination by the sponsor is to be carried out without major public attention, but there is still media interest, the strategy of restrained information is appropriate. In this case, proactive communication is avoided, but internal communication guidelines are defined in advance (and, if necessary, coordinated with the cultural partner) to be provided in the event of journalistic inquiries.
7. **Strategy of concealing the cause:** This strategy is chosen when the sponsor expects that communicating the actual reasons for terminating a cooperation will be negatively received by the target groups and there is a risk of reputational damage. The reasons for termination are not only concealed from the general public, but sometimes also from the cultural institution, which may not receive a transparent explanation for the end of the collaboration. For outsiders, this strategy is difficult to identify, as concealment is usually combined with another strategy. For example, a sponsor may publicly state that a cultural institution is no longer supported due to the sponsor's new positioning. However, without internal knowledge, it is difficult to verify whether this is actually the decisive reason for ending the cooperation.

The above explanations make it clear that when selecting arts and cultural sponsorships, various strategic as well as operational decisions must be made. This applies especially to the initial and detailed selection when a corporate sponsor wishes to engage as a cultural sponsor. However, the end must also often be considered, so at the appropriate time, the termination of cultural partnerships should be taken into account.

The following provides an insight into the strategic considerations and practical implementation of the work of "Bayer culture," the cultural sponsorship commitment of the Bayer Group, using Bayer AG as an example.

8.4.1 Case Study: Strategy of arts and cultural sponsorship at Bayer AG

Initial Situation

Bayer AG is a life science corporate sponsor founded in 1863 with three divisions: Crop Science, Pharmaceuticals, and Consumer Health. The group sees its core competencies in the fields of health and nutrition. With "Science for a better life," the corporate sponsor also defines its purpose. Through the development of innovations in medical care and agriculture, Bayer aims to realize its mission "Health for all, Hunger for none."

Bayer's corporate headquarters are located in Leverkusen. In 2023, the group had 22,231 employees at 13 locations in Germany. Globally, in 2022, Bayer was represented in 83 countries with a total of over 101,400 employees and generated sales of around EUR 50.7 billion.

Organization of arts and cultural sponsorship at Bayer AG

The cultural sponsorship activities are grouped under the term **"Bayer culture"**. Bayer culture is part of the Corporate Positioning department and is assigned to Corporate Communications. Arts and cultural funding has a long tradition at Bayer AG, as an inherent corporate commitment to the urban community, initially at the Leverkusen site and later at other company locations: As early as 1901, a company orchestra was founded, and in 1907, a dedicated cultural department was established.

Today's Bayer culture department is the successor to the education department and shapes the company's overall social engagement in the field of art and arts and cultural funding for Bayer AG.

Bayer culture sees itself as an **art and culture mediation department** for everyone, with a focus on addressing employees as well as children and young people: evolving from the former education department through a modern event operation to today's mission of making art and culture accessible to all. The art and arts and cultural funding is differentiated into activities of arts and cultural sponsorship (Leverkusen Jazz Days, stARTacademy, orchestra in residence l'arte del mondo, former company associations such as Bayer Philharmonic, Bayer Men's Choir, etc.) as well as its own cultural and art projects (nationwide stARTfestival, art in urban spaces with "Lost Places") (see Fig. 8.4).

Objectives and Target Groups of Arts and Cultural Sponsorship

Bayer culture represents Bayer AG's commitment to society as a whole in the field of arts and cultural funding and is part of the company's brand identity.

Fig. 8.4 Singer-songwriter Wallis Bird with the band Spark at the stARTfestival 2023 in the Erholungshaus Leverkusen (Photo: Hanne Engwald)

The company's cultural engagement does not yield any direct economic advantages for corporate sponsorship. The activities in arts and cultural funding are understood as a **commitment to the respective locations** and as a means of strengthening the local cultural actors. Consequently, the target groups of arts and cultural sponsorship are not defined analogously to the target group segments of the various sales markets. Rather, Bayer AG's cultural offerings are aimed at culturally interested people at the respective company locations and—depending on the offerings—also at culture enthusiasts throughout Germany and international cultural tourists.

In addition to these external target groups, arts and cultural funding at Bayer has a long tradition for the **internal target group of employees** of the company: The Erholungshaus (rest home) was opened in Leverkusen at the beginning of the 20th century and offered employees a wide range of leisure activities. It thus served as an instrument to increase Bayer's attractiveness as an employer. Today, the Erholungshaus is an established cultural institution in Leverkusen with around 30 of its own events per year—in addition to numerous events by external organizers and independent company clubs, some of which also rehearse on site. By supporting the cultural scene at its company locations, Bayer AG's arts and cultural sponsorship also serves employer branding.

Selection of Arts and Cultural Sponsorships

The supported **cultural offerings** can be divided into three categories:

1. **Long-term support** is provided to local cultural actors with whom Bayer AG has developed partnerships over many years. This includes actors that, for example, originated from former company clubs. The main funding criteria are artistic excellence, regional relevance, and sustainability.
2. **Medium-term engagements** usually extend over several calendar years. These are projects curated by Bayer culture itself, such as the stARTfestival. In the selection of these projects, evaluations from audience surveys are also taken into account.
3. **Short-term sponsorship cooperations** generally have a contract term of one calendar year. However, contract extensions are not fundamentally excluded for these projects.

Agreement of Sponsorship Benefits

The **budget** for Bayer AG's corporate arts and cultural funding is subject to fluctuations and is renegotiated annually. Projects and institutions that benefit from financial support enter into a **sponsorship contract** with Bayer AG. These agreements on cultural sponsorship activities are negotiated by Bayer culture in consultation with the company's legal department.

In return for the financial contributions from Bayer culture, it is agreed as a **consideration** that Bayer AG's corporate engagement is sufficiently acknowledged in images and text.

Furthermore, the agreements ensure that additional sponsorship commitments by the sponsored party can only be made with companies from other industries. As a rule, the sponsorship benefits stipulated in the agreements require that Bayer AG or Bayer culture must be named as sponsor, and that logos and/or wordmarks are published in press releases. In addition, the logo must be placed in print and online media. The inclusion of logos is also emphasized for reasons of transparency.

Integration of Arts and Cultural Sponsorship into Overall Communication

In the activities of partner institutions supported by Bayer AG, care is taken to ensure **integration into overall communication**. Whenever possible, they are included in nationwide reporting on Bayer AG's activities in the field of corporate social responsibility. Own projects are promoted and presented both within and outside the company on its own online channels such as Instagram, Facebook, LinkedIn, and the corporate website (see Figs. 8.5, 8.6 and 8.7).

Fig. 8.5 Communication of Bayer AG's cultural engagement on LinkedIn

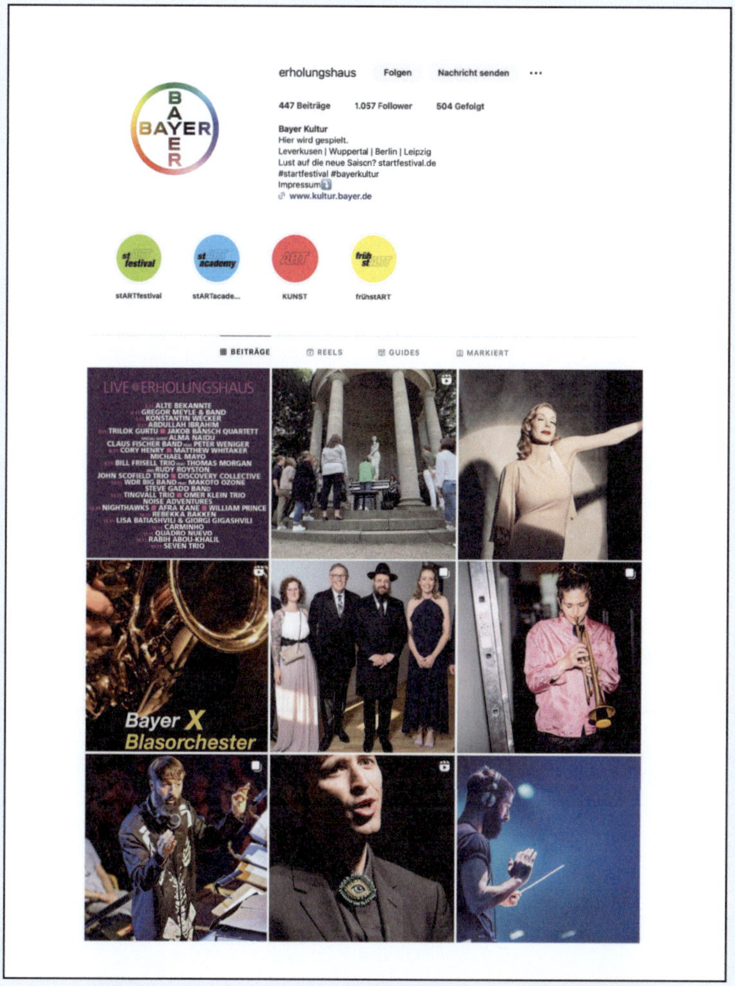

Example 3: Instagram profile of the Bayer recreation center in Leverkusen (as of 23.07.2023).

Fig. 8.6 Communication of Bayer AG's cultural engagement on Instagram

Effects and Performance Evaluation

With its corporate arts and cultural funding activities, Bayer AG's corporate sponsorship aims to reach as many people as possible—employees, culture enthusiasts, children, and young people at the respective locations and beyond. In doing so, Bayer AG aspires to

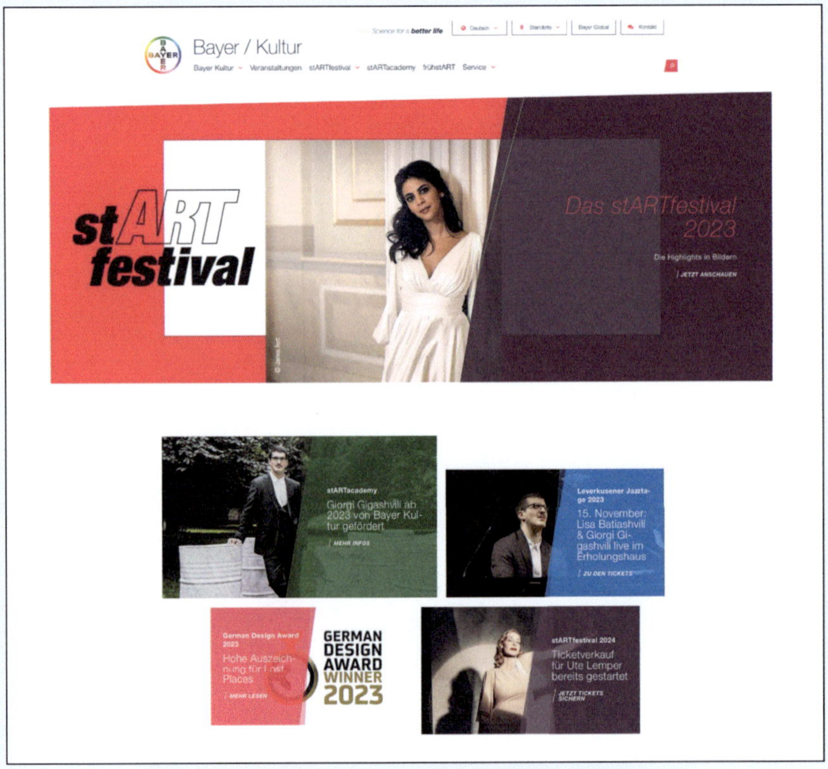

Example 4: Presentation of the cultural events and projects supported by Bayer on the Group's homepage.

Fig. 8.7 Communication of Bayer AG's cultural engagement on the Bayer culture homepage

have an impact on society as a whole and to help shape it. Monetary measurability or a cost-benefit analysis of these activities is not considered necessary.

Key Points

1. **Conduct sponsorship selection:** The selection of a sponsorship is generally carried out based on a multi-stage process, beginning with a preliminary selection as a strategic decision and continuing with a detailed selection as an operational decision.
2. **Define criteria:** As part of the preliminary selection of cultural sectors, criteria must be established on the basis of which the suitability of cultural fields

and institutions for the company's communication objectives can be assessed (e.g., affinity concept, proximity to location, etc.).

3. **Analyze cultural audience:** The role of the cultural audience in sponsorship selection should be examined by determining the level of sponsorship acceptance among target groups as well as the size of the fan base associated with a cultural offering.
4. **Consider durability and sustainability:** When deciding between engagements in mainstream cultural offerings or niche cultural offerings, the issues of durability and sustainability should also be evaluated.
5. **Examine sponsorship alternatives:** During the detailed selection, the various sponsorship alternatives within the chosen cultural sectors should be analyzed. This includes decisions on whether individual artists, ensembles, institutions, and/or events could be suitable partners.
6. **Take competition criteria into account:** Competition-related criteria must be considered when selecting a cultural sector and an organizational unit to sponsor. These help to differentiate from competitors and to build unique image dimensions.
7. **Prepare for termination in advance:** Every sponsorship engagement has a contractual term. If a decision to end the relationship is pending, preparations for the termination of the sponsorship relationship should be made in good time.
8. **Communicate termination decision:** Professional conduct is generally standard when terminating a contract between sponsorship partners. The public and private communication of a termination decision should be carried out in a coordinated manner in terms of content, timing, and form.
9. **Initiate termination in a timely manner:** It is helpful to hold discussions with the sponsored party during the final phase of a partnership in order to send timely signals regarding termination.
10. **Use exit and communication strategies:** Special exit and communication strategies should be considered to help a departing sponsor avoid negative side effects.

Operational Design of Arts and Cultural Sponsorship

9

Contents

9.1 Development of Individual Measures for Arts and Cultural Sponsorship 202
9.2 Valuation of Sponsorship Benefits 210
9.3 Calculation of the Sponsorship Budget 214
9.4 Legal Framework of Arts and Cultural Sponsorship (in Germany) 217
9.5 Elements of a Cultural Sponsorship Contract (With Case Study Beatbox Germany) 222

Abstract

In the operational design of arts and cultural sponsorships, the sponsor's specific contributions as well as the sponsorship benefits for the cultural partner are defined. While the sponsor provides the cooperation partner with financial, material, or immaterial resources, in return they primarily receive communicative benefits. The sponsor's contributions are determined by the available budget and the calculated media value of the sponsorship benefits. Once both cooperation partners reach an agreement, the exchange of services is contractually regulated in a sponsorship contract. When structuring the cooperation, it is important to consider the legal framework, such as the general legal and tax assessments of cultural sponsorship, as well as compliance regulations in the sense of laws, guidelines, and voluntary codes. The aspects of operational design are explained in the following chapter and illustrated with various practical examples as well as the Beatbox Germany case study.

M. Bruhn and L. Pöllmann, *Arts and Cultural Sponsorship*,
https://doi.org/10.1007/978-3-658-50079-5_9

9.1 Development of Individual Measures for Arts and Cultural Sponsorship

In developing individual measures for arts and cultural sponsorship, both the sponsor's contributions and the benefits provided by the sponsee must be compared. The services of external specialists, who provide support within the arts and cultural sponsorship program, should also be taken into account.

9.1.1 Contribution and Consideration in Arts and Cultural Sponsorship

When planning individual measures for arts and cultural sponsorship, the specific **framework conditions of a cultural partnership** must be considered. These specific features include in particular:

- With the exception of music events in the rock and pop sector, arts and cultural sponsorship is less able to reach a mass audience. It is particularly suitable for addressing smaller, but for corporate sponsorship attractive, target groups (e.g., opinion leaders, major clients, and journalists).
- Arts and cultural sponsorship enables a more exclusive appearance for the sponsor than in other areas. Sponsorship in conjunction with many other sponsors (e.g., at sports events) is rather the exception and is mainly observed at festivals.
- Among the sponsored parties, there are sometimes barriers and concerns about entering into a partnership with corporate sponsorship, as there is a fear of influence and restriction of cultural or artistic freedom. Here, it is important to clarify mutual expectations in advance.
- Corporate sponsorship requires engagement with the artistic or cultural mission. Only if the support is credibly communicated to the target groups can a positive communicative effect for the corporate sponsorship be achieved.
- The planning and implementation of arts and cultural sponsorship requires a responsible person within the corporate sponsorship who is personally committed to the sponsorships. Only through the personal commitment of individuals can the prerequisites for successful arts and cultural sponsorships be established.

Arts and cultural sponsorship is not equivalent to the purchase of advertising space or media for a fee, where the communicative benefit for the corporate sponsorship "automatically" occurs. Rather, the use of **arts and cultural sponsorship as a creative instrument** is understood as something that must be developed largely independently and tailored to the company, in order to be used for communicative purposes. Fig. 9.1 provides an overview of the diverse possibilities of sponsorship in various arts and cultural sectors.

Arts and culture	Characteristics	Sponsored	Sponsoring measure, object
Music	• Pop • Rock • Folk music • country music • Jazz • Hip hop • rap • house music • techno • Punk • Classical music • Baroque • Light music, etc.	• Singers • Choirs • Musicians • Groups • Orchestras • Festivals • Concert halls etc.	• Individual concerts • Concert series • Tours • Festivals etc.
Visual arts	• Graphics • architecture • Photography • Painting • Sculpture, etc.	• Painters • Sculptors • Art gallery • Exhibition house • Museum etc.	• Promotion of individual artists • Own museum and foundation • Exhibitions • Loans • Competitions etc.
Performing arts	• Drama • Opera • Operetta • Musical • ballet • Children's theater • cabaret • Variety etc.	• Performers • Theater or ballet groups • Theaters • Festivals etc.	• Performances • Performance series • Events • Tours • Charity events etc.
Media Art	• Film • Television • Video • Multimedia etc.	• Filmmakers • Films • Museums/ exhibition venues • Festivals etc.	• Individual artists • Performances • productions • exhibitions Competitions etc.
Literature	• Books • magazines	• Authors • Houses of literature etc.	• Readings • Competitions etc.
Architecture	• Architectural monuments • Monument preservation etc.	• Objects etc.	• Individuals • Exhibitions • Individual construction measures for restoration
Design	• Object design • Graphic design etc.	• Exhibition houses • Designers • Design schools etc.	• competitions • exhibitions
Leisure culture	• Folk festivals • Preservation of customs and local history • Cultural weeks • Adventure parks etc.	• Organizers etc.	• Overall event • Individual events, -attractions • Groups • Program points

Fig. 9.1 Possibilities for sponsorship in various arts and cultural sectors. (*Source* Bruhn, 2018a, p. 260)

A central task in the planning of sponsorships is to specify the **contributions and sponsorship benefits** between both partners.

On the side of the **sponsors**, it must be clarified which contributions the corporate sponsorship provides to the sponsored party or parties. These may include the following **individual contributions**:

- Financial grants for overall funding,
- Announcement of awards with various endowments,
- Provision of scholarships,
- Purchase of art objects for cultural organizations,
- Acquisition of art objects for the company's own interior design,
- Establishment of foundations with a cultural focus,
- In-kind contributions from the company's service portfolio (e.g., free flights, complimentary vehicle fleet, free video equipment),
- Provision of in-kind services by the corporate sponsorship (e.g., printing of posters, tickets, and exhibition catalogues, infrastructure),
- Provision of services by the corporate sponsorship (e.g., public relations, administration, event management, logistics, mailing of programs and tickets),
- Release of employees to support the cultural institution, among others (corporate volunteering).

On the side of the **sponsored parties** or **recipients**, it must be clarified which sponsorship benefits are provided or "tolerated." The following **sponsorship benefits** are given as examples:

- Personal mention of the sponsors by the recipient,
- Opportunity for a company representative to address the audience,
- Mention of the sponsor on posters, programs, tickets, social media platforms (e.g., LinkedIn, Instagram), websites, and other publications,
- Advertisements in the program booklet,
- Provision of opportunities for hospitality measures,
- Complimentary tickets to certain events,
- Product presentations and distributions during events as well as product placement,
- Events for company employees at the recipient's venue or within the corporate sponsorship,
- Toleration of (exclusive) advertising measures in the context of the event,
- Use of designations, titles (e.g., "supporter") in media advertising and public private relations,
- Mention of arts and cultural sponsorships in press releases and annual reports as well as on the company's website, among others.

The individual contributions of the cultural institution can be divided into three overarching **categories of sponsorship benefits**:

1. **Image transfer:** The sponsor benefits from an association with the image of the cultural brand by being allowed to use the cultural brand in its own communication, or by being mentioned in the context of cultural communication.
2. **Reach:** The sponsor increases its reach among its target groups by having its brand and marketing messages communicated by the cultural institution (e.g., through logo integration in cultural communications).
3. **On-site advantages:** The sponsor can present itself to its target groups as a co-host at an event, for example by distributing complimentary tickets or creating its own areas at an event (e.g., VIP lounge).

These three categories do not automatically arise for cultural institutions in a quality that is attractive to potential sponsors. This means that strategic cultural management must work towards developing these categories in order to formulate competitive sponsorship offers.

In order to be able to offer one's own (brand) **image as consideration**, the **development of a strong cultural brand** is necessary—one that is clearly positioned and can articulate its values precisely. The professional implementation of the individual components of a corporate identity, such as corporate design, corporate communication, or corporate behavior, is also among the prerequisites for developing the cultural brand as a suitable cooperation partner for potential sponsors. However, branding of cultural organizations should not be promoted solely with the aim of sponsor acquisition, but rather understood as an element of professional cultural management and based on an authentic profile. For an artificially created cultural brand that is not credible and is not accepted by the target groups would harm both the cultural organization and any potential cooperation partner equally.

The **reach** consists of the number and quality of contacts achieved by the cultural organization. On the one hand, it is important for cultural organizations to be able to offer sponsors a high number of media contacts that are reached through their own communication channels. On the other hand, it is important to avoid significant wastage, as otherwise the offered reach would not provide efficient value for the sponsors. Therefore, it makes sense for cultural organizations to build up high reach within their target group by establishing their own media, such as social media channels, program booklets, magazines, podcasts, blogs, newsletters, etc. Their own **media channels of the cultural organization** also have the advantage that cultural organizations can largely determine and shape the integration of sponsors themselves. For example, they can conduct interviews with sponsors, integrate sponsors' advertisements, or develop their own media formats in collaboration with the sponsor (e.g., a series of TikTok videos produced with representatives of the cultural organization on the sponsor's premises).

Especially **high-reach social media channels** offer cultural organizations the potential for valuable sponsorship benefits, as these channels not only provide access to the target groups, but also enable cultural organizations to advise sponsors on the best tone and media staging for presenting their marketing messages. Consulting and producing social media content thus increases the value of the consideration. The alternative to having their own media channels would be to book advertising space, for example in outdoor advertising, by placing online banners, or by purchasing ad space in magazines. However, sponsors can also book this form of "paid media" themselves.

If a cultural organization offers a sponsor logo integration on media that the organization itself has booked (e.g., when announcing an event through poster advertising with an outdoor advertising company), this does not provide the sponsor with any special access to target groups. The sponsor could also book this reach themselves as part of their media planning. In this case, the actual consideration would again be reduced to the image transfer, since the sponsor would be communicated in the context of the cultural organization's brand through logo presence or other mention in the booked reach. This highlights the necessity for cultural organizations to establish their own media and build their own reach.

For offers of possible **on-site benefits**, it is helpful for cultural organizations to analyze the "service bundle" of the cultural offering, taking into account the various benefit dimensions (Klein 2011), and to identify possible additional services that can be offered to sponsors as part of a cooperation proposal. These are particularly found in service offerings, for example through special catering options, the provision of shuttle services, VIP parking, dedicated areas on the premises, etc. But special services that are part of the core offering can also be offered as sponsorship benefits, such as access at special times that enable an exclusive experience, e.g., a guided tour after opening hours in a museum.

Based on these three categories, extensive and detailed sponsorship benefits can be developed to attract sponsors for a partnership with a cultural organization. The following example from the Zelt-Musik-Festival Freiburg illustrates a **service package** offered to potential main sponsors.

Example: Service Offering of the Zelt-Musik-Festival Freiburg

Founded in 1983, the **Zelt-Musik-Festival** offers a music, culture, and leisure program for various age groups in Freiburg (Germany) over nearly three weeks in the summer. The festival has a special unique selling proposition (USP) thanks to its various tents and open-air stages, which are erected each year as temporary festival locations on an open area at the Freiburg Mundenhof. The festival is attended by around 120,000 people, including approximately 50,000 concertgoers. Of the roughly 200 program items, 80 are free of charge, and entry to the festival grounds is also free.

As **consideration**, the ZMF offers its main sponsor:

- Use of the ZMF logo for their own communication activities,
- Printing of the sponsor's logo in the program booklet (print run of 180,000),
- Logo mention and link on the website zmf.de,
- Logo mention on a large on-site poster listing all sponsors, in the program folder (print run of 60,000), on announcement posters, on the welcome banner at the entrance, on side stage banners,
- Social media posts (coordinated between ZMF and sponsor),
- Priority for ticket reservations,
- Placement of a full-page ad in the ZMF program booklet with advance booking rights for the cover page,
- Priority to host sponsor meetings,
- Mention at official occasions,
- Invitation to the press conference,
- Opportunities for advance sale of festival tickets in the sponsor's own business premises,
- Industry exclusivity,
- 5 invitations to the opening reception,
- Concert tickets worth up to €3500,
- 2 festival cards (admission to all concerts) price category 1,
- 2 festival cards (admission to all concerts) price category 2,
- 4 parking permits,
- 10% discount on the purchase of concert tickets for employees,
- Garden tickets,
- Opportunity for promotional activities on the festival grounds,
- A permanent presentation stand on site,
- A billboard on the festival grounds.

In addition, **additional services** can be booked, such as:

- Logo integration on concert tickets (approx. 25,000 units),
- Publication of an editorial article in the ZMF newsletter (approx. 5000 subscribers),
- Advertising message on the back of employee ID cards (approx. 250 units),
- Booking of a backstage tour for 12 people,
- Rental of a special tent (mirror tent) for special events before the start of the festival,
- Engagement of musicians as a program item at a sponsor's event for their customers,
- Creation of a photo documentation of the sponsor's special events,
- Additional billboards on the festival grounds,
- Additional promotional stands on site ◀

Arts and cultural sponsorship is not an isolated instrument of marketing and corporate communication; rather, **arts and cultural sponsorship should be viewed as an integrative instrument** that, as a cross-sectional tool, touches on many areas of corporate communication (see in detail Chap. 10). The examples of possible sponsorship benefits shown above illustrate how a sponsorship partnership can fulfill the functions of other corporate communication instruments: The number of events produced in-house as part of event marketing can be reduced by engaging as a presenting partner or co-organizer in cooperation with cultural institutions. In addition, part of the **social media posts** to be produced can be replaced with content resulting from a sponsorship partnership. For some corporate sponsors, sponsorship engagements are an important source for generating attractive content for their social media communication, as the company's everyday activities do not generate sufficiently usable narratives for communication policy.

Certain **media advertising measures** can also be covered to some extent through sponsorship activities, provided the sponsor's brand is communicated with sufficient prominence in the cultural institution's external advertising, or if, as part of the consideration, advertisements and similar traditional advertising measures are implemented. However, the effort for the sponsor is only partially reduced, since in order to make the most effective use of the media contacts acquired through sponsorship, individual advertisements and promotional materials must also be designed and produced in the context of a sponsorship partnership. However, the costs for advertising space, which would otherwise be paid to another advertising medium such as a magazine or an online advertising platform, are eliminated.

The extent to which **communication budgets are allocated to arts and cultural sponsorship** and thus potentially diverted from other channels is an individual decision and depends on the expected benefit of arts and cultural sponsorship compared to available alternatives. Instead of building a new social media channel, it may seem more efficient to first benefit from the know-how of a cultural institution and present oneself to the target audience through a partnership on their channels. Similarly, the market launch of a new beverage may be more cost-effective and impactful through cooperation with several large festivals than by organizing numerous events independently. Despite these considerations, arts and cultural sponsorship should not be understood as a competing instrument to other communication tools. Rather, sponsorship (see also Chap. 10) only unfolds its full effect when it is activated by the additional use of further instruments by corporate communication. The operational design of arts and cultural sponsorship therefore does not end with the implementation of the sponsorship benefits offered by the cultural partner, but is accompanied by additional measures taken by the sponsor itself.

9.1.2 Services Provided by External Specialists

The planning and implementation of arts and cultural sponsorships requires specialized knowledge, experience, and expertise. Since the diverse tasks involved in planning and executing individual measures are often not covered by in-house staff in corporate sponsorship, it is possible to engage external specialists (see also Sect. 12.2.4). In this context, two different **types of specialists in arts and cultural sponsorship** can be distinguished:

Cultural Sponsorship Intermediaries

Cultural sponsorship intermediaries are usually agencies that typically work for a cultural organization and act as classic intermediaries in the search for sponsors. These agencies often have **exclusive rights** when awarding sponsorships. If, on the other hand, an agency does not have exclusive rights, it can be assumed that, in addition to the cultural sponsorship intermediary, the cultural institution itself will also search for potential partners. In the worst case, this can lead to conflicts if the sponsors ultimately do not match. For example, a few years ago, a sponsorship agency secured a premium automotive brand for a music event. The organizers themselves also looked for sponsors and secured a fashion brand whose brand positioning was clearly *not* in the premium segment. The fact that both sponsors appeared at the event was, at least for the automotive brand, not advantageous. Therefore, for sponsors, not only the possibility of industry exclusivity is fundamentally important, but also the issue of so-called "**brand safety**." This means that the sponsor's brand is not presented in an environment that contradicts the brand's values—whether due to unsuitable other partners or the sponsor's placement at an event (e.g., not placing promotional stands near restrooms or waste collection points).

Arts and cultural sponsorship consultant

Arts and cultural sponsorship consultants operate in two directions: On the one hand, they may act as **advisors to a cultural organization**, supporting them, for example, in developing a marketing and sponsorship concept. On the other hand, the **consulting service may relate to corporate sponsorship**, for instance by developing a company-specific cultural sponsorship concept based on the company's communication situation. In both areas—advising a company or a cultural organization—sponsorship consultants provide support both in the conceptual planning of a cultural engagement and in its implementation. Cultural sponsorship consultants include, for example, art historians and gallery owners, as well as art consultants and agencies, or even artists themselves.

The most important **service provided by arts and cultural sponsorship consulting** is to develop a mutual understanding of the starting point, goals, and possibilities of both partners (cultural institution and sponsor). Such understanding supports efficient cooperation negotiations by reducing misunderstandings or even conflicts. In practice, a recurring problem is that the sponsorship motive of sponsors is overestimated by cultural institutions, resulting in too few sponsorship benefits being offered to fulfill the goals of marketing and corporate communication. Consulting for cultural institutions can help them better understand the company's marketing perspective and develop the sponsorship offer with greater consideration for target group segments, number of contacts, and the communication of specific brand values.

Cultural institutions, on the other hand, sometimes wish in practice for sponsors to have a better understanding of the special production processes and artistic content. The **understanding of processes in cultural management** can be differentiated by various levels of complexity, as illustrated by three possible **practical examples** that can lead to conflicts:

1. **Example 1:** A sponsor books a promotional stand at an exhibition. During setup, the sponsor's representatives spontaneously decide to expand the stand area a bit, since there is still plenty of space next to them. The event management of the cultural institution is not particularly enthusiastic and explains, referring to the venue regulations, that the area must remain clear as it is an escape route. The sponsor's stand should therefore be limited to the assigned area.
2. **Example 2:** A sponsor wants to invite key account partners to a theater premiere at which they are presenting themselves as a supporter. For the design of their invitation cards, they ask the theater's press office for photos of the stage set to give their guests a preview of the performance. The press office explains that the director does not want any images published in advance, as this would spoil the surprise effect when the curtain rises. Additionally, she does not want the media to report on the stage production before the premiere.
3. **Example 3:** A sponsor would like to address a brief welcome to the audience before the start of a concert. However, the conductor rejects the proposal, explaining that this would destroy the mystical moment before the concert begins, which is an integral part of the performance's staging.

In **Example 1**, the sponsor's request cannot be reconciled with the legal requirements of event organization. In **Example 2**, the sponsor's request conflicts with the theater's PR strategy. In **Example 3**, the sponsor's proposal is at odds with the artistic staging concept. Understanding the need to comply with legal requirements may initially seem less problematic than understanding staging objectives. Nevertheless, in practice, there are occasionally only partially reasonable negotiation proposals, for example, with the argument "in an emergency, we'll just quickly move the stand away." Experienced cultural sponsorship managers who themselves have expertise in culture or event management generally bring greater empathy for the cultural institution. When cooperating with unfamiliar cultural sectors, prior consultation or more in-depth research—including into production processes—is advisable.

9.2 Valuation of Sponsorship Benefits

For sponsors as well as cultural institutions, assessing the offered or desired sponsorship benefits often presents a challenge. However, in order to agree on a cooperation, a financial **valuation of individual services or service packages** is essential. Various aspects are considered in the valuation, which can be determined with varying degrees of precision. A **quantification of the evaluation criteria** is comparatively straightforward:

- **Total expected reach:** The reach can be derived from the circulation of printed media (posters, flyers, program booklets, etc.) as well as the number of fans and followers on the social media channels (of the cultural institution), the number of addresses on the newsletter distribution list, the page impressions per month on the cultural institution's website, the expected number of visitors, and so on.
- **Quality of expected contacts:** Contact quality depends, on the one hand, on the number of wasted contacts, which can be forecast from the distribution channels of the communication media. On the other hand, contact quality is determined by the attractiveness of the target group reached. Attractiveness increases, for example, with the purchasing power or influence of the target group. Thus, contacts with a target group with high household income or with a target group with significant influence (e.g., media representatives, influencers, political decision-makers) are generally more expensive than contacts with consumers with low household income.
- **Event services:** The value of complimentary tickets and other services can be determined relatively easily, especially if regular tickets for an event are available for public sale and thus concrete comparison prices exist.

However, **difficulties in quantifying evaluation criteria** for certain factors must also be taken into account. This is the case, for example, with the following criteria:

- **Image of a cultural brand:** For an evaluation, the brand value of a cultural institution is less decisive than the value generated for the sponsor through an image transfer. In addition to the general reputation of the cultural institution, the specific brand values are particularly important, as these are the values from which the sponsor hopes to benefit through image transfer. For example, a cultural organization may stand for high artistic standards, while the sponsor does not wish to be perceived as "artistic" but instead hopes for an image transfer of values such as "passion" and "perfection." Whether this succeeds ultimately depends on the credibility and the manner in which the sponsorship cooperation is staged, so that this value (in contrast to reach) can vary between different corporate sponsorships.
- **Artistic and cultural value:** Since the motivation to support culture is significant for many corporate sponsorships, the question arises as to what monetary value the support of a particular sector or cultural offering has. This question can be debated with quite opposing arguments. One could argue that supporting a rare or unique cultural offering provides greater added value than widely available offerings, as it promotes cultural diversity. Conversely, it could be argued that partnerships with mainstream cultural offerings have a higher value, as they maintain cultural access for broad segments of the population. Another approach is to attempt to determine artistic quality based on awards and prizes received, which would mean that professional cultural

practitioners could command ever higher sponsorship prices than cultural engagements in children's and youth work. However, referring to awards ultimately leads back to an assessment of reputation and thus the image of the cultural practitioners. Ultimately, it must be acknowledged that attempts to quantify artistic achievements for a sponsorship cooperation are unlikely to be successful.

The most important **evaluation criteria for sponsorship benefits** in arts and cultural sponsorship are the reach to relevant contacts in connection with the image transfer from the cultural institution to the sponsor. Since reach is "sold" in conjunction with image, the cultural organization can either demand more than a sponsor would have to pay for the same reach and contact intensity through another medium. Or the cultural organization offers the reach at a similar price but is more attractive to the sponsor than other advertising media, since there is also an image transfer and the opportunity to support culture. In both cases, the sponsor must know the value of the offered reach and contact quality. Cultural organizations should also know the value of their sponsorship benefits. Often, sponsorship requests are sent to corporate sponsors without specifically naming the prices for the services offered, so that the offer cannot be evaluated by the sponsors, making decision-making impossible.

An important **reference for the evaluation of sponsorship benefits** in arts and cultural sponsorship is the pricing of other corporate communication instruments. For more complex sponsorship benefits, this can lead to a "make-or-buy" decision, where the sponsor considers whether to organize an event themselves or realize it through a partnership. The evaluation is simpler when only comparing reach-based prices. In this case, the offer of a cultural organization is compared with the media data of other media that could reach a similar target group.

For example, sponsorship offers can be compared with the costs of outdoor advertising or advertisements in cultural media. For **costs as references**, such as in an outdoor advertising campaign, the costs of billboard or public transport advertising can be determined. For instance, advertising on a city bus in Berlin costs 3101 EUR per month without route binding and 6636 EUR with route binding in city areas for year-round placement. Advertising on a tram costs 5794 EUR per month without route binding. The very popular bus lines 100/200, which pass by numerous Berlin landmarks, cost 14,077 EUR per month (WallDecaux, 2023, pp. 83 f.).

As an **example of advertising rates** for an art magazine, the following shows the costs for various ad formats in Arte Magazin (see Fig. 9.2). Arte Magazin reaches an above-average culturally engaged audience and is therefore suitable as a reference. The circulation is 98,993 copies (IVW, 2022), reaching 475,000 readers per issue (IfDA, 2022).

CPM – The cost per mille (CPM)

Both examples provide an initial reference for evaluating the prices of outdoor advertising or ad placements in cultural media. Since public transport advertising is not easily

Fig. 9.2 Advertising rates Arte Magazin. (*Source* Arte Magazin, 2023)

Format	Price
2/1 page	24,500.00 EUR
U4 (4th cover page)	15,490.00 EUR
U2 (2nd cover page)	15,490.00 EUR
1/1 page	14,490.00 EUR
1/2 page	7,690.00 EUR
1/3 page	5,390.00 EUR
1/4 page	4,390.00 EUR

comparable to a magazine ad, corporate sponsors will request the **cost per mille (CPM)** for better comparability (see also Sect. 11.1). This price is a key figure in marketing communications that indicates the price per thousand contacts. The price is calculated according to the following formula:

$$\text{CPM} = \frac{\text{Price of ad placement}}{(\text{Sum of contacts} \div 1.000)}$$

For Arte Magazin, the following CPM results for an ad on the 4th cover page:

$$\frac{15.490 \text{ EUR}}{(475.000 \div 1.000)} = \frac{15.490 \text{ EUR}}{475} = 32.61 \text{ EUR}$$

The cost per mille (CPM) for an ad on the back cover of Arte Magazin is therefore 32.61 EUR.

A distinction must be made between a **gross** and a **net CPM**, as the CPM can be calculated based on both gross and net media contacts: If a person sees an online banner three times, this results in three gross contacts. However, it is only one net contact, as the purchasing power does not change. The gross reach thus reflects the number of contacts, while the net reach indicates the number of individuals.

Obviously, there are significant differences in the **quality of contact intensity**. If visitors to a festival see a sponsor's banner next to the main stage for several hours, this measure generates a higher contact intensity than a fleeting glance at a poster at a bus stop. The German Sponsorship Association (FASPO) has therefore decided, for the evaluation of events, to add the number of visitors every 30 minutes for the duration of the event to the contact values. So if an event is attended by 10,000 people and lasts three hours, the calculation is $10{,}000 \times (3 \text{ h} \div 30 \text{ min}) = 10{,}000 \times 6 = 60{,}000$ contacts. These considerations show that contact values can be calculated in various ways and therefore should not be adopted as absolute figures without scrutiny, but require critical interpretation. Nevertheless, the number of contacts and the indication of the CPM are important in order to better interpret and compare offers.

Sponsorship Packages

Typically, potential sponsors of cultural organizations are offered various service packages, which differ in terms of the scope of communicative sponsorship benefits and, consequently, in price. A common distinction is the **categorization of sponsors** into:

- **Presenting partner:** The sponsor presents the event and receives the most prominent placement.
- **Main sponsor:** The sponsor is given special prominence over other partners and receives more sponsorship benefits than the co-sponsors.
- **Co-sponsor:** The sponsor is involved to a lesser extent and therefore only receives basic benefits.

If a corporate sponsorship provides the cultural organization primarily with **goods and services**, the partners are often classified according to the type of contribution, for example into:

- **Media partners:** The sponsor is a media company and supports the cultural institution with its reach, for example through advertising space, announcements, or post-event coverage.
- **Logistics partner:** The sponsor is a logistics service provider and supports the cultural organization with transportation services for the setup and dismantling of events or by providing a shuttle service.
- **Catering partner:** The sponsor is a catering business that provides the catering (or parts of the catering).

The Zelt-Musik-Festival Freiburg presented above divides the offered packages and prices into the following **categories:**

Patron	500 EUR
Partner	2,500 EUR
Basic Sponsor	5,000 EUR
Sponsor	10,000 EUR
Premium Sponsor	25,000 EUR
Main sponsor	Price on request (>25,000 EUR)

9.3 Calculation of the Sponsorship Budget

When calculating the sponsorship budget, the first step is to determine the costs of the individual measures for cultural sponsorship. In addition, an overall budget must be established (including activation costs) in order to allocate the total budget appropriately in terms of content and timing.

Costs of Cultural Sponsorship Measures

Given the wide range of possible engagements in the fields of art and culture, it is difficult to provide universally valid information about the **costs of sponsorships**. Costs vary depending on media presence, performance level, the benefits provided by the sponsee, the market value of the artists, and other factors. As with other forms of sponsorship, a general trend of rising costs for corporate sponsorship can also be observed in arts and cultural sponsorship. The frequently expressed assumption that arts and cultural sponsorship can achieve a great impact with minimal resources is ultimately disproved, at the latest, when cultural engagements are used to cultivate relationships with elite target groups, as is especially the case in exhibition sponsorship. Financial expenditures as well as the provision of in-kind contributions and know-how here lead to very high cost per thousand contacts, and such engagements often reach six-figure or even million-euro amounts (Walter, 2008).

However, opportunities for relatively cost-effective engagement arise from the increasing number of cultural institutions that, due to declining public funding, are willing to cooperate with sponsors. The following figures serve as rough **guidelines for the costs of arts and cultural sponsorships** with regard to the expenses incurred in the context of cultural engagement:

- Supporting a theater performance of supraregional significance costs between EUR 25,000 and EUR 80,000.
- The promotion of artists involves costs between EUR 2,000 and EUR 5,000 per month.
- Subsidies for exhibition catalogs amount to costs between EUR 5,000 and EUR 40,000, depending on the significance of the exhibition.
- The announcement of cultural awards is more cost-intensive: total expenses are expected to range between EUR 40,000 and EUR 250,000.
- In-kind contributions for cultural events are less cost-intensive. Internal company services should be budgeted at costs between EUR 2000 and EUR 25,000.
- The costs for purchasing art objects to design a company's premises depend on the market value of the objects to be purchased and start at around EUR 2,500.
- Sponsoring an exhibition costs—depending on the size and significance of the exhibition and the scope of the sponsorship benefits—between EUR 6,000 and EUR 80,000.
- Sponsoring international top-level art events involves amounts between EUR 150,000 and several million euros.

Budgeting of Arts and Cultural Sponsorship

The budgeting of a company's cultural engagement involves determining the budgets to cover the costs of all cultural measures within a planning period. It reflects the objectives, strategies, and measures defined as part of the planning and decision-making process, taking into account the company's own financial constraints and the anticipated activities of competitors. Partial decisions to be made as part of budgeting include both the **determination of the total amount** of the cultural sponsorship budget and the **allocation of the budget** in terms of timing and content.

From a theoretical perspective, the optimal solution to these decision problems would have to be made simultaneously. In practice, however, for reasons of complexity reduction, this approach is deviated from in such a way that the individual planning problems are always solved successively. The starting point of budgeting is the determination of the total amount of the cultural sponsorship budget. In a subsequent step, as part of the distribution planning, the budget is then allocated to the individual sponsorships in terms of content and timing.

In the **budget calculation for arts and cultural sponsorship**, not only those amounts that go to the sponsored party must be estimated. Rather, the total amount required for arts and cultural sponsorship must be calculated, which, in addition to the costs for supporting the sponsored party, also includes, among other things, the so-called activation costs (costs to increase the impact of arts and cultural sponsorships), as well as consulting fees, personnel costs, honoraria, advertising costs, insurance costs, commissions, and follow-up costs. As a guideline, it can be assumed that every **"sponsor euro/dollar"** (funds for the sponsor) requires at least one additional **"marketing euro/dollar"** (additional costs for the preparation, implementation, and follow-up of cultural sponsorships). In individual cases, this may even mean two or three additional euros (resp. Dollar).

In connection with budgeting, it is of particular interest from which **company budgets** the funds for arts and cultural sponsorships are drawn. While the financial resources for patronage in most cases come from the donation budgets of corporate sponsorship, arts and cultural sponsorship draws on different budgets depending on the company. In most cases, in addition to the public relations budget, the sponsorship and advertising budgets are particularly affected. With increasing professionalism and regularity of arts and cultural sponsorship, however, the importance of individual budgets shifts, and a dedicated sponsorship budget gains in significance.

As a consequence, not only are different departments responsible for managing the budgets, but, depending on the specific objectives, different priorities are also set in arts and cultural sponsorship. In general, it can be observed that in numerous corporate sponsorships—with the intention of more targeted cultural engagement—there is a partial reallocation of cultural funding budgets from the donation budget to the communications budget (**"From donation to arts and cultural sponsorship"**).

On the part of the recipients as well, an increasing **professionalization of cultural institutions** can be observed. While in 2010, approximately 16.5% of sponsorship income of sponsored institutions was invested in marketing or advertising/public relations, expenditures in this area rose by about 0.7% to 17.2% in 2013. Increased investment in marketing ensures the continuous development of the cultural umbrella brand. A further 19.2% of income is spent on art or material resources, and 12.7% on personnel costs (Causales Agentur für Marketing und Kommunication, 2010, 2013).

9.4 Legal Framework of Arts and Cultural Sponsorship (in Germany)

When examining the legal framework of arts and cultural sponsorship in detail, both general legal and tax aspects as well as compliance regulations in corporate sponsorship are of importance. These will be discussed in detail below.

9.4.1 General Legal and Tax Assessment of Arts and Cultural Sponsorship

Statutory provisions regarding arts and cultural funding can be found in various places. The Basic Law (German constitution) states in Art. 5 para. 3: "Art and science, research and teaching are free." Art. 35 of the Unification Treaty regulates the area of culture in detail, and the Treaty on European Union contains several provisions relating to culture. According to these, the promotion of culture is to be regarded as one of the sovereign duties of the state.

However, since the state has recognized that comprehensive arts and cultural funding can no longer be provided by it alone, it allows corporate sponsorship, within certain limits, the opportunity to promote cultural activities through the targeted use of financial and material resources. The use of the communicative effect created by art and cultural content for one's own communicative purposes is permitted. This includes, for example, a company's efforts to improve its image with regard to certain dimensions conveyed by culture. The **limit of legal admissibility** of cultural engagement by corporate sponsorship is exceeded when there is an influence on cultural content and dependencies are created that are prohibited by the legal system (Bruhn & Mehlinger, 1999, p. 75 ff.).

Another legal complex that affects arts and cultural sponsorship is **foundation and foundation tax law.** On October 9, 2007, the "Act to Strengthen Civic Engagement" (Bundesgesetzblatt I, 2007 p. 2332) came into force retroactively at the beginning of 2007. It serves to strengthen and expand the improved tax deductibility of donations to foundations, which has been in place since 2000 with the "Act to Further Promote the Tax Deductibility of Foundations" (Bundesgesetzblatt I, 2000 p. 1033). The Act to Further Promote the Tax Deductibility of Foundations aims to create a more foundation-friendly environment in Germany and thus contribute to the preservation of cultural offerings. For example, since the law came into force, donations to foundations of up to EUR 20,450 per year have been fully tax-deductible. If a private individual or a partnership established a new foundation, under the old law, donations made to the foundation's capital up to an amount of EUR 307,000 could be claimed for tax purposes until the end of the first year after establishment (Bundesgesetzblatt I, 2000 p. 1033). The above maximum amount deductible from income is increased by the new "Act to Strengthen Civic Engagement" and the restriction to the founding year is lifted. The 2000 law created a special incentive for establishing foundations, while under the new law, not only the initial endowment of a foundation is tax-privileged, but also subsequent donations to existing foundations. Accordingly, it is possible to claim donations to charitable private foundations as well as to public and church foundations as a special deduction reducing taxes up to EUR 1,000,000 every ten years (Bundesgesetzblatt I, 2007 p. 2332).

In connection with the **tax treatment of arts and cultural sponsorships**, both questions of deductibility as business expenses for advertising costs for the sponsor and the question of charitable status for the sponsored parties are addressed. The income tax treatment of arts and cultural sponsorship—just like the treatment of other forms of sponsorship—is regulated in the "Act to Strengthen Civic Engagement" (Bundesgesetzblatt I, 2007). Since patronage is more widespread in arts and cultural sponsorship than in sports sponsorship, it is of particular interest whether the donations made in connection with sponsorship are to be classified as business expenses or donations. The following two **tax-relevant assessments** are necessary for corporate sponsorship:

1. Assessment of the intention to achieve an economic benefit with the expenses, in order to deduct them as **business expenses** under § 4 para. 4 of the Income Tax Act (EStG) for tax purposes.
2. Assessment of the requirements for a **donation** under § 10 b of the Income Tax Act (EStG) as well as § 9 no. 3 of the Corporation Tax Act (KStG) and § 9 no. 5 of the Trade Tax Act (GewStG), in order to deduct the donations for tax purposes.

Expenses of the sponsor are considered **business expenses**, if the sponsor seeks economic advantages, particularly in securing or enhancing its corporate reputation, through its corporate sponsorship or advertises products of its company. This is especially the case when the recipient of the benefits refers to the corporate sponsorship or the sponsor's products in an advertising-effective manner on posters, event notices, or in exhibition catalogs. Furthermore, media coverage in newspapers, radio, or television also constitutes an economic advantage for the sponsor. The prerequisite is that the media coverage is integrated into the sponsor's public relations activities or the sponsor participates in press conferences or other public events of the sponsored party and makes its own statements about its corporate sponsorship or its products.

Economic advantages for the sponsoring company are also achieved when the sponsor draws public attention to itself by using the name, emblems, or logos of the sponsored party or in other ways. It is irrelevant whether the expenses are necessary, customary, or appropriate. The expenses are also deducted as business expenses if the sponsor's monetary or material contributions and the intended advertising objectives are not equivalent. However, if there is an extreme disproportion between the sponsor's contributions and the sought economic benefit, the deduction as a business expense is denied.

Donations by a sponsor that are not recognized as business expenses are tax-deductible as **donations** if certain conditions are met. The prerequisite for tax deductibility is that the donations are made voluntarily or on the basis of a voluntarily assumed legal obligation to promote tax-privileged purposes. In addition, the donations must not be compensation for specific services provided by the recipient. Furthermore, the donations must not be in an actual economic relationship with the recipient's services (Bundesgesetzblatt I, 2007).

Sponsorship expenses that are not deducted as business expenses or donations are, according to § 12 no. 1 sentence 2 of the Income Tax Act (EStG), considered costs of private living. In addition, in the case of corresponding donations by a corporation, hidden profit distributions exist if the shareholder is favored by the donations.

9.4.2 Sponsorship and Compliance Regulations

If a cultural institution offers a sponsor special advantages at an event, such as complimentary tickets for very good seats, exclusive tours, and other service and hospitality benefits, the sponsor, as co-host, can pass these advantages on to selected partners. However, these opportunities are restricted by **compliance regulations** of many corporate sponsors or by **provisions on the acceptance of donations** in the public sector or in private companies. Sponsors and guests of sponsors must therefore clarify in advance when an invitation is appropriate and when there is a risk of unauthorized acceptance of benefits or suspicion of improper influence.

The regulations for **employees of the federal administration** include, for example, the following legal provisions regarding the acceptance of invitations from sponsors:

- **Federal Civil Servants Act (Bundesbeamtengesetz, BBG), § 71 (1):**
  Civil servants may not, even after termination of their civil service relationship, demand, be promised, or accept any rewards, gifts, or other advantages for themselves or a third party in connection with their office. Exceptions require the approval of the highest or last highest service authority. The authority to grant approval may be delegated to other authorities. (…)
- **Collective agreement for the public private sector (Tarifvertrag für den öffentlichen Dienst, TVÖD), § 3 (2):**
  Employees may not accept rewards, gifts, commissions, or other benefits from third parties in connection with their work. Exceptions are only possible with the employer's consent. If such benefits are offered to employees, they must notify the employer immediately.
- **Criminal code § 331 (Acceptance of Benefits):**
  (1) A public official, a European public official, or a person with special obligations to the public service who demands, is promised, or accepts a benefit for themselves or a third party for the performance of their duties shall be punished with imprisonment of up to three years or a fine.
  (2) A judge, member of a court of the European Union, or arbitrator who demands, is promised, or accepts a benefit for themselves or a third party as consideration for

having performed or for performing a judicial act shall be punished with imprisonment of up to five years or a fine. Attempted acts are also punishable.
(3) The act is not punishable under paragraph 1 if the perpetrator is promised or accepts a benefit not demanded by them and the competent authority, within its powers, has either approved the acceptance in advance or the perpetrator immediately reports it to the authority and it grants approval.

- **Criminal code § 332 (Bribery):**
(1) A public official, a European public official, or a person with special obligations to the public service who demands, is promised, or accepts a benefit for themselves or a third party as consideration for having performed or for performing an official act and thereby has violated or would violate their official duties shall be punished with imprisonment from six months to five years. In less serious cases, the penalty is imprisonment of up to three years or a fine. Attempted acts are also punishable.
(2) A judge, member of a court of the European Union, or arbitrator who demands, is promised, or accepts a benefit for themselves or a third party as consideration for having performed or for performing a judicial act and thereby has violated or would violate their judicial duties shall be punished with imprisonment from one year to ten years. In less serious cases, the penalty is imprisonment from six months to five years.
(3) If the perpetrator demands, is promised, or accepts the benefit as consideration for a future act, paragraphs 1 and 2 shall already apply if the perpetrator has indicated to the other party their willingness to violate their duties in the act or, insofar as the act is at their discretion, to be influenced in the exercise of discretion by the benefit.

Despite these restrictive regulations, the **acceptance of gifts and invitations** is not fundamentally prohibited. There are often tacit approvals for minor gifts with a value of up to 25 EUR, which, however, must be reported. For gifts and invitations valued above 25 EUR, approval is required. The work of political decision-makers also includes the performance of representative duties, which are often associated with the acceptance of invitations and hospitality services. Furthermore, public sector employees must be enabled to participate in events relevant to their professional duties.

The Initiative Group for Combating Corruption in Business and Federal Administration has therefore developed a "Question/Answer Catalogue on the Acceptance of Rewards, Gifts, and Other Benefits (Gratuities)" (BMI, n. d.). This also includes regulations on dealing with invitations and hospitality.

With regard to hospitality services, such as the acceptance of catering offers, reference is made to appropriateness in the context of the event and participants: "For hospitality, the **principle of social adequacy** applies, according to which a customary and appropriate range of food and beverages is permissible. Appropriateness is also determined by the function of the employee and the context of the event (e.g., occasion, duration, location, content, participants). (…) If the hospitality is customary and appropriate, tacit approval can generally be assumed." (BMI, n.d., p. 27).

Regulations are also specified for participation in (cultural) events for representative purposes: "The participation of employees in annual summer festivals, annual receptions, opening events, anniversaries, or similar occasions is permissible if the respective event provides an opportunity and reason to represent the federal administration in public and the participating employee, due to their position, can represent their authority at such an event and is specifically expected to fulfill this social obligation. (…).

Acceptance of an invitation to other events, such as cultural or sporting events, may only be permissible in particularly exceptional cases if there is a plausible reason and any appearance of influencing the employee's official duties is avoided (e.g., invitation of a high-ranking employee in their representative function by the sponsor of an event). It should be noted, however, that the employee usually requires prior approval from the competent authority within their organization (BMI, n.d., p. 30). If the invitation to an event is associated with special exclusive benefits, such as access to a VIP lounge, approval is only possible "… in exceptional cases and, if applicable, subject to transferring the value of the invitation to the federal treasury or a charitable organization" (BMI, n.d., p. 31). Bringing (spousal) partners is only permitted in exceptional cases, for example, if this is in line with the conventions of the event (e.g., invitation to a ball).

Private sector corporate sponsorships also often commit themselves through **compliance guidelines** (voluntary codes) to a restrained approach to gifts, invitations, and other benefits, in order to prevent corruption and avoid the appearance of active or passive bribery. For example, Mercedes-Benz defines in its code of conduct: "As employees, we may not solicit, request, or demand gifts, invitations, personal services, or favors from business partners for ourselves or others. We decline benefits if even the mere appearance of undue influence could arise. We also pay attention to the appropriateness of discounts and benefits. Voluntarily granted promotional and occasional gifts of appropriate value may be accepted. Invitations from business partners to meals or events are only accepted if they are unsolicited, serve a business purpose, are not repeated with undue frequency, and are proportionate to the occasion. As a guideline for what can be considered appropriate, we refer to a value of 50 EUR for gifts from third parties and 100 EUR for invitations from third parties. In case of doubt about the appropriateness of gifts or invitations, we consult with our supervisor." (Mercedes Benz, 2023, pp. 38 f.)

The Berlin compliance model for arts and cultural sponsorship invitations

Representatives from culture, administration and politics, business, as well as experts, have developed guidelines for dealing with cultural sponsorship offers under the leadership of the Cultural Circle of German Industries within the BDI e. V. and the Rheingau Music Festival. These guidelines were published under the name **Berlin compliance model** and are intended to provide legal and planning certainty to those involved in the cultural sponsorship process. Below are the **key recommendations** of the Berlin Compliance Model that should be taken into account when planning cultural sponsorship offers (BDI and RMF, n. d., p. 4):

- Hotel and travel expenses should be borne by the invitees themselves.
- The value of admission tickets should generally not exceed 70 EUR.
- Catering offers should not be of a luxurious standard and should not significantly exceed a value of 30 EUR.
- This results in a total value of 100 EUR per invited person.
- Invitations are not permitted if a contract or other business relationship with the invited person is imminent.
- Invitations to public officials must be examined separately.
- Since the invited person may incur tax obligations as a result of the benefits received, the sponsor should cover this taxation on a flat-rate basis for their guests. This is possible through a flat-rate taxation in accordance with § 37b EstG and should already be noted in the invitation. ◀

9.5 Elements of a Cultural Sponsorship Contract (With Case Study Beatbox Germany)

With regard to the **contractualdesign** of sponsorships, there are no universally applicable rules. This is due to the fact that, depending on the content of the legal issues to be addressed, either the **General or Special Law of Obligations** must be applied, and that the matters to be regulated extend into various areas of art and culture. A sponsorship contract, for example, may have the nature of a lease agreement if the corporate sponsor is provided with premises for the design of a VIP lounge for the duration of a cultural event. The sponsorship contract may also have the nature of a purchase agreement if the sponsor is guaranteed event tickets and media services for a specific price.

If the cultural institution and the corporate sponsor have agreed to collaborate, a **letter of intent** may follow as needed, which in turn leads to a sponsoring contract. In general, contracts can be distinguished according to the support of individual services as well as the support of projects and events. The following points can be listed as **contents of individually customizable sponsorship contracts**:

- **Contracting parties, contacts:** A contract should not only define the legal contracting parties, but also specifically name those responsible for operational implementation of the cooperation on the side of both the sponsor and the cultural institution. For more complex projects, it can also be helpful to define representatives for the main contacts. This is necessary, for example, if certain approval processes are agreed upon (e.g., print approval for advertising materials) and the phases of media production fall during the vacation periods of the main contacts.
- **Services and sponsorship benefits:** The services should be defined as concretely as possible. This includes, for example, information about the print run and size of advertising media (e.g., 1000 posters in DIN A1 format).

- **Payment terms:** If a financial contribution by the sponsor is agreed upon, payment after the cooperation has taken place is advantageous for the sponsor, as their expenses are incurred later and they can be sure the sponsorship benefits have been delivered. Cultural institutions, on the other hand, often prefer the earliest possible payment of sponsorship funds, since costs are incurred even before events and other offerings take place, thus supporting the institution's liquidity. It is therefore necessary to contractually regulate at what point or after which partial services payments are to be made.
- **Place of performance:** When supporting cultural events, the venue must also be specified precisely.
- **Industry exclusivity:** For the sponsor, it is important to be assured of industry exclusivity. Additional exclusive rights can also be defined; for example, that no other sponsor may donate a prize at the event, or that no other sponsor will give a welcome speech.
- **Good conduct, information, confidentiality:** The contracting parties commit to mutual respect, transparent communication of relevant information, and confidentiality towards third parties.
- **Disclaimer of liability and insurance:** Apart from liability issues involving gross negligence and intent, liability for other contingencies must also be regulated. This may include the requirement to take out insurance for damages (for example, it must be clarified how damages to vehicles provided for a shuttle service are to be handled).
- **Regulation of conflicts of interest and brand safety:** In the implementation of larger cultural events with numerous partners, conflicting interests may occasionally arise. For example, a cultural event is sponsored by a beverage manufacturer whose logo is present at the event. However, a catering provider who has purchased a booth license brings refrigerators bearing the logo of a competitor of the sponsor. In this case, the cultural institution would need to point out that, in the interest of brand safety, event partners should not display brand messages from competitors of the sponsor at the event. Since the contract with a caterer may be concluded before the contract with the beverage sponsor, and thus the conditions for the catering partner could change, a regulation for such cases must be found.

  When regulating potential conflicts of interest, risks of **ambush marketing** can also be taken into account (Bruhn & Ahlers, 2003, 2004; Nufer & Simmerl, 2008; Nufer, 2020). Ambush marketing refers to marketing activities in which a brand leverages the media reach of an event without participating as a sponsor. This could occur, for example, if a brand distributes free T-shirts with its logo to the audience of a festival at the entrance, while a competitor of the brand is the official sponsor of the event. While ambush marketing activities are uncommon at traditional cultural events and the risk is considered low, it is worthwhile to discuss preventive measures against ambush marketing at pop culture festivals that attract significant media attention.
- **Term:** The term regulates the commencement and termination of the contract.

- **Premature termination of contract:** The conditions for early termination must be clarified, especially for cultural events, as it may happen that, for example, an event cannot take place due to insufficient ticket sales.
- **Written form, severability:** The contract should state that all provisions are documented in writing and that there are no verbal side agreements. It should also be noted that if individual contractual provisions are invalid, the entire contract does not become invalid ("severability clause").
- **Applicable law:** Cooperations between corporate sponsors and cultural institutions in Germany are generally subject to German law. The regulation of applicable law is particularly important in cooperations with foreign partners and in international or multinational collaborations.
- **Jurisdiction:** Depending on the applicable law, the place of jurisdiction in the event of disputes must also be clarified.
- **Annexes:** The contract may include annexes such as seating plans or design samples of advertising materials.

The operational design of arts and cultural sponsorship is associated with numerous decision-making factors in the **implementation of arts and cultural sponsorships**. This not only concerns the careful selection of individual measures to increase the effectiveness of arts and cultural sponsorships. From a corporate perspective, important questions regarding the evaluation of sponsorship packages and the internal calculation of the necessary budgets must also be considered. Last but not least, legal and tax issues as well as compliance regulations are of particular importance. In the management process of arts and cultural sponsorship, the implementation questions listed here involve considerable effort. They form the basis for the performance evaluation of arts and cultural sponsorship.

The following example provides more detailed insights into the implementation of cultural sponsorship concepts. The **Beatbox Germany case study** presents the perspective of the sponsored party and shows the criteria used to select cooperation partners and the role that versatile social media activities can play as a possible consideration for sponsors.

9.5.1 Case Study Beatbox Germany: Arts and Cultural Sponsorship from the Perspective of a Cultural Event

Initial Situation

Beatbox Germany was founded in 2018 by Marvin Pöttgen and Tanita Helm and is a cultural organizer for beatbox events. Beatbox Germany sees itself as a point of contact and network builder for the hip-hop and beatbox scene. In addition to events, they also offer artist placement and workshops.

Beatboxing refers to the imitation and creation of sounds using the mouth, nose, and throat, which can be assigned to the rhythm sections of hip-hop music. This means that beatboxers produce sounds that, for example, resemble drum rhythms, electronic drum sets, or scratching, and by varying different vocal effects, create their own musical pieces that are performed live.

Founder Marvin Pöttgen is a beatboxer, beatbox coach, and event organizer, as well as a member of Germany's most successful beatbox ensemble, "The Razzzones." While Pöttgen, as managing director, is particularly responsible for the commercial management of Beatbox Germany, co-founder Tanita Helm acts as Creative Director. Helm is a graphic and communications designer, DJ, and producer.

The **collaboration with sponsors** takes place especially at the **events**, including:

- German Beatbox Championship in Berlin (see Fig. 9.3)
- West German Beatbox Championship in Dortmund
- North German Beatbox Championship in Hamburg
- South German Beatbox Championship in Stuttgart
- East German Beatbox Championship in Berlin

All the events mentioned are musical competitions in which beatboxers compete in the categories unter-18 (U18), Solo, Loopstation (beatboxing that enables multitrack performances using an audio recording or playback device), Tag-Team, and Crew.

Objectives of arts and cultural sponsorship at Beatbox Germany

The **decision to cooperate with sponsors** is based, on the one hand, on the desire for more resources for the events. On the other hand, integrating sponsors is intended to provide up-and-coming artists with low-threshold access to relevant corporate sponsorship, thereby strengthening the scene. The events are fundamentally not designed for profit maximization. Rather, the events are aimed at covering the costs incurred in order to enable many people from the beatbox scene to participate and to promote the establishment of networks within the scene. At the same time, resources are needed to realize the

Fig. 9.3 Cultural event German Beatbox Championship in Berlin

events, which is why the financing model, in addition to own revenues from ticket sales, merchandising, and beverage sales, also includes cooperation with sponsors.

Target groups

The founders of Beatbox Germany estimate the number of people interested in beatboxing in Germany as the **target group** at around one million. Based on the evaluation of event audiences and users of social media offerings, they state that 88% of beatbox fans are between 18 and 34 years old. Notably, the target group has a clear focus on younger men, with 90% male and 10% female fans.

From a consumer typology perspective, the **target group in the Sinus Milieus** is primarily assigned to the adaptive-pragmatic middle, the hedonistic milieu, and the performers. To better communicate the target groups to potential cooperation partners, the organizers have also developed the **persona "Julian"**. This defines a 22-year-old engineering student in Berlin who works as a student trainee and plays in a band. He is characterized, among other things, as a musical, sociable, and tech-savvy person who regularly attends events, dresses in a sporty-casual style, and seeks self-fulfillment. His media usage behavior is particularly shaped by social media (TikTok, YouTube) and WhatsApp for maintaining contacts.

The **acceptance of the target groups towards sponsors** is generally present, especially since they are used to the integration of sponsors at similar events. However, the target group is also sensitive to the potential commercial appropriation of the events and may develop reactance if a cooperation is perceived as too dominant or not a good fit in terms of content.

Strategic orientation

Collaboration with sponsors is understood not only as the acquisition of resources but also as **strategic networking**. The basic attitude is that as the number of cooperation partners increases, the visibility and relevance of beatboxers also rises, which in turn enhances and strengthens the scene. At the same time, this does not mean that all corporate sponsorships are suitable as sponsors. Since Beatbox Germany sees itself as a cultural organizer "from the scene for the scene," there are limits to the use of sponsors. For individual events, these limits are, on the one hand, quantitative, as the impression of a commercial event should be avoided by having too many sponsors. On the other hand, they are qualitative, as the connection between a corporate sponsorship and Beatbox Germany must be accepted by the organizers and the target groups. For this purpose, potential sponsors are divided into four **categories of sponsors**:

1. Corporate sponsorships that have a direct connection to beatboxing: e.g., manufacturers of microphones, music software, music hardware (loopstations, speakers).
2. Corporate sponsorships that have an indirect connection to beatboxing: e.g., music streaming providers or hip-hop fashion brands.

3. Corporate sponsorships that have no connection to beatboxing but are accepted by the target group as sponsors: e.g., beverage manufacturers, telecommunications providers, car brands, financial service providers.
4. Corporate sponsorships that have no connection to beatboxing and are *not* accepted by the target group as sponsors: e.g., weapons manufacturers, as well as brands that are viewed critically within the scene due to their business practices.

Corporate sponsorships in the last category are excluded as sponsors, as they are not compatible with the values of the Beatbox Germany brand and would therefore damage the image of the institution and the event.

Selection of Sponsors

Decisions regarding sponsors and the structuring of the cooperation are always discussed and made as a team. For the **decision on a sponsorship cooperation**, there are two processes:

1. If, in the **first process**, a corporate sponsorship approaches Beatbox Germany and offers sponsorship, the corporate sponsorship is first analyzed according to the criteria mentioned above. In addition, it is checked whether a cooperation would conflict with other sponsors (for example, if another corporate sponsorship from the same industry has already been granted industry exclusivity). The number of existing contracts with other sponsors is also taken into account in the review. If a cooperation is fundamentally deemed possible, negotiations are initiated regarding the specific services and sponsorship benefits, and a contract is concluded upon agreement.
2. The **second process** applies when Beatbox Germany itself actively approaches potential sponsors. In this case, only corporate sponsorships that have already been evaluated in advance according to the aforementioned criteria are contacted. These are offered various cooperation models based on different sponsorship benefits (see below) and, if interested, negotiations are conducted up to the conclusion of a contract.

Sponsorship contracts are generally tied to one or more events, so the duration is determined by the dates of the events. In principle, a renewal of the collaboration is sought in order to reduce transaction costs through the integration of new partners and to give the Beatbox Germany brand greater consistency.

Performance and Consideration

Beatbox Germany is supported by **services from sponsors** such as financial resources, material goods, and services. Financial resources are preferred, as they can be used flexibly as needed in the implementation of events. However, a cooperation below a value of EUR 5,000 is generally not efficient due to the organizational effort involved. In addition, there is always a need for material prizes for the winners of the competitions.

Services, for example for logistical tasks and various consulting needs, also arise in the organization of the events and are partially covered through sponsorship cooperations.

The **sponsorship benefits for the sponsors** can be distinguished as follows:

- Benefits at the events themselves,
- Media benefits before and after the events.

At the events, sponsors receive, for example, the following **advertising opportunities:**

- Logo print on admission tickets,
- Logo presence on stage (integration into the stage branding, see Fig. 9.4),
- Promotional stands at the event,
- Presentation of prizes by representatives of the sponsor to the winners of the competitions,
- On-site branding, for example by hanging banners,
- Distribution of promotional gifts (e.g., via a "goody bag" to visitors after the event).

Beatbox Germany continuously engages in active **social media work**, which enables outreach to interested parties beyond the event audience. Sponsors are offered this reach with various integration options, such as:

- Logo mention in the opening or closing credits of videos,
- Selection of camera angles in photos and videos during the event that show the presence of sponsors,
- Interviews with sponsor representatives,
- Individually produced clips communicating sponsors' offers.

Fig. 9.4 Logo integration of sponsors at the German Beatbox Championship in Berlin

The **use of the reach** of the Instagram, YouTube, and TikTok channels is offered. This provides Beatbox Germany with attractive potential in negotiations, as a specific and hard-to-reach target group with a large reach can be addressed. This is evident from selected **key figures** (as of July 2023, see Fig. 9.5):

- Instagram channel Beatbox Germany: 15,500 followers,
- YouTube channel Beatbox Germany: 668,000 subscribers, 137 million views, 188 million impressions,
- TikTok channel Beatbox Germany: 2.4 million followers, 20.5 million likes.

Impact and Evaluation

An **evaluation** is conducted for the sponsorship cooperation, firstly to capture the audience's response and thereby improve the quality of the events. Secondly, the evaluation is used in debriefings with sponsors as well as in the acquisition of new partners. In the evaluation of sponsorship, a distinction is also made between events and media integration.

At the **events**, in addition to the number of visitors, the overall atmosphere and feedback from conversations with individual guests are relevant. A systematic survey is not currently conducted. Conversations with the audience are held on a random basis on site

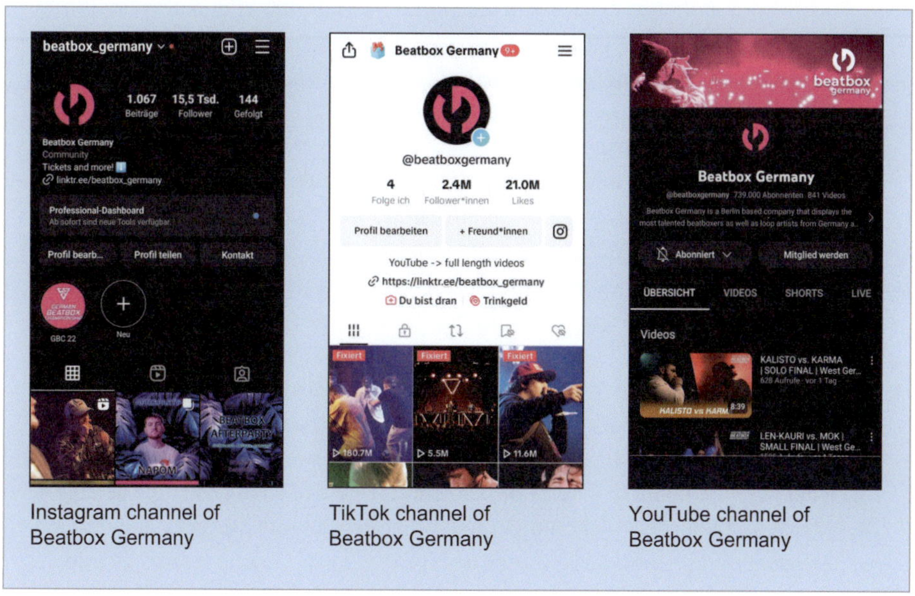

Fig. 9.5 Social media channels of Beatbox Germany (as of July 2023)

and sometimes after the event. In addition, the satisfaction of the sponsors with the event is evaluated afterwards in a discussion. The mood and atmosphere at the promotional stands, satisfaction with the visibility of the sponsors, and the assessment of the organizational processes are inquired about.

The **integration of sponsors into the online channels** is evaluated more precisely, as concrete figures on views and interactions are collected. Comments on the posts are also analyzed. Sponsors are first informed as soon as a post featuring their integration is online, which usually fulfills Beatbox Germany's contractual obligations. As a rule, the sponsor also receives information on relevant key figures regarding the achieved reach after three months.

Key Points

1. **Understand the artistic or cultural objective:** Engaging with the objective is necessary for sponsors to ensure credible communication to the target groups and to achieve a positive communicative effect.
2. **Analyze the sponsorship benefits of cultural institutions:** Sponsorship benefits should be divided into reach, image transfer, and local advantages in order to understand their impact.
3. **Leverage the expertise of sponsorship intermediaries:** Sponsorship intermediaries and consultants with knowledge of cultural production should be involved if in-house expertise is lacking, to ensure the efficient execution of the sponsorship cooperation.
4. **Evaluate the consideration:** The sponsorship benefits should be assessed based on the offered reach, quality of contacts, and the expected image transfer to determine their significance.
5. **Compare cost per mille (CPM):** The cost per mille should be used as a key figure to compare various sponsorship offers with other communication instruments.
6. **Analyze service packages:** Cultural sponsorship offers should be divided into different service packages, with pricing based on the scope of communication services provided.
7. **Consider budgeting:** When budgeting for cultural sponsorship expenditures, it should be noted that, in addition to the direct costs of sponsorship, further costs for the implementation and communication of the engagement arise, which often amount to at least the same as the cost of a sponsorship package.
8. **Check tax aspects:** It should be noted that expenditures for arts and cultural sponsorship are considered business expenses for tax purposes and not donations, provided that the corporate sponsorship results in economic advantages.

9. **Observe compliance regulations:** Company compliance guidelines and legal requirements regarding the design of invitations and hospitality services by sponsors must be observed when designing and invoicing sponsorship offers.
10. **Understand the sponsorship contract:** Since the sponsorship contract is not a distinct type of contract but is composed of provisions from general contract law, the specific services and sponsorship benefits on which the contract is based must be taken into account when drafting the agreement.

Classification of Arts and Cultural Sponsorship in Marketing and Corporate Communications

10

Contents

10.1 Integration of Arts and Cultural Sponsorship into Marketing and Corporate Communication 234
10.2 Integration of Arts and Cultural Sponsorship into the Communication Mix of Corporate Sponsorship 237
10.3 Integration of Arts and Cultural Sponsorship into the Sponsoring Mix of Corporate Sponsorship 249
10.4 Decision Levels in the Corporate Hierarchy 251

Abstract

Arts and cultural sponsorship is not an isolated marketing measure, but rather a communication tool that must be integrated into a company's other communication activities. Only through the planned interplay within the communication mix can the potential of a cultural sponsorship commitment be activated. This chapter highlights the various approaches to integration and explains the roles that individual communication instruments (e.g., public private relations, media advertising, social media, etc.) play in the integration of arts and cultural sponsorship. In addition, the content-related, formal, and temporal decision dimensions in the integration of arts and cultural sponsorship into the sponsorship mix of corporate sponsorship are discussed.

M. Bruhn and L. Pöllmann, *Arts and Cultural Sponsorship*,
https://doi.org/10.1007/978-3-658-50079-5_10

10.1 Integration of Arts and Cultural Sponsorship into Marketing and Corporate Communication

Particular attention must be paid during the planning process to the networking of arts and cultural sponsorship with the other instruments of marketing and corporate communication. Only if arts and cultural sponsorship is linked with the other communication instruments will it be possible to achieve a synergistic amplification of the overall effect of communication. To this end, it is necessary to examine in detail which opportunities exist for deploying sponsorship in combination with the other communication instruments.

Integration Approaches

When planning and implementing sponsorships, the following **integration approaches for arts and cultural sponsorship** into marketing and corporate communication are important and must be observed:

(1) Strategic Integration

Strategic integration focuses on the question of what contribution sponsorships make to solving the company's communication tasks. The strategic contribution of sponsorship, for example, lies in increasing awareness of the company or a brand, profiling its image, or reaching specific target groups — and, more generally, the contribution of arts and cultural sponsorship to the positioning of the company or brand.

(2) Instrumental Integration

The primary objective of instrumental integration is to leverage synergy potential by linking sponsorships with other communication instruments. In particular, the use of sponsorship, which is at risk of being implemented in isolation and without a long-term concept, requires systematic planning and networking with the other instruments of marketing and corporate communication — within the so-called **communication mix** of the company. Furthermore, integration of arts and cultural sponsorship into the company's **sponsoring mix** must be ensured, i.e., both among arts and cultural sponsorships themselves and with the company's other sponsorship engagements (e.g., sports sponsorship, environmental sponsorship).

(3) Content Integration

The subject of content integration is the thematic alignment with the company's communication mix. The aim of this approach is to ensure a consistent appearance and to achieve a synergistic increase in communication effects. To this end, uniform core messages, key arguments, and more are formulated, and the content statements about the company's services are focused. The communication of these statements can take place either directly in textual form or indirectly through symbols and key visuals. It is particularly important to ensure that the image attributes targeted through sponsorship are also picked up as central messages in the other communication instruments.

(4) Formal Integration

In addition to content integration of arts and cultural sponsorship, formal coordination processes are also required. Based on the application of uniform design principles, sponsorship should be linked with other communication instruments in such a way that a formally consistent appearance is created. Among other things, it is important to ensure that (written) corporate design guidelines are adhered to in communication. In particular, the use of uniform slogans, fonts, colors, and sizes, e.g., for logos, must be ensured. The goal is to maintain a homogeneous perception of the company from the recipients' perspective.

(5) Temporal Integration

Temporal integration of arts and cultural sponsorship into the communication mix encompasses all activities aimed at coordinating communication instruments and media both within and between different planning periods. As a rule, the annual plan is considered the planning period. In the context of the temporal networking of sponsorship with other communication instruments, it is therefore necessary to analyze to what extent a parallel, successive, intermittent, or substitutive use of sponsorship within a planning period appears sensible in order to strengthen the perception of marketing and corporate communication as a unified whole.

(6) Internal Integration

Internal integration refers to the in-house coordination of arts and cultural sponsorship with other sponsorship engagements (e.g., sports sponsorship) as well as with the activities of other company departments. Here, coordination processes with departments such as media advertising, sales promotion, public private relations, event marketing, market research, product management, sales, human resources, and others are particularly relevant. To ensure this, it is advisable to appoint a person responsible for the internal coordination of sponsorship activities.

(7) External Integration

The planning, implementation, and follow-up of sponsorships usually involve a wide range of external individuals and organizations. To ensure the smooth execution of all activities within the framework of sponsorship, intensive coordination is required not only with the sponsored parties themselves but also with sponsorship, advertising, and public private relations agencies, media, and government authorities.

If a particular sponsorship engagement constitutes a key focus within a company's communication policy, its strengths can be best exploited when sponsorship is developed into a comprehensive "communication platform." When **sponsorship is positioned as a communication platform**, it is assumed that sponsorship forms the thematic centerpiece of various supporting communication instruments, which are coordinated with each other. It is a central component of a company's communication strategy and serves as a vehicle for conveying the core communication messages.

Sponsorship as a communication platform thus creates events and occasions whose content is picked up and further disseminated by other instruments of corporate and marketing communication (Bruhn, 2003; Lorenz, 2003; Schmidt & Holze, 2003).

The general objective of corporate sponsorship will be to **develop new forms of arts and cultural sponsorship** that are capable of initiating a dialogue with target groups. The aim is to achieve experience-oriented sponsorship, in which brands and products are directly integrated into the sponsorships, in order to enable the closest possible connection between the content of the sponsorships or cultural offerings and the company's range of services. In addition, established forms of sponsorship should be more strongly integrated into the communication mix than before. In this context, particular importance is attached to the company's social media communication as well as to the communication activities of the cooperating cultural institution. Due to the dynamic development of media and communication markets and changing consumer behavior, it is no longer sufficient to present one's own brand solely in the context of a cultural event—for example, by integrating the logo on advertising media or banners. In order to enable the desired image transfer, it is much more important to place, pick up, and actively communicate these sponsorship engagements and the associated experiential values and image dimensions in other communication instruments (for example, through media advertising or social media communication).

The goal should be to attract consumers' attention, **generate emotions through arts and cultural sponsorship**, and project these onto the corporate sponsorship or the advertised brand by establishing concrete lines of connection. In addition, visitors to cultural events should also be seen as multipliers and influencers who can communicate sponsor messages within their private networks through their own social media posts.

(8) Integration into the Communication Mix and Sponsoring Mix of Corporate Sponsorship

Every corporate sponsorship seeks to communicate with its current and potential customers, the public, its employees, and other target groups in various ways. To ensure the efficient and effective use of marketing and corporate communication, integration must take place on two levels (Bruhn, 2014):

- On a **first level**, it is necessary to coordinate the communication instruments used both in terms of content, form, and timing as part of the integration of arts and cultural sponsorship into the **communication mix** of corporate sponsorship. Sponsorship should always be seen in conjunction with other communication instruments, as it creates events whose content is picked up and further disseminated by other communication instruments.

- Furthermore, on a **second level**, integration of arts and cultural sponsorship into the **sponsoring mix** of corporate sponsorship is necessary. This requires the coordination and alignment of the various sponsorship activities with each other — both within arts and cultural sponsorship and with other manifestations and engagements of the company's sponsorship (e.g., in the areas of sports, environment, social affairs).

10.2 Integration of Arts and Cultural Sponsorship into the Communication Mix of Corporate Sponsorship

The objective of integrating arts and cultural sponsorship into a company's communication mix is to link sponsorship activities in a specific way with other communication instruments, so that a **synergistic amplification of the overall communication effect** is achieved (Bruhn, 2018a, p. 35). As shown in Fig. 10.1, there are various ways to deploy sponsorship in combination with the communication instruments of media advertising, sales promotion, direct marketing, public private relations, internal communication, online communication, event marketing, trade fairs and exhibitions, as well as personal communication.

However, a corporate survey among German, Swiss, and Austrian corporate sponsors on the practice of integrated communication makes it clear that a strong **integration of sponsorship into the communication mix** — in contrast to other instruments (such

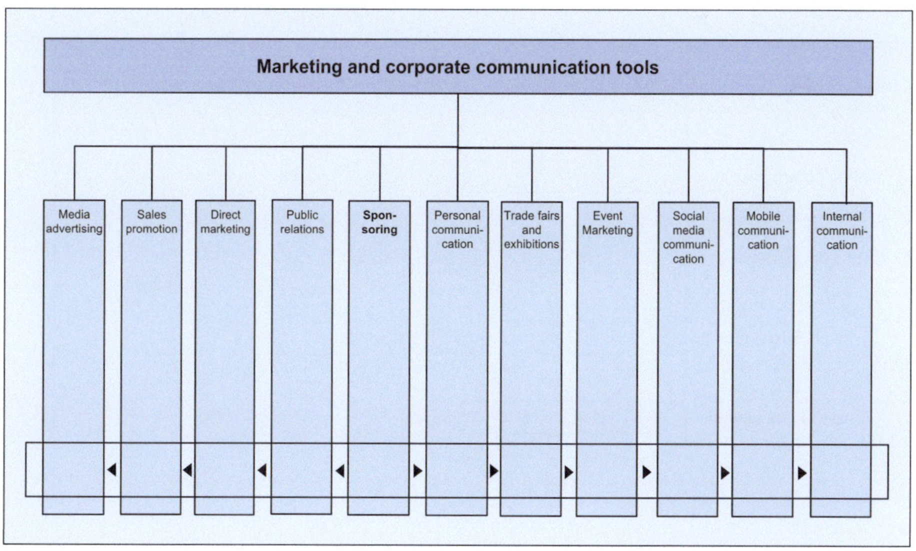

Fig. 10.1 Sponsorship in combination with other instruments of the communication mix. (Source: Bruhn, 2018a, p. 39)

as media advertising, PR/public relations, and sales promotion)—is not a given (Bruhn et al., 2014). These results refer both to the inclusion and the significance of sponsorship within the framework of integrated communication. The reasons for this may include, among others, that those responsible for sponsorship are less frequently involved in the implementation of integrated communication than those responsible for other communication disciplines (with the exception of social media communication, online marketing, and customer relationship management/CRM). Nevertheless, sponsorship is categorized by the surveyed corporate sponsors as an **"integration instrument"** that neither exerts a major influence on other instruments nor is strongly influenced by them. Accordingly, sponsorship is very well suited for integration purposes, but its potential has yet to be fully realized (Bruhn et al., 2014).

Despite the often relatively low integration of sponsorship with other communication instruments, corporate sponsors who network their instruments focus on certain communication tools. As shown in Fig. 10.2, instruments such as public relations, employee

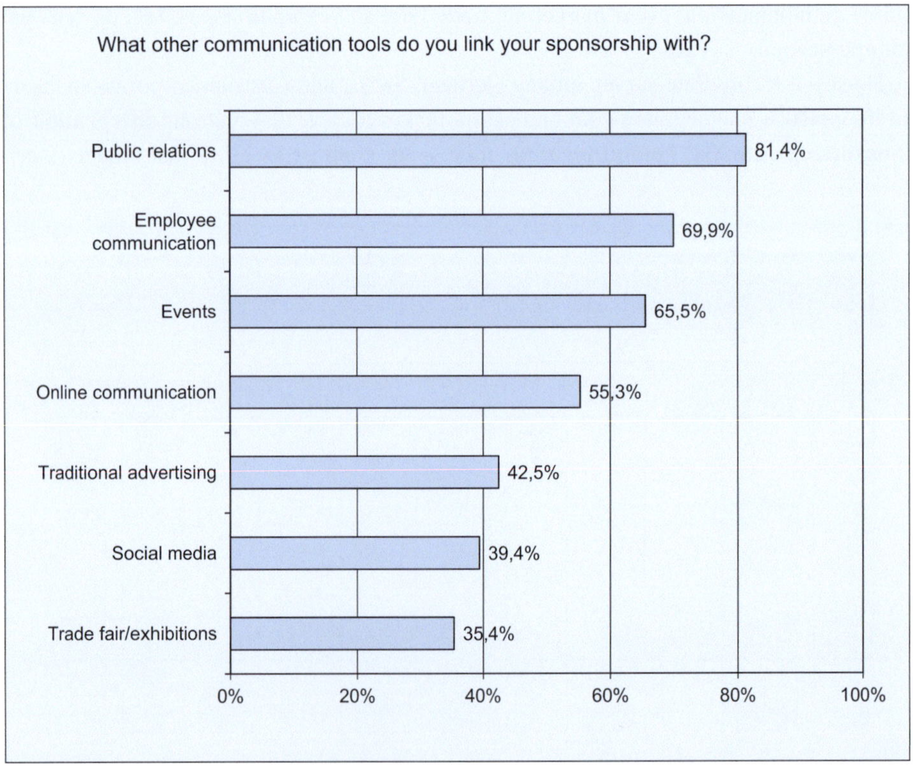

Fig. 10.2 Integration of sponsorship with other communication instruments. (Source: Bagusat, 2013, p. 26)

communication, events, and online communication are preferably networked with sponsorship (Bagusat, 2013, p. 26).

For the communication practice of corporate sponsors, it will be crucial in the future to professionally advance the integration of sponsorship into the communication mix and to leverage the creative opportunities for addressing target groups that arise from the use of sponsorship in combination with other communication instruments.

More so than in sports sponsorship, corporate sponsors must demonstrate a certain sensitivity when integrating their cultural activities into marketing and corporate communication. If arts and cultural sponsorship is used as part of an aggressive corporate communication strategy, visitors to the sponsored events perceive this as intrusive, leading to reactance. The following section outlines the possible applications of arts and cultural sponsorship in combination with the communication instruments of public private relations, media advertising, sales promotion, direct marketing, internal communication, online communication, event marketing, trade fairs and exhibitions, as well as personal communication (Bruhn, 2018a, pp. 269 f.).

Arts and Cultural Sponsorship and Public Private Relations

In many cases, the planning and implementation of arts and cultural sponsorship in corporate sponsorship is assigned to the public private relations department. This is due in no small part to the fact that, especially in small and medium-sized corporate sponsors, decisions about cultural engagement are often made by company management, and the public private relations department is usually assigned to management as a staff unit. Thus, the first approach for integrating arts and cultural sponsorships is to assign them to public relations. This could be achieved, for example, through the following **measures**:

- Integration of arts and cultural sponsorships into all press relations,
- Organization of exhibitions in business premises as well as events within the corporate sponsor's own facilities,
- Endowment of prizes or competitions for arts and cultural funding with dedicated announcements and organization of award ceremonies,
- Invitations to sponsored cultural events for customers and business partners with the aim of maintaining contact with company-relevant groups,
- Mention of arts and cultural sponsorships in corporate media activities such as annual reports, company magazines, brochures, internet, and social media,
- Mention of arts and cultural sponsorships in lectures and publications as well as during company tours.

The inclusion of arts and cultural sponsorship in the public private relations work of corporate sponsors is standard practice. By supporting a cultural event often initiated by a third party, the corporate sponsor demonstrates its cultural responsibility and builds

"goodwill" among socially relevant groups. However, relatively passive measures still predominate, especially the use of sponsorships for press releases. For the public relations work of corporate sponsors, it is important that cultural engagement also generates news value (so-called "news value") that is considered newsworthy by other media. Therefore, sponsorship activities that are directly and significantly causally linked to new artistic or cultural activities, such as commissions to artists or the awarding of cultural prizes, are particularly advantageous.

For example, the fashion manufacturer Hugo Boss regularly awards the Hugo Boss Prize to artists. The award is communicated through the company's own public private relations work with press releases and on the company's online press portal. The art prize has been awarded since 1996 in cooperation with the Solomon R. Guggenheim Museum and the foundation of the same name to promote contemporary art.

Arts and Cultural Sponsorship and Media Advertising

In Germany, the integration of cultural engagements into media advertising is becoming increasingly important. First, let us refer to some possibilities for **advertising integration**:

- References in institutional communication advertisements to explain and justify (especially externally initiated) arts and cultural sponsorships,
- References in advertisements for the announcement of cultural awards and calls for participation in competitions,
- Mention of sponsorships within image or product advertising through titles or symbols,
- References in product advertising to the connection between arts and cultural sponsorship and company performance,
- Placement of advertisements in program booklets, brochures, or catalogs used as part of cultural sponsorships (see Figs. 10.3 and 10.4),
- Mention of cultural engagement in commercials presenting the company,
- Mention of cultural engagement on/in other advertising media such as radio, posters, cinema, television, and websites,
- Mention of cultural engagement by printing on various promotional materials (product and company brochures, beer mats, etc.),
- Use of sponsored artists as so-called "testimonials" or of projects as exemplary product applications in media advertising.

The main reason for the increasing integration of the instruments media advertising and arts and cultural sponsorship is that corporate sponsors are becoming more aware of the positive effects and **opportunitiesof media communication** associated with cultural engagement. The mobile network provider Vodafone integrates its sponsorship of the casting show "Voice of Germany" into its media advertising, for example on the internet, on its social media channels, in advertisements, and commercials. With the claim "Nonstop dabei sein!" ("Be there nonstop!"), Vodafone announces that it is the official

Fig. 10.3 Example of integration of sponsorship into media advertising: Advertisement by Hirslanden Klinik St. Anna in the program booklet of the Lucerne Symphony Orchestra for the 2022/2023 season

Fig. 10.4 Example of integration of sponsorship into media advertising: Advertisement by Luzerner Kantonalbank in the program booklet of the Lucerne Symphony Orchestra for the 2022/2023 season

partner of the music show. On the news channel live.vodafone.de, Vodafone reports on the results of the competition and refers to the possibility of listening to the songs of the judges and award winners via the Vodafone Music streaming service.

Arts and Cultural Sponsorship and Sales Promotion

One way to **integrate the instruments arts and cultural sponsorship and sales promotion** is to involve artists supported as part of a cultural engagement in sales promotion activities, for example by having them (discreetly) perform at dealer presentations. In addition, the instruments are networked in such a way that, in the context of sales promotion competitions, a link is established to the existing cultural sponsorship. Through prize draws, sweepstakes, and other forms of lotteries, consumers or dealers are, for example, given the chance to participate in events initiated or sponsored by corporate sponsorship, such as theater performances or concerts. For example, Deutsche Telekom raffles tickets for its concert series "Telekom Street Gigs," featuring famous artists such as Coldplay, Linkin Park, or Adel Tawil. As part of the "Telekom Street Gigs Community," members can win tickets for an upcoming concert in a sweepstake. As a consolation prize, an exclusive livestream of the concerts is available (Deutsche Telekom

AG, 2016d). Another example is provided by Coca-Cola: In 2023, the beverage brand raffled tickets for major music festivals such as Tomorrowland, Openair Frauenfeld, Lakelive Festival Biel/Nidau, among others, as well as non-cash prizes (see Fig. 10.5). To participate in the raffle, interested parties had to download the Coca-Cola app to their smartphone and take part in a game.

Arts and Cultural Sponsorship and Direct Marketing

The **integration of the instruments arts and cultural sponsorship and direct marketing** takes place in such a way that various direct marketing media are used to draw attention to a cultural engagement. For example, selected target groups are invited to exhibitions supported by corporate sponsorship through the mailing of "mail-order packages." Individual tours and hospitality offers during and after the exhibition provide opportunities for customer care. In addition, it is possible to send documentation about the contents of the exhibition after the event. Of central importance for the use of direct marketing in the context of arts and cultural sponsorships is the maintenance of the customer-specific database with corresponding information on individual cultural interests. This applies primarily to a company's A and B customers.

Arts and Cultural Sponsorship and Internal Communication

Since arts and cultural sponsorship aims for substantive engagement with the supported cultural sectors at all levels of the company, the integration of employees is of particular importance. To enhance credibility, employees must also "live" the arts and cultural

Fig. 10.5 Integration of sponsorship into sales promotion: Landing page of the Coca-Cola sweepstake. (Source: Coca-Cola, 2023)

funding, so internal communication is assigned important tasks. The possibilities for **using arts and cultural sponsorships within the framework of internal communication** are being recognized by an increasing number of corporate sponsors. The interconnection of these instruments takes place, for example, through the following **measures**:

- Inviting executives and employees to sponsored cultural events,
- Implementing arts and cultural sponsorships within the company's own corporate sponsorship for employees,
- Involving employees in the implementation of local and national sponsorships within the organization or as supporters of cultural institutions (corporate volunteering),
- Development of employees' own artistic activities through accompanying measures related to arts and cultural sponsorship,
- Involving employees in decisions regarding arts and cultural sponsorships,
- Involving employees in online communication activities (e.g., the company's social media presence, blog posts),
- Supporting cultural initiatives that have been started by employees,
- Development of special cultural initiatives to promote trainees and future leaders,
- Fostering dialogue between executives and employees about the reasons for cultural engagement,
- Establishing a "cultural circle" or "cultural representative" within the company's own corporate sponsorship, who considers improvements in arts and cultural sponsorship and develops proposals.

Here, too, the list of possible internal measures could be continued. The involvement of employees in the company's arts and cultural sponsorship is initially of particular importance for legitimization as well as for the **anticipation of internal criticism of arts and cultural sponsorship**. Such criticism will always arise when the decision is made too much in isolation by top management, the lines of connection to corporate sponsorship and the justifications are not convincing, and inconsistencies in cultural engagement occur.

An **example** of integrating employees into arts and cultural funding is provided by Bayer AG, which founded its own musical company clubs decades ago, including today the Bayer Philharmonic Orchestra. BASF SE also supports the Young Choir in the choral society, which consists mainly of BASF employees and regularly performs concerts featuring gospel, spirituals, and well-known melodies from musicals and folk music at the BASF Feierabendhaus (after-work house).

Arts and Cultural Sponsorship and Online Communication

In recent years, the **networking of arts and cultural sponsorship and online communication** has experienced very high growth rates, particularly in the form of social media communication via Instagram, TikTok, LinkedIn, and similar platforms. The possibilities range from a simple mention on the sponsor's homepage or social media presence about the supported event, to offering online registration for participation in cultural events, all the way to integrating sponsored artists into a "celebrity chat" and presenting entire events via livestream or photo galleries — such as concerts — on the internet. In addition, the internet and social media pages of a sponsored event also reference the sponsors by integrating their logo and a link to the sponsor's homepage or social media presence.

The following **example** may be mentioned: On the website of the Berlin Philharmoniker, a link leads to their main sponsor, Deutsche Bank. Vice versa, Deutsche Bank uses its Facebook page to inform about events of the Berlin Philharmoniker and posts excerpts from concerts in the form of videos (see Fig. 10.6). For Deutsche Bank's art collection, the corporate sponsorship created its own homepage (www.deutsche-bank-kunst.com/collection/), where, among other things, artworks are displayed and information about the artists is provided (see Fig. 10.7). Another tool for linking in social media channels is the hashtag "#", which makes terms available for keyword searches. In this way, current trends are quickly spread and interconnected on the internet. This service is especially interesting for sponsors, as it allows them to achieve a wide reach and directly associate their sponsored cultural projects with their corporate sponsorship.

In addition to using the internet for communication of cultural engagements, it is also conceivable that corporate sponsorship supports specific **cultural projects on the internet**. This means providing a cultural project with an online presence, announcing cultural awards directly online, or offering a cultural association a communication platform on the internet (Doemich, 2016). A project specifically conceived as an internet project is the "BMW Tate Live" initiative by BMW in cooperation with the Tate Modern art museum in London. This subproject of "BMW Tate Live" is a purely digitally curated "Performance Room" that exists exclusively online. The performances presented there form part of the museum's collection, thus enabling a virtual visit regardless of the viewer's actual location. To date, ten online works have been created for "BMW Tate Live." In total, over 165,000 people from 90 countries have visited the performance room. More than 330,000 people have participated in a performance or talk event, and over 72,000 people have watched the documentaries offered (Tate, 2023).

In addition to this use of the internet, in the area of online communication it is also conceivable that **company-specific applications (apps)** are made available for download for supported events, giving event visitors the opportunity to obtain further information about the supporting corporate sponsorship. In addition, sponsors can provide customers with videos or photo galleries of an event within the app and use push notifications to inform them about news and current cultural events in which the corporate sponsorship acts as sponsor.

Foundations, backed by private corporate sponsorship, also integrate the internet as a platform into their communication mix. Examples include the Deutsche Bank Foundation (www.deutsche-bank-stiftung.de), the Allianz Foundation founded in 2022 (www.allianzfoundation.org), and the Dresden Cultural Foundation of Dresdner Bank (https://www.commerzbank.de/de/kulturstiftungdresden/home_2/index.html). It is noteworthy that

Fig. 10.6 Reciprocal references between sponsor and sponsored party using the example of Deutsche Bank and Berlin Philharmoniker (2023)

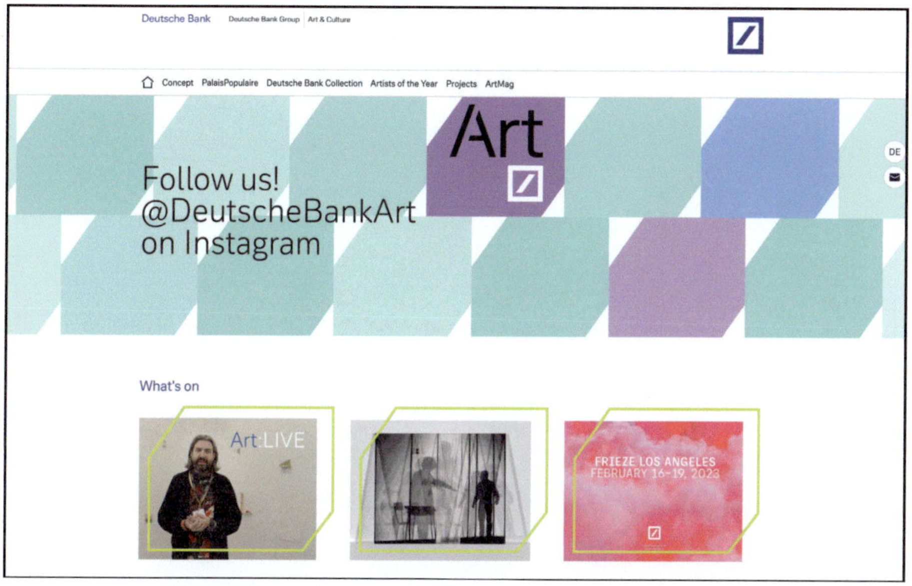

Fig. 10.7 Dedicated website for communication of arts and cultural sponsorship using the example of the Deutsche Bank art program

the Dresden Cultural Foundation of Dresdner Bank continues to exist and is active, even though Dresdner Bank merged with Commerzbank back in 2009 and is no longer visible as an independent brand in the financial sector.

The foundations use their online presence, for example, to inform about their foundation activities, to intensify relationships with key sponsors, or to conduct internet campaigns. At the same time, the corporate sponsorship behind the foundation benefits from the additional publicity for its cultural engagement. It is also conceivable to integrate a link to the company's website and vice versa from the company's site to the foundation's homepage.

Arts and Cultural Sponsorship and Event Marketing

An **integration of the instruments arts and cultural sponsorship and event marketing** is achieved by engaging groups or ensembles that have been supported over a longer period to participate in independently initiated events. For example, a sponsored music ensemble might accompany introductory events for a newly launched product in various cities. Furthermore, it is possible to independently design parts of the program at sponsored events to draw attention to the company's engagement. For instance, the logistics company Hermes supported the Lollapalooza music festival in Berlin in 2022 and presented its services on site at the festival grounds with a pop-up parcel shop. At the shop, festival visitors could send Hermes parcels from the festival free of charge. With this event action, Hermes aimed to emphasize its message "always near you" and to win festival visitors as multipliers for Hermes' services (see Fig. 10.8).

Fig. 10.8 Connection of arts and cultural sponsorship and event marketing using the example of Hermes

Arts and Cultural Sponsorship and Trade Fairs & Exhibitions

The **integration of cultural sponsorships with trade fairs and exhibitions** is conceivable, for example, in the form of having supported groups or artists available at the company's exhibition stands to engage in conversations with visitors. In addition, they are also integrated into the program of the trade fair. Such integration would be conceivable, for example, for the corporate sponsorship BMW and its "Art Car Collection." Since 1975, the Munich-based automobile manufacturer has commissioned exclusive special editions designed by famous artists such as Jeff Koons, Frank Stella, and others (see the case study in Chap. 2). It would also be possible to exhibit these "Art Cars" at well-known automotive trade fairs and invite the respective artists to personally interact with trade fair visitors. It is also possible for the company's exhibition stands to highlight its cultural activities, and for visitors, for example, to have the opportunity to purchase discounted tickets for supported performances or concerts. The BMW Group, for example, is represented as a sponsor at all major art fairs in order to engage with potential customers.

Arts and Cultural Sponsorship and Personal Communication

A company's cultural engagement provides a solid foundation for the **integration of cultural sponsorships with personal communication**, especially with a target group that has been carefully selected through corporate sponsorship. For example, Audi AG emphasizes that by supporting renowned cultural festivals, it specifically secures access to tickets for high-end customers. According to corporate sponsorship, special advantages of such invitations lie in the unifying nature of music and the lasting memorability of glamorous events, such as attending a prestigious festival. The invitations are further enhanced by offering an exclusive Audi chauffeur service for the company's VIP guests (Audi AG, 2016a).

Furthermore, there are additional approaches to leveraging cultural engagement within corporate sponsorship. This includes the impact of arts and cultural sponsorship on the company's **product policy**, particularly product design. Artistic engagement by executives and employees with questions of aesthetics and design heightens awareness of art within corporate sponsorship. This, in turn, facilitates internal discussions about improving product design.

Likewise, dialogue with an art sector supported by arts and cultural sponsorship intensifies the discussion about **art in corporate sponsorship**. This includes, for example, questions of architecture, art in and on buildings, office and workplace design, as well as libraries, company museums, and much more. Moreover, cultural engagement can also spark a discussion about corporate identity.

10.3 Integration of Arts and Cultural Sponsorship into the Sponsoring Mix of Corporate Sponsorship

Another key to achieving a high impact with arts and cultural sponsorship is the **integration of arts and cultural sponsorship into the company's sponsoring mix**. The starting point for this integration is the question of how the individual sponsorship activities can be interconnected so that, by developing a holistic concept, the various communication instruments are used in such a way that the overarching communication objectives are achieved as effectively as possible. The integration of arts and cultural sponsorship into the sponsoring mix must take place in two areas:

- Integration of the various sponsorships within the field of arts and cultural sponsorship,
- Integration of cultural sponsorships with the company's other engagements (e.g., sports, environment, social, media).

These interconnections in arts and cultural sponsorship do not mean that every communication activity within the framework of sponsorship must be carried out in exactly the same way, but rather that, for example, an overarching **"umbrella theme"** ensures the integration of individual communication measures within sponsorship. A practical example of successful integration is the arts and cultural sponsorship of the innogy Foundation for Energy and Society (formerly RWE Foundation). All engagements are united under the umbrella theme of "energy," and within this framework, the foundation supports, for example, the International Light Art Prize, the art festival Strom, or the event series "Conversations on Light Culture" (innogy Stiftung für Energie und Gesellschaft gGmbH, 2016).

With regard to the area of integration decisions, the following **decision dimensions** are distinguished, which must be considered in both forms of integration:

- Content dimension,
- Formal dimension,
- Temporal dimension.

The **content dimension** of integrating arts and cultural sponsorship into the company's sponsoring mix involves the thematic coordination of the individual sponsoring activities within a planning period. For example, if a corporate sponsorship aims to position itself as particularly creative, progressive, or more classically traditional, the thematic focus of the sponsorship engagement should be on entering into partnerships that ensure a corresponding image transfer. When selecting the overarching theme, such as supporting emerging artists, it is important to consider the needs and wishes of the targeted **target groups** in order to ensure the necessary topic-related **acceptance**. The selection of the thematic spectrum thus also represents a significant strategic decision that sets the framework for all further planning and implementation decisions. Approaches for linking the thematic messages of various other company sponsorship engagements, such as in sports or the environment, include the use of consistent slogans, core messages, key arguments, and key visuals.

Closely linked to the content decision is the **formal dimension** of integrating arts and cultural sponsorship into the sponsoring mix. Here, the alternatives regarding the degree of formal integration of individual sponsoring activities must be evaluated. For example, it must be decided to what extent it makes sense to adopt an identical communication approach for every sponsorship activity. Furthermore, within this decision dimension, the specific **design** of sponsoring activities must be defined, i.e., the integration of formal design principles such as the use of colors, font sizes, or symbols according to the design manual.

Finally, all communication measures must also be continuously coordinated within a **temporal dimension**. On the one hand, corporate sponsorship implements integrative measures to ensure mutual support of all communication instruments in their timing. On the other hand, temporal continuity of the communication instruments must be ensured and too frequent changes in the communication concept should be avoided. The temporal dimension here refers to short- to medium-term coordination of the communication instruments used, in order to reinforce key communication objectives, such as the perception of a consistent corporate image.

10.4 Decision Levels in the Corporate Hierarchy

When using arts and cultural sponsorship as an integrative tool of marketing and corporate communication, both sponsored parties and sponsoring agencies face the question of which **entity within the corporate hierarchy** is responsible for sponsorships. Experience in recent years has shown that responsibilities and competencies regarding the undertaking of a sponsorship commitment are distributed very differently depending on the company. Figure 10.9 shows, as the result of a company survey, the organizational positions of the persons with primary responsibility for the area of sponsorship.

In order for a company's cultural engagement to be implemented into a holistic sponsorship strategy, it is advisable to differentiate between the various sponsorship areas (sports, culture, social/environmental, media). In addition, the functions (initiation, planning, decision-making, implementation) that different company departments perform in the development of sponsorship must be distinguished. The **responsibilities and tasks of the various hierarchy levels and departments** should be considered with regard to the phases of initiation, planning, decision-making, and implementation. In arts and cultural sponsorship, the functions of initiation, planning, and implementation often lie with the public private relations department (technical promoters), while the decision itself is often made at the executive board level (power promoters). Marketing and advertising departments are also regularly involved in arts and cultural sponsorship.

Responsibilities in corporate sponsorship can, however, vary depending on the sponsorship area. For example, sports sponsorship is more frequently assigned to marketing and advertising departments than arts and cultural sponsorship. Sponsorship activities are therefore not necessarily the domain of a specific communications department. Rather, responsibility varies depending on the sponsorship area, the company's communication situation, the power of individual departments, and the personal interests of managers.

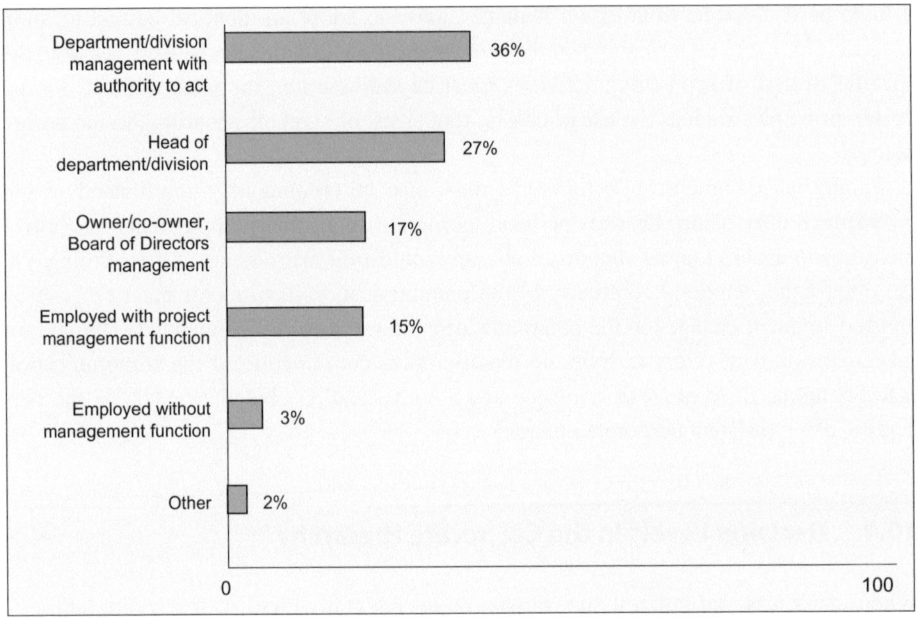

Fig. 10.9 Organizational position of the person with primary responsibility for sponsorship. (Source: ZHAW, 2015, p. 11)

Key Points

1. **Integration of arts and cultural sponsorship is necessary:** Arts and cultural sponsorship is not independent of other communication instruments and must therefore be integrated into a company's communication mix.
2. **Examine criteria for integration:** The strategic, instrumental, content-related, formal, temporal, internal, and external aspects of integrating arts and cultural sponsorship must be taken into account.
3. **Promote cooperative collaboration:** The numerous partners such as agencies, media, and cultural institutions must be coordinated for effective external integration of arts and cultural sponsorship.
4. **Leverage synergy effects:** Arts and cultural sponsorship should be used in conjunction with other communication instruments such as advertising, PR, and events to enhance its impact.
5. **External and internal integration:** In addition to integrating arts and cultural sponsorship into external corporate communication, integration into internal communication must also be considered.
6. **Relevance of integration into the sponsorship mix:** Intra-instrumental integration of the individual communication instruments is necessary. This

includes the alignment and coordination of various sponsorship activities with each other.

7. **Focused arts and cultural sponsorship:** In terms of the content dimension for integrating arts and cultural sponsorship into the sponsorship mix, it makes sense to focus on a thematic priority for the cultural sponsorship commitment.
8. **Professional integration through uniform design:** In terms of the formal dimension of integration, attention should be paid to a uniform design of communication, taking design manuals into account.
9. **Importance of continuity in communication:** When integrating, attention must be paid to the continuity of communication measures to ensure mutual reinforcement of the attention generated by the communication activities.
10. **Decision levels are not uniformly regulated:** Responsibilities and tasks of the various hierarchy levels and departments for implementing arts and cultural sponsorship measures must be clarified, as they are not the same for all corporate sponsorships and can also vary within a company depending on the sponsorship area (e.g., arts and cultural sponsorship vs. sports sponsorship).

Performance Evaluation in Arts and Cultural Sponsorship

11

Contents

11.1 Methods of Performance Evaluation in Arts and Cultural Sponsorship 256
11.2 Questionnaire for Performance Evaluation in Arts and Cultural Sponsorship 265
11.3 Problems of Performance Evaluation in Arts and Cultural Sponsorship. 273
11.4 Criteria and Award Winners of Successful Sponsorship Activities 275

Abstract

The management process of arts and cultural sponsorship traditionally concludes with an evaluation of the sponsorship cooperation in order to determine its performance metrics and thus its success. This involves assessing not only the organizational process but also the impact and cost-effectiveness of the activities. The chapter presents various methods and instruments of performance evaluation, particularly for process, effectiveness, and efficiency control. In addition, the problems and limitations of performance evaluation in arts and cultural sponsorship are discussed. For practical application, a sample questionnaire is provided as a basis for implementing control within the framework of audience studies. Finally, award winners of successful arts and cultural sponsorships are mentioned.

The performance evaluation of arts and cultural sponsorship in terms of the degree to which the set objectives are achieved concludes the planning process and at the same time marks a starting point for planning considerations regarding the use of arts and cultural sponsorship in subsequent periods. The focus of the **assessment of the**

M. Bruhn and L. Pöllmann, *Arts and Cultural Sponsorship*,
https://doi.org/10.1007/978-3-658-50079-5_11

effectiveness of arts and cultural sponsorship centers on the questions of what communicative impact the engagement has achieved among the target groups, and whether the financial investment in corporate sponsorship has "paid off."

As with other forms of sponsorship, the subject of performance evaluation distinguishes between **process controls**, which deal with monitoring the implementation of arts and cultural sponsorships, and effectiveness as well as efficiency controls, which relate to the measurement of tangible results. An example of process control is a systematic analysis of the course of an arts and cultural sponsorship, including critical phases that could influence the success of the project. Within the **effectiveness control**, corporate sponsorships, for example, examine what media impact was achieved and to what extent the support of an artist contributed to achieving the communicative objectives. In the context of **efficiency control**, the focus is on an economic evaluation of individual sponsorship measures and resources, whereby corporate sponsorships compare the costs incurred for all sponsoring activities with the realized benefits.

When measuring impact, it is also advisable in arts and cultural sponsorship to distinguish between **long-term communication effects**, which are learned by an individual over the long term, and **immediate communication effects**, which manifest as short-term reactions in a specific situation. Surveys to determine image and awareness levels are particularly suitable for measuring long-term communication effects. In addition to surveys using representative samples, methods such as individual explorations and group discussions can also be considered, as they provide insights into the communication effects caused by arts and cultural sponsorship. Furthermore, impact measurement is supported by comparative quantitative and qualitative analysis of media coverage as well as evaluation of social media posts. Immediate communication effects can be captured using various survey methods, as well as through procedures for calculating media values, recall and recognition tests, group discussions, and more.

In addition to reviewing processes and goal achievement, performance evaluation is also used for a more in-depth **analysis of the cost-benefit ratios** of a cultural sponsorship engagement. This enables the evaluation of different arts and cultural sponsorships, as well as a comparison with other communication instruments, providing insights into the economic assessment of cultural engagements.

11.1 Methods of Performance Evaluation in Arts and Cultural Sponsorship

Within the framework of arts and cultural sponsorship, the following presents three areas of performance evaluation: process, effectiveness, and efficiency control.

(1) Process control

The analytical tools used in process control examine the individual **planning and implementation steps of a cultural sponsorship engagement**. Accordingly, there is a targeted focus on monitoring the necessary activities for preparing a cultural sponsorship measure, adherence to schedules, and control of the procedures and measures used. The following **process control methods** are used for this purpose:

- Test catalogs (checklists),
- Bar charts/network planning technique,
- Point evaluation procedure (scoring models),
- Mini audit,
- Process audit,
- Calculation of an integration index,
- Quality of integration assessment profile,
- EFQM excellence model,
- Communication scorecard/corporate communications scorecard,
- Advertising success chain.

Test question catalogs (checklists)
Test question catalogs or checklists are a method for systematically reviewing specific aspects of a project or process. They contain predefined questions or criteria that are worked through to ensure that all relevant points have been considered. In arts and cultural sponsorship, checklists can be used to verify whether all necessary measures for planning and implementing a sponsorship event have been taken, such as whether the sponsor's brand presence is appropriate or whether contractual obligations have been fulfilled.

Bar charts and network planning technique
Bar charts, also known as Gantt charts, are visual representation methods for planning and providing a timeline overview of project schedules. They show the duration of activities and their temporal sequence. The network planning technique is a project management tool that takes into account the dependencies between individual tasks. In the evaluation of cultural sponsorship projects, bar charts can be used to plan and track the milestones and phases of marketing and advertising activities, while the network planning technique can help identify critical paths and potential delays in project implementation.

Point evaluation procedure (scoring models)
Point evaluation procedures, also known as scoring models, are quantitative methods for evaluating and comparing projects or decision options. Various criteria are weighted and assessed to arrive at an overall evaluation. For example, in arts and cultural sponsorship, the integration of sponsorship into corporate, marketing, and brand communication can be examined. This would require, as part of developing a scoring model, defining criteria as indicators, assigning weighting factors, and evaluating them on a point scale. It is advisable to conduct the scoring procedure regularly in order to obtain comparative values and thus assess not only the status quo but also the development of sponsorship activities.

Mini audit
A mini audit is a focused review of a specific part of a company or project. It is less comprehensive than a full audit but still provides insights into the effectiveness and efficiency of processes. In the context of arts and cultural sponsorship, a mini audit can be used to assess the effectiveness of specific sponsorship measures, such as the visibility of the brand during an event or customer satisfaction.

Process audit
A process audit is a detailed examination of the procedures within a project or organization to ensure their compliance with specified standards or best practices. In arts and cultural sponsorship, a process audit can be used to examine the processes of planning, implementing, and following up on sponsoring activities and to assess whether these processes are efficient and effective and meet the objectives of the sponsorship.

Calculation of an integration index
An integration index is a quantitative measure that assesses how well various marketing and sponsorship activities are integrated into an overall concept. It evaluates the consistency and harmony between sponsoring activities and the company's other marketing measures. For example, for a cultural sponsorship project, an integration index can be determined by assessing how well the sponsorship aligns with the overall brand strategy.

Quality of integration assessment profile
This profile is an evaluation scheme that also assesses the quality of the integration of sponsorship activities into corporate communication or the marketing strategy of a specific product (in the case of corporate sponsorship with multiple brands). It includes factors such as creative implementation, consistency of messages, and interaction with the target groups. For cultural sponsorship activities, such an assessment profile can be used to evaluate how well the sponsorship messages have been incorporated into the various marketing and communication channels and whether they have reached the cultural audience in a coherent and engaging manner.

EFQM Excellence Model
The EFQM Excellence Model is a quality management tool (named after the European Foundation for Quality Management, EFQM) that provides a holistic view of an organization's performance. It is based on a self-assessment in various areas such as leadership, strategy, people, partnerships, resources, and processes. When evaluating cultural sponsorship activities, the model can be used to assess the extent to which the sponsoring activities contribute to achieving excellence or a particular quality within the organization, such as improving the company's image and increasing employee engagement.

Communication Scorecard/Corporate Communications Scorecard
The communication scorecard/corporate communications scorecard is a variation of the classic Balanced Scorecard (BSC), a strategic planning and management system used to align activities with an organization's vision and strategy. It considers multiple perspectives such as finance, customers, internal processes, among others. For cultural sponsorship projects, such a scorecard can be used to measure and balance the performance of the sponsorship across various dimensions. These dimensions may include, for example, the following aspects:

- Brand image,
- Audience response,
- Cost efficiency,
- Contribution to corporate culture.

Advertising Success Chain
The advertising success chain is a concept that maps the steps along the entire customer journey from the consumer's initial perception of the advertising message to the purchase and beyond. It takes into account various stages from initial attention to the after-sales phase. When applied to arts and cultural sponsorship, the chain of effectiveness can help measure the effectiveness of sponsorship at each stage—from increasing brand awareness and interest in products to brand loyalty. It is important to consider not only the company's communication measures to activate the arts and cultural sponsorship, but also the communication activities of the cooperating cultural institutions.

These methods are capable of monitoring schedules and critical activities in the planning process of sponsorship, even in the short term.

(2) Effectiveness Control
Effectiveness controls refer to the realization or the **degree of achievement of the intended communicative effects** among the individual target groups of arts and cultural sponsorship. By comparing with the predefined objectives, the degree of achievement and thus the success of the cultural sponsorship engagement is assessed. For arts and cultural sponsorship, the fundamental aim is to achieve higher levels of impact among recipients through the integrated use of other communication instruments than through the isolated use of various communication measures. The measurement of impact is carried out for arts and cultural sponsorship, the entire sponsorship engagement, as well as at the level of overall communication.

The following **effectiveness control methods** have proven themselves as analytical tools in the context of effectiveness controls:

- Measurement of the perception of sponsorship activities,
- Measurement of recall effect,

- Conducting image studies,
- Determination of number of contacts.

Measurement of the Perception of Sponsorship Activities

In the context of effectiveness analyses, various methods of impact measurement are used to assess cognitive, affective, and conative responses among the target groups. Since the perception of the sponsoring message has a significant influence on the effectiveness of sponsorship, but is usually exposed to numerous competing stimuli, corporate sponsorship must pay particular attention to this aspect of impact measurement. Using an **eye-tracking device** (also known as the **eyetracking method**), which measures the pupil's response to specific elements of a projection surface, sponsors can determine, for example, whether their logo in a program booklet or on tickets is noticed at all and, if so, with what intensity (Hermanns & Marwitz, 2008, p. 151). By using a tachistoscope, corporate sponsorship can check whether a company logo is correctly recognized and which elements, for example in an advertisement, are perceived earlier or later. The strength of attention can be derived from the level of activation and measured using various apparatus-based methods (measurement of electrodermal and psychogalvanic response). Through these methods, sponsors obtain information, among other things, about how much the design of a poster attracts attention and how it affects logo placement.

Measurement of Recall Effect

To measure recall effect in arts and cultural sponsorship, recall and recognition tests are primarily used.

Recall Tests assess the communicative memory effect, i.e., how well the audience of a cultural event remembers the sponsors (and their messages). To measure this, a survey is conducted after an event, in which respondents are asked, without further prompting, to name from memory who the sponsors of the cultural offering were. A distinction can be made between short-term recall results, obtained through surveys conducted immediately after an event, and medium- to long-term recall results from surveys conducted several days or even weeks after an event. Generally, recall tests are limited to surveys conducted directly after an event, by integrating them into general feedback questionnaires (see Fig. 11.1).

Recognition Tests in contrast, measure recognition values. In this case, test subjects are shown sponsor logos or promotional materials from cultural sponsorship (e.g., posters) and are asked which corporate sponsorships and activities they recognize. This form of aided questioning generally yields higher values than unaided recall tests.

Fundamentally, it is necessary to examine whether and to what extent the **recall rate of cultural sponsors** is present in specific arts and cultural sponsorships at all. As shown in Fig. 11.2, in eight out of thirteen events examined in the study by the Working Group on Arts and Cultural Sponsorship (Arbeitskreis Kultursponsoring, AKS), sponsorship

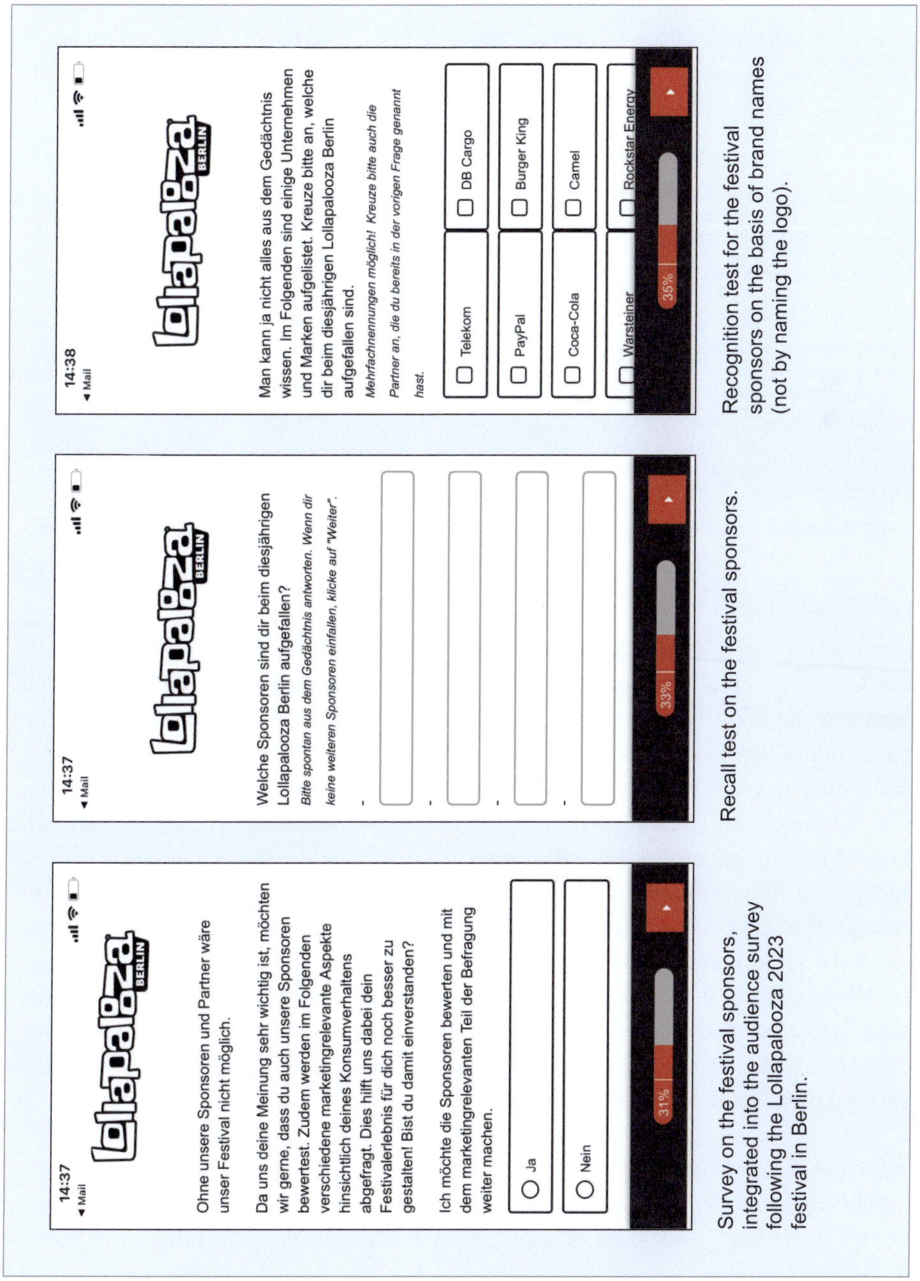

Fig. 11.1 Example of an audience survey on sponsor impact: excerpts from the Lollaplooza 2023 Berlin questionnaire

Company and project	Surveyed people	Sponsorship perceived	Aided recall
Audi: Salzburg Festival	234	82,9%	50,9%
Beiersdorf: tesafilm-fest	123	93,5%	84,6%
BMW Group: Jazz & More	185	53,5%	42,7%
Deutsche Bahn: Literature	265	27,9%	12,1%
Express Ford: Cologne Music Triennial	187	90,9%	83,4%
Jenoptik: Georges Rousse exhibition	72	87,5%	87,5%
Montblanc: Menuhin Festival Gstaad	105	71,4%	42,9%
Philip Morris: F6 Graphics Prize	74	71,6%	58,1%
Siemens: Late Freedoms	101	30,7%	14,9%
Siemens: The Injured Diva	101	12,9%	10,9%
United KV: Zeralda's Journey	119	79,0%	57,1%
VW-Soundfoundation: Music Festival on the Ring	150	87,3%	6,0%
LMU: Writing and Image in Motion	110	34,5%	n.a.

Fig. 11.2 Attention values of sponsorship for selected cultural events. (Source: Schwaiger, 2001, 2006, p. 12)

was noticed by over 70% of respondents, and in at least six of the events, unaided recall was at least 50%. Of all respondents at the 13 evaluated cultural events, 63% of visitors noticed that the event was sponsored, and as many as 88.4% of respondents rated the arts and cultural sponsorship very positively (Schwaiger, 2001, 2006). Furthermore, individual studies revealed that male visitors perceive sponsors more frequently than female visitors. In some cases, a clear correlation was also demonstrated between unaided recall values and the number of visitors to the event.

In addition to querying recall values in face-to-face interviews, a modified form of the recognition test is used in arts and cultural sponsorship, the so-called **folder test**. In this test, the subject receives, for example, an exhibition catalog in which logos of various exhibitors appear in different placements, sizes, and frequencies. After reviewing the catalog, both aided and unaided recall of the sponsors by the subject is determined. The folder test provides the sponsor, among other things, with insights into the impact of different logo placements on recall effectiveness.

Conducting Image Studies

To easily capture a person's general attitude toward a cultural sponsor, simple **rating scales** are used. These scales, for example, ask about a company's likability or its sense of social responsibility.

A step further is the use of the **"semantic differential"**, which enables the assessment of a sponsor with regard to individual image attributes (e.g., modernity, originality)

(Christensen, 2006; Hermanns & Marwitz, 2008). In this way, corporate sponsorships can **compare their image with other sponsors** of a cultural event and examine whether there are image differences between sponsors and non-sponsors. Furthermore, it is possible to ask about the company's image among people who are aware of the corporate sponsorship as a sponsor and those who are not aware of the cultural involvement. The results of these questions provide valuable insights into the effectiveness of sponsorship activities in terms of image change.

Such a survey can be conducted using a semantic differential or polarity profile, in which both groups rate the extent of defined attributes with regard to the sponsor's brand. Figure 11.3 shows an example of such a **polarity profile** (Pöllmann, 2021a, p. 115) and possible results from a survey of two groups. For the use of this method, the attributes must be individually adapted to the relevant attributes of the sponsor brand.

Surveys on the **acceptance of arts and cultural sponsorships** were conducted as part of a study by the Working Group on Arts and Cultural Sponsorship and found that almost all respondents expressed positive attitudes toward the sponsors (Schwaiger, 2006). It is noteworthy that acceptance proved to be independent of possible lines of connection (product affinity, image affinity, etc.) between the sponsor and the sponsored event.

To investigate the short-term **effect of arts and cultural sponsorship on a sponsor's image**, the exhibition "Surrealism 1919–1944" in Düsseldorf, supported by Deutsche

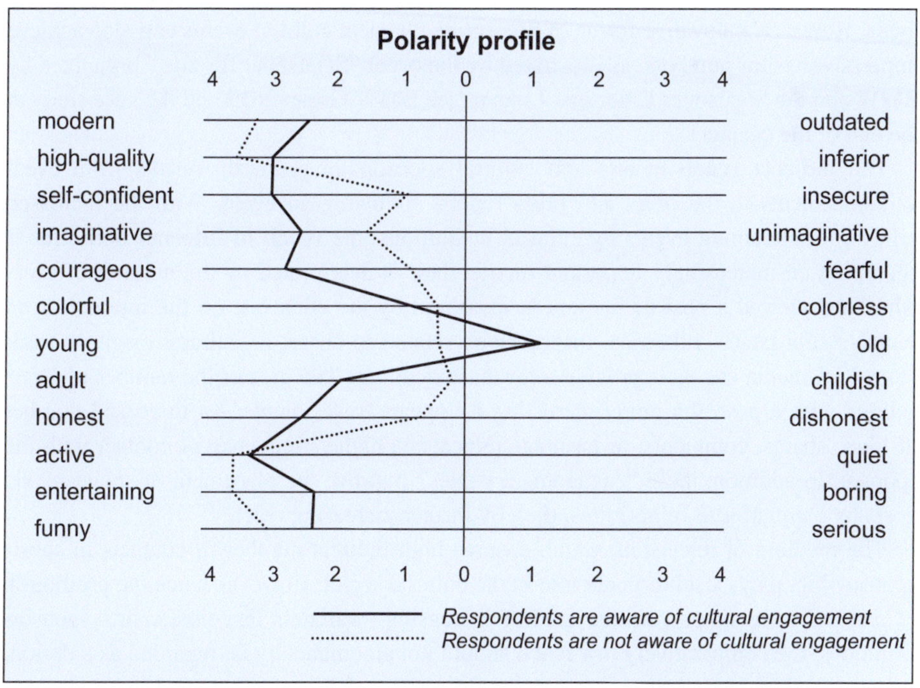

Fig. 11.3 Example of a polarity profile in the context of a sponsorship image study

Renault AG in 2002, and the opera performance "Die Meistersinger von Nürnberg" at the Bavarian State Opera in Munich, sponsored by Siemens in 2004, were analyzed. The study demonstrates that arts and cultural sponsorship can at least temporarily achieve positive effects on attitudes toward a sponsor. In particular, the constructs of responsibility and performance are positively influenced (Schwaiger & Unterreitmeier, 2003; Schwaiger et al., 2005). In a long-term study, the long-term effect of arts and cultural sponsorship on reputation judgment was examined in over 3000 subjects. Although, after intensive information about the engagements of four corporate sponsors over a longer period, the individual sponsorship activities of corporate sponsors were rated significantly higher over time, no clear increase in reputation assessment could be demonstrated (Schwaiger, 2006).

Determining the Number of Contacts

While the measurement of recall effectiveness and perception of sponsorship activities as well as image studies aim at a qualitative evaluation of arts and cultural sponsorship, determining the number of contacts serves as a quantitative impact control. A distinction is made between the direct reach of an event, which can be determined from the number of visitors to a sponsored cultural event, and the indirect reach, which can be derived from media coverage.

The **direct reach** is comparatively low for most cultural events compared to sports events. Exceptions include the sponsorship of rock and pop concerts or international festivals. However, innovative forms of presenting classical cultural events can also achieve impressive visitor numbers, as illustrated by the event "Staatsoper für alle," organized by BMW and the Staatsoper Unter den Linden (see BMW Group 2022 and the case study at the end of the chapter).

The **indirect reach** in arts and cultural sponsorship primarily results from event announcements in the press and press reports following an event. With the increased offering of streaming events by cultural institutions, the **reach of internet activities** is becoming an increasingly important metric. This is determined by the number of users who have viewed a post online and is measured by the click rate on the internet or on social media pages. Likewise, **interactions** related to an art or cultural event on various social media channels provide relevant indications. The greater the number of interactions with a post, the more interesting it appears to recipients. An increased number of likes, shares, comments, or hashtags indicates a higher frequency of contact with the sponsor. In addition, these "engagement values" improve the placement of social media posts by the platforms' algorithms, thereby further increasing reach.

The medium of television, which ensures high indirect number of contacts in sports sponsorship, plays a subordinate role in the cultural sector. However, since the promotion of cultural interests pursues the goal of increasing awareness less than sports sponsorship does, the comparatively low reach should not automatically be regarded as a deficit. Although quantitative impact control should not be neglected in arts and cultural sponsorship, the focus is on determining qualitative effects.

(3) Efficiency control

The starting point of efficiency control within the framework of a cost-benefit analysis is a comparison of the resources used ("costs") and the communication impact achieved ("benefit") of arts and cultural sponsorship.

- **Costs of sponsorship:** The costs are recorded as the expenditure for the respective sponsorship.
- **Benefits of sponsorship:** The benefits of sponsorships are often determined by media equivalency analyses, i.e., the media impact achieved is calculated using prices that would "normally" be spent on comparable advertising (e.g., placements in commercial television, so-called opportunity costs).

Theoretically, it would also be conceivable, following the opportunity cost approach, to estimate and evaluate the "advertising benefit" forgone from other communication tools as costs. Another possibility is the calculation of media values, e.g., the **sponsoring cost per mille (SCPM)**. This essentially corresponds to the cost per mille (CPM), which was already explained in Chap. 10 for the evaluation of sponsorship offers. However, these comparisons often fail because the necessary empirical information is not available, resulting in highly subjective estimates that are hardly meaningful. In principle, it is assumed that, measured by cost per thousand contacts, the instrument of arts and cultural sponsorship does not compete with media advertising or sports sponsorship. The strengths of cultural activities in corporate sponsorship are seen more in **contact quality** than in quantity, as well as in image improvement and the retention of attractive customers (Schwaiger, 2006, pp. 117 ff.). However, empirical findings on these assumptions are not yet available.

Due to methodological problems that make a **systematic impact assessment in arts and cultural sponsorship** difficult, impact models and empirical studies are so far only available in isolated cases (Walliser, 2003; Colbert et al., 2005). For example, a study was commissioned by the working group on arts and cultural sponsorship between 1999 and 2006, which surveyed 1826 visitors to 13 cultural events. Another study surveyed 472 people regarding their reaction or opinion about the sponsorship engagement of 16 corporate sponsors at 12 cultural events (Christensen, 2006; Schwaiger, 2006).

11.2 Questionnaire for Performance Evaluation in Arts and Cultural Sponsorship

A low-threshold form of performance evaluation is a written **survey of the audience at cultural events**. This can be defined and implemented as a basic measure for evaluating cultural engagement. Since cultural organizations often conduct audience surveys, it is generally possible to integrate questions about the presence of sponsors into these surveys (see again Fig. 11.1). The advantage of this method is that the survey can be conducted with very little effort. The disadvantage, however, is that only a few questions can be asked specifically about sponsorship, since other aspects of the event must also be considered in the survey.

In principle, sponsors should consider whether a survey should focus solely on their individual brand presence or whether the evaluation should cover sponsorship activities as a whole. An **overall evaluation** has the advantage for sponsors that they can compare their own activities with those of other sponsors and thus better derive implications for future engagements.

The audience survey should ideally cover three **survey areas**:

- **Part 1: Audience cultural attendance behavior**
  Cultural attendance behavior can be divided into the phases before, during, and after the visit. It is of interest what attitude the audience has towards the cultural offering, how they inform themselves, and how they use the cultural offering. Based on this information, the target group segments of the cultural offering can be derived and compared with one's own target groups. In addition, the answers provide numerous possibilities for bivariate analysis procedures by cross-tabulating the answers from Part 1 with the questions on sponsorship (Part 2).
- **Part 2: Evaluation of sponsorship activities**
  These are the core questions of the survey, which can be used to determine the success of the activities. In addition to recall and recognition values, a comparison with other sponsors as well as key figures on recommendation behavior (e.g., based on the Net Promoter Score) can also be derived.
- **Part 3: Sociodemographic information**
  Information on the sociodemographic composition of the audience is essential for any audience survey, provides important insights into the target group reached, and also plays a special role in bivariate analysis. These questions are placed at the end of the questionnaire design, as they are particularly "easy" for respondents to answer and thus offer a simple and quick conclusion to the survey.

Below, a total of 34 possible questions are presented for all three areas, which can be used in the development of an audience study (Pöllmann, 2022). The questions are formulated using the **example of a music festival** and capture an evaluation of several sponsors.

Part 1: The cultural attendance behavior of visitors

1. Through which sources do you find out about music festival offerings?

Multiple answers possible

- □ Daily newspaper
- □ City magazine

- □ Radio
- □ Online event calendar
- □ Blogs
- □ Posters
- □ Flyers
- □ Facebook
- □ YouTube
- □ Instagram
- □ TikTok
- □ X (formerly Twitter)
- □ Festival website
- □ Newsletter
- □ Recommendations from friends and acquaintances
- □ Other: _______________

2. Did you attend the festival with other people? If yes, with whom?

Multiple answers possible

- □ I was alone
- □ Spouse/partner
- □ Friends/acquaintances
- □ Own children
- □ Other family members
- □ Organized groups
- □ Other: __________

3. What is your motivation for attending the festival?

Multiple answers possible

- □ An extraordinary experience
- □ To see my favorite musicians
- □ Intellectual stimulation
- □ To share something with the people I am with
- □ To meet new people
- □ To be surprised
- □ Attending festivals is part of my lifestyle
- □ Good entertainment
- □ To experience something I can tell others about
- □ Inspiration on political or social topics
- □ Education
- □ The feeling of breaking out of everyday life

4. Before attending the festival, I gathered detailed information (e.g., reviewed the music program and entertainment offerings)
- □ Fully applies
- □ Mostly applies
- □ Partly applies
- □ Applies somewhat
- □ Does not apply at all

5. Before attending the festival, I made a plan for which concert or event I would attend and when
- □ Fully applies
- □ Mostly applies
- □ Partly applies
- □ Applies somewhat
- □ Does not apply at all

6. Your expectations for a festival visit were met during your attendance
- □ Fully applies
- □ Mostly applies
- □ Partly applies
- □ Applies somewhat
- □ Does not apply at all
- □ No answer

Part 2: Evaluation of Sponsorship Activities

7. Did you notice the presence of sponsors during the festival?
- □ Yes, very strongly
- □ Yes, occasionally
- □ No

8. Please name the sponsors you can remember
- □ Answer A
- □ Answer B
- □ Answer C
- □ Answer D

9. Which of the following sponsors do you remember (please also check sponsors you already named in the previous question)
- □ Brand/Logo A
- □ Brand/Logo B

□ Brand/Logo C
□ Brand/Logo D

10. Which activities or advertising measures by the sponsors do you remember?
□ Activity Sponsor A
□ Activity Sponsor B
□ Activity Sponsor C
□ Activity Sponsor D

11. Which of the following festival sponsors were you aware of before the festival?
□ Sponsor A
□ Sponsor B
□ Sponsor C
□ Sponsor D

12. How do you rate the presence of the sponsors on the festival grounds?
□ The presence was an asset to the festival
□ The presence was rather appropriate
□ The presence was rather inappropriate
□ The presence was disruptive

13. Which sponsor activities do you consider to provide the greatest added value?

Multiple answers possible
□ Activities by Sponsor A
□ Activities by Sponsor B
□ Activities by Sponsor C
□ Activities by Sponsor D

14. How do you rate the quality of interactions with the sponsors (e.g., prize draws, product samples, special promotions)?
□ Very good
□ Rather good
□ Rather poor
□ Very poor

15. Has the event's sponsorship increased your interest in the sponsors' products or services?
□ Yes
□ Rather yes

- □ Rather no
- □ No

16. What expectations did you have of the festival sponsors

Multiple answers possible

- □ … that the sponsor supports the festival financially or through other contributions.
- □ … that the sponsor offers visitors free products or services.
- □ … that the sponsor organizes entertainment activities during the festival.
- □ … that the sponsor enhances the festival's image through their presence.
- □ … that the sponsor creates photo and selfie opportunities on the festival grounds through their installations.
- □ … that the sponsor provides information about new products and services.
- □ … that the sponsor presents themselves in a reserved manner.
- □ … other, namely: ______________________

17. Which of the sponsors best met your expectations?

- □ Sponsor A
- □ Sponsor B
- □ Sponsor C
- □ Sponsor D

18. Did the event's sponsorship influence you to purchase products or services from the sponsors?

- □ Yes
- □ Rather yes
- □ Rather no
- □ No

19. In your opinion, which of the sponsors best addressed the festival's target audience?

Multiple answers possible

- □ Sponsor A
- □ Sponsor B
- □ Sponsor C
- □ Sponsor D

20. Were you able to obtain promotional materials or information from the sponsors during the festival?

□ Yes
□ Rather yes
□ Rather no
□ No

21. How well did the sponsors enhance the festival experience?

not improved at all									very improved
1	**2**	**3**	**4**	**5**	**6**	**7**	**8**	**9**	**10**
□	□	□	□	□	□	□	□	□	□

22. Did the sponsorship influence your opinion of the sponsors?

Opinion very deteriorated									Opinion very much improved
1	**2**	**3**	**4**	**5**	**6**	**7**	**8**	**9**	**10**
□	□	□	□	□	□	□	□	□	□

23. In your opinion, which sponsor brands best fit the festival's brand?
Multiple answers possible

□ Sponsor A
□ Sponsor B
□ Sponsor C
□ Sponsor D

24. How likely are you to use or purchase products or services from the festival's sponsors in the future?

very unlikely									very likely
1	**2**	**3**	**4**	**5**	**6**	**7**	**8**	**9**	**10**
□	□	□	□	□	□	□	□	□	□

25. How likely are you to recommend Sponsor A's products or services to others as a result of the festival's sponsorship?

very unlikely									very likely
1	**2**	**3**	**4**	**5**	**6**	**7**	**8**	**9**	**10**
□	□	□	□	□	□	□	□	□	□

26. Did you participate in any sponsor activities or events?

□ Yes, in many
□ Yes, in a few
□ No

27. Did the sponsorship influence your overall satisfaction with the festival?

□ Yes, very positively
□ Yes, rather positively
□ Yes, rather negatively
□ Yes, very negatively
□ No influence on satisfaction

28. How well did the sponsors contribute to the festival atmosphere?

□ Very positively
□ Rather positively
□ Rather negatively
□ Very negatively
□ No influence on the atmosphere.

Part 3: Sociodemographic Information

29. Your age?

______

30. Your gender?

□ Female
□ Male
□ Diverse

31. Are you employed?

(Multiple answers possible)

□ Employed (not self-employed, e.g., salaried employee, civil servant)
□ Employed (self-employed, freelance professions)
□ Homemaker
□ School student
□ University student
□ Apprentice
□ Voluntary social year
□ Currently not employed
□ Other: ____________

32. What is your highest level of educational attainment?
- □ I am still in school
- □ Lower secondary school leaving certificate
- □ Intermediate school leaving certificate, Realschule diploma
- □ Higher education entrance qualification
- □ University degree
- □ Other school leaving certificate

33. What is your monthly net income?
- □ 0–100 EUR
- □ 101–450 EUR
- □ 451–1000 EUR
- □ 1001–1500 EUR
- □ 1501–2000 EUR
- □ 2001–2500 EUR
- □ 2501–3000 EUR
- □ 3001–3500 EUR
- □ 3501–4000 EUR
- □ over 4000 EUR

34. Would you please provide your postal code?
Postal code: ___________

11.3 Problems of Performance Evaluation in Arts and Cultural Sponsorship

Although the preceding discussion shows that there are indeed suitable instruments for performance evaluation, consistent success measurement is not implemented everywhere in practice. Surveys on performance evaluation in sponsorship indicate that more than two-thirds of corporate sponsorships now conduct control measures (Pilot Checkpoint, 2008; Bagusat, 2013). However, these studies were not conducted specifically for arts and cultural sponsorship and also show that the instruments used often involve either simple media resonance analysis methods or qualitative assessments. In practice, the **measurement of communicative effects of arts and cultural sponsorships** is sometimes carried out through the following measures:

- Collection of “clippings,” i.e., gathering newspaper excerpts or online articles that report on the company’s cultural engagement,
- Recording the circulation figures of printed materials, catalogs, program booklets, etc., that featured the company’s branding,

- Recording the broadcast duration of TV or radio commercials per day,
- Clicks on online advertisements,
- Recording the number of newsletter subscribers for specific cultural events with reference to sponsors (e.g., sponsored music festivals),
- Recording the number of company giveaways distributed at sponsored cultural events,
- Measurement of recall values regarding which corporate sponsorships are active in arts and cultural sponsorship (recognition tests),
- Recording cultural attribute manifestations in connection with the measurement of corporate image,
- Surveying opinion leaders regarding the assessment and acceptance of arts and cultural sponsorships,
- Recording social media metrics, including:
  - reach of posts,
  - number of likes,
  - number of shares/retweets,
  - number of comments,
  - tonality and content of comments,
  - click-through rate (CTR),
- Recording leads (number of contact details received from potential customers).

A frequently cited **reason for the lack of performance evaluation** is the issue of insufficient cause-and-effect relationships between the cultural engagements of corporate sponsorships and the achievement of communication policy objectives, or the distortion of effects due to external conditions. However, these deficits also exist for other communication instruments, whose effectiveness is nonetheless professionally monitored. The problem of impact control is therefore not solely attributable to the characteristics of arts and cultural sponsorship, but also lies in the behavior of the cultural sponsors themselves. In particular, when setting the objectives of an arts and cultural sponsorship, many corporate sponsors still lack professionalism, and objectives are often described as "global goals" or are only formulated retrospectively. However, the definition and operationalization of clear objectives is a prerequisite for any type of performance evaluation.

This raises the question of the general **benefit of performance evaluation** in arts and cultural sponsorship. Certainly, precise statements regarding the efficiency of arts and cultural sponsorship will hardly be evaluable. Similar problems arise here as with the measurement of the efficiency of public relations. As a rule of thumb, for smaller expenditures on arts and cultural sponsorships (up to about EUR 50,000 or up to 3% of the company's communications budget), comprehensive performance evaluation is unprofitable for financial reasons alone. If the budget exceeds 3% of the communications budget, a corporate sponsor must regularly record the effects of its cultural engagement and align its activities accordingly. Even then, the available techniques must be reviewed in each case for their costs and benefits. Especially with technical methods, whose use is often associated with high costs, careful consideration is required in arts and cultural sponsorship.

It can be expected that the **requirements for impact and performance evaluation** in arts and cultural sponsorship will continue to increase overall. The main focus will be on obtaining more precise information on the following aspects:

- Continuous recording of image (transfer) effects through arts and cultural sponsorship,
- Measurement of effects in medium- to long-term cultural engagements over time (learning and forgetting effects),
- Measurement of synergy effects of arts and cultural sponsorship in combination with other communication instruments,
- Comparison of the impact of arts and cultural sponsorship with other communication instruments,
- Effects of sponsorship on the perception of corporate identity and culture by target groups,
- Acceptance of arts and cultural sponsorship by employees,
- Acceptance of arts and cultural sponsorship by customers as an expression of the company's social responsibility,
- Continuous image affinity checks, especially for long-term sponsorship engagements, to exclude inappropriate or undesirable image effects and ensure a fit with the desired corporate image,
- Consideration of possible risks of sponsorship in the arts and cultural sector that could have negative effects on the corporate sponsor and its image (e.g., accidents at cultural events, scandals in the private lives of sponsored artists, data protection issues when using customer or participant data).

The possibilities for determining the effects of arts and cultural sponsorship will, as past progress shows, continue to develop steadily in the coming years, and will increasingly offer corporate sponsors the opportunity to review the results of their cultural engagement.

11.4 Criteria and Award Winners of Successful Sponsorship Activities

For corporate sponsors who are engaged as sponsors, as well as cultural institutions distinguished by their cultural management, there are numerous awards for which sponsors, cultural institutions, or the supporting agencies can apply (see, among others, ARCult Media, 2023; Marketingbörse, 2023; Bundesverband Marketing Clubs, 2023; W&V, 2023). Two awards are examined in more detail below: the International Sponsoring Award and the Kulturmarken Award.

International Sponsoring Award

The **Association of Sponsoring Agencies and Service Providers e. V. (FASPO)** is the representative body for service providers within the sponsorship market of the DACH region and presents the "International Sponsoring Award (ISA)" (FASPO, 2023). The ISA serves as a distinction for outstanding quality and professionalism in the field of sponsorship for agencies as well as corporate sponsorship and was last awarded in 2019 (as of December 2023). The association honors particularly successful and creative sponsorship engagements in the project-specific categories of sports, culture, media, and public-private sponsorship, as well as innovation, which have been planned and implemented by corporate sponsors, agencies, and institutions in Germany, Austria, and Switzerland. In addition, in the company-specific category, the "Newcomer of the Year" and the "Agency/Service Provider of the Year" are also recognized. To ensure that smaller and regional projects also have a chance at the coveted ISA, the award is given regardless of project size or investment volume and is evaluated by a renowned expert jury.

A criterion for submitting a sponsorship project is its active market implementation in Germany, Austria, or Switzerland and an attached **brief description of the project**. The brief description must include the following information:

- Task, objectives,
- Target groups,
- Integrated sponsorship strategy,
- Measures, networking,
- Performance control and impact measurement,
- Project implementation period,
- Justification for the proposed sponsorship.

Furthermore, the jury evaluates based on a fact-based rationale, the reason why, an initiative, and the performance/impact data of the respective project. For the awards "Newcomer of the Year" and "Agency/Service Provider of the Year," additional criteria such as the positioning of the company are also considered.

Past award winners include, for example, in 2017 Fraport and the agency 2 bp communications for the project "Dorian Gray 2.0 — Sponsoring of the BigCityBeats World Club Dome 2016." In 2016, Telekom Deutschland together with the agency DO IT! received the award for the project "Unsere Lieder werden EINS."

Kulturmarken Award

An award specifically aimed at cultural sponsors and cultural promoters is the **"European Cultural Investor of the Year"**, which has been presented as part of the Kulturmarken Awards since 2010. The prize honors private individuals, corporate sponsors, and organizations for their sustainable investments in and support of cultural institutions and cultural creators.

The award is presented based on the following **criteria** (Kulturmarken, 2021):

Social benefit	Sustainability of arts and cultural sponsorship
Innovative strength	Creative integration of the sponsor into the project
Implementation	Integration into internal and external communication
Impact	Presentation of the benefits for the corporate sponsor
Sustainability	Implementation of economic, ecological, and social criteria

The following **award winners** have been honored with the Kulturmarken Award to date (Kulturmarken, 2021):

- 2010: Migros Kulturprozent
- 2011: Bayer Culture
- 2012: The Young ClassX (in addition, the BMW Group was awarded the "Trend Brand of the Year" prize in 2012 for the BMW Guggenheim Lab project)
- 2013: Sparkassen Finanzgruppe
- 2014: RWE
- 2015: Colours International Dance Festival
- 2016: Guggenheim UBS MAP
- 2017: Würth
- 2018: AVL Cultural Foundation
- 2019: Art Stations Foundation
- 2020: Deutsche Post DHL Group
- 2021: European Cultural Foundation

In the years 2022–2024, the competition was paused due to a temporary change in the organizers of the awards. The continuation of the Kulturmarken Awards is planned for 2025.

Key Points

1. **Conduct process control:** The implementation of arts and cultural sponsorships should be reviewed through effectiveness and efficiency controls in order to measure tangible results.
2. **Differentiate impact measurement:** When evaluating the effects of sponsorship, a distinction should be made between lasting and momentary communication impacts.
3. **Evaluate individual planning steps:** The planning steps of the sponsorship cooperation should be assessed using project management techniques such as checklists and network diagrams.

4. **Measure perception and recall effects:** Measurements of perception, recall, and image formation of the sponsorship should be conducted, as well as determining the number of contacts achieved.
5. **Conduct standard measurements:** Unprompted recall tests and prompted recognition tests should be used as standard measurements in sponsorship.
6. **Analyze costs and benefits:** The costs and benefits of the sponsorship cooperation should be recorded and compared to each other for efficiency control.
7. **Consider the profitability of performance evaluation:** Professional performance evaluation should be carried out once a certain budget share or a defined project budget is reached.
8. **Collaborate with cultural institutions:** Effectiveness controls should be conducted in cooperation with cultural institutions, and, where possible, questions should be integrated into general audience surveys.
9. **Use questionnaires for success measurement:** Questionnaires should be used to capture cultural attendance behavior, evaluation of sponsorship activities, and sociodemographic information.
10. **Consider applying for sponsorship awards:** The potential for media utilization and increased reach of an arts and cultural sponsorship should be taken into account by applying for sponsorship awards.

Trends in the Use of Arts and Cultural Sponsorship 12

Contents

12.1 Sponsorship from the Perspective of the Involved Stakeholders 279
12.2 Tendencies from the Perspective of Sponsors 281
12.3 Tendencies from the Perspective of Cultural Organizations 290
12.4 Tendencies from the Perspective of Cultural Policy 295

Abstract

Arts and cultural sponsorship is influenced by economic, social, artistic, technological, as well as (cultural) political developments. As a communication tool, it interacts with other media and instruments of marketing and corporate communication, particularly in light of the ever-evolving opportunities for activating sponsorship engagements. This results in arts and cultural sponsorship being in a state of continuous, dynamic development, which repeatedly gives rise to opportunities and risks, as well as the necessity for a deliberate design of sponsorship management. This chapter discusses developments in arts and cultural sponsorship from the perspective of sponsors, cooperating cultural institutions as sponsored parties, and cultural policy.

12.1 Sponsorship from the Perspective of the Involved Stakeholders

From the perspective of the stakeholders involved in the sponsorship process, various developments can be observed that lead to changing framework conditions and influence strategic decisions regarding the use of arts and cultural sponsorship. The key **factors**

M. Bruhn and L. Pöllmann, *Arts and Cultural Sponsorship*,
https://doi.org/10.1007/978-3-658-50079-5_12

influencing the dynamics of future development include market, societal, competitive, financing, technological, and jurisdictional dynamics.

1. Market Dynamics
Arts and cultural sponsorship has led to the emergence of a "market" in the fields of communication, promotion, and leisure, where prices are determined by supply and demand. Even though this market is not always transparent, **its own market rules** apply, which the participants must adapt to. Since arts and cultural sponsorship is a communication tool, the design of offerings and pricing is influenced by developments in other communication instruments.

2. Societal Dynamics
The development of arts and cultural sponsorship is closely linked to the demand for cultural offerings. If certain cultural offerings are less attended and perceived as less important by society, this reduces the reach and potential image transfer and has significant effects on the willingness of corporate sponsors to engage in cultural sponsorship. Thus, arts and cultural sponsorship also depends on the cultural education and cultural activity of society. Another influencing factor derives from the development of societal trends and values. In recent years, the issue of ecological sustainability has gained considerable importance in public perception, which is why many corporate sponsors align their engagements in the areas of corporate social responsibility (CSR) with ecological criteria. At the same time, the general public has become more sensitive to inauthentic engagements and actions suspected of **"greenwashing"** or **"whitewashing"**. Arts and cultural sponsorships with ecological connections are intensely discussed in the media and on social networks, making a sustainably considered selection of sponsorships necessary.

3. Competitive Dynamics
Sponsorship tends to lead to **increased competition among market participants**, that is, among sponsors for sponsorships, among sponsored parties for sponsorship funds, and among media outlets for coverage of attractive leisure events. Excessive competition in arts and cultural sponsorship can result in negative side effects (e.g., ambush marketing, influence on the sponsorship, excessive sponsor presence, reactance). These should be anticipated in advance and factored in as risk considerations when planning cultural engagements.

4. Financing Dynamics
Arts and cultural sponsorship leads to cultural institutions increasingly counting on sponsorship funds and, in some cases, relying on them. However, the **funding volumes of sponsors** depend on the economic success of the corporate sponsors. Poor economic conditions, industry-specific problems, and financial constraints of corporate sponsors reduce their ability to significantly increase investments in cultural sponsorship. There

is even a risk of reduced engagement. Therefore, in medium- and long-term planning, it is advisable for cultural institutions to avoid financial dependence on a single sponsor in favor of a multidimensional funding mix.

5. Technology Dynamics
Arts and cultural sponsorship is used in conjunction with other media to draw attention to a sponsor and its initiatives. Therefore, the attractiveness and practical possibilities of arts and cultural sponsorship are directly linked to the **technological development of communication media**. Through digital media and especially social media, sponsors and cultural institutions have, in recent years, been able to free themselves from dependence on traditional mass media and build their own reach. This development will intensify in the future through the expansion of their own channels and the use of newer media (e.g., TikTok, BeReal) or new features in existing media (e.g., WhatsApp Channels, VR offerings, AI-generated content).

6. Jurisdictional Dynamics
The implementation of sponsorships may involve various legal norms in individual cases, such as constitutional law, tax law, media law, competition law, or association law. These legal norms are continuously adapted to new requirements and developments. Therefore, the parties involved are called upon to monitor the relevant national and European legal regulations and, if necessary, anticipate them in their engagements.

The changes in the framework conditions listed above influence the activities of sponsors, sponsored parties, and government agencies in the various areas of sponsorship. For all parties involved in sponsorship, this results in a continuous **adaptation process** to changing environmental conditions.

12.2 Tendencies from the Perspective of Sponsors

Due to the necessity of using marketing budgets efficiently, further professionalization of arts and cultural sponsorship can be expected. From a corporate perspective, various **critical areas of development** can be identified regarding the successful use of sponsorship. One challenge is the planning foundation and creative use of sponsorships. Additional difficulties arise from combining sponsorship activities into a sponsorship mix, collaborating with sponsorship agencies, and measuring effectiveness.

12.2.1 Planning Basis of Sponsoring

The successful use of the communication instrument sponsoring requires similar planning considerations as the use of media advertising, sales promotion, or other communication instruments. The foundation for the conception and implementation of sponsoring is a **systematic planning process** that supports decision-makers in ensuring the effective and efficient use of sponsoring.

In the development of a sponsorship concept and its consistent implementation in communication practice, problems repeatedly arise. The typical **mistakes in sponsorship planning and implementation** can be characterized as follows:

- Lack of formulation of operational objectives that are specifically to be achieved through sponsoring,
- Lack of consistent orientation towards the target groups to be addressed through sponsorships,
- Lack of conceptual orientation in sponsoring with a focus on selected sponsorship areas and types,
- Lack of critical review of historically developed sponsorship engagements based on changed communicative tasks,
- Lack of integration of sponsorship into the other instruments of marketing and corporate communication,
- Lack of internal and external coordination of sponsoring activities,
- Insufficient substantive alignment of individual sponsorships,
- Lack of success controls for sponsoring in general as well as for individual sponsorships.

Some corporate sponsors still reject a systematic planning of sponsoring even today. These are mainly corporate sponsors whose patronage has developed historically over decades and whose decision-makers—despite the strong communicative impact of their "patronage" activities—refuse to base their activities on a systematic planning process. However, this does not change the fact that these corporate sponsors are publicly perceived as classic sponsors.

However, in recent years there has been a significant shift in awareness regarding the necessity of a **goal-oriented basis for sponsoring**. Sponsoring corporate sponsors are increasingly using planning methods (Bagusat, 2013, p. 21). The planning basis, however, is not limited to quantification, such as of target group overlaps and success data. Rather, qualitative assessments and derivations, such as identifying affinities and determining usage potentials, are also necessary for a planning basis.

Such planning is supported by the increasing **professionalization of cultural institutions**, as corporate sponsors receive more meaningful offers. Sponsorship offers are increasingly modeled after media data from other media (e.g., newspapers, radio programs, online offerings), including information on the target group reached and specific reach figures. This also enables sponsors to plan their engagement more concretely based on relevant economic criteria.

One aspect that will be given greater consideration in the future when planning arts and cultural sponsorships is the topic of **brand safety**. As already mentioned (see

Chap. 9), corporate sponsors are paying more attention to how their brand is presented in order to avert potential reputational damage. The need for brand safety measures arises, on the one hand, from the economic necessity of efficient sponsorship activities. If a corporate sponsor is associated with an event that is publicly criticized, this can also cause significant reputational damage for the sponsor and thus lead to a counterproductive effect, i.e., a negative image transfer. The example of Documenta Fifteen (2022) has already been mentioned (see Chap. 6)—here, the sponsors distanced themselves in press statements. Another example is the terminated cooperation between the sponsor BMW and the Regensburg Castle Festival. The Süddeutsche Zeitung interprets BMW's withdrawal as a reaction to the public and private criticism of patron Gloria von Thurn und Taxis. Her controversial statements led to calls for a boycott of the festival (Süddeutsche Zeitung, 2023).

Another aspect of brand safety concerns the **implementation of negotiated sponsorship benefits by cultural partners**. Promotional sponsorship benefits are often organized by the cultural institutions themselves. It is important to pay attention to how precisely the agreed services are implemented. For example, it must be clarified how professionally social media posts are produced by the cultural institutions or how advertising media (e.g., posters) are distributed. There is a significant difference between posters being published by professional outdoor advertising companies and the form of so-called guerrilla or wild posting—particularly popular among smaller cultural institutions (see Fig. 12.1). The latter often leads to brand presentations that are only partially compatible with the desired image of the sponsors.

12.2.2 Sponsoring as a Creative Instrument of Marketing and Corporate Communication

The possibilities that sponsoring offers as an exceptionally creative instrument of marketing and corporate communication are often not fully exploited. The reason for this is that some managers still have "mental barriers": they associate sponsoring merely with various options for logo integration on the media of a cultural institution and hardly with its creative communication potential.

The **creative possibilities** of sponsoring relate to various measures:

- Development of new and previously industry-unusual sponsorships,
- Use of new advertising opportunities at cultural events,
- Testing new possibilities for networking with other communication instruments,
- Involving employees in the sponsorships,
- Cooperation with third parties (e.g., co-sponsors),
- Creation of platforms for customer events,
- Use of licenses for new products and services of the company.

Guerrilla poster advertising for cultural events on glass recycling containers.

Staging of sponsor logos.

Fig. 12.1 Example of wild posting in an environment unfavorable to the sponsor's image

Reducing the use of arts and cultural sponsorship to the display of a company logo does not do justice to the potential of this communication instrument. In addition, the development of good **storytelling** is necessary to achieve the intended sustainable image transfer and to create lasting memories through the sponsorship commitment. It is important to ensure that cultural sponsorship measures are perceived as authentic in order to prevent accusations of "whitewashing." Therefore, it can be assumed that sponsors will increasingly collaborate with cultural institutions in the future to develop suitable measures.

The innovation potential is understandably particularly high in arts and cultural sponsorship. Especially with self-initiated commitments, there is the opportunity to develop company-specific sponsorship concepts in collaboration with the sponsored parties, which are capable of contributing to the achievement of communication objectives, as has already been illustrated by the examples presented in the case studies in the preceding chapters.

In addition to the creative design possibilities and the innovation potential of arts and cultural sponsorship, the **analytical potential of arts and cultural sponsorship** should not be neglected. With the ongoing digitalization of media that accompany sponsoring, as well as the digital transformation of areas of event organization, the evaluation and measurement of the impact of sponsorship measures will also become easier in the future. On the one hand, it is increasingly possible to determine simple and concrete number of contacts as well as other key figures regarding the reach of communicated sponsorship messages. The measurement of achieved **leads** and **conversions** within the framework of sponsorship projects is also simplified by tracking methods of a **digital customer journey**. On the other hand, digital methods of audience surveys facilitate evaluation and impact measurement by collecting opinions from the target groups (see Sect. 11.3). It is to be expected that in the future, the use of artificial intelligence or machine learning will provide improved forecasting methods based on the collected data. This will also improve the assessment of implemented sponsorship measures and support decisions for further cultural collaborations. Thus, in addition to the creative possibilities, the analytical possibilities are also required in arts and cultural sponsorship.

12.2.3 Development of a Sponsoring Mix for Corporate Sponsorship

In many corporate sponsorships, a large number of different sponsorship commitments can be observed, which are initiated and carried out by various departments. The larger and more diversified a company is, the more heterogeneous the sponsorships. For these corporate sponsorships, it is advisable to develop a **sponsoring mix**.

A sponsoring mix refers to the meaningful combination and coordination of different sponsorships for a corporate sponsorship. With the horizontal and vertical sponsoring mix — as shown in Fig. 12.2 — two levels of the **development of a sponsoring mix** can be distinguished:

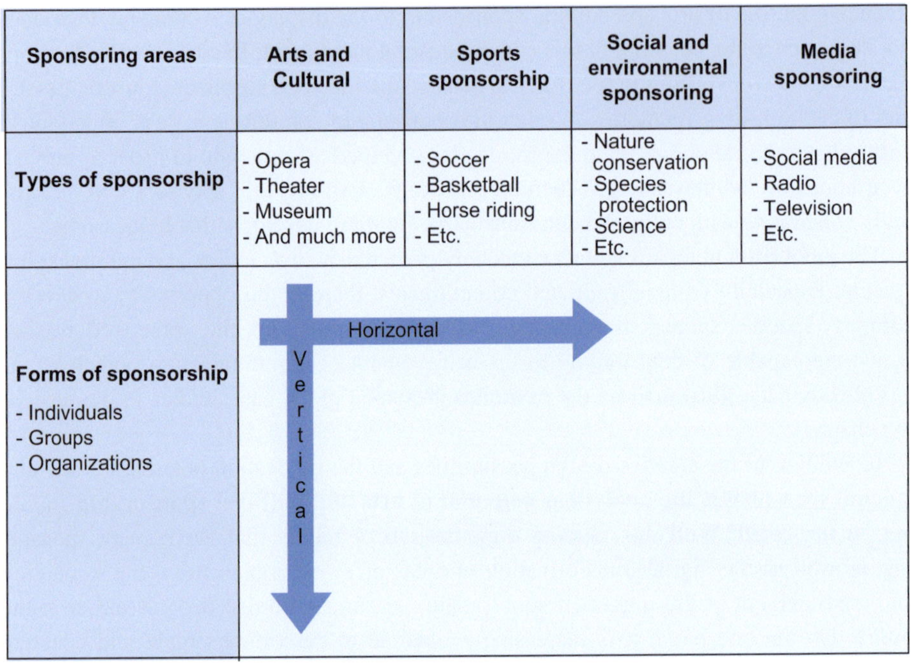

Fig. 12.2 horizontal and vertical sponsoring mix

1. A **horizontal sponsoring mix** combines and coordinates the various sponsoring areas in which the corporate sponsorship wishes to be active.
2. A **vertical sponsoring mix** coordinates the activities within a sponsoring area.

Horizontal coordination problems arise when different departments within the corporate sponsorship are responsible for individual sponsoring areas. For many corporate sponsorships, however, the main problem lies in insufficient **vertical coordination** of their sponsoring activities. While in the past there were often good reasons for engaging in different types of sponsoring, today, due to rising costs, there is a risk of "spreading too thin" and causing confusion among the target groups if no clear priorities are set, for example with regard to a cultural sector. Here, a consistent conceptual orientation and clear guidelines are necessary to ensure a focus of sponsoring resources.

In the future, the marketing department will increasingly be expected to **define an overarching main objective** with the resulting sub-goals as well as to formulate an integrated sponsoring message. Based on this, the corresponding sponsorships are to be selected and the message communicated across all communication instruments and media. Sponsors with diverse cultural commitments will therefore increasingly distinguish between an **overarching strategic sponsoring message** and more specific messages tailored to a particular sponsorship. This means that a guiding idea is defined for the overall cultural engagement, and concrete campaign messages for individual cultural sponsorship collaborations are derived based on the respective cultural partners and target groups (see Fig. 12.3).

12.2.4 Collaboration with Sponsoring Agencies

The professionalization of sponsoring has led to corporate sponsorships now regularly involving specialized agencies in the planning and implementation of sponsorships (see Sect. 10.1.2). Basically, three **types of sponsoring agencies** are distinguished:

1. **Consulting agencies**: They specialize in conceptual consulting for sponsors and cultural organizations.
2. **Intermediary agencies**: They acquire usage rights (e.g., broadcasting rights or licenses) and/or mediate between sponsors and/or sponsored parties.
3. **Implementing agencies**: They assist in the implementation of sponsorships, such as in press relations or event management.

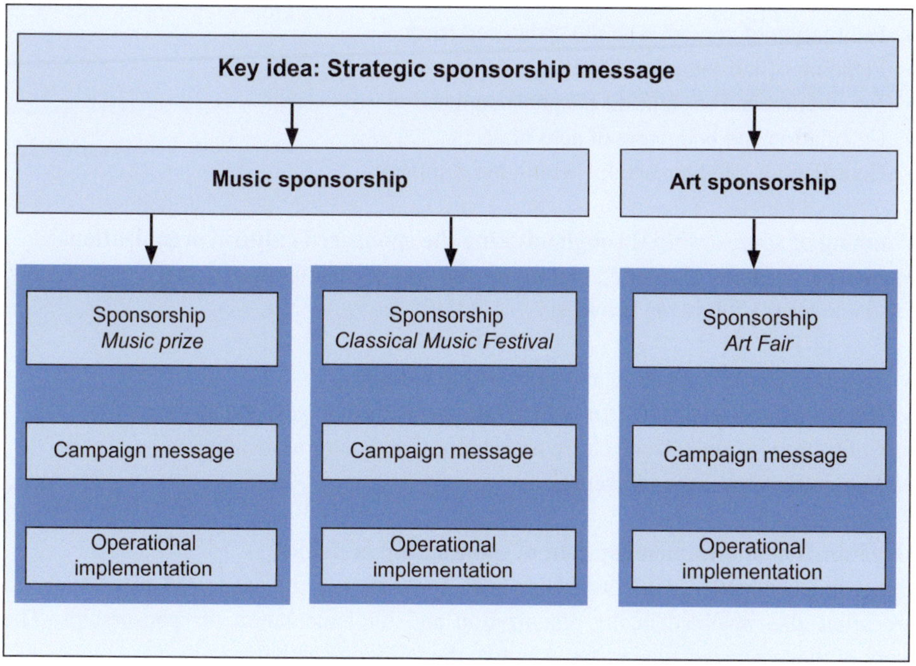

Fig. 12.3 Example of a hierarchy of guiding idea and campaign messages in various cultural sponsorship areas

The significance of intermediary agencies is less pronounced in arts and cultural sponsorship than in other areas of sponsorship, such as sports sponsorship. Instead, agencies and service providers that support corporate sponsorship in the implementation and activation of sponsorships play a greater role. Due to the necessity of employing more creative measures (see above), it can be expected that specialized service providers will be increasingly involved in the future, as especially smaller corporate sponsors often lack the expertise for their conception and realization.

If one considers the **services provided by sponsoring agencies**, the following (partial) tasks can be distinguished, which are specified in detail below:

- Planning of sponsorship through advising the sponsor,
- Planning of sponsorship through advising the sponsored cultural organizations,
- Organization and implementation of sponsorship activities,
- Monitoring of sponsorship activities.

Planning of sponsorship through advising the sponsor
Depending on the agency's range of services (specialist agency or full-service agency), the following consulting services are provided:

- Development of sponsorship concepts for corporate sponsors and brands,
- Search for suitable cultural partners,
- Facilitation of contact with the sponsored party,
- Planning of individual measures,
- Negotiation and structuring of sponsorships,
- Calculation and budgeting of activities,
- Coordination of sponsorships within the company.

Planning of sponsorship through advising the sponsored cultural organizations
Numerous agencies also offer consulting services to the sponsored party. Specifically, this includes the following services:

- Development of marketing and sponsorship concepts,
- Marketing and consulting for individuals (investment, taxes, and insurance),
- Consulting for organizers, clubs, associations, and cultural institutions,
- Marketing of events and licenses.

Organization and implementation of sponsorship activities
Either independently or in cooperation with sponsors and the sponsored party, agencies are often also involved in the organization and implementation of sponsorships. The work of the agencies includes, for example, the following activities:

- Use of advertising materials,
- Handling of official events,
- Organization of their own events, happenings, or projects,
- Promotional activities during events,
- Press relations.

Monitoring of sponsorship activities

Another important activity of sponsoring agencies, as part of ongoing collaboration with a corporate sponsor, is the regular performance evaluation of sponsorship activities. Specifically, the following measures are carried out, among others:

- Monitoring of the various sponsorship activities with regard to effectiveness and efficiency.
- Estimation of the market value of the sponsored party after the sponsorship has ended.
- Development of suggestions for improvement for the sponsor and the sponsored party for future engagements.

Collaboration with sponsoring agencies is a subject of controversial discussion. The following **advantages** are cited for a **partnership with external consultants**:

- Subject matter experts contribute time, know-how, and experience that are conducive to systematic and professional work.
- Consultants have a network of contacts that is brought into the work.
- By using consultants, the parties involved are able to understand the specific mindset of their counterpart and take it into account in their own decisions.
- Independent consultants provide sponsors and sponsored parties with objective and realistic recommendations regarding entering into sponsorships, based on their knowledge of the sponsorship market.

On the other hand, **disadvantages** are also mentioned that are associated with such collaboration. For example:

- The use of consultants incurs additional costs.
- Cultural organizations often lack the funds to finance the necessary initial services of the agency (development of a sponsorship concept) from their own resources.
- The sponsored parties may become dependent on consultants or intermediaries if they have been granted certain exclusive rights.

There are also **"dubious" intermediaries and consultants** active in the sponsorship market, who jump on the sponsorship bandwagon as a trend topic and are not able to provide solid and well-founded work. Classic creative and media agencies are rarely engaged; instead, specialized sponsoring agencies are used. While sponsorship planning is predominantly carried out by internal departments—but in many cases also by specialist agencies—specialist agencies for sponsorship or events are particularly engaged for implementation. For contract drafting, corporate sponsors also seek support from lawyers and law firms, while for performance evaluation, market research institutes and specialist institutes for recording and evaluating media presence are primarily used (Pilot Checkpoint, 2002, pp. 69 f.).

When **selecting sponsoring agencies**, sponsors and sponsored parties must develop a requirements profile in order to find the right consultant. For example, the following **requirements** should be taken into account (Hermanns & Marwitz, 2008, pp. 61 ff.):

- Experience in the fields of marketing, communication, and arts and cultural sponsorship,
- Insider knowledge regarding the areas of cultural sponsorship relevant to the individual company,
- Contacts with cultural institutions, associations, relevant personalities, and media,
- Full-service offering regarding the planning, implementation, and monitoring of sponsorship activities,
- Consulting without specific marketing interests,
- Integrity and credibility of the individuals, organization, and concepts.

Despite the large number of agencies that have now added sponsorship to their range of services, there is still a **deficit of consulting or communications agencies** that, as full-service providers, are able to develop cultural sponsorship concepts and at the same time integrate them with other communication instruments (e.g., performance marketing measures such as SEA — Search Engine Advertising and paid reach on social media) in terms of content, form, and timing. However, since corporate sponsors will increasingly demand integrated sponsorship strategies in the future, agencies are also coming under increasing pressure to meet these requirements.

12.3 Tendencies from the Perspective of Cultural Organizations

If one considers **sponsorship from the perspective of the sponsored**, an international comparison reveals that in Germany, arts and cultural sponsorship is still in a developmental phase compared to other Western countries. Overall, the support of high art dominates, such as the backing of art exhibitions and museums, as these are particularly attractive to sponsors in terms of experience value and are relatively “risk-free.” In addition, music festivals are preferred by sponsors, as corporate sponsorship encounters a target audience that is open to sponsorship, offering greater potential for creative staging by the sponsors. In the future, it is expected that sponsorship will open up to additional art forms and arts and cultural sectors.

The **risks for art and culture** associated with sponsorship focus on the accusation of interference in the arts and the growing dependence on business. However, it should be noted that the public-private debate and criticism of arts and cultural sponsorship are in a diametrically opposite relationship to the actual sponsorships and negative side effects. No serious sponsor has any interest in directly interfering with the arts. At most, one speaks of indirect interference when certain art forms are preferred by corporate sponsorship.

Some **further trends in arts and cultural sponsorship** can be observed and are explained in more detail below.

Dealing with Critical Partners

More dangerous than sponsor influence on artistic decisions is the potential damage to the image of a cultural institution through the **selection of unsuitable sponsors**. Criticism of sponsors is now also quickly and widely disseminated by third parties via social media and other media channels. For example, some partnerships of the Salzburg Festival in 2022 were described in interviews by director Yana Ross and writer Lukas Bärfuss as **"toxic sponsorship"** and this was widely picked up by numerous media outlets. The background to the public criticism was the Salzburg Festival's collaboration with the mining company Solway, which has been accused of human rights violations (Siebenhaar, 2022; Höbel, 2022; BR Klassik, 2022). In response to the criticism, the Salzburg Festival has since ended its collaboration with Solway (FAZ, 2022).

The years-long partnership between the Tate Gallery and the corporation British Petroleum was also repeatedly criticized in the public eye (Serafini & Garrard, 2019; Chong, 2012). The artist collective Liberate Tate staged performances in the museum in which artists, among other things, poured dark paint over themselves to draw attention to the environmental damage caused by the sponsor. In 2017, British Petroleum finally ended its collaboration with the museum.

Criticism of partnerships with unsuitable sponsors led Austria's Secretary of State for Arts and Culture, Andrea Mayer, to introduce a **guideline for how cultural institutions should handle sponsorship** at the end of 2022 (BMKÖS, 2022a). This guideline defines criteria for assessing potential partnerships as well as decision-making processes. For example, exclusion criteria are specified, which are also to be applied to existing partnerships (BMKÖS, 2022b, p. 7).

These **guidelines** state verbatim: "Provisions that exclude a partnership or the acceptance of third-party funds concern the following potential partners:

- Corporate sponsors and foundations that are based in a country against which Austria or the European Union has imposed sanctions and that operate in sectors affected by these sanctions,

- Private individuals and their foundations who are listed on Austria's or the European Union's sanctions lists,
- Partners whose financial resources predominantly and demonstrably originate from countries listed on the EU list of non-cooperative jurisdictions for tax purposes (guidelines for anti-money laundering and counter-terrorism financing)."

In addition, the guideline makes it clear: "Partnerships that could damage the reputation of a cultural institution are to be avoided." (BMKÖS, 2022b, p. 8).

The debate about "toxic arts and cultural sponsorship" and the publication of the guideline show that cultural organizations will in future be subject to greater scrutiny regarding their partnerships, and will have to weigh these decisions more carefully in advance. It is to be expected that cultural organizations will increasingly define their criteria for partnership decisions through their own **code of conduct**.

Professional Sponsorship Management

In some cases, arts and cultural sponsorships do not materialize because cultural institutions are characterized by **a lack of professionalism in sponsorship management** when seeking sponsors. Many cultural professionals looking for a sponsor are essentially seeking patronage-like support from corporate sponsors. In addition, from the perspective of interested corporate sponsors, personal and written requests are often too short-term and insufficiently targeted to specific audiences.

A change in mentality is necessary for the future. Cultural professionals need to develop a greater willingness to engage with sponsorship as a source of funding and to adopt a positive or at least constructive attitude toward this communication tool. They need to develop a stronger interest in the industries of the sponsors and make efforts to put themselves in the position of the corporate sponsors. Only with this **change of perspective** and under these conditions can individual communicative solutions be developed that meet the interests of the sponsors (Causales Agentur für Marketing & Kommunikation, 2007). Artistic directors, theater and museum directors, festival managers, etc., must address arts and cultural sponsorship more proactively and develop their own concepts for their area in order to actively take advantage of the opportunities offered by arts and cultural sponsorship.

Against the backdrop of increasing discussions about climate change, sustainability, poverty reduction, and the current refugee issue, the area of social and environmental sponsorship has become significantly more important for sponsors. As corporate sponsors increasingly focus their support on these areas, **ecologically and socially sustainable cultural management** will also become more important for attractiveness to sponsors in the future. Cultural organizations will have an advantage in negotiations with potential sponsors if they can demonstrate that a partnership not only supports artistic work but also contributes to social and ecological sustainability.

Cultural Audiences after COVID-19

During the pandemic, numerous cultural events could not take place, which significantly reduced the opportunities for sponsorship benefits and thus the attractiveness of cultural institutions for sponsors. The 2022/2023 season and especially the 2023 festival season showed that cultural audiences have returned in many places, as illustrated by the **attendance rates of selected classical music festivals**:

Bayreuth Festival	97% attendance (Crescendo, 2023)
Kissinger Sommer	80% attendance (Kissinger Sommer, 2023)
Lausitz Music Festival	80% attendance (Münchner Merkur, 2023)
Rheingau Music Festival	93% attendance (RMF, 2023)
Salzburg Festival	98.5% attendance (Salzburg Festival, 2023)
Schleswig–Holstein Music Festival	94% attendance (SHMF, 2023)

These figures provide an optimistic outlook for the development of attendance at cultural events. They show that the feared long-term **collapse in visitor numbers** due to the COVID-19 pandemic has not materialized, at least for festivals. However, the positive festival results cannot be generalized to all cultural events. Despite the high attendance rates at renowned cultural institutions and events, many cultural organizations continue to face pressure from insufficient audience numbers. In addition, rising production costs are making the economic conditions for organizing cultural events more challenging, as the purchasing power and willingness to pay of audiences are not increasing to the necessary extent. Nevertheless, it should be emphasized that the situation for cultural event organizers has developed better in many places after the pandemic than was feared during the lockdowns (see also Glaap, 2023, for the discussion on the development of cultural audiences).

The certainty of once again being able to plan and hold events after the pandemic-related restrictions will provide cultural organizations with an important basis for argumentation. This should be used to regain communication budgets that were shifted from arts and cultural sponsorship to other communication instruments during the pandemic.

New Potential for Arts and Cultural Sponsorship through Digitalization

During the pandemic, many cultural organizations developed additional **digital offerings** and established channels for streaming services. In doing so, they laid the foundation for expanding their target groups, as attendance is no longer tied to geographic criteria and people with physical limitations can more easily participate in cultural offerings.

In addition, new **opportunities for audience interaction based on digital media** have been created (Pöllmann, 2021c, d; Spelleken, 2023). These digital offerings open up new possibilities for the development of arts and cultural sponsorship, particularly for integrating partners, as can be illustrated using the affinity concept:

- **Product affinity:** New digital media and streaming services offer numerous opportunities to authentically integrate various industries and corporate sponsors as partners who have expertise in digital communication media. The market for digital communication media grew significantly during the pandemic and expanded its target groups through increased use of video conferencing. A successful example is the cooperation between Telekom and numerous music festivals, where Telekom acts as a streaming service provider for the digital distribution of cultural performances.
- **Know-how relevance:** In addition to hardware and software manufacturers, digital cultural offerings create further opportunities to credibly integrate corporate sponsors with expertise in digital transformation and communication as cultural sponsors. This relates on the one hand to the technical aspects of digital offerings, but also, for example, to questions of content conception and the design of cultural mediation (e.g., through apps, virtual worlds, online games, etc.).
- **Responsibility affinity:** Digital cultural offerings provide new approaches for cultural sponsors to demonstrate their sense of responsibility, particularly in two respects. First, digital offerings generally have a lower CO_2 footprint than regular events, since audience travel—which accounts for a significant portion of event-related CO_2 emissions—is eliminated. Second, many digital offerings facilitate cultural participation because access is not associated with physical barriers, for example. Thus, sponsors of digital cultural offerings enable new target groups to access cultural education.
- **Target group affinity:** The new target groups reached by digital offerings also create new opportunities to reach regional, national, and international audiences, as well as individuals who have not previously attended cultural institutions due to various barriers (e.g., uncertainty about behavior on site, physical barriers, lack of companionship, etc.). This opens up further potential cooperation partners who were not sufficiently attractive due to the limited reach of analog cultural offerings. However, it should be noted that there are still significant discrepancies between the potential of new audiences and the actual reach. While some cultural institutions succeed in reaching an international audience with their digital offerings—as demonstrated by the success of the Berlin Philharmonic's Digital Concert Hall—for many other streaming offerings, the potential reach still needs to be activated through additional arts marketing measures.
- **Image affinity:** Digital opportunities have led to numerous new cultural formats. These innovations, as well as the technology-oriented use of digital applications, provide cultural sponsors with additional image-related touchpoints that were not always available with analog productions.

Overall, the examination of different sponsorship areas reveals a wealth of opportunities for corporate sponsors to become involved as cultural sponsors. However, the **differentiation of various sponsorship alternatives** and the resulting allocation of sponsorship budgets across the areas of cultural, sports, social, environmental, and media sponsorship has also led to increasing competition among sponsorship providers. This competitive pressure is further intensified by the growing concentration of funds on a few major activities and the challenging economic climate. These developments pose risks for those cultural institutions that do not provide a platform for effective public presence or a positive, impactful image transfer. This affects individual sponsorships whose topics often attract only limited interest from their target audiences and for which sponsorship-specific communication measures are also limited due to credibility issues.

12.4 Tendencies from the Perspective of Cultural Policy

Government agencies at the federal, state, or municipal level are affected in various ways by the increased use of sponsorship. Three main **areas of focus** should be mentioned here:

- Relief of the state's own financial expenditures resulting from its sovereign mandate,
- Promotion of sponsorship and patronage through legal regulations,
- Promotion of sponsorship through the development of new forms of cooperation involving government agencies.

The **contribution to relieving government budgets** through the activities of sponsors is relatively minor in Germany. Elsewhere, the significant government expenditures on culture to support institutions and cultural offerings have already been discussed (see Chap. 3). Government spending far exceeds the sums provided by arts and cultural sponsorship. Furthermore, it should be noted that corporate sponsorships do not intend their cultural engagement to serve as a "gap filler" for reductions in public cultural spending, but rather to support additional offerings.

A reduction in cultural spending in the hope that missing funds will be compensated by sponsors cannot be in the interest of cultural policy, since ensuring regular support is generally difficult to plan. The **provision of cultural offerings** would thus depend on the economic success or funding strategies of sponsors, which can change at any time.

Nevertheless, an **expansion of sponsorship collaborations** is of interest to cultural policy for two reasons: On the one hand, additional resources increase the scope of action for the sponsored parties, leading to an expanded range of cultural offerings. On the other hand, the acquisition of sponsors means that cultural organizations build their financing on several pillars, thereby also developing their business management competence. Collaboration with sponsors thus generally supports the professionalization of cultural management in general and arts marketing in particular, and promotes economic efficiency. Of course, the economic efficiency of cultural organizations is not subordinate to the goal of artistic quality. Quite the opposite is true.

A recurring demand is the **improvement of the framework conditions for sponsorship and patronage** by legislators. The legislative measures called for also include increasing the maximum donation amounts and facilitating the recognition of sponsorship funds as business expenses, which have now been implemented. Further general legal and tax relief, including in case law, would be beneficial for arts and cultural sponsorship. This also concerns a more attractive design of foundation law, which is extremely restrictive in many areas and does little to encourage private individuals to make foundation capital available from inheritances or other assets. The legislative measures called for also include increasing the maximum donation amounts and facilitating the recognition of sponsorship funds as business expenses, which have now been implemented.

Sponsorship is primarily a partnership between sponsors and the sponsored. However, collaborations involving additional parties are also conceivable. For example, private and public funds could be used jointly in cooperation with government agencies. Regional government cultural authorities are particularly suitable for this. However, this raises a number of legal questions (e.g., regarding competition law) that must be clarified in advance. One example of this is **public private partnerships (PPP)** (see Chap. 3). This refers to a partnership-based collaboration between the state and private industry with the aim of finding optimal solutions for public-private issues. While public private partnerships are usually associated with the establishment of (cultural) institutions, there are other models of cooperation between public authorities and sponsors, such as so-called **matching funds**, in which funds raised by cultural organizations are supplemented by public funds (e.g., for every sponsor euro, there is an additional euro of public funding). For growth impulses in the cultural sponsorship market, the development of further cooperative incentive models between government agencies and corporate sponsors would be a promising initiative. This would also promote collaboration between corporate sponsors and the cultural sector.

Key Points

1. **Monitor developments in sponsorship:** Corporate sponsors must take into account that the attractiveness of a sponsorship or a sponsored party can change very quickly from the perspective of audiences and the media.
2. **Differentiate manifestations of sponsorship:** When deriving behavioral recommendations for sponsorships, the various areas of sponsorship must be considered separately.
3. **Develop a sponsorship mix:** Different sponsorships within a company should be sensibly combined and coordinated both horizontally and vertically in a sponsorship mix.
4. **Consider new forms of sponsorship:** Corporate sponsors must always monitor developments regarding new forms of sponsorship, such as AI-supported communication, and weigh their use.

5. **Leverage cooperation with government agencies:** Sponsorship is a partnership between sponsors and the sponsored. In addition, opportunities for cooperation with government cultural authorities can be utilized.
6. **Professionalize sponsorship:** Corporate sponsors must quantify and qualitatively assess success data and derive potential for use. Cultural organizations must understand the framework conditions and objectives of cooperating corporate sponsors and should not reduce sponsorship to its patronage character.
7. **Integrate sponsorships into the communication mix:** For sponsorships, overarching main objectives and the resulting sub-goals must be defined, and an integrated sponsorship message formulated. Based on this, the appropriate sponsorships should be selected and the message communicated across all communication instruments and media.
8. **Consider collaboration with agencies and consultants:** Depending on the size of the arts and cultural sponsorship, collaboration with external parties in various areas should be considered. The advantages and disadvantages of involving external parties must be weighed.
9. **Select credible partners:** Cooperations must be critically examined for credibility by both corporate sponsors and cultural organizations. It is advisable for cultural organizations to define a code of conduct for the selection of partners.
10. **Leverage digitalization:** Digital cultural offerings enable numerous new opportunities for collaboration with corporate sponsors, which should be utilized.

References

A

Ackermann, J. (2008). Deutsche Bank – Mehr als Geld. *Soziales Kapital schaffen*. http://www.kulturmarken.de/content/view/252/306/. Accessed 7 Nov 2008.

Ahlert, D., Vogel, V., & Woisetschläger, D. (2007). Ist Sponsoring der Zaubertrank einer starken Marke? In D. Ahlert, D. Woisetschläger, & V. Vogel (Eds.), *Exzellentes Sponsoring. Innovative Ansätze und Best Practices für das Markenmanagement* (2nd ed., pp. 3–32).

Alfred Kärcher Vertriebs-GmbH. (2016). https://www.kaercher.com/de/inside-kaercher/kultursponsoring.html. Accessed 21 July 2016. Wiesbaden.

Alfred Kärcher Vertriebs-GmbH. (2023). *Kultursponsoring*, https://www.kaercher.com/de/inside-kaercher/unternehmen/sponsoring/kultursponsoring.html. Accessed 9 May 2023.

Allianz Foundation. (2022). *Jahresbericht 2022*, https://allianzfoundation.org/de/reports/jahresbericht-2022. Accessed 9 Aug 2023.

Altdorfer, H., Graber, H., Gremaud, T., Rogger, B., & Zumbrunnen, F. (2014). *Migros-Kulturprozent. Eine Kultur des Kulturförderns*. Migros-Kulturprozent.

ARCult Media. (2023). *Onlineausgabe des Handbuchs der Kunstpreise*, https://www.kulturpreise.de/web/preis-suche.php?sind=0&keyw=kulturmarken&x=0&y=0. Accessed 1 Oct 2023. Zürich.

Arte Magazin. (2023). *Mediadaten*, https://www.arte-magazin.de/media/2022/09/ARTE-Magazin-Mediadaten-2023.pdf. Accessed 28 May 2023.

Asongu, J. J. (2007). The legitimacy of strategic corporate social responsibility as a marketing tool. *Journal of Business and Public Policy, 1*(1), 1–12.

Audi AG. (2016). http://www.audi.de/de/brand/de/audi-artexperience.html#page=/de/brand/de/audi-artexperience.html. Accessed 15 Mar 2016.

Audi AG. (2023). *Kulturengagement der Audi AG,* https://www.audi.de/de/brand/de/audi-artexperience.html. Accessed 9 Aug 2023.

B

Baetzgen, A. (Ed.). (2022). *Brand Purpose*. Wie Marken nachhaltig Wert schaffen. Stuttgart

Bagusat, A. (2013). *Sponsoring Trends 2012*, https://www.ostfalia.de/export/sites/default/de/ispm/Blickpunkt_Sportmanagement/Sponsoring_Trends_2012.pdf. Accessed 17 Feb 2016.

M. Bruhn and L. Pöllmann, *Arts and Cultural Sponsorship,*
https://doi.org/10.1007/978-3-658-50079-5

Bagusat, A., & Marwitz, C. (2008). Sponsoring. Faszinierendes Instrument der Marketingkommunikation. In Bagusat, A., Marwitz, C., & Vogl, M. (Eds.), *Handbuch Sponsoring* (pp. 3–15). Erfolgreiche Marketing- und Markenkommunikation.

Barta & Partner. (2016). http://www.barta.co.at/links/index.php?cmd=setLanguage&language=en. Accessed 22 Mar 2016.

BASF SE. (2023). *BASF-Kulturengagement – Projekte,* https://www.basf.com/global/de/who-we-are/organization/locations/europe/german-sites/ludwigshafen/gesellschaftliches-engagement/woran-wir-arbeiten/arts-and-culture/Projekte.html. Accessed 9 Aug 2023.

Batt, V., Holzer, M., Bruhn, M., & Tuzovic, S. (2021). Effects of sponsorship quality and quantity on employee brand behavior. *Journal of Brand Management, 28*(4), 495–509. https://doi.org/10.1057/s41262-021-00242-w.

BBDO Live GmbH. (2010). Sponsoring Trends 2010, Studie in Zusammenarbeit mit dem Institut für Marketing, Universität der Bundeswehr München, Bonn.

BDI und RMF (o. D.). Berliner Compliance Modell, o. O.

Bendixen, P. (2010). *Einführung in das Kulturmanagement* (4th ed.). Wiesbaden.

BfS (Bundesamt für Statistik). (2022). *Öffentliche Kulturfinanzierung*, https://www.bfs.admin.ch/bfs/de/home/statistiken/kultur-medien-informationsgesellschaft-sport/kultur/kulturfinanzierung/oeffentliche.html. Accessed 4 Jan 2023.

BMEL (Bundesministerium für Ernährung und Landwirtschaft). (2020). *Neue Werbeverbote für Tabakerzeugnisse und E-Zigaretten und Nachfüllbehälter*, https://www.bmel.de/DE/themen/verbraucherschutz/tabak/tabakwerbeverbot.html. Accessed 1 Jan 2023.

BMI (o. D.). *Initiativkreis Korruptionsbewältigung Wirtschaft und Bundesverwaltung, Fragen-/Antwortenkatalog zum Thema Annahme von Belohnungen, Geschenken und sonstigen Vorteilen (Zuwendungen),* https://www.bmi.bund.de/SharedDocs/downloads/DE/publikationen/themen/moderne-verwaltung/korruptionspraevention/faqs-korruptionspraevention.pdf?__blob=publicationFile&v=3. Accessed 29 May 2023.

BMKÖS (Bundesministerium Kunst, Kultur, öffentlicher Dienst und Sport). (2022a). *Leitfaden für Kultursponsoring*, https://www.bmkoes.gv.at/Kunst-und-Kultur/Neuigkeiten/leitfaden-fuer-kultursponsoring.html. Accessed 10 Jan 2023.

BMKÖS (Bundesministerium Kunst, Kultur, öffentlicher Dienst und Sport). (2022b). *Leitfaden für Kultureinrichtungen im Umgang mit Drittmitteln aus Sponsoring und sonstigen Zuwendungen.* Wien.

BMW. (2008). *Olafur Eliasson – Your mobile expectations: BMW H2R project. Das 16. BMW Art Car*, veröffentlicht unter: https://www.press.bmwgroup.com/austria/article/detail/T0031216DE/olafur-eliasson-your-mobile-expectations:-bmw-h2r-project-das-16-bmw-art-car?language=de. Accessed 18 Dec 2023.

BMW AG. (2015). *Kulturengagement der BMW Group.* https://www.bmwgroup.com/content/dam/bmw-group-websites/bmwgroup_com/responsibility/downloads/de/2015/BMW_Group_Kulturengagement_de.pdf. Accessed 24 Mar 2016.

BMW AG. (2016a). *Das Kulturengagement der BMW Group.* https://www.bmwgroup.com/content/bmw-group-websites/bmwgroup_com/de/verantwortung/gesellschaftliches-engagement/kultur.html. Accessed 22 Mar 2016.

BMW AG. (2016b). *BMW Art Car.* http://www.artcar.bmwgroup.com/en/art-car/. Accessed 12 July 2016.

BMW AG. (2023). *Presseclub: Oper für alle begeistert Münchner Publikum seit 25 Jahren*, veröffentlicht unter: https://tinyurl.com/7s6rzjjt. Accessed 6 Feb 2023.

BMW Group. (2022). *Presseclub Deutschland. Über 22.000 Besucher bei „Staatsoper für alle" 2022 am 18. und 19. Juni auf dem Bebelplatz. Nach zwei Jahren endlich wieder für alle und dank BMW kostenfrei,* https://www.press.bmwgroup.com/deutschland/article/detail/

T0400473DE/ueber-22-000-besucher-bei-„staatsoper-fuer-alle“-2022-am-18-und-19-juni-auf-dem-bebelplatz-nach-zwei-jahren-endlich-wieder-fuer-alle-und-dank-bmw-kostenfrei?language=de. Accessed 3 June 2023.

Bob Bomliz Group. (2008). Sponsoring Trends 2008, Studie in Zusammenarbeit mit dem Institut für Marketing, Universität der Bundeswehr München, Bonn.

Bortoluzzi Dubach. (2011). Kultursponsoring. In: A. Klein (Ed.), *Kompendium Kulturmanagement* (pp. 476–502). München.

Boseman & Phatak. (1989). *Strategic Management: Text and Cases* (2nd ed.). New York.

BR Klassik. (2022). *Protest gegen „toxisches" Sponsoring*, https://www.br-klassik.de/aktuell/news-kritik/salzburger-festspiele-sponsor-solway-kritik-yana-ross-lukas-baerfuss-100.html. Accessed 20 Apr 2022.

Bruhn, M. (1987). Sponsoring. Mäzenatentum oder Schleichwerbung? *Harvard Manager, 9*(3), 46–52.

Bruhn, M. (2003). Denk- und Planungsansatz der Integrierten Marketing-Kommunikation. In A. Hermanns & F. Riedmüller (Eds.), *Sponsoring und Events im Sport. Von der Instrumentalbetrachtung zur Kommunikationsplattform* (pp. 23–44). München.

Bruhn, M. (2006). Integrierte Kommunikation in den deutschsprachigen Ländern. Bestandsaufnahme in Deutschland, Österreich und der Schweiz, Wiesbaden.

Bruhn, M. (2012). *Marketing für Nonprofit-Organisationen. Grundlagen, Konzepte, Instrumente* (2nd ed.). Stuttgart.

Bruhn, M. (2014). *Integrierte Unternehmens- und Markenkommunikation* (6th ed.). Stuttgart.

Bruhn, M. (2015). *Kommunikationspolitik. Bedeutung, Strategien, Instrumente* (8th ed.). München.

Bruhn, M. (2016). Corporate Sponsoring. In M. Urselmann (Ed.), *Handbuch Fundraising* (pp. 121–143). Wiesbaden.

Bruhn, M. (2018a). *Sponsoring. Systematische Planung und integrativer Einsatz* (6th ed.). Wiesbaden.

Bruhn, M. (2018b). Einsatz des Kultursponsoring für die Marketing- und Unternehmenskommunikation. In M. Bruhn (Ed.), *Sponsoring: Systematische Planung und integrativer Einsatz* (pp. 219–314). Wiesbaden: Springer Gabler.

Bruhn, M. (2018c). *Kommunikationspolitik. Systematischer Einsatz der Kommunikation für Unternehmen* (9th ed.). München.

Bruhn, M. (2022). *Relationship Marketing. Das Management von Kundenbeziehungen* (6th ed.). München.

Bruhn, M. (2024). *Marketing. Grundlagen für Studium und Praxis* (16th ed.). Wiesbaden: Springer Gabler.

Bruhn, M., & Ahlers, G. M. (2003). Ambush Marketing. „Angriff aus dem Hinterhalt“ oder intelligentes Marketing? *Jahrbuch der Absatz- und Verbrauchsforschung, 49*(3), 271–294.

Bruhn, M., & Ahlers, G. M. (2004). Ambush Marketing. „Attack from Behind“. *Yearbook of Marketing and Consumer Research, 2*(1), 40–61.

Bruhn, M., Martin, S., & Schnebelen, S. (2014). *Integrierte Kommunikation in der Praxis – Entwicklungsstand in deutschsprachigen Unternehmen.* Wiesbaden.

Bruhn, M., & Mehlinger, R. (1999). *Rechtliche Gestaltung des Sponsoring. Sport-, Kultur-, Sozial-, Umwelt- und Programmsponsoring. Band 2: Spezieller Teil* (2nd ed.). München.

Bruhn, M., & Wieland, T. (1988). Sponsoring in der Bundesrepublik. Ergebnisse einer Unternehmensbefragung, Arbeitspapier Nr. 10, Institut für Marketing, European Business School, Schloß Reichartshausen/Rheingau.

Bühler, S. (2020). Reputation. Visibilität. Glaubwürdigkeit. Über die Vorteile, die ein Unternehmen aus dem Engagement in Kunst ziehen kann. Ein Interview mit Prof. Dr. Thomas Girst, Leiter BMW Group Kulturengagement. weißBLAU, Ausgabe 01/2020, https://www.

marketingclub-muenchen.de/wp-content/weissblau/2020_01_weissblau.pdf. Accessed 18 Dec 2023.

Bulut, D., & Bulut Yumrukaya, C. (2009). Corporate social responsibility in culture and art. *Management of Environmental Quality, 20*(3), 311–320. https://doi.org/10.1108/14777830910950702.

Bundesgesetzblatt, I. (2000). *Gesetz zur weiteren steuerlichen Förderung von Stiftungen* (Jg. 2000, Nr. 3).

Bundesgesetzblatt, I. (2007). *Gesetz zur Stärkung des bürgerschaftlichen Engagements* (Jg. 2007, Nr. 50). Bonn.

Bundesverband Marketing Clubs. (2023). *Awards*, https://www.marketingverband.de/awards. Accessed 1 Oct 2023. Bonn.

Bunk, B. (2003). Corporate Citizenship und Marketing. Wie Synergien erschlossen werden. *Absatzwirtschaft, 46*(10), 26–31.

C

Causales Agentur für Marketing & Kommunikation. (2006). Corporate Cultural Responsibility (CSR), Studie 2006, Berlin.

Causales Agentur für Marketing & Kommunikation. (2007). Kultursponsoringmarkt Deutschland 200, Berlin.

Causales Agentur für Marketing & Kommunikation. (2008). *Fachbeiträge Kultursponsoring*. http://www.kulturmarken.de/content/blogcategory/133/356/. Accessed 15 Nov 2008.

Causales Agentur für Marketing & Kommunikation. (2013). Studie Kultursponsoringmarkt in Deutschland, Österreich, Schweiz und Luxemburg 2013, Berlin.

Causales Agentur für Marketing & Kommunikation. (2016). *Fachbeitrag: Kultur als Standortfaktor*. http://kulturmarken.de/wissen/kulturfinanzierung/achbeitrag-causales-7. Accessed 24 Mar 2016.

Chong, D. (2012). Institutions Trust Institutions Critiques by Artists of the BP/Tate Partnership. *Journal of Macromarketing, 33*(2), 104–116.

Christensen, S. R. (2006). Measuring consumer reactions to sponsoring partnerships based upon emotional and attitudinal responses. *International Journal of Market Research, 48*(1), 61–80.

Ciconte, B. L., & Jacob, J. G. (2009). *Fundraising basics. A complete guide* (3rd ed.). Burlington.

Cirque du Soleil. (2023). *Discover the extraordinary*, https://www.cirquedusoleil.com. Accessed 9 May 2023.

Coca Cola. (2023). *Festival Promo*, https://www.coca-cola-deutschland.de/gewinnen/coke-studio/festival-promo. Accessed 10 Feb 2023.

Colbert, F., Astous, A., & Parmentier, M.-A. (2005). Consumer perception of private versus public sponsorship of the arts. *International Journal of Arts Management, 8*(1), 48–60.

Cornwell, B. T., & Maignan, I. (1998). An international review of sponsorship research. *Journal of Advertising, 27*(1), 1–21.

Cornwell, T. B., & Coote, L. V. (2005). Corporate sponsorship of a cause. The role of identification in purchase intent. *Journal of Business Research, 58*(3), 268–276.

Cresendo. (2023). *Bayreuther Festspiele erreichen 97 Prozent Auslastung*, https://crescendo.de/news-29-08-2023-bayreuther-festspiele-erreichen-97-prozent-auslastung/. Accessed 21 Sept 2023.

D

Daimler AG. (2013). *Take the Wheel: Ein Fotowettbewerb geht auf die Straße*. https://www.mercedes-benz.com/de/mercedes-benz/lifestyle/kultur/take-the-wheel-ein-fotowettbewerb-geht-auf-die-strasse/. Accessed 13 July 2016.

DBV (Deutscher Bühnenverband). (2022). *Theaterstatistik 2019/2020*. Köln.

de Alcântara, J. N., de Benedicto, G. C., & da Silva, S. S. (2019). Possible key factors for Brazilian publicly traded companies to adopt a sponsorship strategy. *Journal of Strategy and Management, 12*(4), 429–446. https://doi.org/10.1108/JSMA-04-2018-0029.

Der Präsident des Bundesrechnungshofes. (2016). *Prüfung der Vergabe und Bewirtschaftung von Zuwendungen – Typische Mängel und Fehler im Zuwendungsbereich* (2nd ed.), https://www.bundesrechnungshof.de/SharedDocs/Downloads/DE/Berichte/BWV-Veroeffentlichung/vergabe-und-bewirtschaftung-von-zuwendungen-volltext.html. Accessed 5 Jan 2023.

Deutsche Bank. (2023). *Plus You. Deutsche-Bank-Mitarbeiter engagieren sich und spenden Zeit und Geld*, https://www.db.com/what-we-do/responsibility/society/employee-engagement?language_id=3. Accessed 7 Jan 2023.

Deutsche Bank AG. (2008). Deutsche Bank Stiftung ins Leben gerufen. Zusammenführung von Deutsche Bank Stiftung Alfred Herrhausen Hilfe zur Selbsthilfe und Kultur-Stiftung der Deutschen Bank. *Bildung wird neuer Förderschwerpunkt*. http://www.db.com/presse/de/content/presse_informationen_2005_2628.htm?month=12. Accessed 4 Aug 2008.

Deutsche Bank Stiftung. (2023a). *Deutscher Buchpreis*, https://www.deutsche-bank-stiftung.de/project/deutscher-buchpreis/. Accessed 9 Aug 2023.

Deutsche Bank Stiftung. (2023b). *Akademie Musiktheater Heute*, https://www.deutsche-bank-stiftung.de/project/akademie-musiktheater-heute/. Accessed 9 Aug 2023.

Deutsche Telekom AG. (2016a). *Engagement im Fußball zahlt sich aus*. https://www.telekom.com/konzern/sponsoring/78180. Accessed 8 June 2016.

Deutsche Telekom AG. (2016b). https://www.telekom-streetgigs.de/home. Accessed 5 Apr 2016.

Deutsche Telekom AG. (2016c). https://www.telekom.com/konzern/sponsoring/78136. Accessed 24 Mar 2016.

Deutsche Telekom AG. (2023a). *Special 250 Jahre Beethoven*, https://www.telekom.com/de/konzern/themenspecials/special-250-jahre-beethoven Accessed 9 Aug 2023.

Deutsche Telekom AG. (2023b). *Telekom Street Gigs*, https://www.t.elekom.com/de/konzern/details/telekom-street-gigs-479736. Accessed 9 Aug 2023.

Deutsche Telekom AG. (2023c). *Telekom Electronic Beats*, https://www.telekom.com/de/konzern/details/telekom-electronic-beats-479746. Accessed 9 Aug 2023.

Deutsche Telekom AG. (2023d). *Marke und Strategie*, https://onboarding.telekom.de/onboarding/mitarbeiter/marke-und-strategie.html. Accessed 6 Mar 2023.

Deutsche Telekom AG. (2023e). *Sponsoring-Engagement*, https://www.telekom.com/de/konzern/telekom-konzern-sponsoring. Accessed 6 Apr 2023.

Deutscher Bundestag. (2006). Public Private Partnerships (PPP) im Kulturbereich: Überblick und aktuelle Erfahrungen, Wissenschaftliche Dienste des Deutschen Bundestag, Reg. Nr. WF X 015/06, Berlin.

Deutscher Bundestag. (2011). Antwort der Bundesregierung auf die Große Anfrage des Abgeordneten Siegmund Ehrmann, Martin Dörmann, Petra Ernstberger, weiterer Abgeordneter und der Fraktion der SPD – Drucksache 17/4901, Berlin.

Deutscher Musikrat. (2023). *60. Wettbewerb Jugend musiziert*, https://www.jugend-musiziert.org/fileadmin/user_upload/ausschreibung_23_WEB_5.pdf. Accessed 6 May 2023.

Deutscher Werberat. (2019). *Verhaltensregeln des Deutschen Werberats über die kommerzielle Kommunikation für alkoholhaltige Getränke*. Berlin.

Deutschlandfunk Kultur. (2022). *Groß-Sponsor der documenta fordert „kraftvolle Veränderungen"*, https://www.deutschlandfunkkultur.de/gross-sponsor-der-documenta-fordert-kraftvolle-veraenderungen-102.html. Accessed 1 Apr 2022.

DHPG Dr. Harzem & Partner KG. (2010). *Studie über die wirtschaftlichen Effekte des Beethovenfestes Bonn im Jahr 2009*, http://www.miz.org/dokumente/Beethovenfest_Bonn_Wirtschaftlichkeitsanalyse_final.pdf. Accessed 12 July 2016.

Dietzmann, A. (2022). Das Europäische Kulturförderprogramm Kreatives Europa KULTUR. In L. Pöllmann, M. Risch-Kerst, G. Röckrath, & O. Scheytt (Eds.), *Handbuch Kulturmanagement*, F 2.11.

Documenta Fifteen. (2022). *Partner und Förder*innen*, https://documenta-fifteen.de/partner-und-foerderinnen/. Accessed 1 Apr 2023. Berlin.

Doemich, C. (2016). *Kultursponsoring im Internet*. http://www.doemich.de/kultursponsoring.html. Accessed 5 Apr 2016.

Dolores, L., Macchiaroli, M., & De Mare, G. (2017). Sponsorship for the sustainability of historical-architectural heritage: Application of a model's original test finalized to maximize the profitability of private investors. *Sustainability, 9*(10), 1–16. https://doi.org/10.3390/su9101750.

Dolores, L., Macchiaroli, M., & De Mare, G. (2019). A model for defining sponsorship fees in public-private bargaining for the rehabilitation of historical-architectural heritage, C3 – Smart Innovation, Systems and Technologies, 3rd International New Metropolitan Perspectives. Local Knowledge and Innovation dynamics towards territory attractiveness through the implementation of Horizon/Europe2020/Agenda2030, 2018, 101 (pp. 484–492). https://doi.org/10.1007/978-3-319-92102-0_51.

Dolores, L., Macchiaroli, M., & De Mare, G. (2021). Sponsorship's financial sustainability for cultural conservation and enhancement strategies: An innovative model for sponsees and sponsors. *Sustainability, 13*(16), 28. https://doi.org/10.3390/su13169070.

Duyster, I., & Pöllmann, L. (2023). Nutzendimensionen digitaler Theaterformate – Ergebnisse einer empirischen Umfrage. In L. Pöllmann, M. Risch-Kerst, G. Röckrath, & O. Scheytt (Eds.), *Handbuch Kulturmanagement* (Nr. 84, pp. 9–24). Berlin.

E

Eick, K.-G. (2008). *Kultur und kulturelle Vielfalt fördern*. http://www.kulturmarken.de/content/view/452/306/. Accessed 5 Nov 2008.

ESB (Europäische Sponsoring Börse). (2008). http://www.esb-online.com. Accessed 14 Apr 2008.

Esch, F.-R. (2014). *Strategie und Technik der Markenführung* (8th ed.). München.

F

FAZ. (2022). *Toxisches Sponsoring*, https://www.faz.net/aktuell/feuilleton/buecher/salzburger-festspiele-trennen-sich-von-umstrittenem-sponsor-solway-18154446.html. Accessed 1 Dec 2023.

Falk, J. H. (2012). *Identity and the museum visitor experience*.

FASPO. (2023). *ISA Profil*, http://www.faspo.de/de/profil_2.html. Accessed 1 July 2023. New York.

Fendius, K., & Otte, J. (2021). *Vor, während und nach dem Besuch*. Visitor Journeys in den Staatlichen Museen zu Berlin.

Festspielhaus Baden Baden. (2023a). *Förderung Förderkreis*, https://www.festspielhaus.de/foerderung/foerderkreis/. Accessed 7 Jan 2023. Berlin.

Festspielhaus Baden Baden. (2023b). *Förderung Freundeskreis*, https://www.festspielhaus.de/foerderung/freundeskreis-festspielhaus-baden-baden-e-v/. Accessed 7 Jan 2023.

Fischer, D., & Schmidli, F. (2022). Kultursponsoring wird interessanter für Unternehmen. Ergebnisse der Studie Sponsor Visions Schweiz 2022. In D. Schütz (Ed.), *Kulturmanagement Magazin* (Nr. 166, pp. 95–100).

Fischer, H. H. (1989). *Kulturförderung durch Unternehmen in der Bundesrepublik Deutschland*. Empirische Bestandsaufnahme und Ausblick.

Föhl, P. S., & Nübel, D. (2016). Das Publikum öffentlicher Theater. Ergebnisse der empirischen Forschung. In P. Glogner-Pilz & P. S. Föhl (Eds.), *Handbuch Kulturpublikum* (pp. 207–255). Forschungsfragen und -befunde. Köln.

Frohne, J., Norwidat-Altmann, B., & Scheytt, O. (2015). *Kultursponsoring, Leitfaden für kreative Allianzen*. Wiesbaden.

Fuchs, W., & Unger, F. (2014). Management der Marketing-Kommunikation, Wiesbaden.

G

Gerlach-March, R., & Pöllmann, L. (2019). *Kulturfinanzierung* (2nd ed.).

Gewandhausorchester. (2023a). *Orchester*, https://www.gewandhausorchester.de/orchester/. Accessed 14 July 2023. Wiesbaden.

Gewandhausorchester. (2023b). *Andris Nelson bleibt bis 20207 Gewandhauskapellmeister in Leipzig*, https://www.gewandhausorchester.de/artikel/andris-nelsons-bleibt-bis-2027-gewandhauskapellmeister-in-leipzig-325/. Accessed 14 July 2023.

GfK und Deutscher Spendenrat e. V. (2021a). *Bilanz des Helfens 2021*, https://www.spendenrat.de/wp-content/uploads/Downloads/Bilanz-des-Helfens/bilanz-des-helfens-2021-deutscher-spendenrat.pdf. Accessed 12 Aug 2023.

GfK und Deutscher Spendenrat e. V. (2021b). *Bilanz des Helfens 2020*, https://www.spendenrat.de/wp-content/uploads/Downloads/Bilanz-des-Helfens/bilanz-des-helfens-2020-deutscher-spendenrat.pdf. Accessed 12 Aug 2023.

GfK und Deutscher Spendenrat e. V. (2022). *Bilanz des Helfens 2022*, https://www.spendenrat.de/wp-content/uploads/Downloads/Bilanz-des-Helfens/bilanz-des-helfens-2022-deutscher-spendenrat.pdf. Accessed 12 Aug 2023.

Gianneschi, M., & Broberg, O. (2019). A history of cultural sponsorship in Sweden: A new market in marketing. In K. M. Ekström (Ed.), *Museum Marketization: Cultural Institutions in the Neoliberal Era* (pp. 208–225). https://www.scopus.com/inward/record.uri?eid=2-s2.0-85104163270&partnerID=40&md5=0c4dc8da248bb8e6bde1d64ca34c1178.

Girst, T. (2022). Kultur: Pflicht für die Politik, Kür für die Wirtschaft? In S. Mösch (Ed.), *Wie viel Mozart braucht der Mensch? Musik im Wertewandel* (pp. 89–117).

Glapp, R. (2023). Publikumsschwund vorbei?, https://publikumsschwund.wordpress.com. Accessed 1 Oct 2023. Kassel.

Gottschalk, I. (2016). *Kulturökonomie: Probleme, Fragen und Antworten* (2nd ed.).

Greenfield, J. M. (2002). *Fundraising Fundamentals. A Guide to Annual Giving for Professionals and Volunteers*. Wiesbaden.

Guggenheim Foundation. (2023). *The Hugo Boss Prize*, https://www.guggenheim.org/hugo-boss-prize. Accessed 9 Aug 2023. New York.

H

Haibach, M. (2012). *Handbuch Fundraising. Spenden, Sponsoring, Stiftungen in der Praxis* (4th ed.).

Haibach, M. (2019). *Handbuch Fundraising: Spenden, Sponsoring, Stiftungen in der Praxis, Frankfurt* (5th ed.). Frankfurt am Main.

Haltern, N. J. (2014). *Jenseits des konventionellen Kultursponsoring, Chancen alternativer Kooperationen zwischen Unternehmen und Kulturorganisationen*. Frankfurt am Main.

Handelsblatt. (2022). *„Kraftvolle Veränderungen": Sparkassen wollen Documenta-Sponsoring nur bei Reformen fortsetzen*, veröffentlicht unter: https://www.handelsblatt.com/finanzen/banken-versicherungen/banken/kunstausstellung-kraftvolle-veraenderungen-sparkassen-wollen-documenta-sponsoring-nur-bei-reformen-fortsetzen/28521014.html. Accessed 1 Apr 2023. Bielefeld.

Handelszeitung.ch. (2016). *Kunstsponsoring: Kunst verleiht der Marke noch mehr Glanz*. http://www.handelszeitung.ch/unternehmen/kunstsponsoring-kunst-verleiht-der-marke-noch-mehr-glanz. Accessed 12 July 2016.

Hausmann, A. (2021). Kulturmarketing. *Wiesbaden*. https://doi.org/10.1007/978-3-658-34785-7_6.

HBPeople. (2022). Hurricane Festival 2022: Zahlen, Daten, Fakten, https://hb-people.de/festivals/hurricane-festival-2022-zahlen-daten-fakten/. Accessed 6 Mar 2023.

Heinze, T. (Ed.). (2008). *Kultursponsoring, Museumsmarketing, Kulturtourismus. Ein Leitfaden für Kulturmanager* (3rd ed.).

Heinze, T. (Ed.). (1999). *Kulturfinanzierung. Sponsoring – Fundraising – Public-Private-Partnership*. Wiesbaden.

Hemer, J. (2011). *A snapshot on crowdfunding*. Arbeitspapiere Unternehmen und Region, No. R2/2011, Fraunhofer-Institut für System- und Innovationsforschung ISI, Karlsruhe. Münster.

Hermanns, A. (2001). Sponsoring 2000. Bestandsaufnahme und Perspektiven. Ergebnisse einer empirischen Studie. *Werbeforschung & Praxis, 46*(1), 2–5.

Hermanns, A., & Marwitz, C. (2008). *Sponsoring. Grundlagen, Wirkungen, Management, Markenführung* (3rd ed.).

Heusser, H.-J., Wittig, M., & Stahl, B. (2008). *Kulturengagement Roland Berger*, http://www.rolandberger.ch/en/publications/local_publications/pdf/Kulturengagement_RB.pdf. Accessed 21 Nov 2008. München.

Hewelt, K. (2008). Systematisierung der Sponsoring-Wirkungskontrolle. In G. Bentele, M. Piwinger, & G. Schönborn (Eds.), *Kommunikationsmanagement* (Art-Nr. 4.32).

Höbel, W. (2022). *„Toxisches Sponsoring betrifft die gesamte Gesellschaft"*, https://www.spiegel.de/kultur/lukas-baerfuss-gegen-die-salzburger-festspiele-toxisches-sponsoring-betrifft-die-gesamte-gesellschaft-a-6851ab31-4433-4ff1-88ed-ce65f4fa6fb2. Accessed 24 Feb 2022. Neuwied.

Hohenauer, R., & Reinecke, S. (2016). *Sponsoring-Wirkung auf das Kaufverhalten*.

Hoppe, B. M., & Heinze, T. (2016). Partner des Kulturmanagements. In B. M. Hoppe & T. Heinze (Eds.), *Einführung in das Kulturmanagement: Themen – Kooperationen – Gesellschaftliche Bezüge* (pp. 103–145). https://doi.org/10.1007/978-3-658-09657-1_4. Wiesbaden.

Howe, J. (2006). The Rise of Crowdsourcing. *Wired Magazine, 14*(6), 1–4. Wiesbaden.

Howe, J. (2008). Crowdsourcing: Why the Power of the Crowd is Driving the Future of Business. *New York*. https://doi.org/10.1177/0276146712470458.

Hugo Boss AG. (2023). *Hugo Boss Prize*, https://group.hugoboss.com/de/sponsoring/kultursponsoring/hugo-boss-prize. Accessed 9 Aug 2023.

Hurricane. (2022). *Das war das Hurricane 2022*, https://hurricane.de/de/. Accessed 6 Mar 2023.

HypoVereinsbank. (2016). http://engagement.hypovereinsbank.de/de/kunst-und-kultur/hvb-kunstsammlung/. Accessed 29 Mar 2016.

I

IfDA (Institut für Demoskopie Allensbach). (2022). AWA (Allensbacher Markt- und Werbeträgeranalyse), Allensbach.

innogy Stiftung für Energie und Gesellschaft gGmbH. (2016). http://www.rwestiftung.com/web/cms/de/2477286/innogy-stiftung/projekte/. Accessed 7 Sept 2016.

Integral. (2019). *Sinus Milieus Schweiz*, https://www.integral.co.at/sinus-milieus/sinus-milieus-schweiz. Accessed 7 Mar 2023.

Integral. (2022). *Sinus Milieus Schweiz*, https://www.integral.co.at/sinus-milieus/sinus-milieus-oesterreich. Accessed 7 Mar 2023.

Ipsos GmbH. (2008). *Großevents beflügeln Wintersport. Milka Nummer 1 im Wintersport*. http://www.ipsos.de/downloads/Ipsos_response_01_2008.pdf. Accessed 27 Nov 2008.

Ipsos GmbH. (2014). *Grundlagenstudie Sponsoring 2014*.

IVW (Informationsgemeinschaft zur Feststellung der Verbreitung von Werbeträgern e. V.). (2022). *Auflagenzahlen des 2. Quartals*, https://www.ivw.de/print/quartalsauflagen/pressemitteilungen/auflagenzahlen-des-2-quartals-2022. Accessed 6 May 2023.

J

Jacob, F., & Schnurbein, M.-T. (2004). Kultursponsoring und gesellschaftliche Verantwortung von Unternehmen. Steigt durch Kultursponsoring die von Konsumenten wahrgenommene Verantwortung eines Unternehmens? *Stiftung & Sponsoring, 2004*(6), 31–34.

Julius Bär. (2013). https://www.juliusbaer.com/de/DE_de/publikationsliste/news-detailseite/item/bildungspartnerschaft-zwischen-staedel-museum-und-bank-julius-baer/. Accessed 29 Mar 2016.

Julius Bär. (2023). *Sponsoring*, https://www.juliusbaer.com/de/ueber-uns/unser-engagement/sponsoring/. Accessed 9 May 2023.

K

Kissinger Sommer. (2023). *Rekordjahr beim Kissinger Sommer*, https://www.kissingersommer.de/festival/aktuelles/43522.Rekordjahr-beim-Kissinger-Sommer-2023.html. Accessed 21 Sept 2023.

Klavier-Festival-Ruhr. (2022). *Erfreuliche Erfolgsbilanz des Klavier-Festivals Ruhr 2022*, https://www.klavierfestival.de/erfolgsbilanz-2022/. Accessed 6 Mar 2023.

Klein, A. (2009). *Kulturpolitik: Eine Einführung*. Wiesbaden.

Klein, A. (2011). *Kulturmarketing* (3rd ed.). München

Kobel, S. (2019). *Schampus, Trüffel und Gedränge. Die VIP-Lounges der Art Basel. Ein Test*, https://www.artmagazine.cc/content107896.html. Accessed 6 Mar 2023. München.

Koth, M. (2000). *Soziosponsoring von Krankenhäusern – Potenzielle Gewinnbringung eines Marketinginstruments.*

Kroeber-Riel, W., & Gröppel-Klein, A. (2019). *Konsumentenverhalten* (11th ed.). München.

Kulturkontakte. (2003). http://www.kulturkontakte.com. Accessed 18 Apr 2008.

Kulturkreis der deutschen Wirtschaft im BDI e. V. (2010). *Unternehmerische Kulturförderung in Deutschland – Ergebnisse einer umfassenden Untersuchung des Kulturkreises der deutschen Wirtschaft im BDI.* Berlin.

Kulturkreis der deutschen Wirtschaft im BDI e. V. (2016). *Kulturkreis – Kulturfinanzierung in Deutschland.* http://www.kulturkreis.eu/index.php?option=com_content&task=blogcategory&id=44&Itemid=177. Accessed 17 Aug 2016.

Kulturmarken. (2021). *Europäische*r Kulturinvestor*in des Jahres 2021*, https://kulturmarken.de/veranstaltungen/kulturmarken-award/ausschreibung/europaeischer-kulturinvestor-des-jahres. Accessed 4 June 2023.

Kunstforum. (2022). *Documenta-Sponsoren stellen Forderungen*, https://www.kunstforum.de/nachrichten/documenta-sponsoren-stellen-forderungen/. Accessed 1 Apr 2022.

Künstlersozialkasse. (2023). *KSK in Zahlen – Durchschnittseinkommen Berufsanfänger*, https://www.kuenstlersozialkasse.de/service-und-medien/ksk-in-zahlen. Accessed 9 Aug 2023.

L

Labaronne, L. (2022). *Prof. Thomas Girst (Global Head of Cultural Engagement, BMW Group): In conversation, Cultural Trends, ZHAW Digital Collection*, https://digitalcollection.zhaw.ch/handle/11475/28422. Zugegriffen 01. Dez. 2023. https://doi.org/10.1080/09548963.2022.2156268.

Lamprecht, W. (2014). *Corporate Cultural Responsibility: Moratorium für Kultursponsoring.*

Landesbank Baden-Württemberg. (2023). *Sponsoring*, https://www.lbbw.de/konzern/lbbw/verantwortung/sponsoring/sponsoring_7vpu2vrzr_d.html. Accessed 9 Aug 2023. Wiesbaden.

Leclerc, F. (2023). *English Theatre in Frankfurt: Vertrag über kulturelle Nutzung ging nicht an Investor*, https://www.fr.de/frankfurt/english-theatre-in-frankfurt-vertrag-ueber-kulturelle-nutzung-ging-nicht-an-investor-92051659.html. Accessed 11 May 2023.

Lee, E.-M., & Yoon, S. (2021). Does Cultural Brand Sponsorship Pay Off? *International Journal of Customer Relationship Marketing and Management (IJCRMM), 12*(2), 1–16. https://doi.org/10.4018/IJCRMM.2021040101.

Leißner, C., & Stolze, J. A. (2016). Zeitspenden-Fundraising. In Fundraising Akademie (Ed.), *Fundraising. Handbuch für Grundlagen, Strategien und Methoden* (pp. 833–838).

Litzel, S., Loock, F., & Brackert, A. (Eds.). (2003). *Handbuch Wirtschaft und Kultur. Formen und Fakten unternehmerischer Kulturförderung.*

Lorenz, R. (2003). Sportsponsoring und Sportevents. Auf dem Weg zu einem konsequenten Themenmanagement. In A. Hermanns & F. Riedmüller (Eds.), *Sponsoring und Events im Sport. Von der Instrumentalbetrachtung zur Kommunikationsplattform* (pp. 273–280). München.

Lund, R., & Greyser, S. A. (2019). Integrated partnerships in Cultural Sponsorship: The cases of Guggenheim-UBS and MFA Boston-Fleet. In K. M. Ekström (Ed.), *Museum Marketization: Cultural Institutions in the Neoliberal Era* (pp. 188–207). https://www.scopus.com/inward/record.uri?eid=2-s2.0-85104166829&partnerID=40&md5=5d582e792cc813daa2bfa2cd55874a12.

M

Maniatis, A. (2017). Cultural sponsorship law. *Civitas et Lex, 15*(3), 23–34. https://doi.org/10.31648/cetl.2467.

Marketingbörse. (2023). *Auswahl renommierter Marketingpreise*, https://www.marketing-boerse.de/marktuebersicht/details/auswahl-renommierter-marketingpreise/143162. Accessed 1 Oct 2023.

McDermott, J. (2014). Mercedes-Benz uses Instagram to sell cars to millennials. *Digiday*. http://digiday.com/brands/mercedes-benz-uses-instagram-sell-cars-millennials/. Accessed 13 July 2016.

Mecking, C. (2010). Corporate Giving. Unternehmensspende, Sponsoring und insbesondere Unternehmensstiftung. In H. Backhaus-Maul, C. Biedermann, S. Näahrlich, & J. Polterauer (Eds.), *Corporate Citizenship in Deutschland: Gesellschaftliches Engagement von Unternehmen* (pp. 371–387). Bilanz und Perspektiven.

Meenaghan, T. (1983). Commercial Sponsorship. *European Journal of Marketing, 17*(2), 5–73. Wiesbaden.

Meenaghan, T., & Flood, P. R. (1983). Commercial Sponsorship. The Misunderstood Corporate Art, Special Report, Dublin College of Marketing & Design, Dublin.

Meenaghan, T., & Shipley, D. (1999). Media Effect in Commercial Sponsorship. *European Journal of Marketing, 33*(3/4), 328–347.

Mercedes-Benz. (2023). *Unsere Verhaltensrichtlinie. Das Richtige tun.*, https://group.mercedes-benz.com/dokumente/konzern/compliance/daimler-verhaltensrichtlinie.pdf. Accessed 29 May 2023.

Merck. (2023). *Gesellschaftliches Engagement*, https://www.merckgroup.com/de/company/merck-in-germany/nachbarschaft/merckengagement.html. Accessed 4 May 2023.

Migros-Genossenschafts-Bund. (2023a). *Kulturprozent*, https://engagement.migros.ch/de/kulturprozent. Accessed 9 Aug 2023.

Migros-Genossenschafts-Bund. (2023b). *Richtlinien Förderbeiträge Kultur*, https://engagement.migros.ch/dam/jcr:E909cadc-cf7c-403a-a9ed-61915c07166a/3600-richtlinien-foerderung-kultur-20211117-de.pdf. Accessed 6 May 2023.

Mobiliar. (2016). *Zoo Zürich*. https://www.mobiliar.ch/die-mobiliar/ueber-uns/sponsoring-und-events/kultur-und-gesellschaft/zoo-zuerich. Accessed 12 July 2016.

Montana Cans. (2016). *Sponsoring Guidelines*, https://www.montana-cans.com/en/sponsoring. Accessed 12 July 2016.

Moysidou, S.-A. (2020). *Cultural Sponsorship*, https://repository.ihu.edu.gr/xmlui/bitstream/handle/11544/29547/st.moysidou_ale_27-4-2020.pdf?sequence=1. Accessed 1 June 2023.

Münch, M. (2006). Das Kulturengagement der Deutschen Bank. In D. Ahlert, D. Woisetschläger, & V. Vogel (Eds.), *Exzellentes Sponsoring. Innovative Ansätze und Best Practices für das Markenmanagement* (pp. 335–345).

Münchner Merkur. (2023). Lausitz Festival zieht positives Resumee, https://www.merkur.de/deutschland/sachsen/lausitz-festival-zieht-positives-resuemee-hohe-auslastung-zr-92514778.html. Accessed 21 Sept 2023.

N

NEA. (2023). *National Endowment for the Arts – quick Facts*, https://www.arts.gov/sites/default/files/NEA-Quick-Facts-8.9.22-two-pager.pdf. Accessed 7 Febr 2023.

Neßler, C., Eimuth, A., & Friedrichs, A. (2015). Kunstförderung im Unternehmen – Der immaterielle Wert von Kunst aus Sicht der Unternehmensführung. *Controlling, 27*(12), 719–724.

Nielsen Sports (ehemals Repucom). (2015). *Sponsor-Trend 2015: Status und Trends im Sponsoringmarkt in Deutschland*, Österreich und Schweiz. http://www.marketing.ch/Portals/0/Wissen/Allgemein/Repucom%20Insights_Sponsor-Trend%202015_DACH_SFS.pdf. Accessed 17 Febr 2016.

Nieschlag, R., Dichtl, E., & Hörschgen, H. (2002). *Marketing* (19th ed.).

Nufer, G., & Simmerl, C. (2008). *Strukturierung der Erscheinungsformen des Ambush Marketing*, https://ub01.uni-tuebingen.de/xmlui/bitstream/handle/10900/44062/pdf/Reutlinger_Diskussionsbeitrag_2008_6.pdf?sequence=1&isAllowed=y. Accessed 10 Nov 2023.

Nufer, G. (2020). *Ambush Marketing – Ein Überblick*, https://publikationen.uni-tuebingen.de/xmlui/bitstream/handle/10900/96929/NACHSPIELZEIT%20-%202020-2.pdf?sequence=1&isAllowed=y. Accessed 1 Nov 2023.

O

Osterwalder, A., & Pigneur, Y. (2011). *Business Model Generation: Ein Handbuch für Visionäre, Spielveränderer und Herausforderer*. Frankfurt am Main.

P

Perdoni, S., & Peitz, C. (2020). *Internationale Filmfestspiele Berlin Audi beendet Sponsoring der Berlinale*, https://www.tagesspiegel.de/berlin/audi-beendet-sponsoring-der-berlinale-6864367.html. Accessed 10 May 2023.

Pilot Checkpoint. (2002). *Sponsor Visions 2002*. Hamburg.

Pilot Checkpoint. (2008). *Sponsor Visions 2008*.

Pöllmann, L. (2011). Sponsoring. In V. Lewinski-Reuter & S. Lüddemann (Eds.), *Glossar Kulturmanagement* (pp. 340–347). Hamburg.

Pöllmann, L. (2013). *Der Einsatz von Social Media in der Kommunikationspolitik von Theatern*. Wiesbaden.

Pöllmann, L. (2021a). *Kulturmarketing. Grundlagen, Konzepte, Instrumente*. Aachen.

Pöllmann, L. (2021b). *Musikfinanzierung*, https://miz.org/de/beitraege/musikfinanzierung. Accessed 7 Feb 2023. Wiesbaden.

Pöllmann, L. (2021c). Alternative Kulturformate als Reaktion auf die Pandemie. In M. Grandmontagne, L. Pöllmann, M. Risch-Kerst, G. Röckrath, & O. Scheytt (Eds.), *Theater. Welten*, Berlin, https://www.theaterwelten-online.de.

Pöllmann, L. (2021d). Größer, diverser, partizipativer?! Das digitale Publikum. In D. Schütz & J. Jakob, (Eds.), *Kulturmanagement Network Magazin – Digitale Besucher:Innen* (Nr. 160, Mai/Juni, pp. 8–14).

Pöllmann, L. (2022). Grundlagen der Publikumsforschung. In L. Pöllmann, M. Risch-Kerst, G. Röckrath, & O. Scheytt (Eds.), *Handbuch Kulturmanagement* (Nr. 79, pp. 71–95). Berlin

Porter, M. E., & Kramer, M. R. (2003). Wohltätigkeit als Wettbewerbsvorteil. *Harvard Business. Manager, 3,* 40–56. Berlin.

Posadowsky, D. V. (2007). Kultursponsoring. Zwischen Corporate Citizenship und Marketing. In D. Ahlert, D. Woisetschläger, & V. Vogel (Eds.), *Exzellentes Sponsoring. Innovative Ansätze und Best Practices für das Markenmanagement* (2nd ed., pp. 347–349).

Presse Augsburg. (2021). *MAN beendet Sponsoring der Augsburger Philharmoniker*, https://presse-augsburg.de/man-beendet-sponsoring-der-augsburger-philharmoniker/712814/. Accessed 11 May 2023. Wiesbaden.

Pundt, A., Martins, E., Horsmann, C. S., & Nerdinger, F. W. (2007). Gesellschaftliche Verantwortung als Unternehmenswert. Qualitative und quantitative Untersuchung der Sicht von Führungskräften, Betriebsräten und Vertretern des HR-Managements. *Wirtschaftspsychologie, 9*(1), 31–39.

PWC Deutschland. (2023). *German Entertainment & Media Outlook 2023–2027*, https://pages.pwc.de/contentform?qs=dc7fcb176550eb1a6d1e950e3a1ac396b5c08c8064100f9d-7340ba2417c51ff729ead2ec6a819a82828b04991d53e0fd10af096dcb5a399d2b3519ced808adf-f7aecd27efe16b2f84e78e7203435a3ef. Accessed 1 Jan 2024.

R

Reichertz, J. (2019). Purpose-Marketing: Unternehmen als Sinn- und Wertelieferanten. Zu einer neuen und alten Entwicklung im Marketing. In J. Kemming & J. Rommerskirchen (Eds.), *Marken als politische Akteure* (pp. 69–89). Wiesbaden.

Riethmüller, C. (2022). Der Preis, den man zahlt, Frankfurter Allgemeine Zeitung, 17.09.2022.

RMF. (2023). *36. Festivalsaison endet mit einem Verkaufsrekord und einer Auslastung von rund 93%*, https://www.rheingau-musik-festival.de/fileadmin/Presse/Pressemitteilungen/08302023_PM_Festivalabschluss.pdf. Accessed 21 Sept 2023.

Rothe, C. (2001). *Kultursponsoring und Image-Konstruktion. Interdisziplinäre Analyse der rezeptionsspezifischen Faktoren des Kultursponsoring und Entwicklung eines kommunikationswissenschaftlichen Imageapproaches*. Bochum.

Rothmair, S. (2010). *Wirkt Sponsoring von Musikfestivals? Magisterarbeit*, University of Vienna. Fakultät für Sozialwissenschaften. http://othes.univie.ac.at/11418/. Accessed 12 July 2016.

Ryan, A. (2018). Practice (mis)matching: Multiple performations of a cultural sponsorship network. *Journal of Marketing Management, 34*(17–18), 1445–1469. https://doi.org/10.1080/0267257X.2018.1556723.

S

S20. (2021). Responsible Sport-Sponsoring. Modernes Sportsponsoring – verantwortungsvoll, nachhaltig und relevant. Whitepaper der S20 e. V. Bonn, August.

SÄBL (Statistische Ämter des Bundes und der Länder). (2014). *Kulturfinanzbericht 2014*. Wiesbaden.

SÄBL (Statistische Ämter des Bundes und der Länder). (2018). *Kulturfinanzbericht*, https://www.destatis.de/DE/Themen/Gesellschaft-Umwelt/Bildung-Forschung-Kultur/Kultur/Publikationen/Downloads-Kultur/kulturfinanzbericht-1023002229004.pdf?__blob=publicationFile. Accessed 1 Jan 2023.

SÄBL (Statistische Ämter des Bundes und der Länder). (2022). *Kulturfinanzbericht*, https://www.destatis.de/DE/Themen/Gesellschaft-Umwelt/Bildung-Forschung-Kultur/Kultur/Publikationen/Downloads-Kultur/kulturfinanzbericht-1023002189004.pdf?__blob=publicationFile. Accessed 2 Jan 2023.

Salzburger Festspiele. (2023). *Das waren die Salzburger Festspiele 2023*, https://www.salzburger-festspiele.at/karteninformation. Accessed 21 Sept 2023.

Salzer, F. (2022). *Beendigungsmanagement von Sponsoringbeziehungen. Konzeption und empirische Analyse eines Wirkungsmodells*.

Schad, F., & Berentzen, J. (2007). „Kärcher reinigt die Welt“ – Kultursponsoring als medienwirksame Unternehmens- und Produktpräsentation. In D. Ahlert, D. Woisetschläger, & V. Vogel (Eds.), *Exzellentes Sponsoring – Innovative Ansätze und Best Practices für das Markenmanagement* (2nd ed., pp. 259–270). Wiesbaden.

Scheytt, O. (2008). *Kulturstaat Deutschland: Plädoyer für eine aktivierende Kulturpolitik*. Wiesbaden.

Schmidt, F., & Holze, B. (2003). Sportsponsoring und Sportevents. Kommunikationsplattform für Marken. In A. Hermanns & F. Riedmüller (Eds.), *Sponsoring und Events im Sport. Von der Instrumentalbetrachtung zur Kommunikationsplattform* (pp. 281–289). Bielefeld.

Schwaiger, M. (2001). *Messung der Wirkung von Sponsoringaktivitäten im Kulturbereich, Zwischenbericht über ein Projekt im Auftrag des AKS (Arbeitskreis Kultursponsoring)*. Schriften zur Empirischen Forschung und Quantitativen Unternehmensplanung: Ludwig-Maximilian-Universität München, München.

Schwaiger, M. (2006). Die Wirkung des Kultursponsoring auf die Unternehmensreputation der Sponsoren. 4. Zwischenbericht über ein Projekt im Auftrag des AKS /Arbeitskreis Kultursponsoring. *Schriften zur Marktorientierten Unternehmensführung der Ludwig-Maximilians-Universität München,* (1), 1–12. München.

Schwaiger, M. (2008). Bedeutung und Wirkung des Kunst- und Kultursponsoring. In A. Bagusat, C. Marwitz, & M. Vogl (Eds.), *Handbuch Sponsoring* (pp. 113–124). Berlin: Erfolgreiche Marketing- und Markenkommunikation. München.

Schwaiger, M., & Bury, A. (2003). Auswirkungen des Kultursponsoring auf Mitarbeitermotivation und Kundenbindung. In P. Strahlendorf (Ed.), *Jahrbuch Sponsoring 2004* (pp. 102–105). Hamburg.

Schwaiger, M., Jonas, P., & Lausberg, M. (2005). Welche Reputationstreiber beeinflussen das Kultursponsoring? Eine Studie in der Bayerischen Staatsoper. *Stiftung & Sponsoring,* (1/2005), 26–30.

Schwaiger, M., & Unterreitmeier, A. (2003). Sponsoringkontrolle in der Kunstsammlung NRW. *Stiftung & Sponsoring, 1*, 36–39.

Schwaiger, M. (2003). Evaluierung von Kultursponsoring-Maßnahmen. In S. Litzel, F. Loock, & A. Brackert (Eds.), *Handbuch Wirtschaft und Kultur. Formen und Fakten unternehmerischer Kulturförderung* (pp. 98–113).

Serafini, P., & Garrard, C. (2019). Fossil fuel sponsorship and the contested museum: Agency, accountability and arts activism. *Museum Activism, 69–79.* https://doi.org/10.4324/9781351251044-7. Berlin.

Settembre Blundo, D., García Muiña, F. E., Fernández del Hoyo, A. P., Riccardi, M. P., & Maramotti Politi, A. L. (2017). Sponsorship and patronage and beyond. *Journal of Cultural Heritage Management and Sustainable Development,* 7(2), 147–163. https://doi.org/10.1108/JCHMSD-08-2016-0045.

SHMF. (2023). »Dank an das beste Publikum der Welt!«, https://www.shmf.de/de/abschluss#:~:Text=Der%20Festivalsommer%20war%20ein%20voller,172%20Veranstaltungen%20waren%20ausverkauft. Accessed 21 Sept 2023.

Siebenhaar, H.-P. (2022). *Geld ist nicht alles*, https://www.sueddeutsche.de/politik/salzburger-festspiele-kultur-sponsoring-1.5621534?reduced=true. Accessed 17 July 2022.

Siemens AG (2023). *Partnerschaften*, https://www.siemens.com/de/de/unternehmen/themenfelder/partnerschaften.html. Accessed 9 Aug 2023.

Sinus Institut. (2023). *Sinus Milieus Deutschland*, https://www.sinus-institut.de/sinus-milieus/sinus-milieus-deutschland. Accessed 7 Mar 2023.

Sixt, A. (2014). *Schwarmökonomie und Crowdfunding. Webbasierte Finanzierungssysteme im Rahmen realwirtschaftlicher Bedingungen.*

Social Impact. (2023). *Unterstützung für Bildende Künstler:Innen*, https://socialimpact.eu/atelier-stipendium. Accessed 9 May 2023. Wiesbaden.

Spelleken, C. (2023). Digitales Theater an der Schnittstelle zur Medienkunst: Neue Kulturvermittlung durch digitale Inszenierungen. In L. Pöllmann, M. Risch-Kerst, G. Röckrath, & O. Scheytt (Eds.), *Handbuch Kulturmanagement* (pp. 59–79).

Staatsministerin für Kultur und Medien. (2021). *Neustart Kultur – Das Rettungspaket für den Kultur- und Medienbereich: NEUSTART KULTUR*, https://www.bundesregierung.de/breg-de/bundesregierung/bundeskanzleramt/staatsministerin-fuer-kultur-und-medien/neustart-kultur-startet-1775272. Accessed 12 Aug 2023. Stuttgart.

Startnext (2023). *„NICHTS" – Ein Film von Jana und Sophia Münster*, https://www.startnext.com/nichts-film?utm_source=projectDetail&utm_medium=pageprojects&utm-campaign=startnext. Accessed 4 Feb 2023.

Statistik Austria. (2022). *Kulturstatistik 2020.*

Süddeutsche Zeitung. (2023). *BMW steigt als Sponsor der Regensburger Schlossfestspiele aus*, https://www.sueddeutsche.de/bayern/regensburg-gloria-von-thurn-und-taxis-schlossfestspiele-sponsor-bmw-ausstieg-1.6241519. Accessed 29 Sept 2023. Wien.

Swisscom AG. (2016). https://www.swisscom.ch/de/about/unternehmen/marke/sponsoring/kultur.html. Accessed 29 Mar 2016.

T

Target Group. (2020). *KULMON. System für Besucher-Monitoring an tourismusaffinen Berliner Kulturinstitutionen*, https://about.visitberlin.de/kontinuierliche-besucherinnen-forschung-fuer-den-kultur-und-freizeitbereich-kulmonr. Accessed 7 June 2020.

Tate. (2023). *BMW Tate live*, https://www.tate.org.uk/whats-on/tate-modern/bmw-tate-live. Accessed 10 Feb 2023.

Theater Basel. 2022. *Geschäftsbericht 2021/2022*, https://issuu.com/theaterbasel/docs/tb_jahresbericht_2122_issuu. Accessed 4 Feb 2023.

Toscani, G., & Prendergast, G. (2019). Arts sponsorship versus sports sponsorship: Which is better for marketing strategy? *Journal of Nonprofit & Public Sector Marketing, 31*(4), 428–450. https://doi.org/10.1080/10495142.2018.1526748.

U

United Nations. (2023). *The 17 goals*, https://sdgs.un.org/goals. Accessed 7 Sept 2023.

Unkelbach, H., & Nill, D. (2014). Kulturelles Engagement von Unternehmen. In R. Henze (Ed.), *Kultur und Management – Eine Annäherung* (2nd ed., pp. 223–233). Wiesbaden.

Urselmann, M. (2023). *Fundraising: Professionelle Mittelbeschaffung für gemeinwohlorientierte Organisationen* (8th ed.). Wiesbaden.

V

Vance, L., Raciti, M. M., & Lawley, M. (2016). Sponsorship selections: Corporate culture, beliefs and motivations. *Corporate Communications: An International Journal, 21*(4), 483–499. https://doi.org/10.1108/CCIJ-11-2015-0072.

VdM (Verband deutscher Musikschulen). (2023). *Schülerzahl und Altersverteilung*, https://www.musikschulen.de/musikschulen/fakten/schuelerzahl-altersverteilung/index.html. Accessed 9 Aug 2023.

Verein zur Förderung der Kunst Stuttgart. (2022). *32. Stuttgarter Kunstausstellung*, https://vereinzurfoerderungderkunst-stuttgart.de. Accessed 9 May 2023.

W

W&V. (2023). *Awards*, veröffentlicht unter: https://www.wuv.de/Tag/Awards. Accessed 1 Oct 2023.

Wacken. (2023). *Sauber! Es wird wieder schmutzig! Die Axe Festival Short auf dem W:O:A*, https://www.wacken.com/de/news-details/sauber-es-wird-wieder-schmutzig-die-axe-festival-shower-auf-dem-woa/. Accessed 4 May 2023.

Waite, N. (1979). *Sponsorship in Context*. Cranfield.

Walldeceaux. (2023). *Mediadaten 2023*. Berlin.

Walliser, B. (1995). *Sponsoring. Bedeutung, Wirkung und Kontrollmöglichkeiten*.

Walliser, B. (2003). An International Review of Sponsorship Research. Extension and Update. *International Journal of Advertising, 22*(1), 5–40.

Weckerle, C., & Söndermann, M. (2004). *Erster Kulturwirtschaftsbericht Schweiz. Das Umsatz- und Beschäftigungspotenzial des kulturellen Sektors*.

Wegner, M. (2007). Das Gesellschaftliche Engagement von Unternehmen in Baden-Württemberg. Ergebnisse einer repräsentativen Studie und weiterführende Deutungen. *Wirtschaftspsychologie, 1*, 48–57. Zürich.

Weiland, A. (2017). *Private Kunst-und Kulturförderung in der Bundesrepublik Deutschland*, https://archiv.ub.uni-heidelberg.de/volltextserver/22617/1/Anna%20Weiland_Private%20Kunst-%20und%20Kulturförderung%20in%20der%20Bundesrepublik%20Deutschland.pdf. Accessed 1 Aug 2023.

Welge, M.K., & Al-Laham, A. (2012). *Strategisches Management. Grundlagen – Prozess – Implementierung* (6th ed.).

Wozniak, J. (2016). On sponsoring and CSR involvement. Two theories explaining their effects on a company's attractiveness for candidates. *Romanian Journal of Communication and Public Relations, 16*(2), 58–72. Wiesbaden.

Z

ZAW (Zentralverband der Deutschen Werbewirtschaft). (2013). *Werbung in Deutschland 2013*. Berlin.

ZAW (Zentralverband der Deutschen Werbewirtschaft). (2015). *Werbung in Deutschland 2015*. Berlin.

ZHAW. (2022). *Sponsor Visions Schweiz*, https://www.zhaw.ch/de/sml/institute-zentren/zkm/forschung-und-beratung/studien-zum-download/sponsor-visions-schweiz/. Accessed 9 Aug 2023.

ZHAW (Zentrum für Kulturmanagement, School of Management and Law, Zürcher Hochschule für Angewandte Wissenschaften). (2015). *„Sponsor-Visions 2014/15" – Eine empirische Studie zum Sponsoringmarkt Schweiz*. http://www.swa-asa.ch/de-wAssets/docs/artikel-printmedien/2015/Studie_Sponsor_Visions_Schweiz_2014-15.pdf. Accessed 17 Feb 2016.

MIX
Papier aus verantwortungsvollen Quellen
Paper from responsible sources
FSC® C105338
FSC
www.fsc.org

If you have any concerns about our products,
you can contact us on
ProductSafety@springernature.com

In case Publisher is established outside the EU,
the EU authorized representative is:
Springer Nature Customer Service Center GmbH
Europaplatz 3, 69115 Heidelberg, Germany

Printed by Libri Plureos GmbH
in Hamburg, Germany